Yona of the Dawn

Oh, shoot. We need to get rid of Lord Hak's grave.

STARE

22

Story & Art by

Mizuho Kusanagi

Yona of the Dawn

Volume 22

CONTENTS

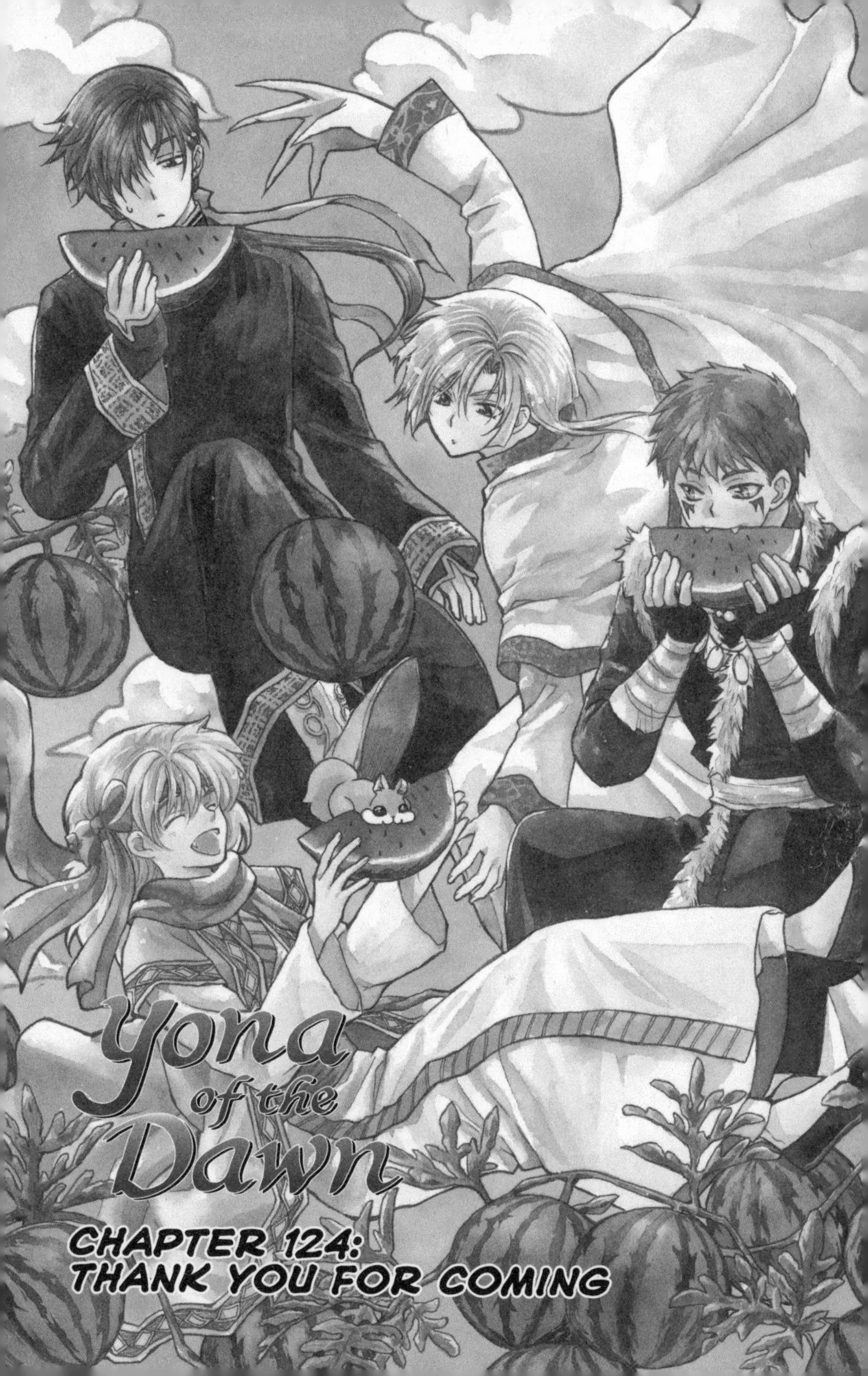
Yona of the Dawn
CHAPTER 124:
THANK YOU FOR COMING

Thank you so much to director Komeda and the staff for their work on the two-part Zeno Arc OAD!

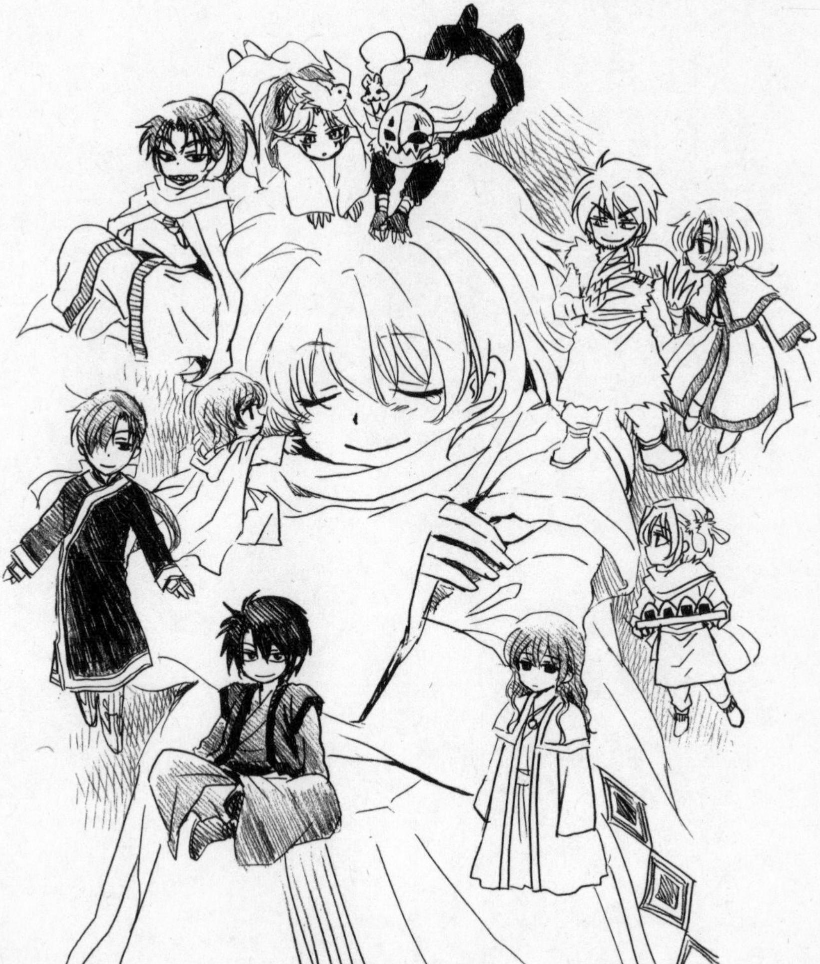

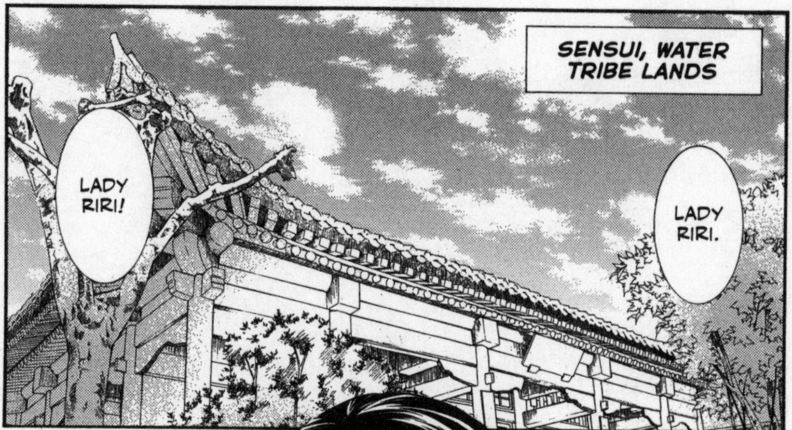
SENSUI, WATER TRIBE LANDS
LADY RIRI.
LADY RIRI!
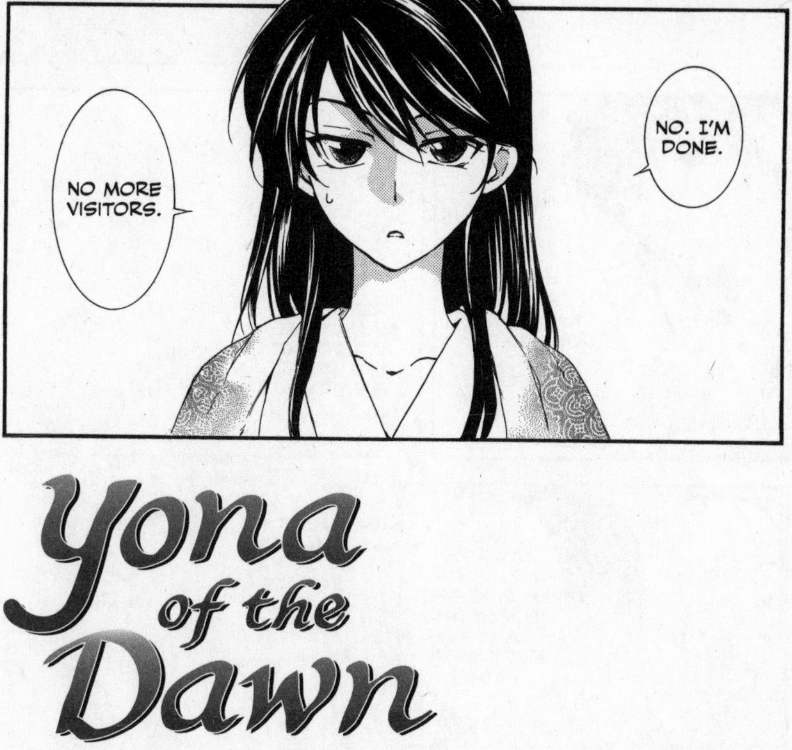
NO. I'M DONE.
NO MORE VISITORS.

Yona of the Dawn

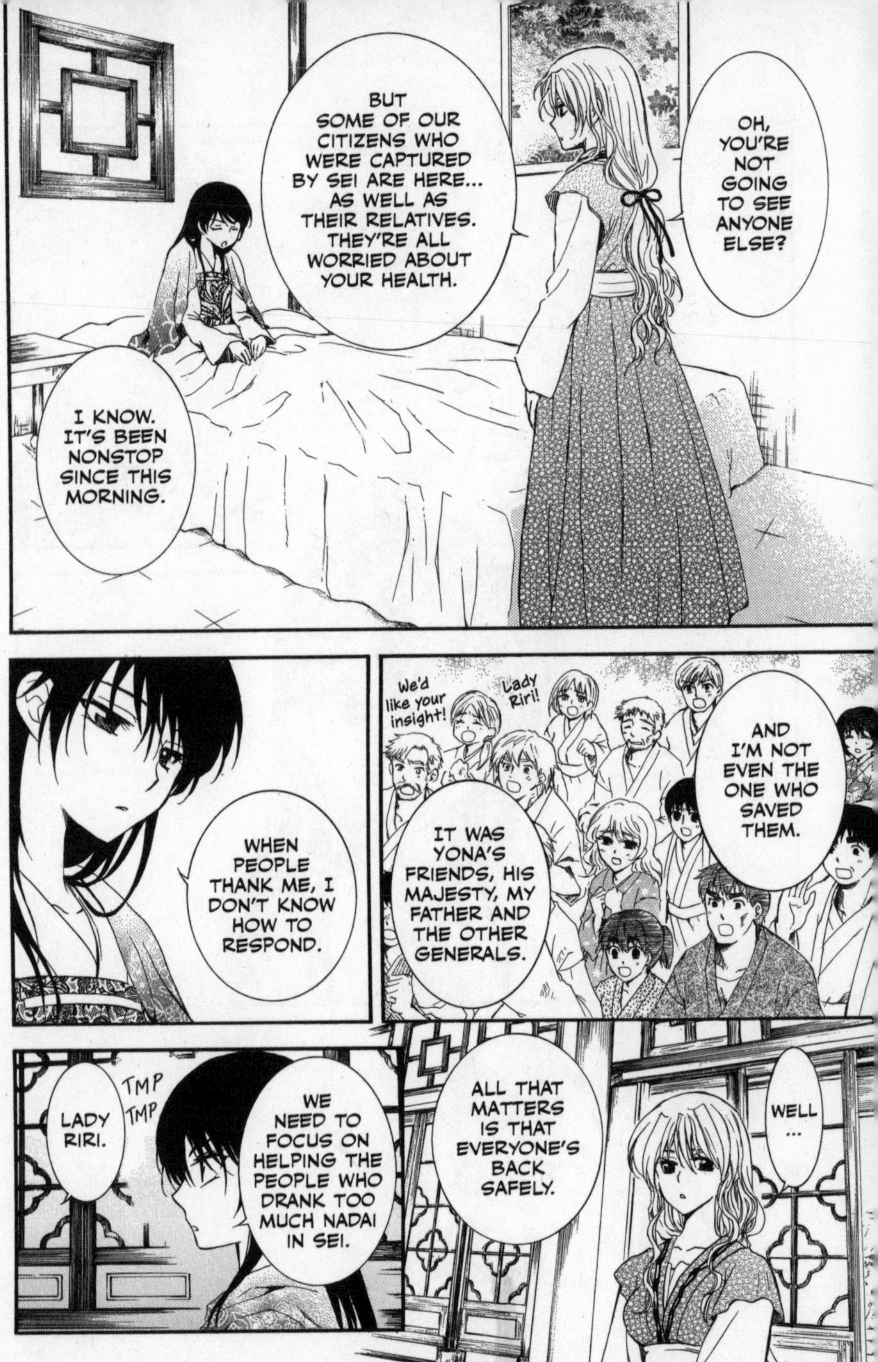
OH, YOU'RE NOT GOING TO SEE ANYONE ELSE?
BUT SOME OF OUR CITIZENS WHO WERE CAPTURED BY SEI ARE HERE... AS WELL AS THEIR RELATIVES. THEY'RE ALL WORRIED ABOUT YOUR HEALTH.
I KNOW. IT'S BEEN NONSTOP SINCE THIS MORNING.
Lady Riri!
We'd like your insight!
AND I'M NOT EVEN THE ONE WHO SAVED THEM.
IT WAS YONA'S FRIENDS, HIS MAJESTY, MY FATHER AND THE OTHER GENERALS.
WHEN PEOPLE THANK ME, I DON'T KNOW HOW TO RESPOND.
WELL ...
ALL THAT MATTERS IS THAT EVERYONE'S BACK SAFELY.
WE NEED TO FOCUS ON HELPING THE PEOPLE WHO DRANK TOO MUCH NADAI IN SEI.
TMP TMP
LADY RIRI.

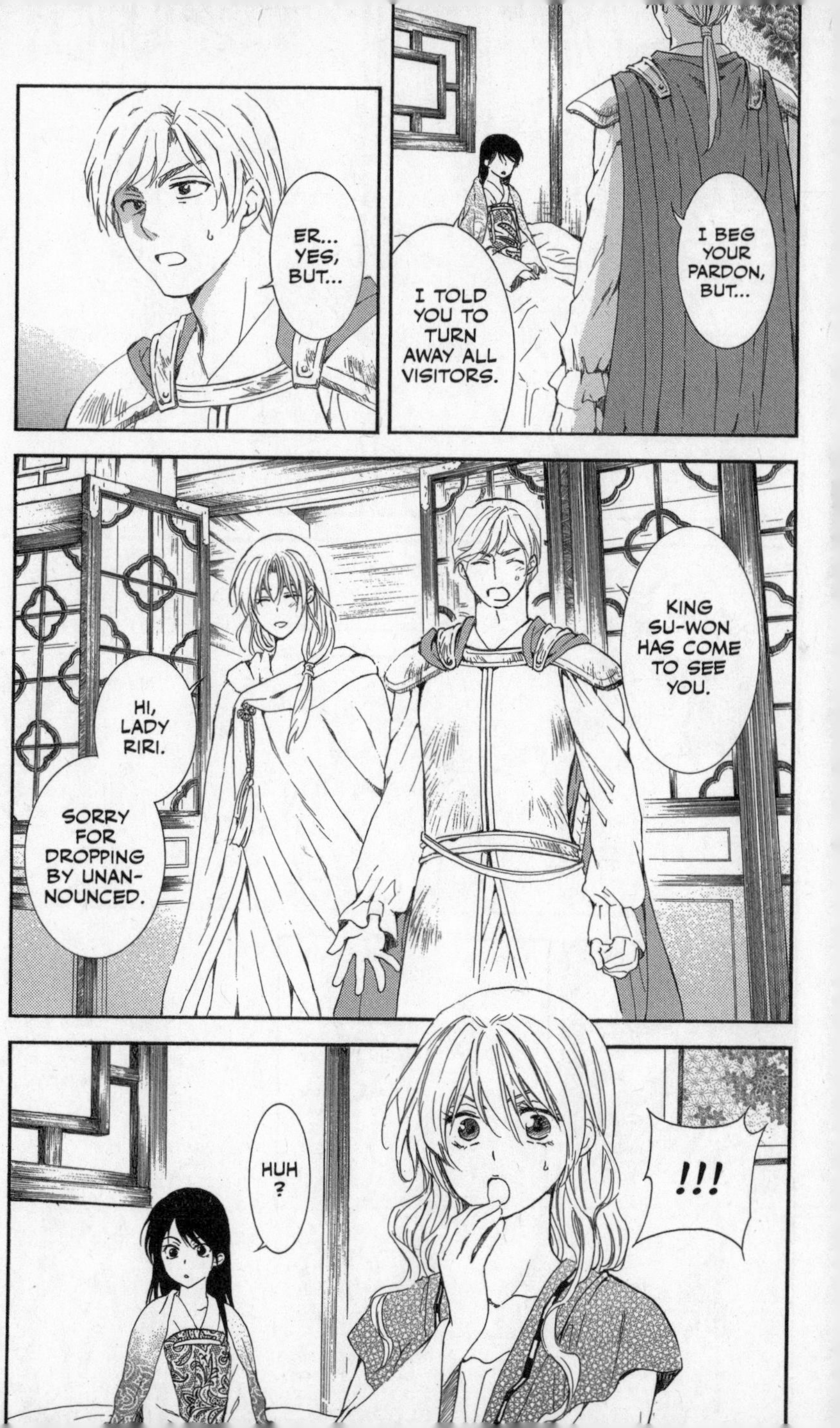
I BEG YOUR PARDON, BUT...
I TOLD YOU TO TURN AWAY ALL VISITORS.
ER... YES, BUT...
KING SU-WON HAS COME TO SEE YOU.
HI, LADY RIRI.
SORRY FOR DROPPING BY UNAN-NOUNCED.
!!!
HUH?

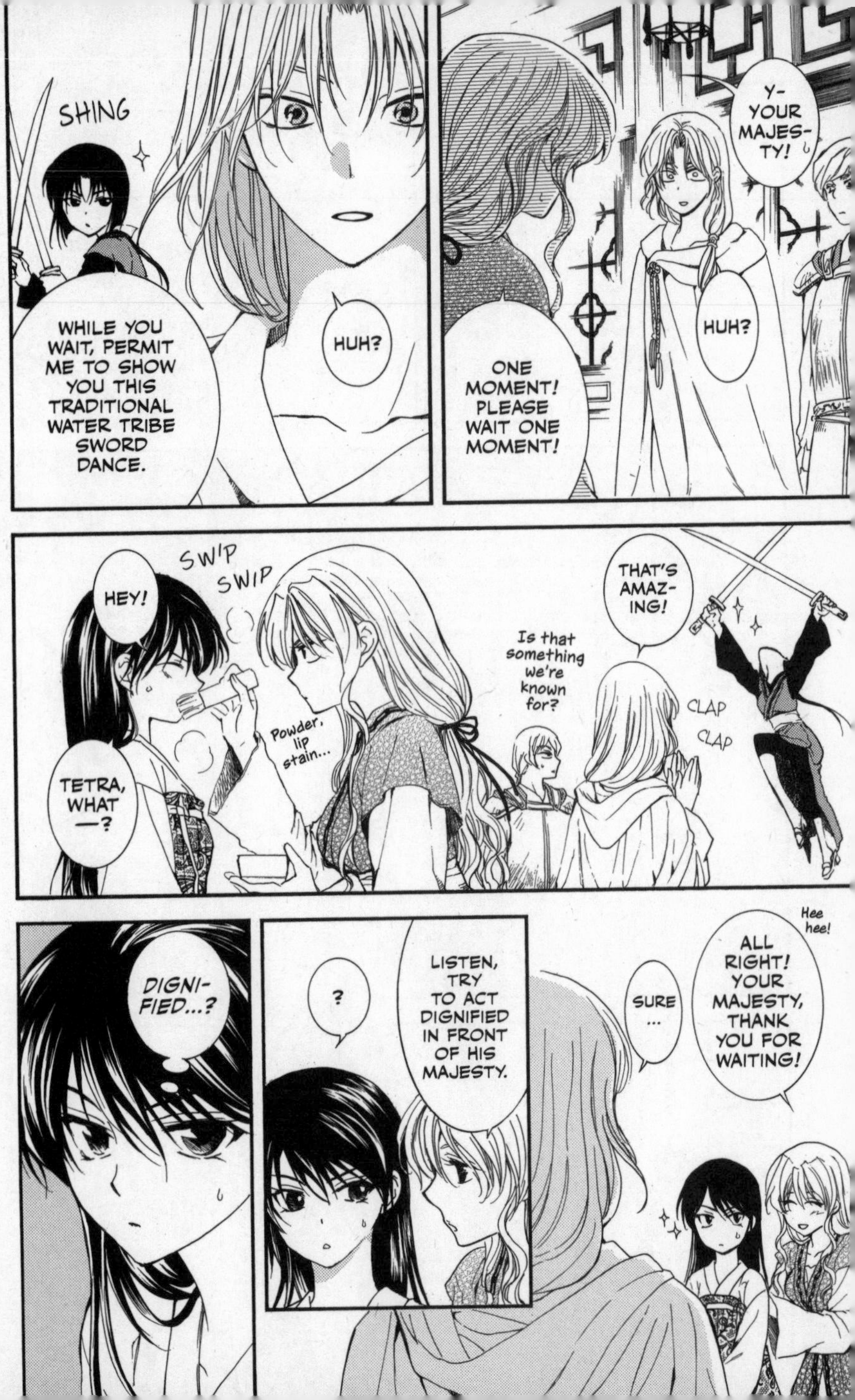
Y-YOUR MAJESTY!
HUH?
ONE MOMENT! PLEASE WAIT ONE MOMENT!
SHING
HUH?
WHILE YOU WAIT, PERMIT ME TO SHOW YOU THIS TRADITIONAL WATER TRIBE SWORD DANCE.
THAT'S AMAZING!
CLAP
CLAP
Is that something we're known for?
SWIP
SWIP
HEY!
Powder, lip stain...
TETRA, WHAT—?
Hee hee!
ALL RIGHT! YOUR MAJESTY, THANK YOU FOR WAITING!
SURE...
LISTEN, TRY TO ACT DIGNIFIED IN FRONT OF HIS MAJESTY.
?
DIGNIFIED...?

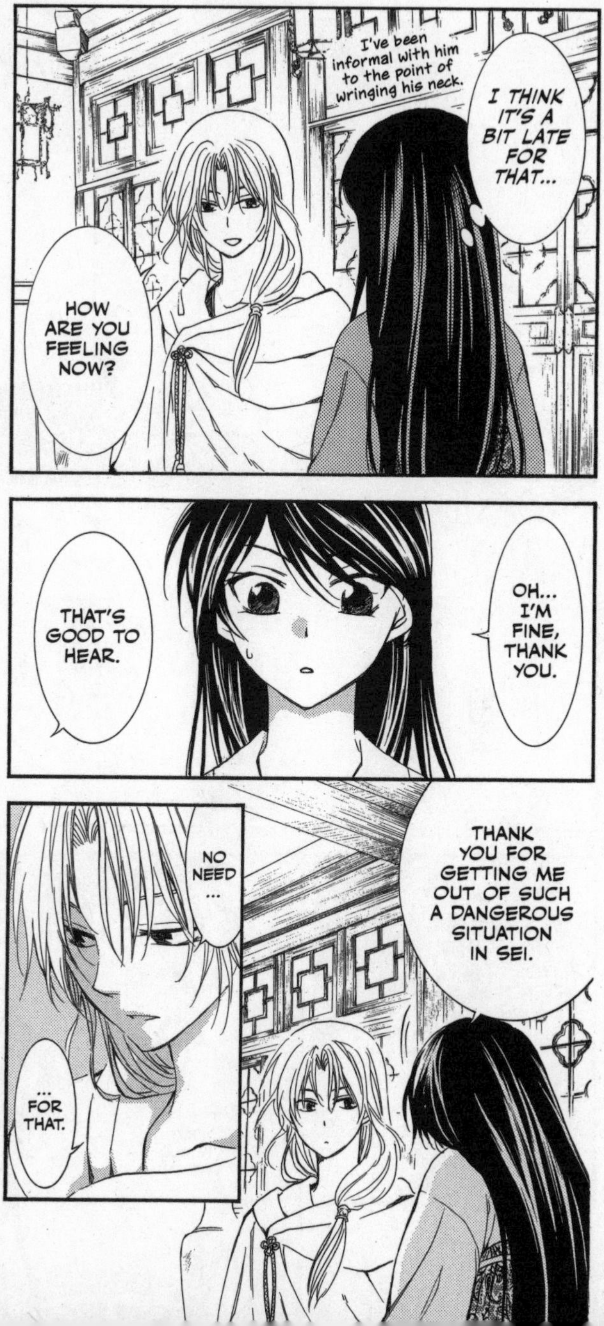
I THINK IT'S A BIT LATE FOR THAT...
I've been informal with him to the point of wringing his neck.
HOW ARE YOU FEELING NOW?
OH... I'M FINE, THANK YOU.
THAT'S GOOD TO HEAR.
THANK YOU FOR GETTING ME OUT OF SUCH A DANGEROUS SITUATION IN SEI.
NO NEED ...
... FOR THAT.

Thank you for picking up volume 22 of Yona of the Dawn! The special edition of volume 22 comes with the Zeno Arc Part 2 OAD. I haven't seen it yet, so I'm really looking forward to it!

Oh yeah—in volume 21, chapter 123, when Yona was thinking back on the fun time she had with Su-won, she thought, "Whereas when I'm with Hak it's a little different." Some readers took this to mean that she always had feelings for Hak...?" but that's not the case! These are Yona's current feelings. I'm sorry if I didn't convey that well enough. Hak's love was really one-sided for a long time. (To put it bluntly...)

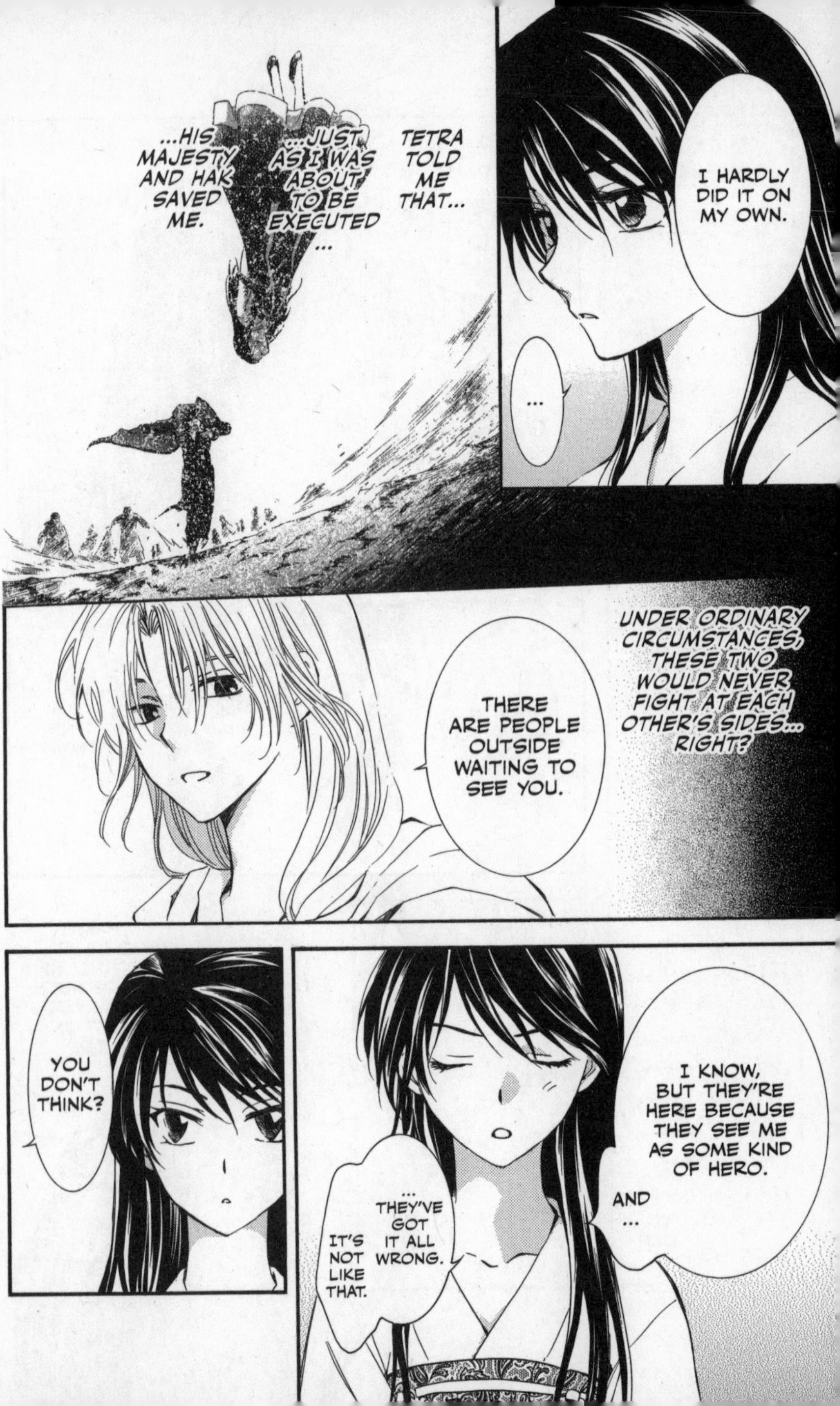
I HARDLY DID IT ON MY OWN.
...
TETRA TOLD ME THAT...
...JUST AS I WAS ABOUT TO BE EXECUTED...
...HIS MAJESTY AND HAK SAVED ME.
UNDER ORDINARY CIRCUMSTANCES, THESE TWO WOULD NEVER FIGHT AT EACH OTHER'S SIDES... RIGHT?
THERE ARE PEOPLE OUTSIDE WAITING TO SEE YOU.
I KNOW, BUT THEY'RE HERE BECAUSE THEY SEE ME AS SOME KIND OF HERO.
AND...
...THEY'VE GOT IT ALL WRONG.
IT'S NOT LIKE THAT.
YOU DON'T THINK?

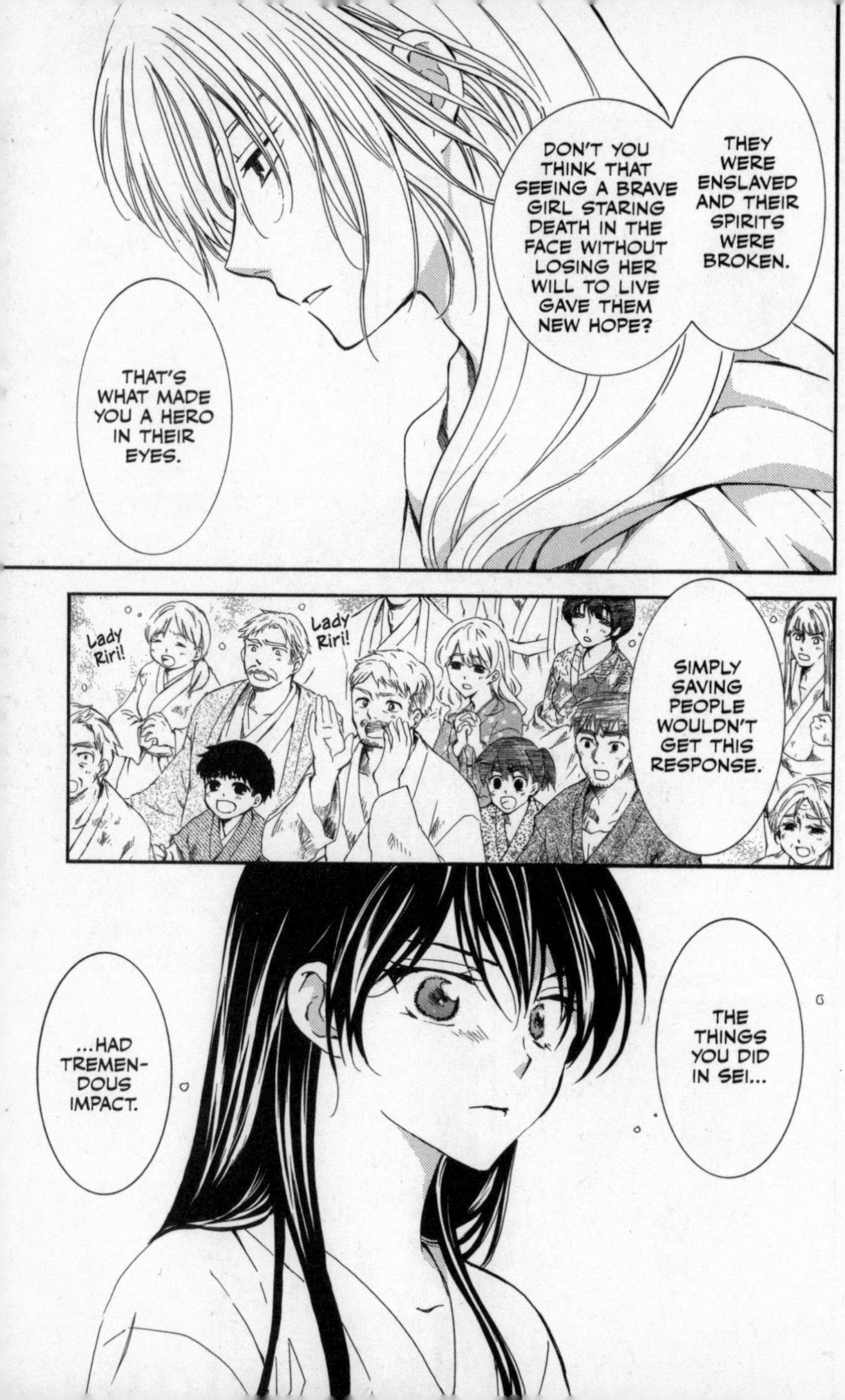
THEY WERE ENSLAVED AND THEIR SPIRITS WERE BROKEN.
DON'T YOU THINK THAT SEEING A BRAVE GIRL STARING DEATH IN THE FACE WITHOUT LOSING HER WILL TO LIVE GAVE THEM NEW HOPE?
THAT'S WHAT MADE YOU A HERO IN THEIR EYES.
SIMPLY SAVING PEOPLE WOULDN'T GET THIS RESPONSE.
Lady Riri!
Lady Riri!
THE THINGS YOU DID IN SEI...
...HAD TREMEN-DOUS IMPACT.

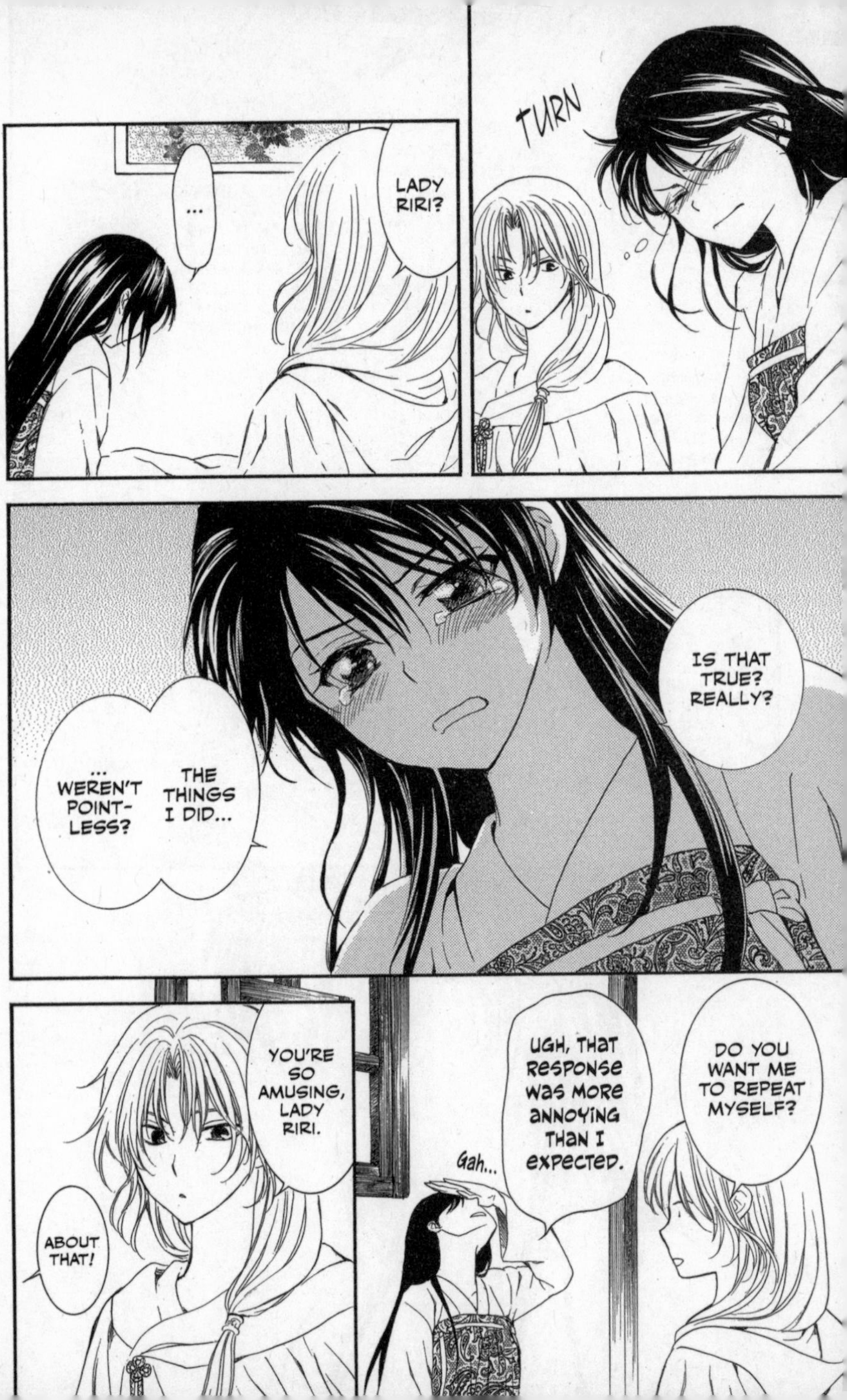
TURN
LADY RIRI?
...
IS THAT TRUE? REALLY?
THE THINGS I DID...
... WEREN'T POINT-LESS?
DO YOU WANT ME TO REPEAT MYSELF?
UGH, THAT RESPONSE WAS MORE ANNOYING THAN I EXPECTED.
Gah...
YOU'RE SO AMUSING, LADY RIRI.
ABOUT THAT!

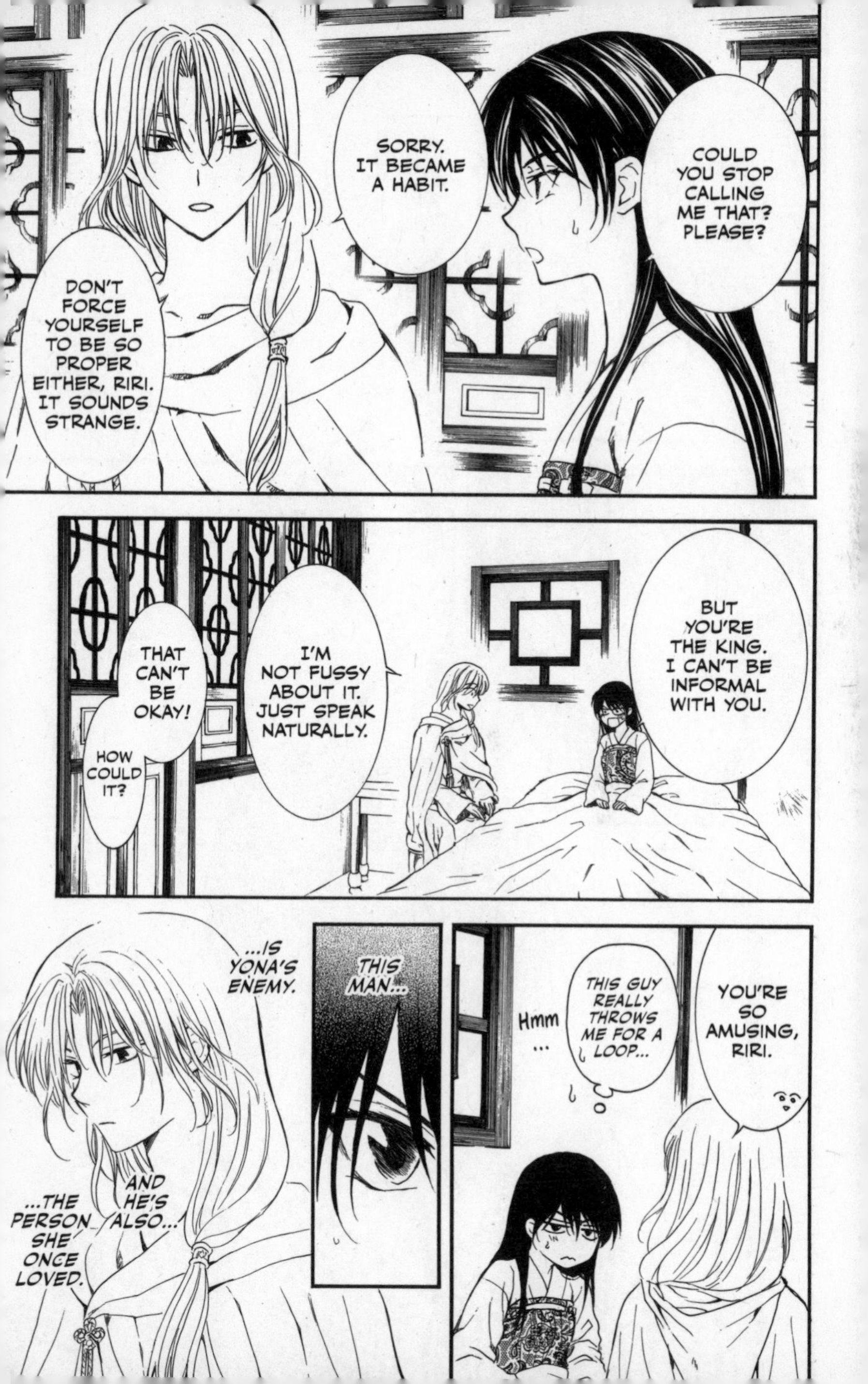
COULD YOU STOP CALLING ME THAT? PLEASE?
SORRY. IT BECAME A HABIT.
DON'T FORCE YOURSELF TO BE SO PROPER EITHER, RIRI. IT SOUNDS STRANGE.
BUT YOU'RE THE KING. I CAN'T BE INFORMAL WITH YOU.
I'M NOT FUSSY ABOUT IT. JUST SPEAK NATURALLY.
THAT CAN'T BE OKAY!
HOW COULD IT?
YOU'RE SO AMUSING, RIRI.
THIS GUY REALLY THROWS ME FOR A LOOP...
Hmm...
THIS MAN...
...IS YONA'S ENEMY.
AND HE'S ALSO...
...THE PERSON SHE ONCE LOVED.

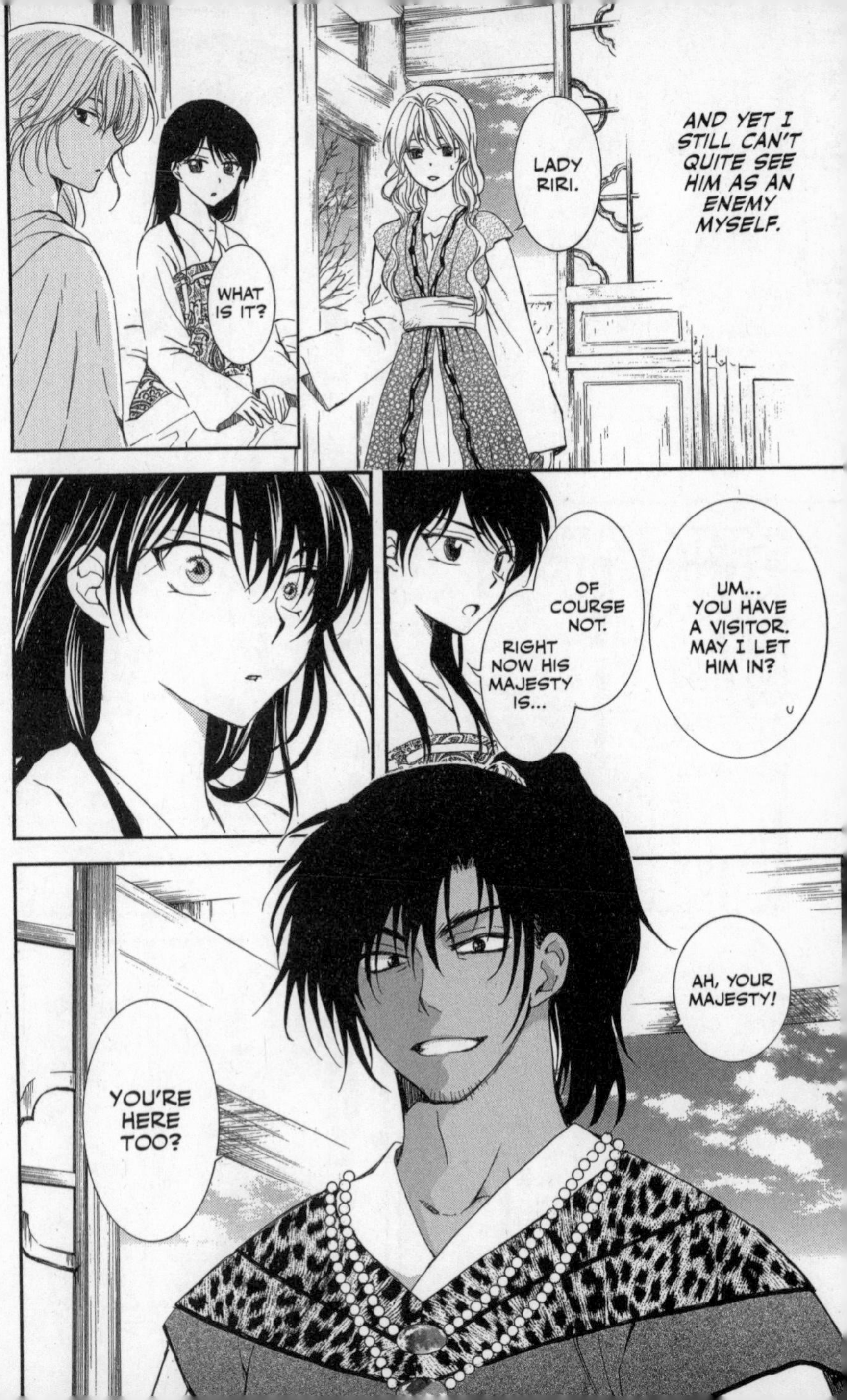
AND YET I STILL CAN'T QUITE SEE HIM AS AN ENEMY MYSELF.
LADY RIRI.
WHAT IS IT?
UM... YOU HAVE A VISITOR. MAY I LET HIM IN?
OF COURSE NOT.
RIGHT NOW HIS MAJESTY IS...
AH, YOUR MAJESTY!
YOU'RE HERE TOO?

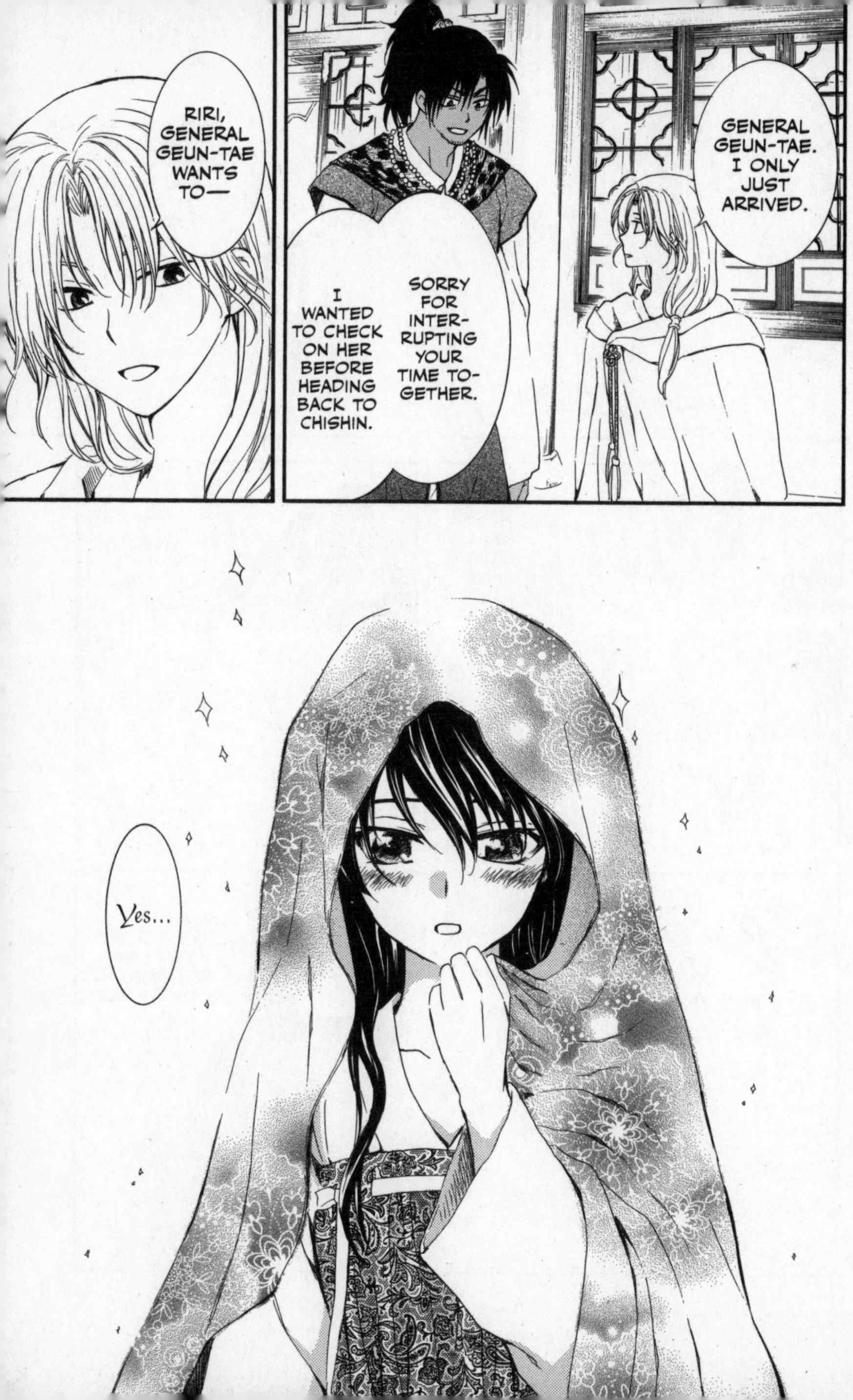
GENERAL GEUN-TAE. I ONLY JUST ARRIVED.
SORRY FOR INTER-RUPTING YOUR TIME TO-GETHER.
I WANTED TO CHECK ON HER BEFORE HEADING BACK TO CHISHIN.
RIRI, GENERAL GEUN-TAE WANTS TO—
Yes...

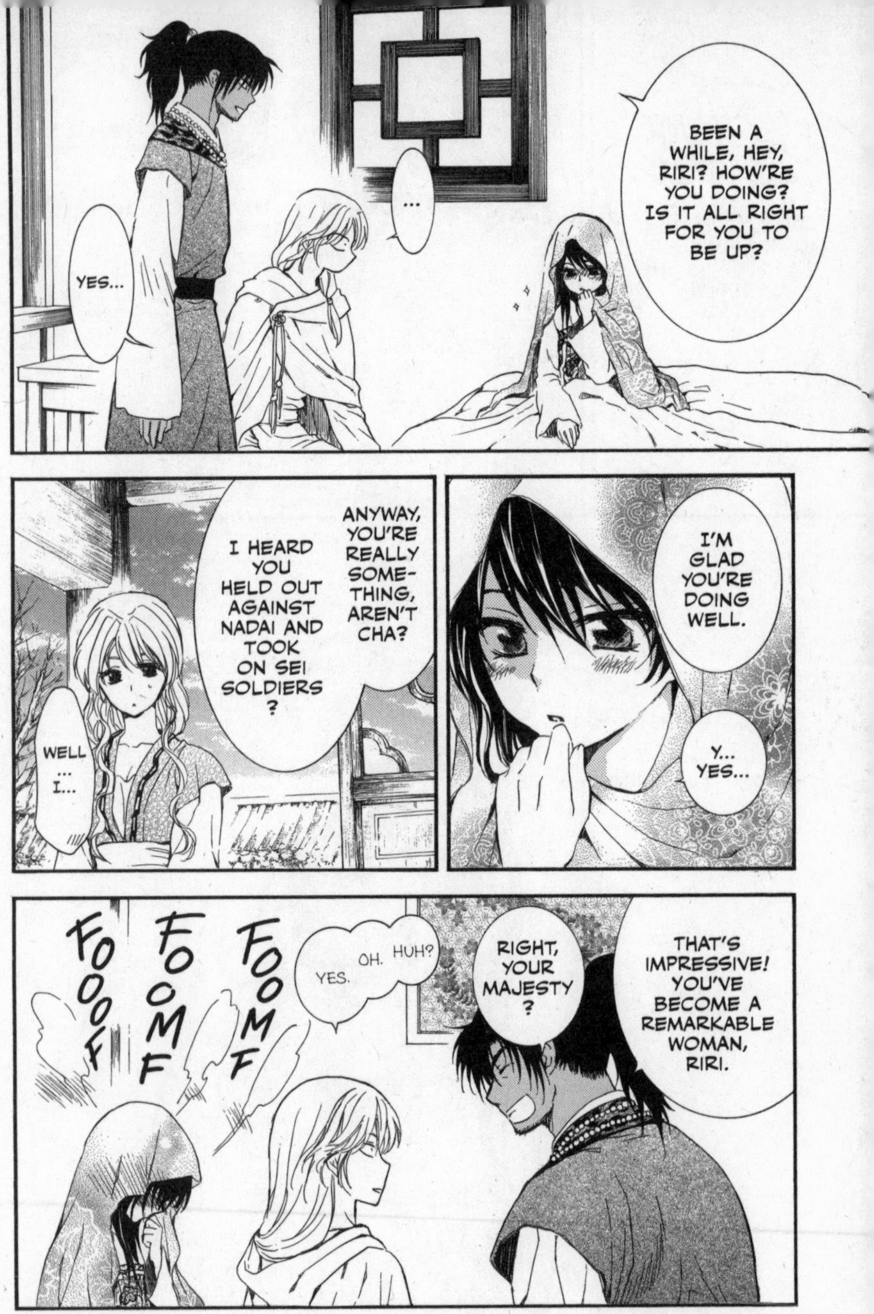
BEEN A WHILE, HEY, RIRI? HOW'RE YOU DOING? IS IT ALL RIGHT FOR YOU TO BE UP?
...
YES...
I'M GLAD YOU'RE DOING WELL.
Y... YES...
ANYWAY, YOU'RE REALLY SOME-THING, AREN'T CHA?
I HEARD YOU HELD OUT AGAINST NADAI AND TOOK ON SEI SOLDIERS?
WELL... I...
THAT'S IMPRESSIVE! YOU'VE BECOME A REMARKABLE WOMAN, RIRI.
RIGHT, YOUR MAJESTY?
HUH?
OH.
YES.
FOOMF
FOOMF
FOOOF

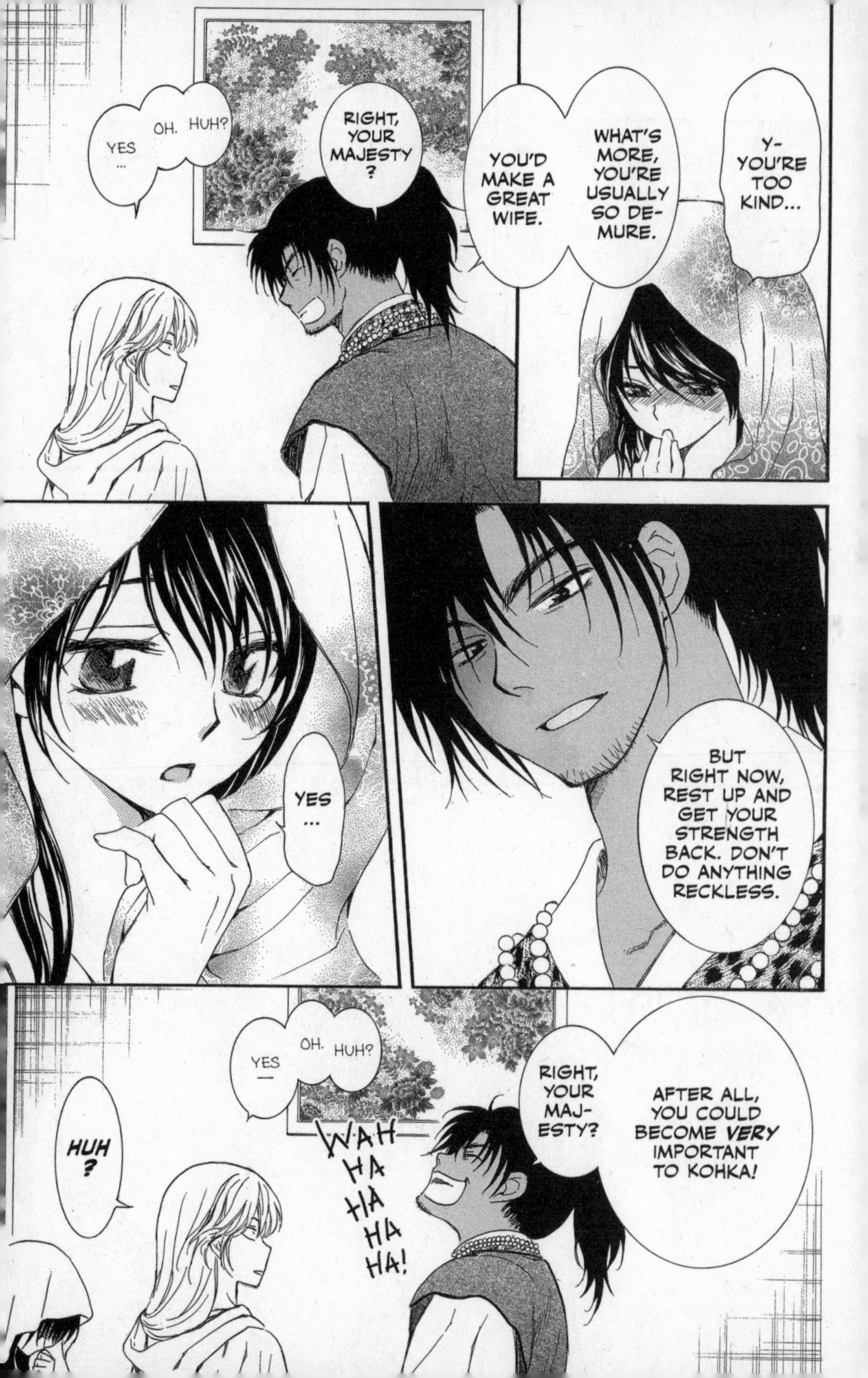
Y-YOU'RE TOO KIND...
WHAT'S MORE, YOU'RE USUALLY SO DE-MURE.
YOU'D MAKE A GREAT WIFE.
RIGHT, YOUR MAJESTY?
OH. HUH? YES ...
BUT RIGHT NOW, REST UP AND GET YOUR STRENGTH BACK. DON'T DO ANYTHING RECKLESS.
YES ...
AFTER ALL, YOU COULD BECOME *VERY* IMPORTANT TO KOHKA!
RIGHT, YOUR MAJ-ESTY?
OH. HUH? YES —
WAH HA HA HA HA HA!
HUH?

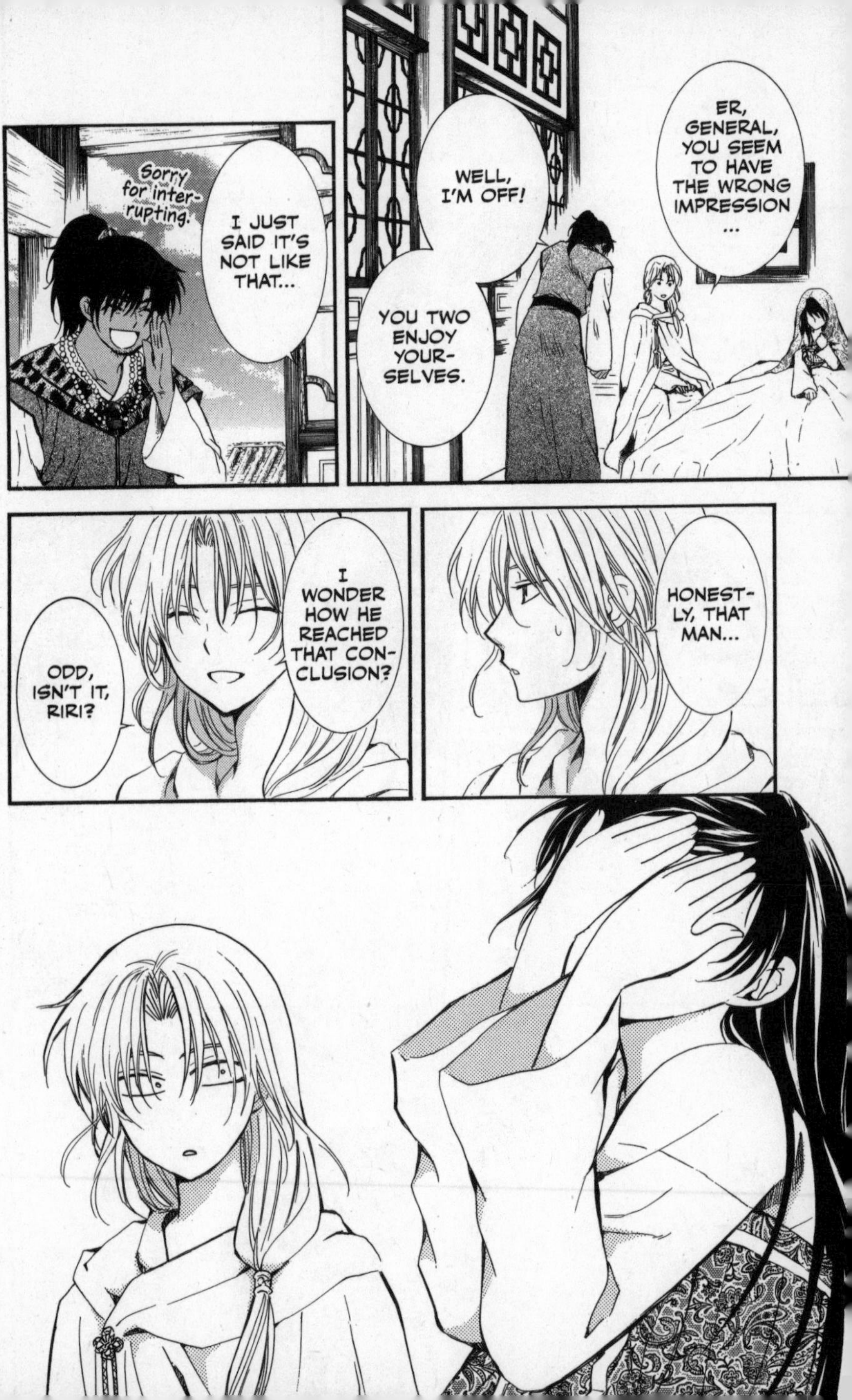
ER, GENERAL, YOU SEEM TO HAVE THE WRONG IMPRESSION ...
WELL, I'M OFF!
YOU TWO ENJOY YOUR-SELVES.
I JUST SAID IT'S NOT LIKE THAT...
Sorry for inter-rupting.
HONEST-LY, THAT MAN...
I WONDER HOW HE REACHED THAT CON-CLUSION?
ODD, ISN'T IT, RIRI?

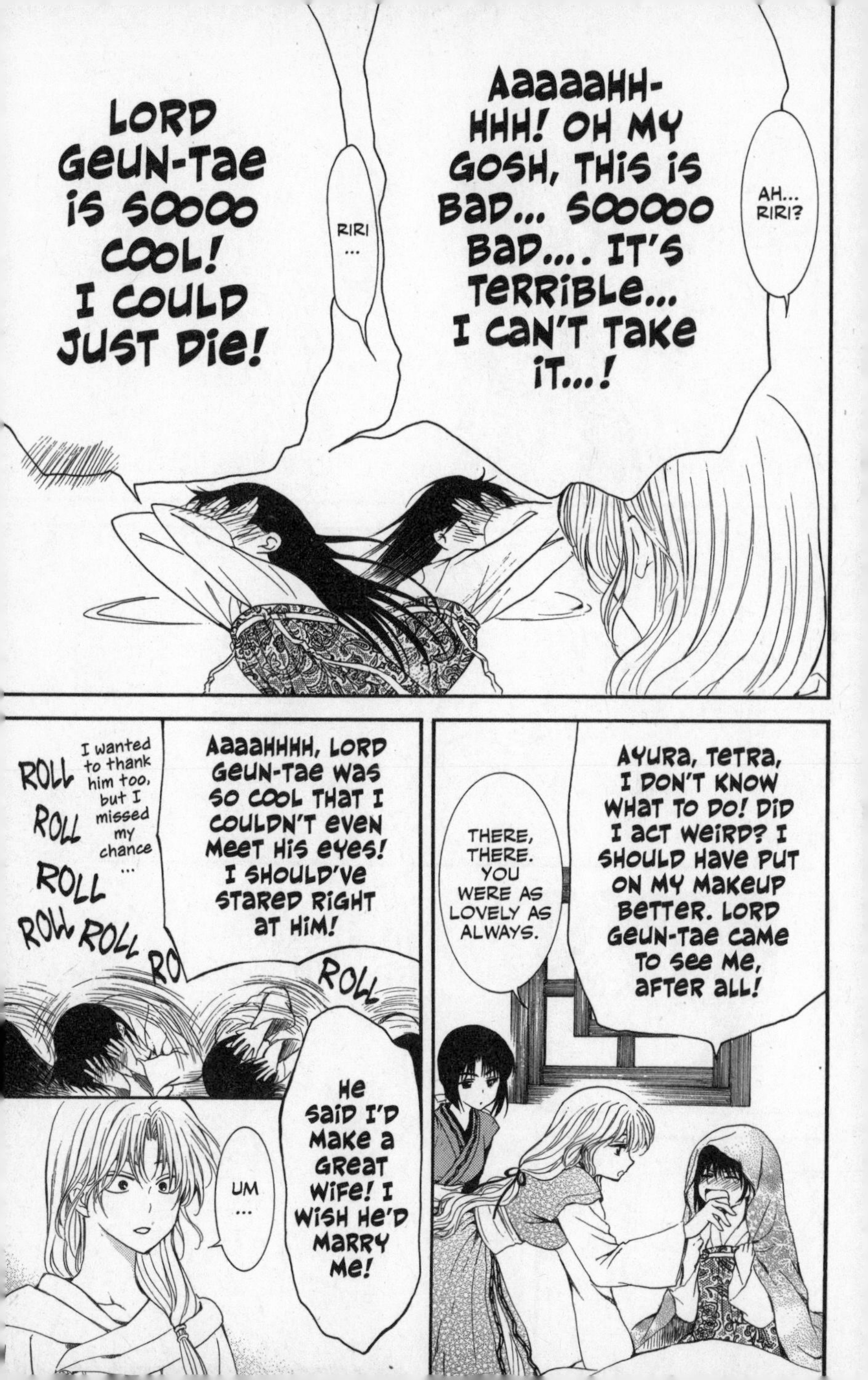
AH... RIRI?
AAAAAHH-HHH! OH MY GOSH, THIS IS BAD... SOOOOO BAD.... IT'S TERRIBLE... I CAN'T TAKE IT...!
RIRI ...
LORD GEUN-TAE IS SOOOO COOL! I COULD JUST DIE!
AYURA, TETRA, I DON'T KNOW WHAT TO DO! DID I ACT WEIRD? I SHOULD HAVE PUT ON MY MAKEUP BETTER. LORD GEUN-TAE CAME TO SEE ME, AFTER ALL!
THERE, THERE. YOU WERE AS LOVELY AS ALWAYS.
AAAAHHHH, LORD GEUN-TAE WAS SO COOL THAT I COULDN'T EVEN MEET HIS EYES! I SHOULD'VE STARED RIGHT AT HIM!
I wanted to thank him too, but I missed my chance ...
ROLL
ROLL
ROLL
ROLL
ROLL
ROLL
RO
HE SAID I'D MAKE A GREAT WIFE! I WISH HE'D MARRY ME!
UM ...

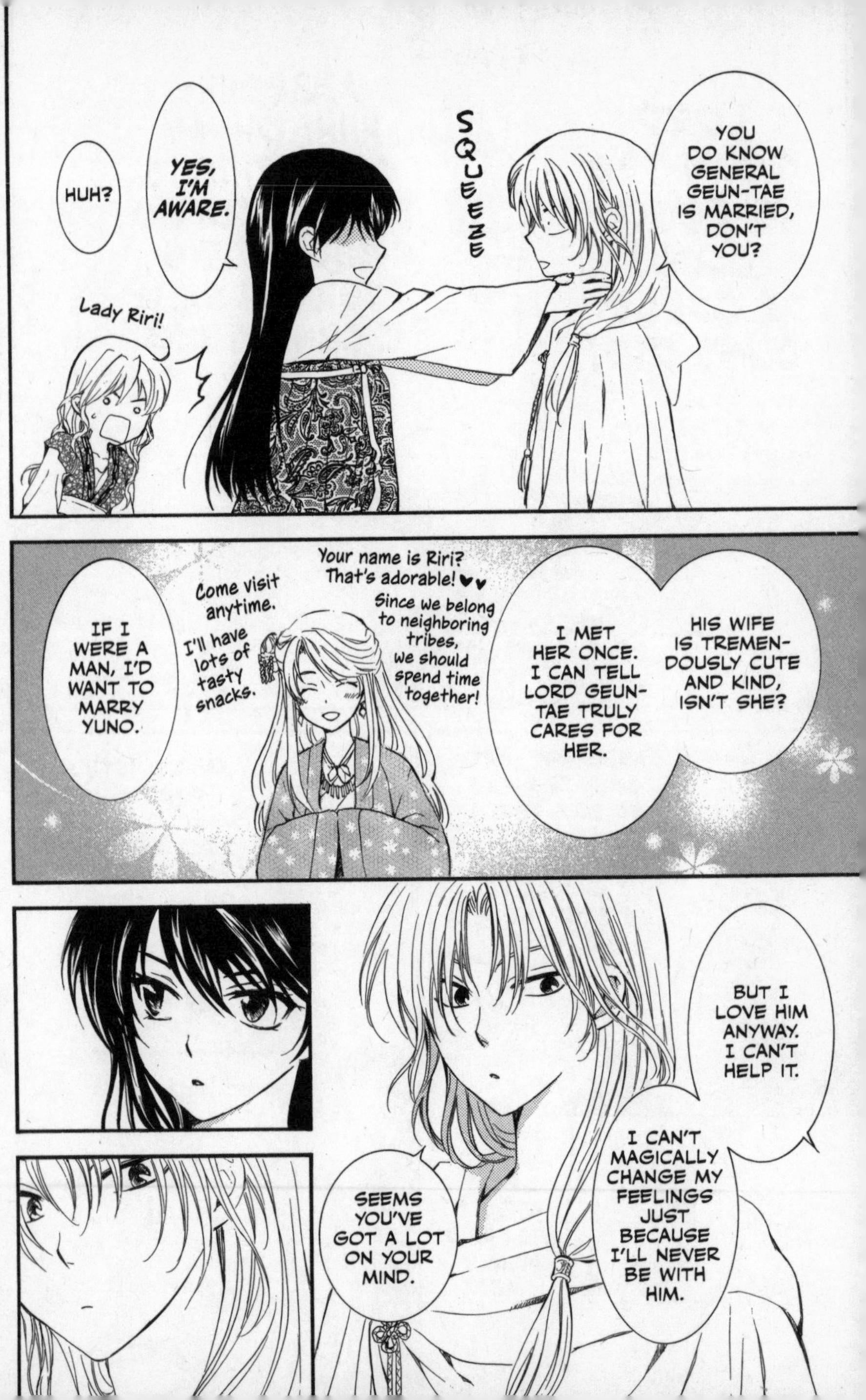
YOU DO KNOW GENERAL GEUN-TAE IS MARRIED, DON'T YOU?
SQUEEZE
YES, I'M AWARE.
HUH?
Lady Riri!
HIS WIFE IS TREMEN-DOUSLY CUTE AND KIND, ISN'T SHE?
I MET HER ONCE. I CAN TELL LORD GEUN-TAE TRULY CARES FOR HER.
Your name is Riri? That's adorable! ♥♥
Since we belong to neighboring tribes, we should spend time together!
Come visit anytime.
I'll have lots of tasty snacks.
IF I WERE A MAN, I'D WANT TO MARRY YUNO.
BUT I LOVE HIM ANYWAY. I CAN'T HELP IT.
I CAN'T MAGICALLY CHANGE MY FEELINGS JUST BECAUSE I'LL NEVER BE WITH HIM.
SEEMS YOU'VE GOT A LOT ON YOUR MIND.

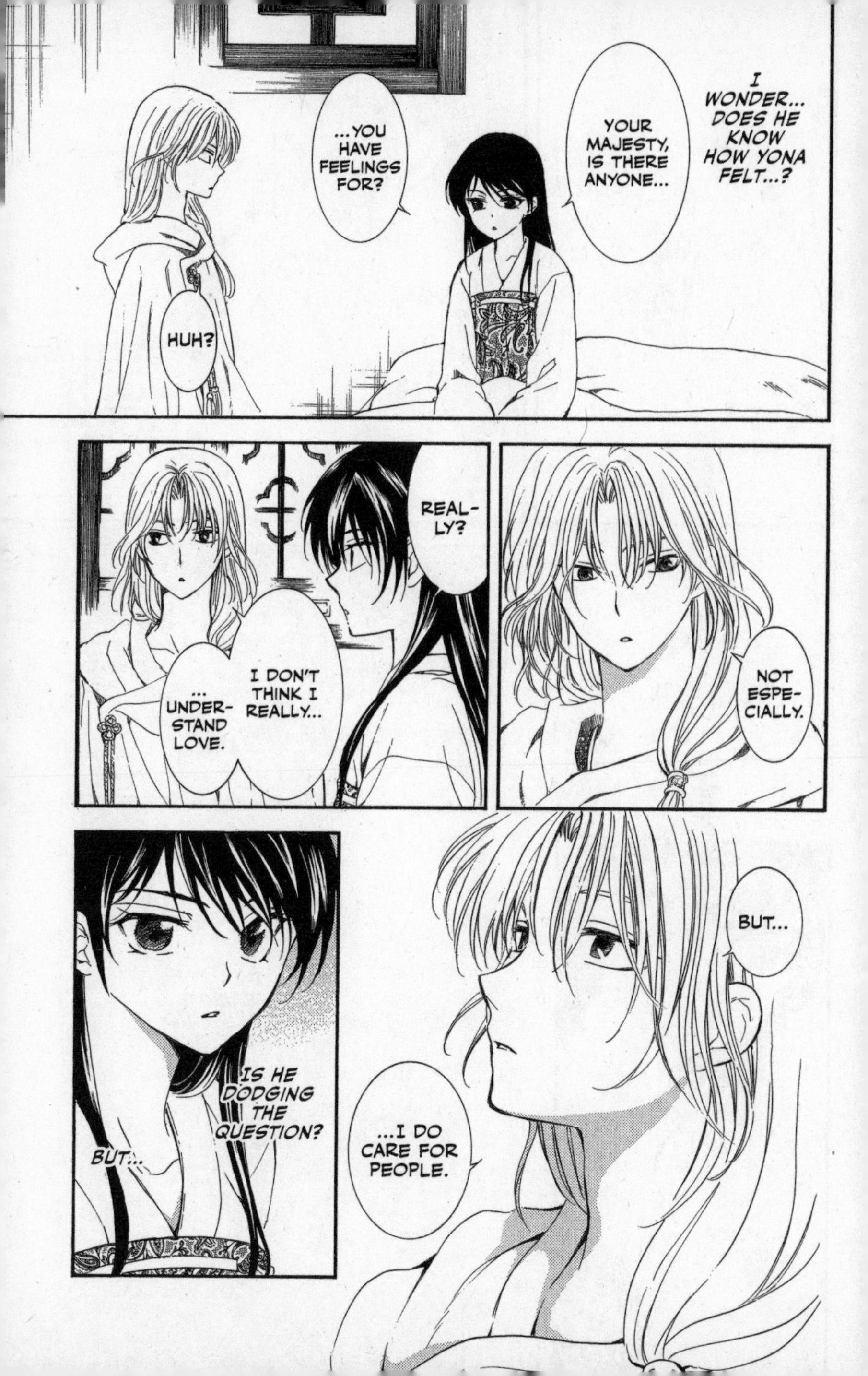
I WONDER... DOES HE KNOW HOW YONA FELT...?
YOUR MAJESTY, IS THERE ANYONE...
...YOU HAVE FEELINGS FOR?
HUH?
NOT ESPE-CIALLY.
REAL-LY?
I DON'T THINK I REALLY...
... UNDER-STAND LOVE.
BUT...
...I DO CARE FOR PEOPLE.
IS HE DODGING THE QUESTION?
BUT...

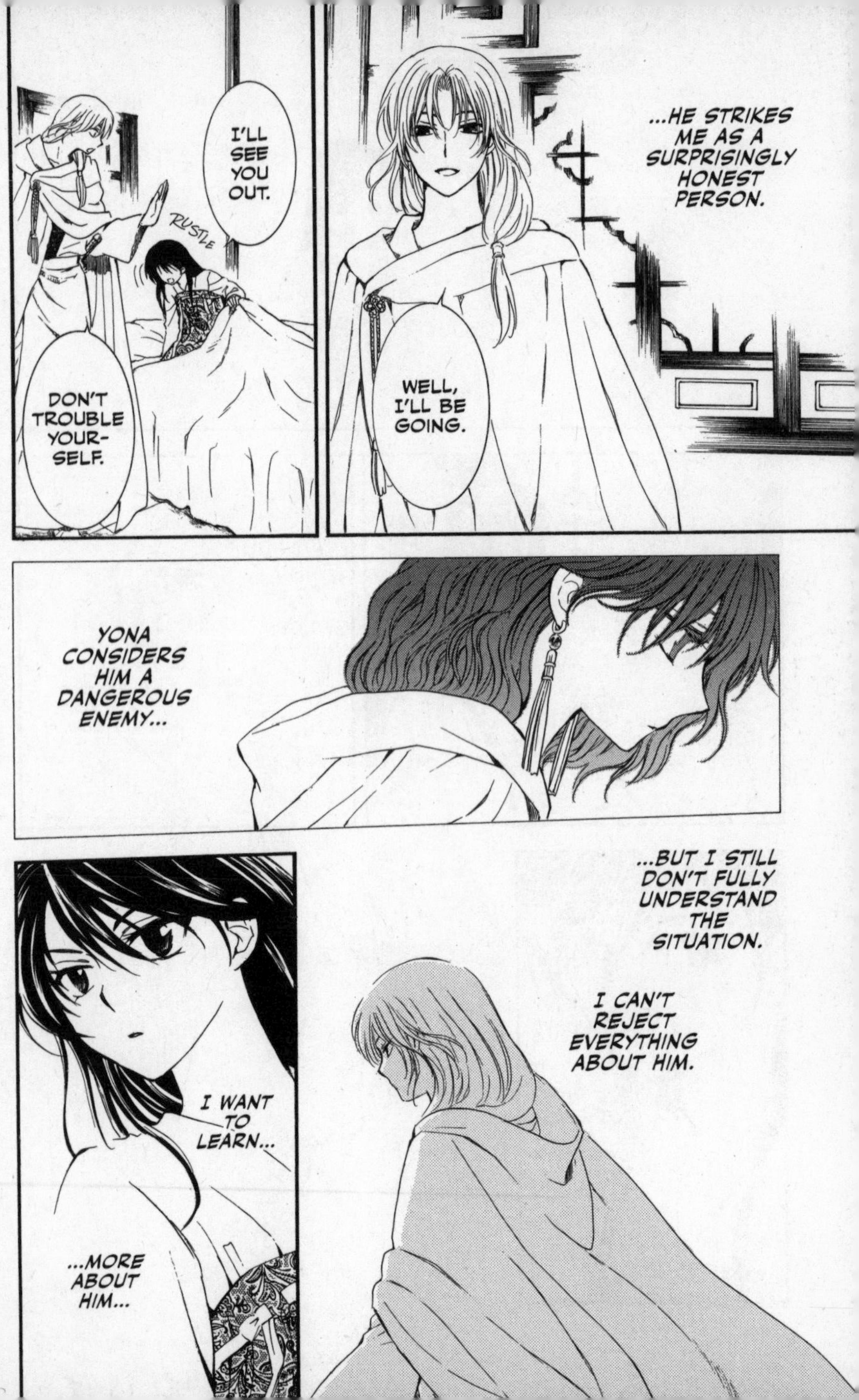
...HE STRIKES ME AS A SURPRISINGLY HONEST PERSON.
WELL, I'LL BE GOING.
I'LL SEE YOU OUT.
RUSTLE
DON'T TROUBLE YOURSELF.
YONA CONSIDERS HIM A DANGEROUS ENEMY...
...BUT I STILL DON'T FULLY UNDERSTAND THE SITUATION.
I CAN'T REJECT EVERYTHING ABOUT HIM.
I WANT TO LEARN...
...MORE ABOUT HIM...

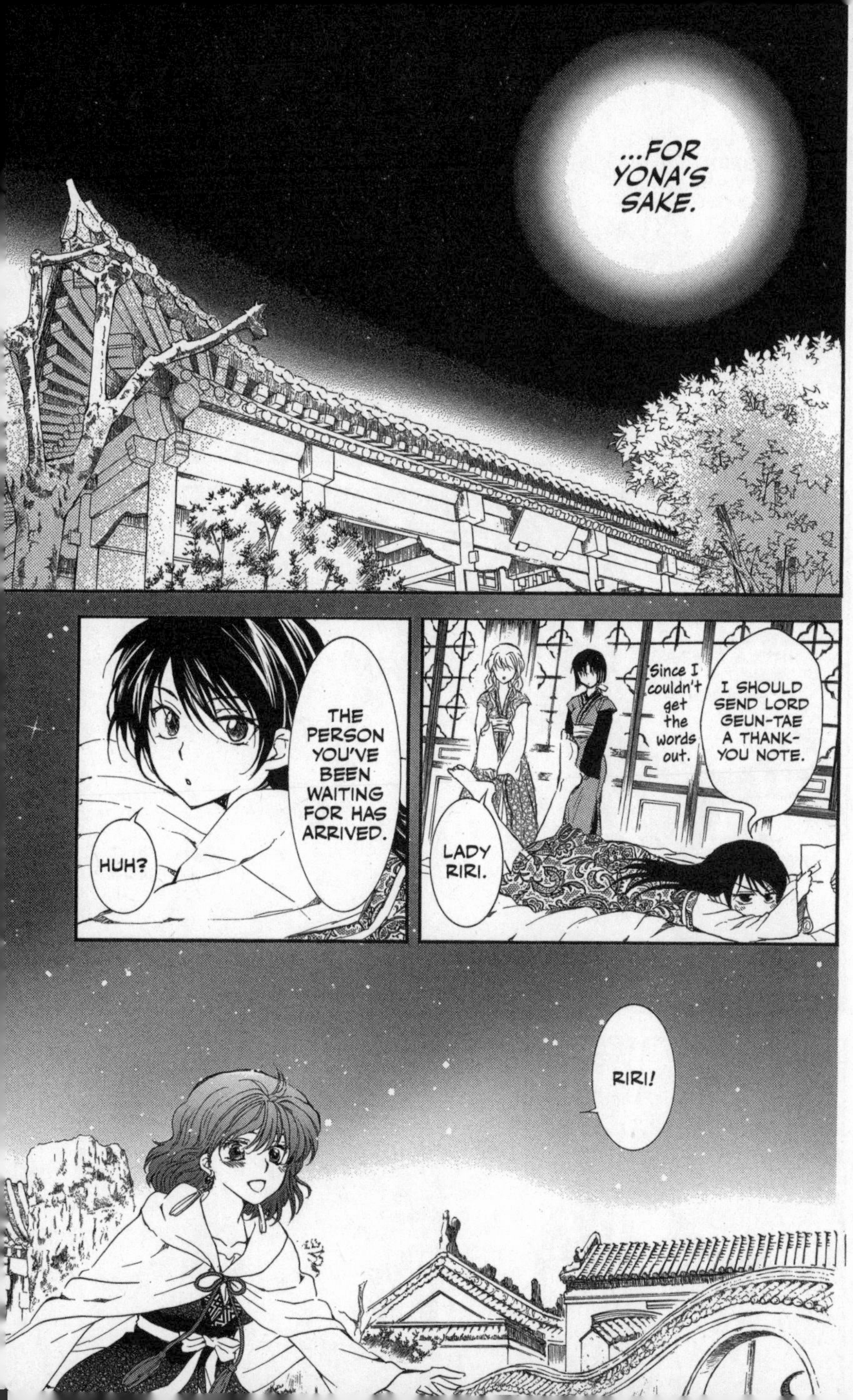
...FOR YONA'S SAKE.
I SHOULD SEND LORD GEUN-TAE A THANK-YOU NOTE.
Since I couldn't get the words out.
LADY RIRI.
THE PERSON YOU'VE BEEN WAITING FOR HAS ARRIVED.
HUH?
RIRI!

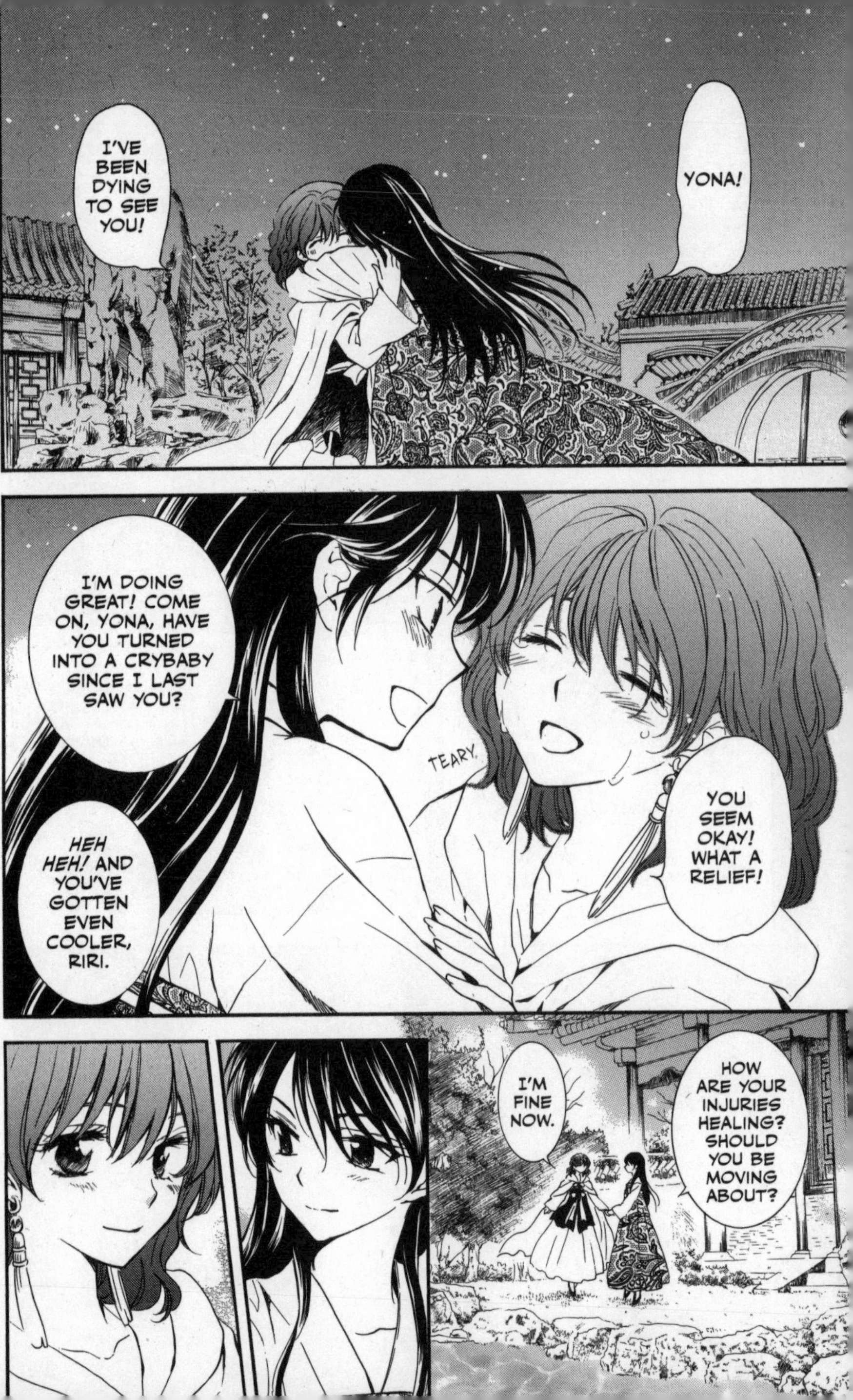
YONA!
I'VE BEEN DYING TO SEE YOU!
YOU SEEM OKAY! WHAT A RELIEF!
TEARY
I'M DOING GREAT! COME ON, YONA, HAVE YOU TURNED INTO A CRYBABY SINCE I LAST SAW YOU?
HEH HEH! AND YOU'VE GOTTEN EVEN COOLER, RIRI.
HOW ARE YOUR INJURIES HEALING? SHOULD YOU BE MOVING ABOUT?
I'M FINE NOW.

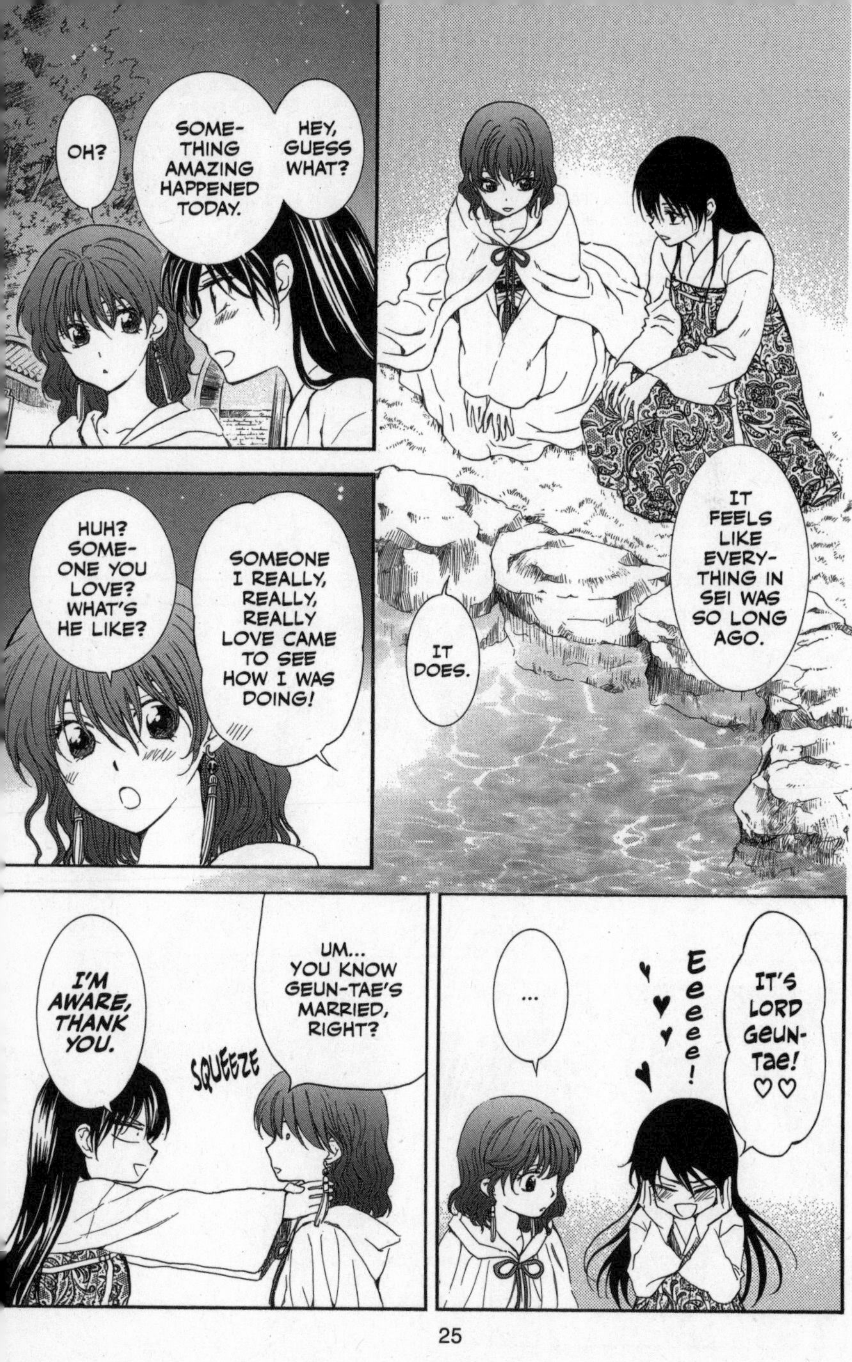
IT FEELS LIKE EVERYTHING IN SEI WAS SO LONG AGO.
IT DOES.
HEY, GUESS WHAT?
SOMETHING AMAZING HAPPENED TODAY.
OH?
SOMEONE I REALLY, REALLY, REALLY LOVE CAME TO SEE HOW I WAS DOING!
HUH? SOMEONE YOU LOVE? WHAT'S HE LIKE?
IT'S LORD GEUN-TAE! ♡♡
Eeeeee!
...
UM... YOU KNOW GEUN-TAE'S MARRIED, RIGHT?
SQUEEZE
I'M AWARE, THANK YOU.

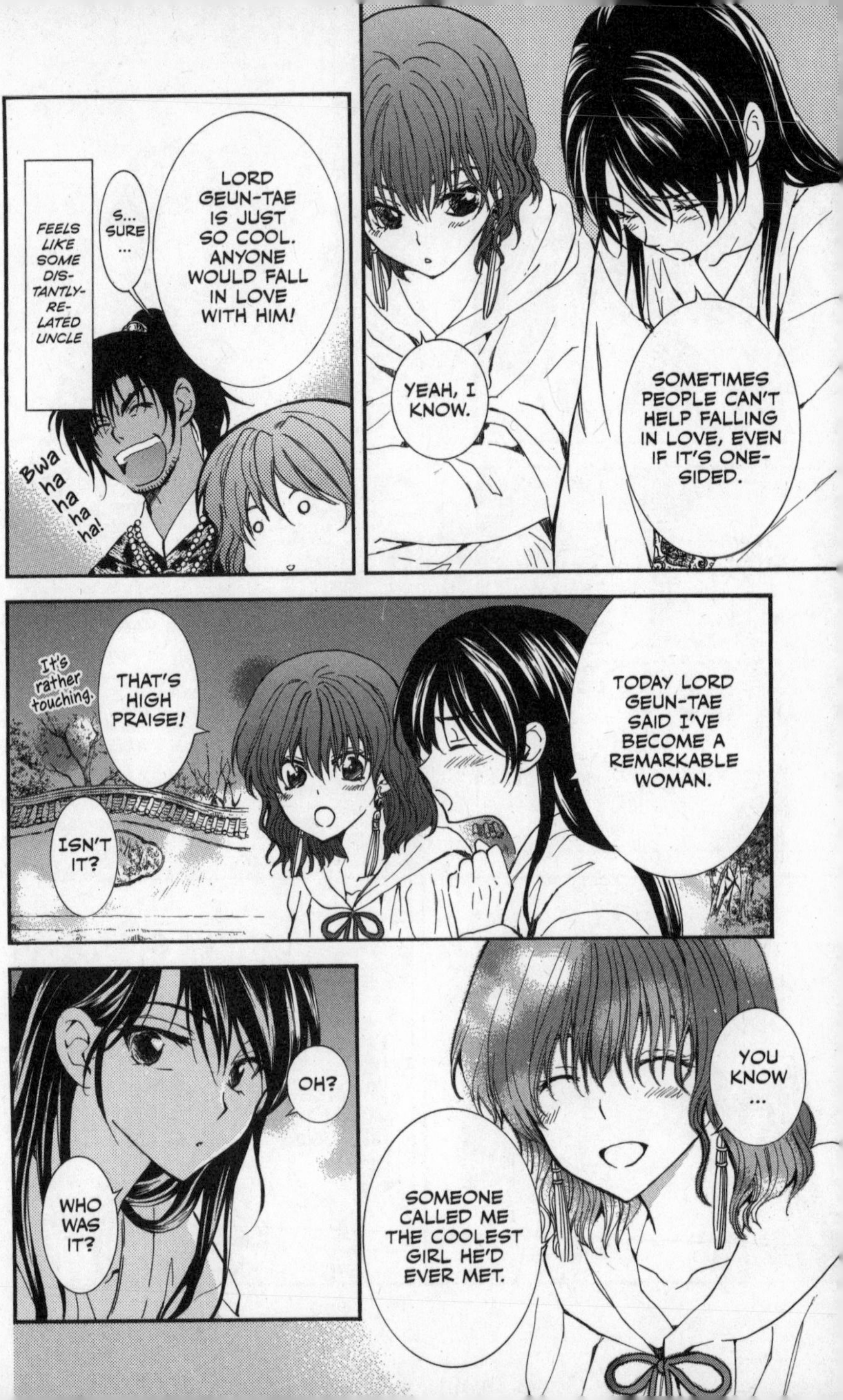
SOMETIMES PEOPLE CAN'T HELP FALLING IN LOVE, EVEN IF IT'S ONE-SIDED.
YEAH, I KNOW.
LORD GEUN-TAE IS JUST SO COOL. ANYONE WOULD FALL IN LOVE WITH HIM!
S... SURE ...
FEELS LIKE SOME DIS-TANTLY-RE-LATED UNCLE
Bwa ha ha ha ha!
TODAY LORD GEUN-TAE SAID I'VE BECOME A REMARKABLE WOMAN.
THAT'S HIGH PRAISE!
ISN'T IT?
It's rather touching.
YOU KNOW ...
SOMEONE CALLED ME THE COOLEST GIRL HE'D EVER MET.
OH?
WHO WAS IT?

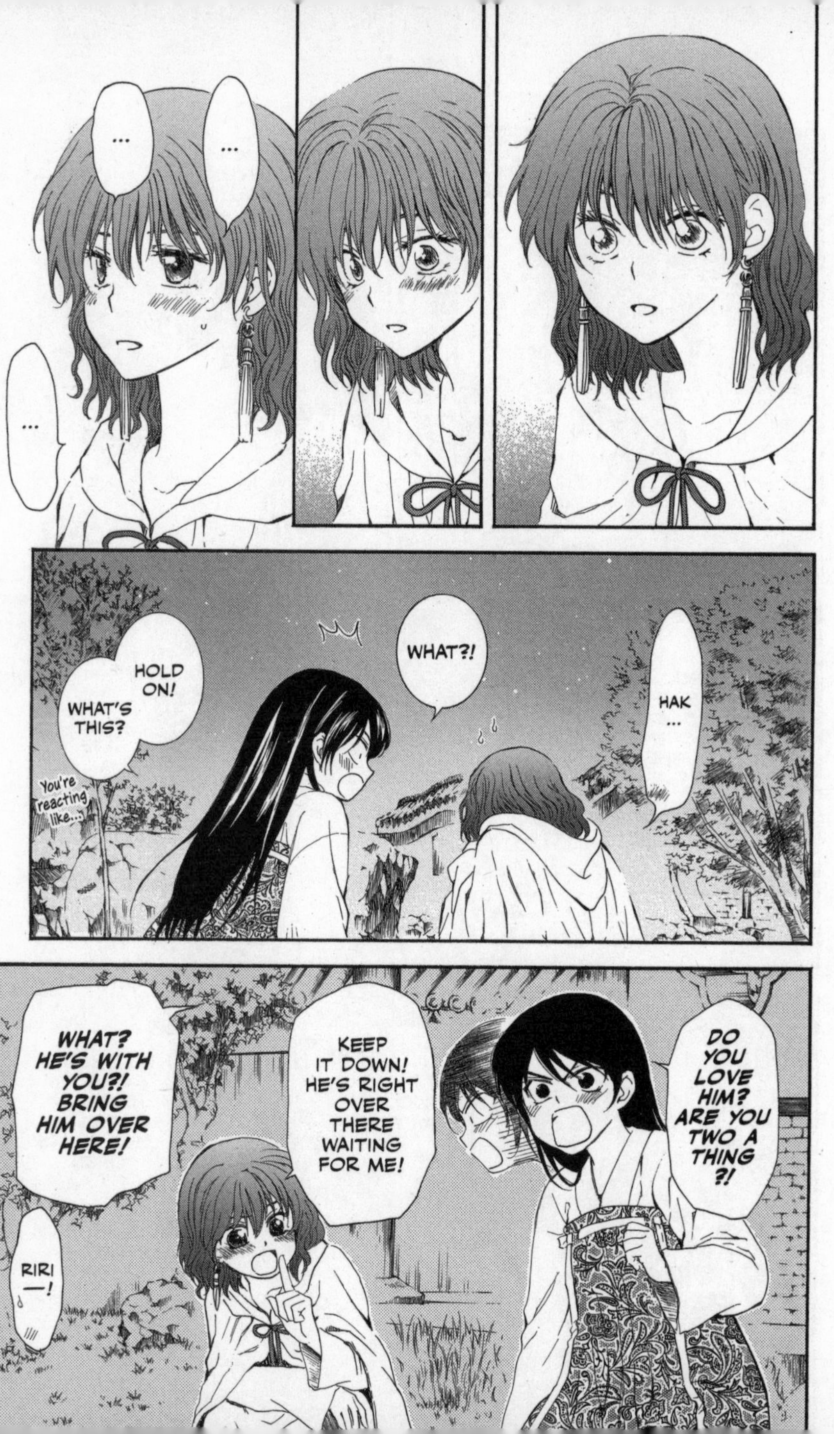
...
...
...
HAK ...
WHAT?!
HOLD ON! WHAT'S THIS?
You're reacting like...
DO YOU LOVE HIM? ARE YOU TWO A THING?!
KEEP IT DOWN! HE'S RIGHT OVER THERE WAITING FOR ME!
WHAT? HE'S WITH YOU?! BRING HIM OVER HERE!
RIRI—!

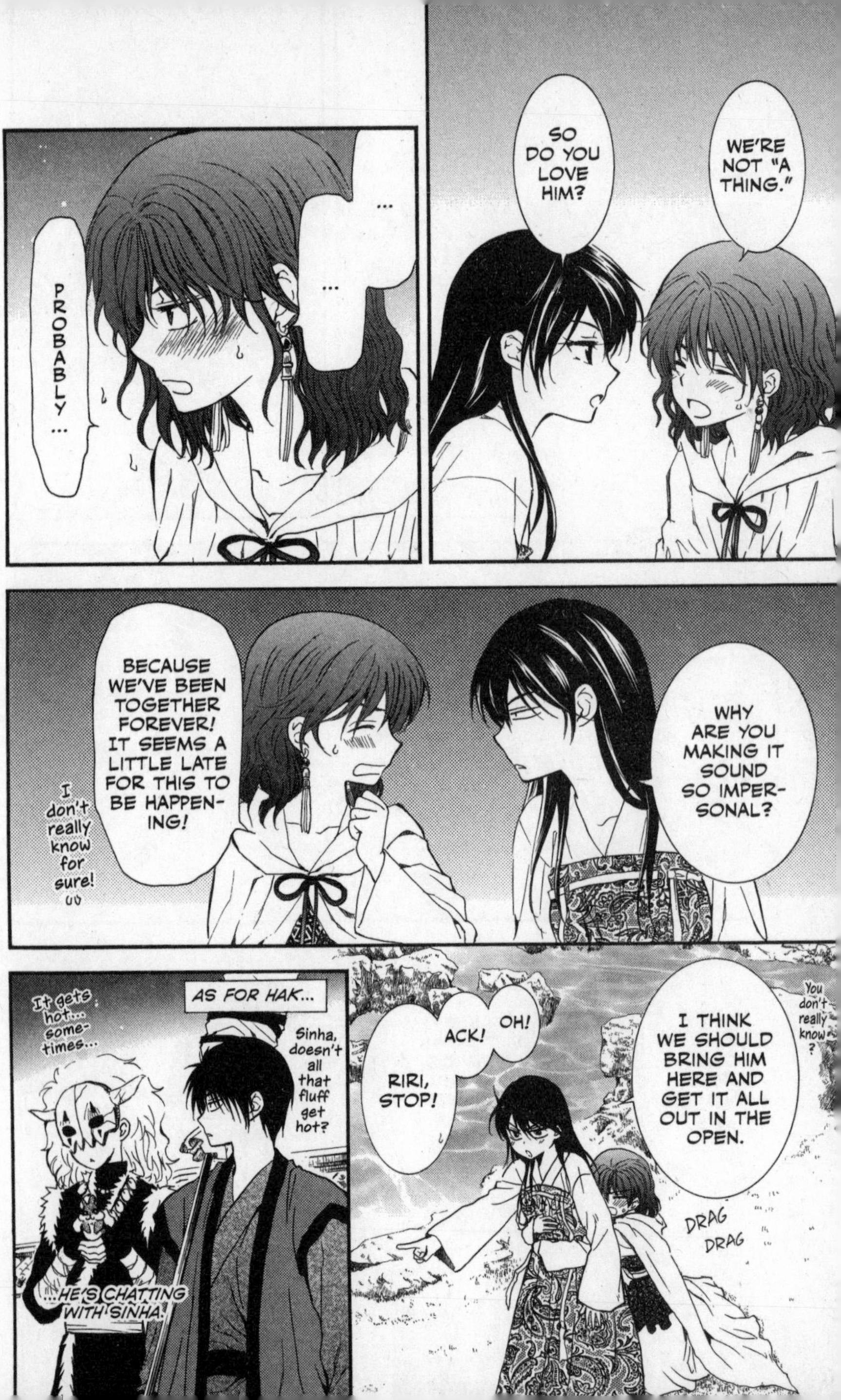
WE'RE NOT "A THING."
SO DO YOU LOVE HIM?
...
...
PROBABLY...
WHY ARE YOU MAKING IT SOUND SO IMPERSONAL?
BECAUSE WE'VE BEEN TOGETHER FOREVER! IT SEEMS A LITTLE LATE FOR THIS TO BE HAPPENING!
I don't really know for sure!
You don't really know?
I THINK WE SHOULD BRING HIM HERE AND GET IT ALL OUT IN THE OPEN.
OH!
ACK!
RIRI, STOP!
DRAG
DRAG
AS FOR HAK...
Sinha, doesn't all that fluff get hot?
It gets hot... sometimes...
...HE'S CHATTING WITH SINHA.

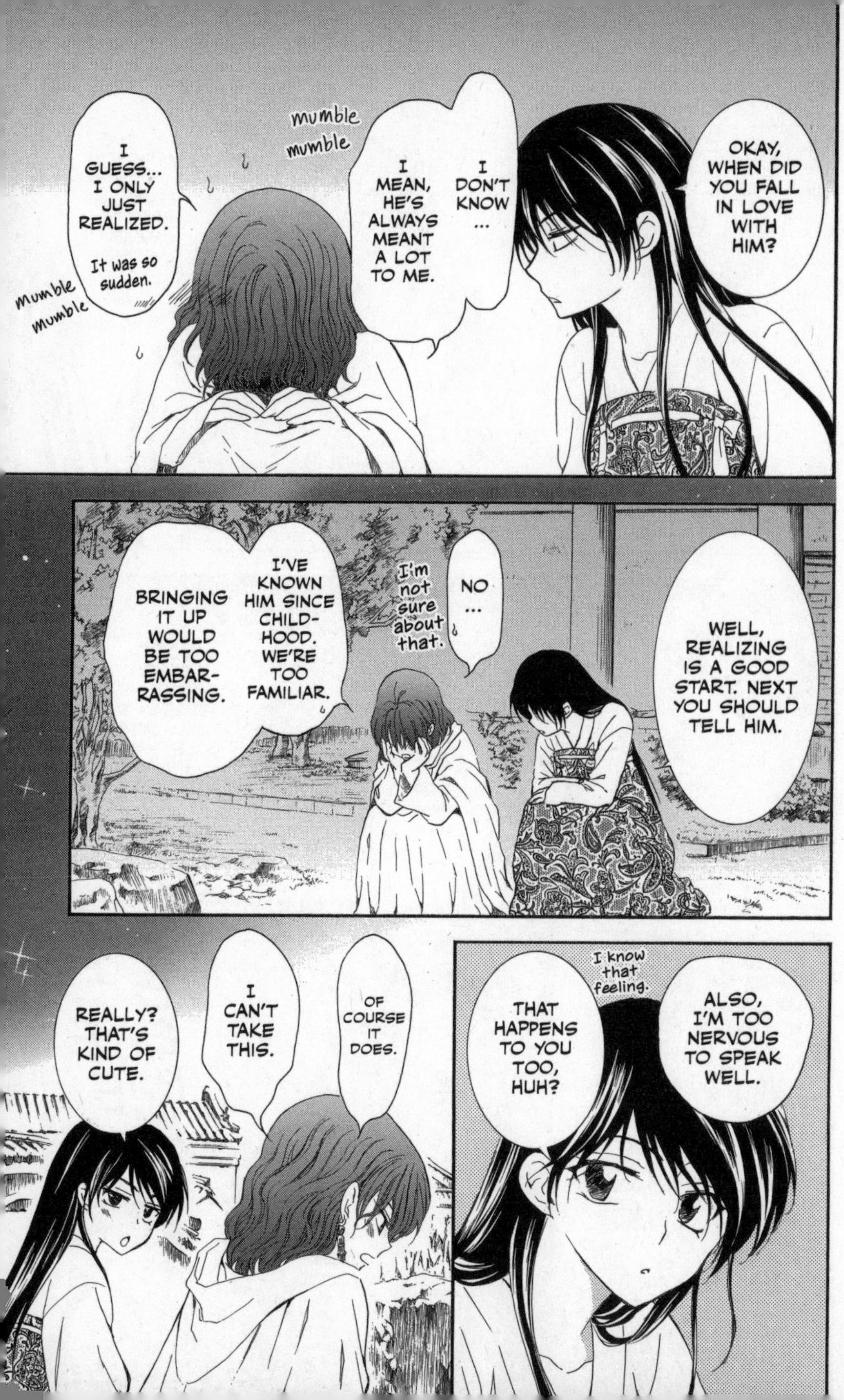
OKAY, WHEN DID YOU FALL IN LOVE WITH HIM?
I DON'T KNOW ...
I MEAN, HE'S ALWAYS MEANT A LOT TO ME.
mumble mumble
I GUESS... I ONLY JUST REALIZED.
It was so sudden.
mumble mumble
WELL, REALIZING IS A GOOD START. NEXT YOU SHOULD TELL HIM.
NO ...
I'm not sure about that.
I'VE KNOWN HIM SINCE CHILD-HOOD. WE'RE TOO FAMILIAR.
BRINGING IT UP WOULD BE TOO EMBAR-RASSING.
ALSO, I'M TOO NERVOUS TO SPEAK WELL.
I know that feeling.
THAT HAPPENS TO YOU TOO, HUH?
OF COURSE IT DOES.
I CAN'T TAKE THIS.
REALLY? THAT'S KIND OF CUTE.

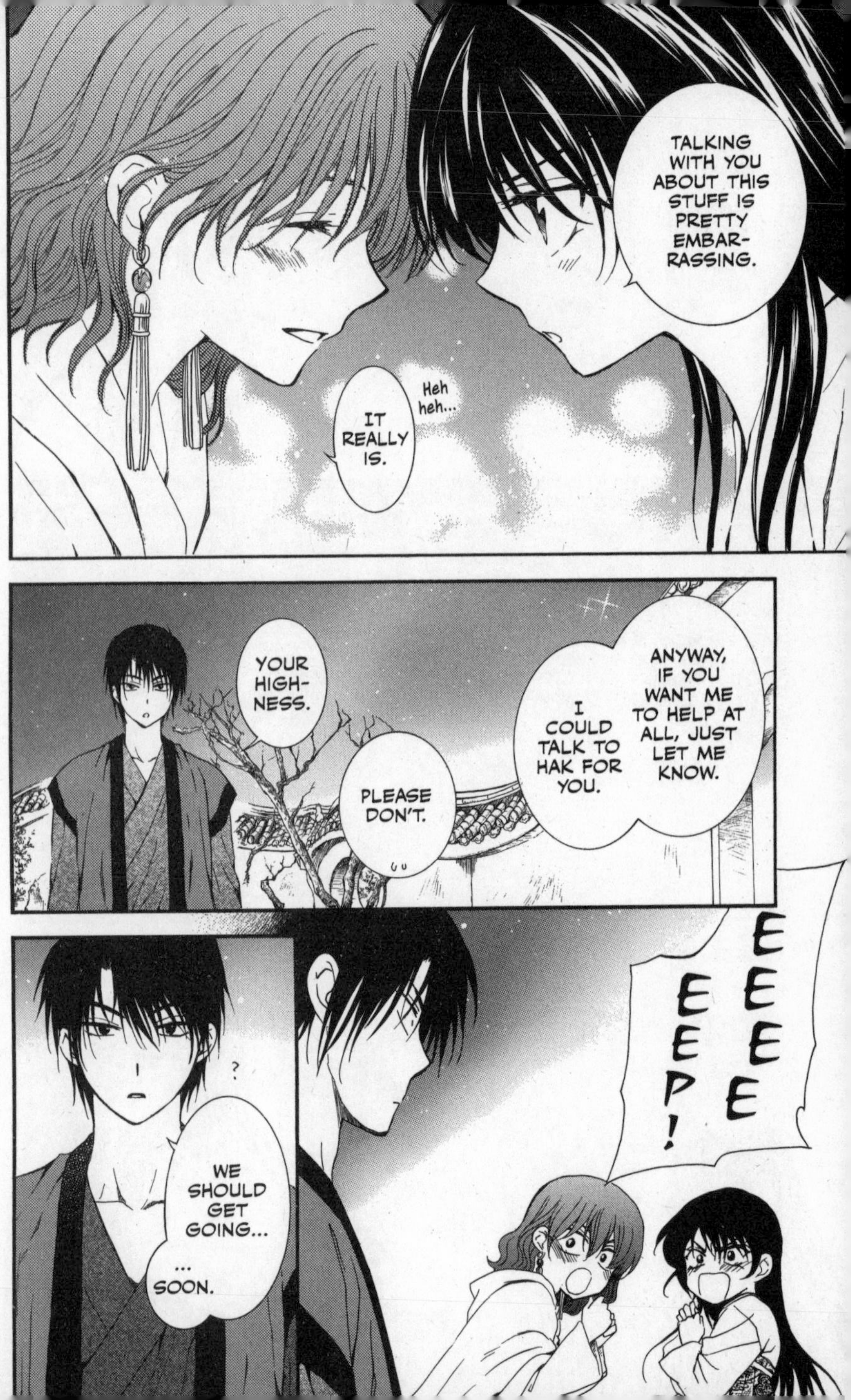

TALKING WITH YOU ABOUT THIS STUFF IS PRETTY EMBAR-RASSING.
Heh heh...
IT REALLY IS.
ANYWAY, IF YOU WANT ME TO HELP AT ALL, JUST LET ME KNOW.
I COULD TALK TO HAK FOR YOU.
PLEASE DON'T.
YOUR HIGH-NESS.
EEEEEEP!
?
WE SHOULD GET GOING...
...SOON.

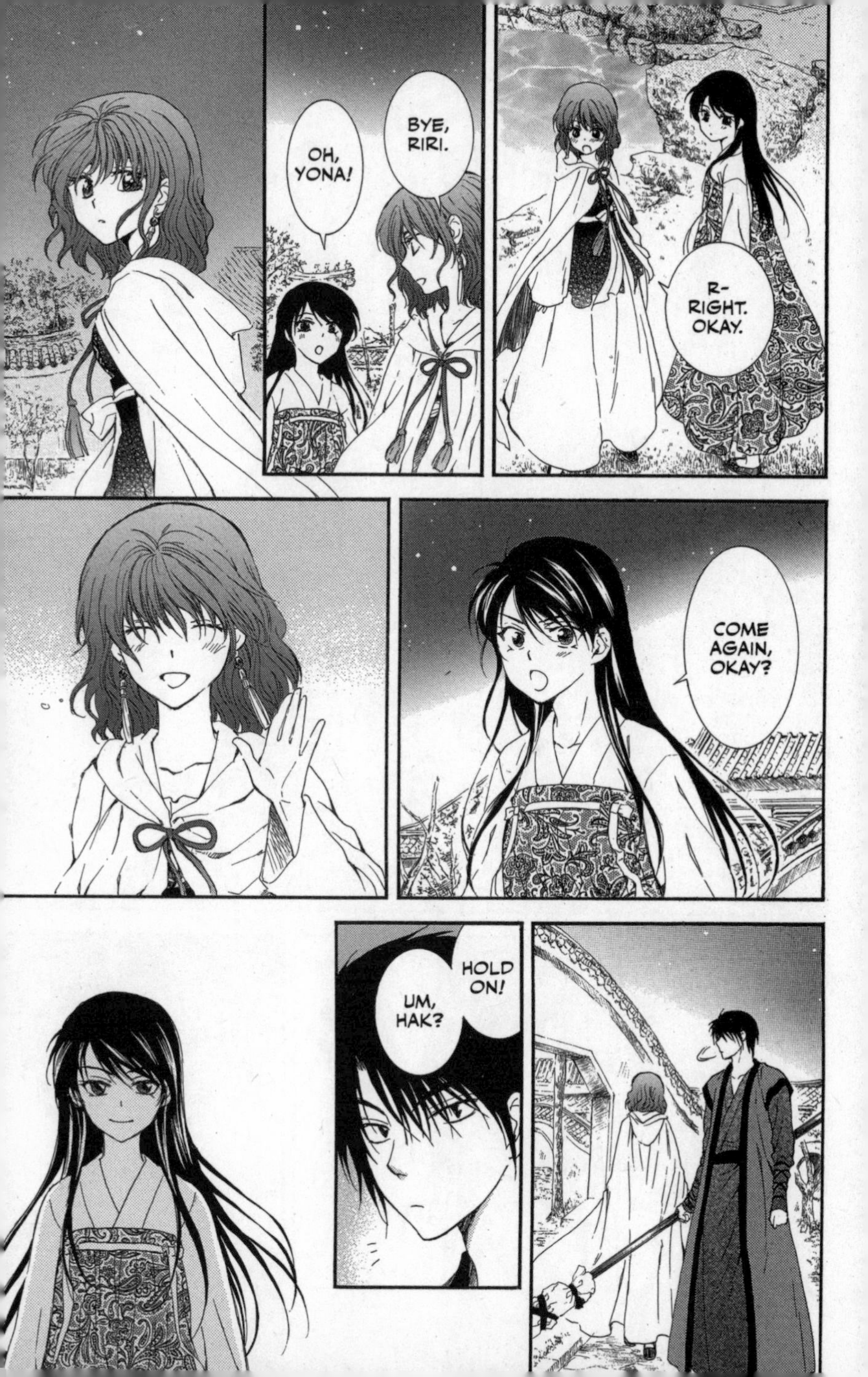
R-
RIGHT.
OKAY.
BYE,
RIRI.
OH,
YONA!
COME
AGAIN,
OKAY?
HOLD
ON!
UM,
HAK?

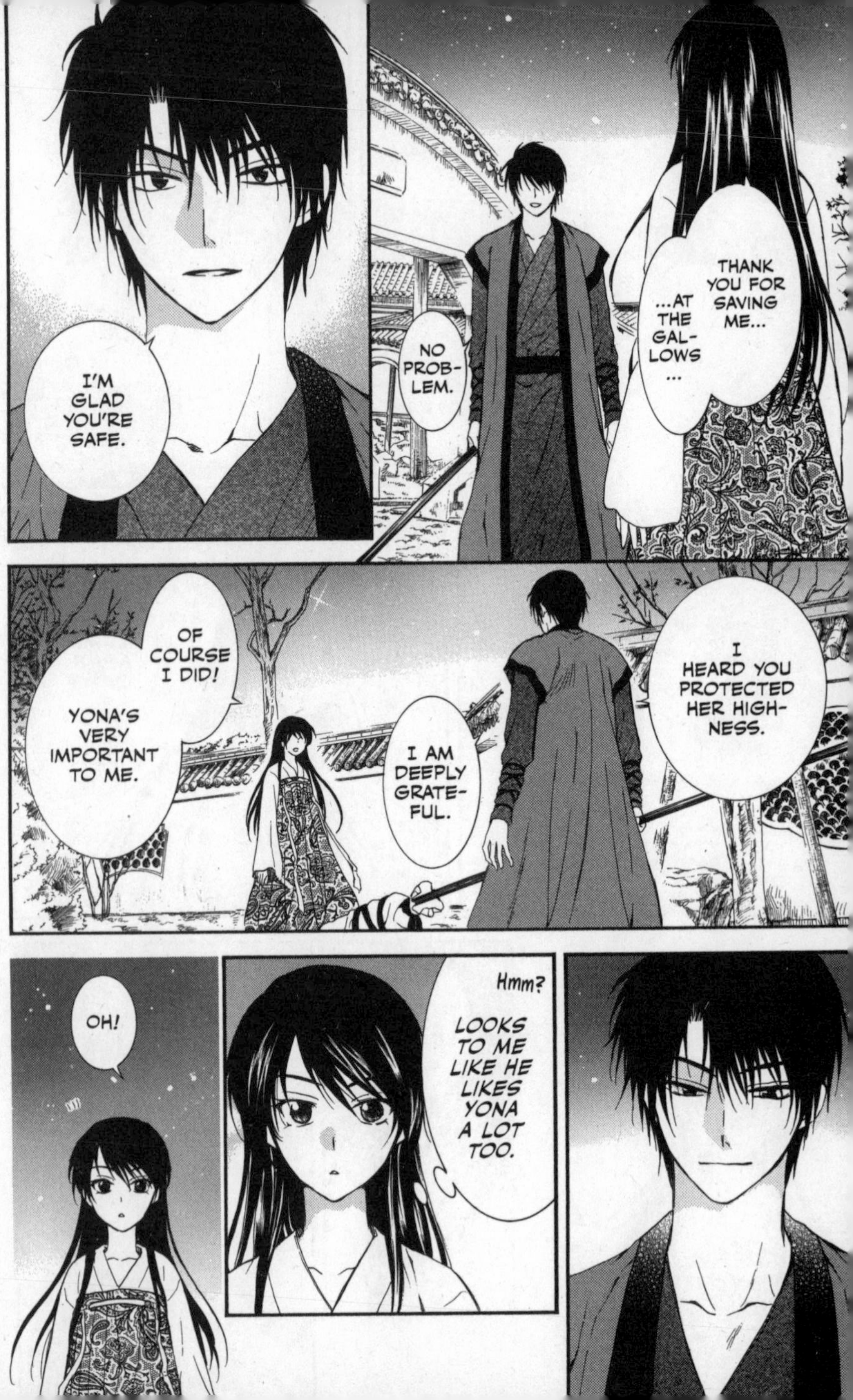
THANK YOU FOR SAVING ME...
...AT THE GALLOWS ...
NO PROBLEM.
I'M GLAD YOU'RE SAFE.
I HEARD YOU PROTECTED HER HIGHNESS.
I AM DEEPLY GRATEFUL.
OF COURSE I DID!
YONA'S VERY IMPORTANT TO ME.
Hmm?
LOOKS TO ME LIKE HE LIKES YONA A LOT TOO.
OH!

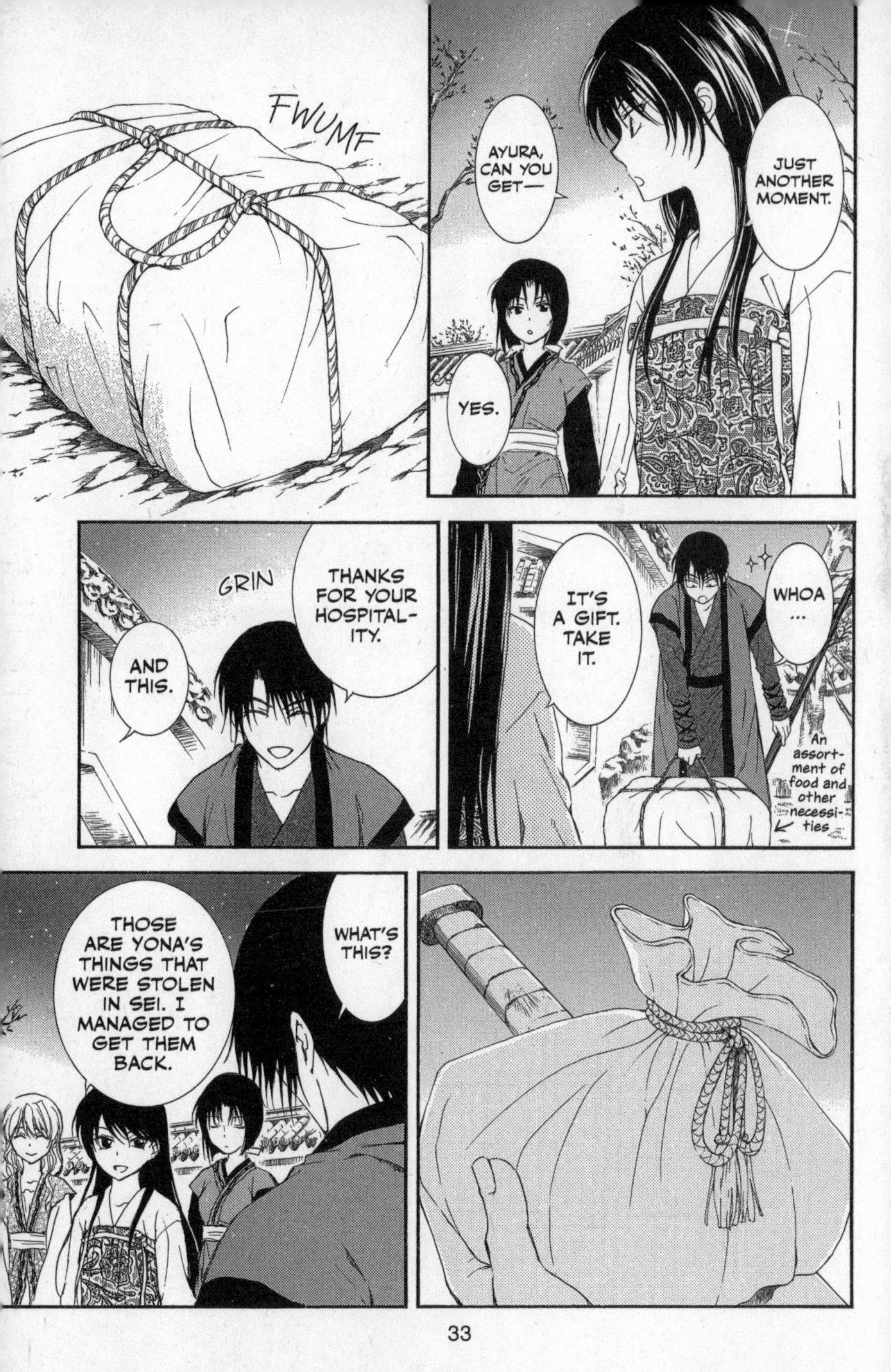
JUST ANOTHER MOMENT.
AYURA, CAN YOU GET—
YES.
FWUMF
WHOA ...
IT'S A GIFT. TAKE IT.
An assortment of food and other necessities
THANKS FOR YOUR HOSPITAL-ITY.
GRIN
AND THIS.
WHAT'S THIS?
THOSE ARE YONA'S THINGS THAT WERE STOLEN IN SEI. I MANAGED TO GET THEM BACK.

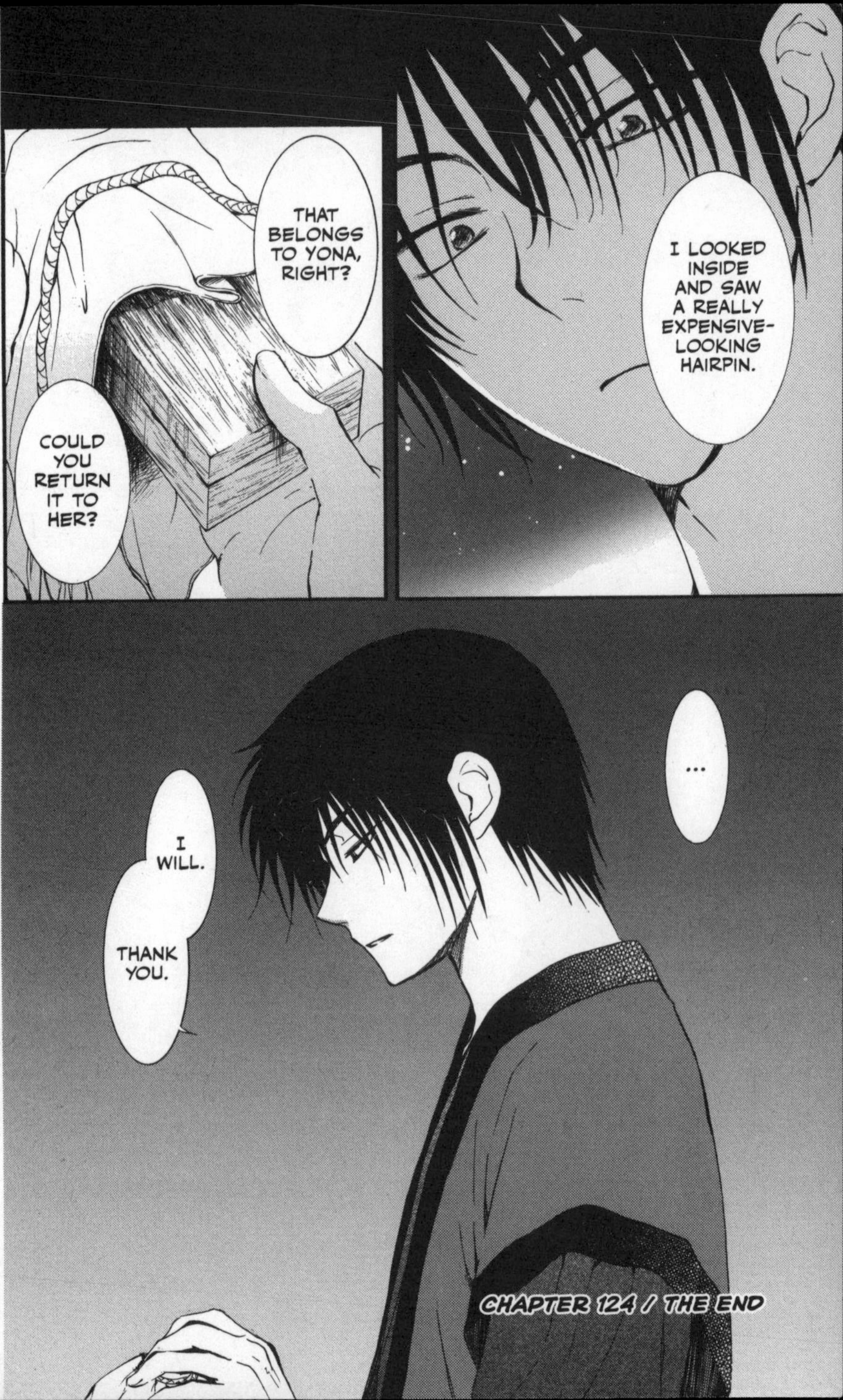
I LOOKED INSIDE AND SAW A REALLY EXPENSIVE-LOOKING HAIRPIN.
THAT BELONGS TO YONA, RIGHT?
COULD YOU RETURN IT TO HER?
...
I WILL.
THANK YOU.
CHAPTER 124 / THE END

CHAPTER 125: THE THING I DREAMED OF

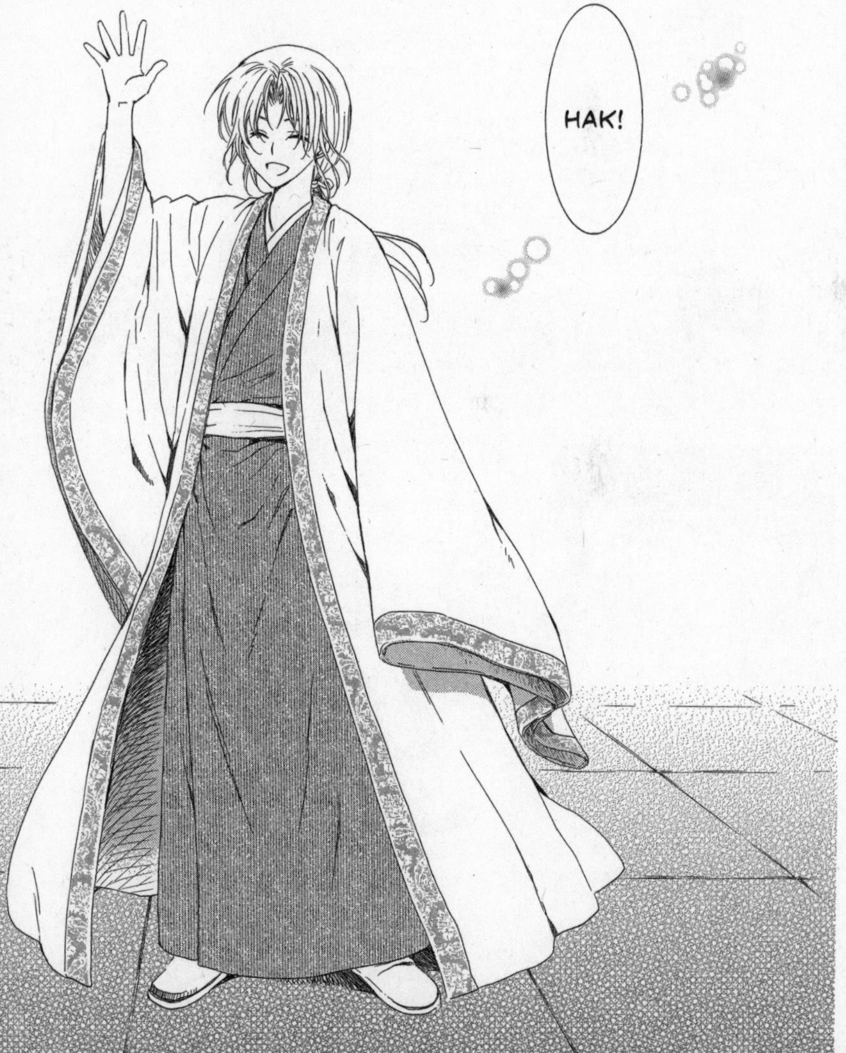
HAK!

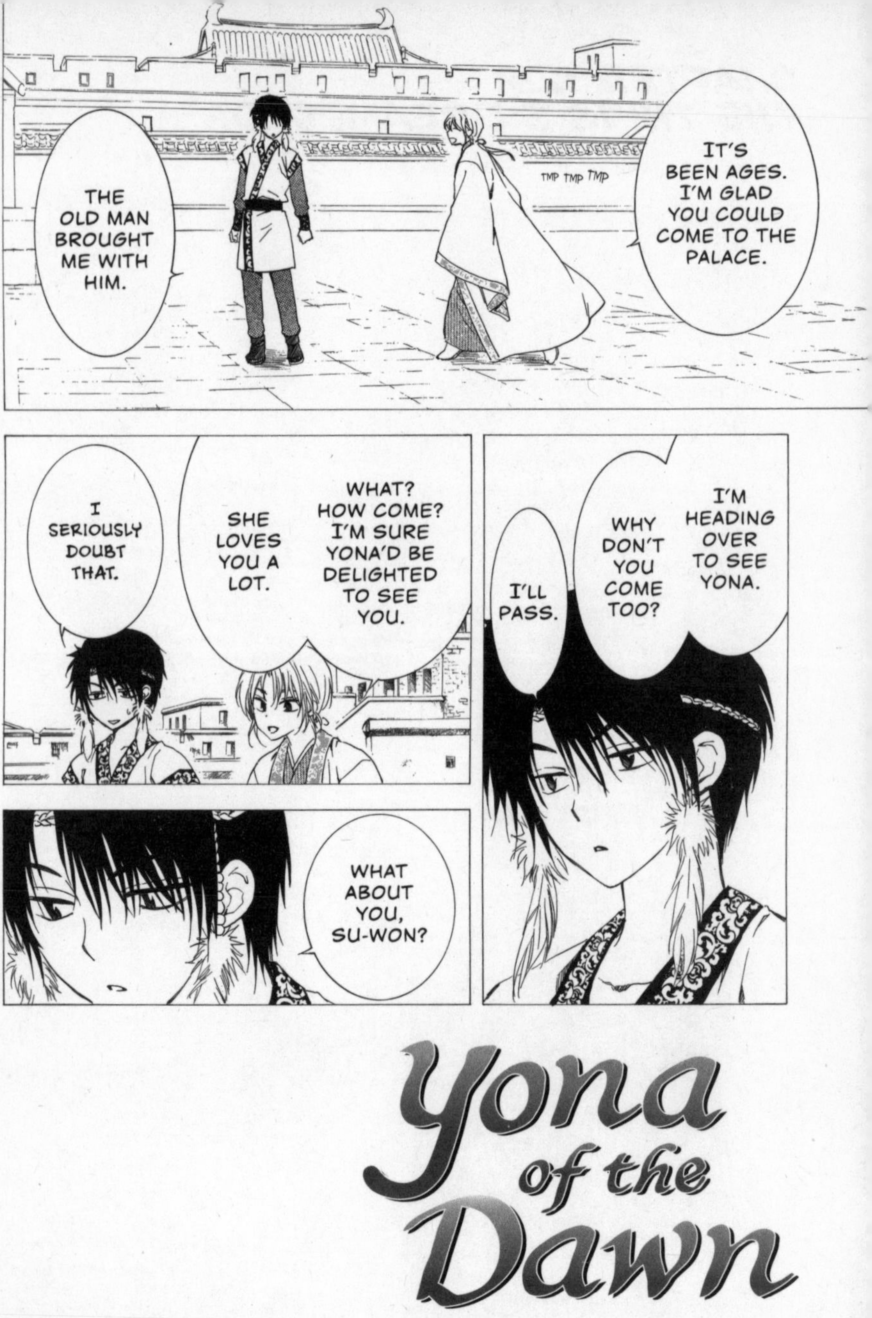
IT'S BEEN AGES. I'M GLAD YOU COULD COME TO THE PALACE.
TMP TMP TMP
THE OLD MAN BROUGHT ME WITH HIM.
I'M HEADING OVER TO SEE YONA.
WHY DON'T YOU COME TOO?
I'LL PASS.
WHAT? HOW COME? I'M SURE YONA'D BE DELIGHTED TO SEE YOU.
SHE LOVES YOU A LOT.
I SERIOUSLY DOUBT THAT.
WHAT ABOUT YOU, SU-WON?

Yona of the Dawn

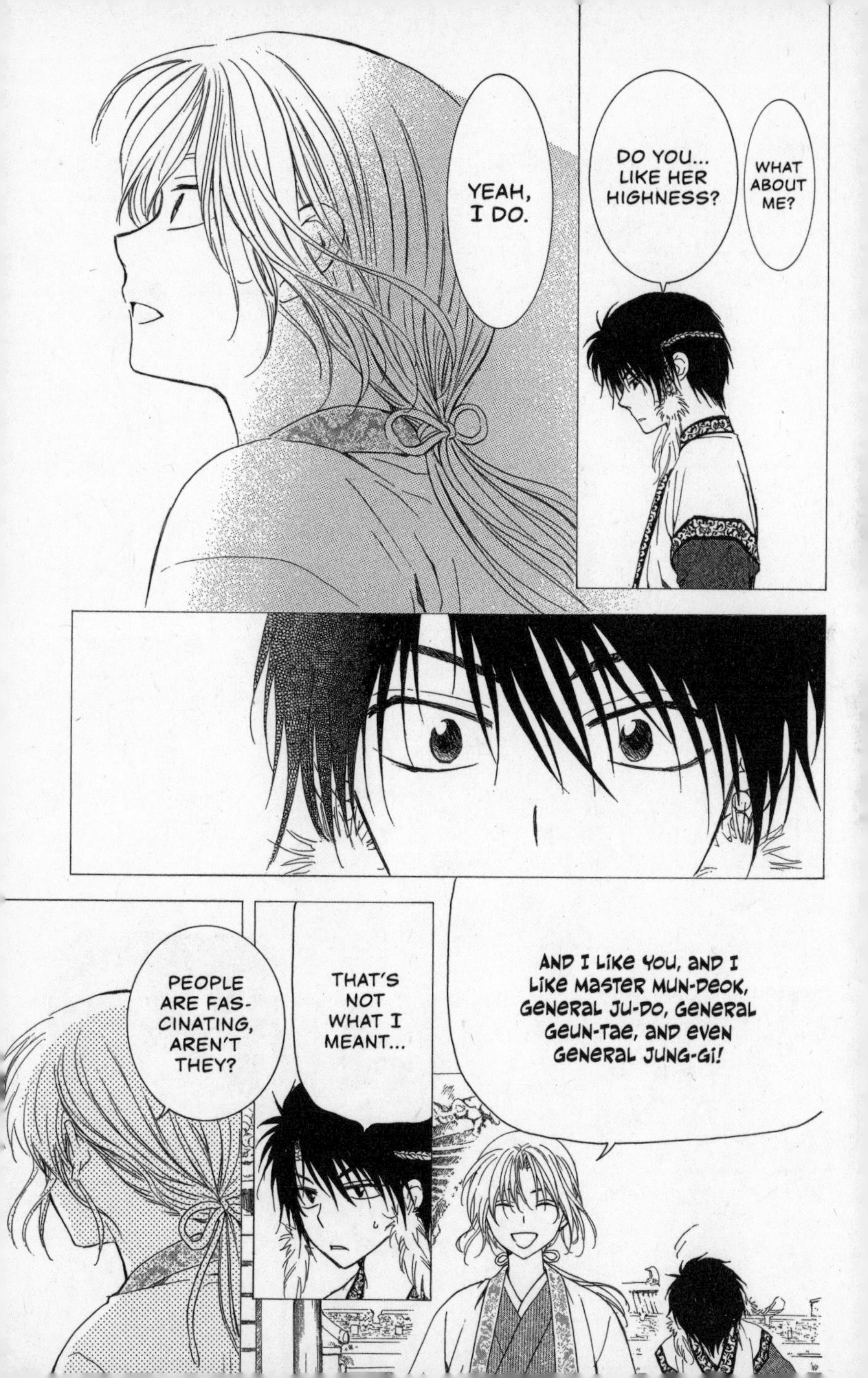
WHAT ABOUT ME?
DO YOU... LIKE HER HIGHNESS?
YEAH, I DO.
AND I LIKE YOU, AND I LIKE MASTER MUN-DEOK, GENERAL JU-DO, GENERAL GEUN-TAE, AND EVEN GENERAL JUNG-GI!
THAT'S NOT WHAT I MEANT...
PEOPLE ARE FAS-CINATING, AREN'T THEY?

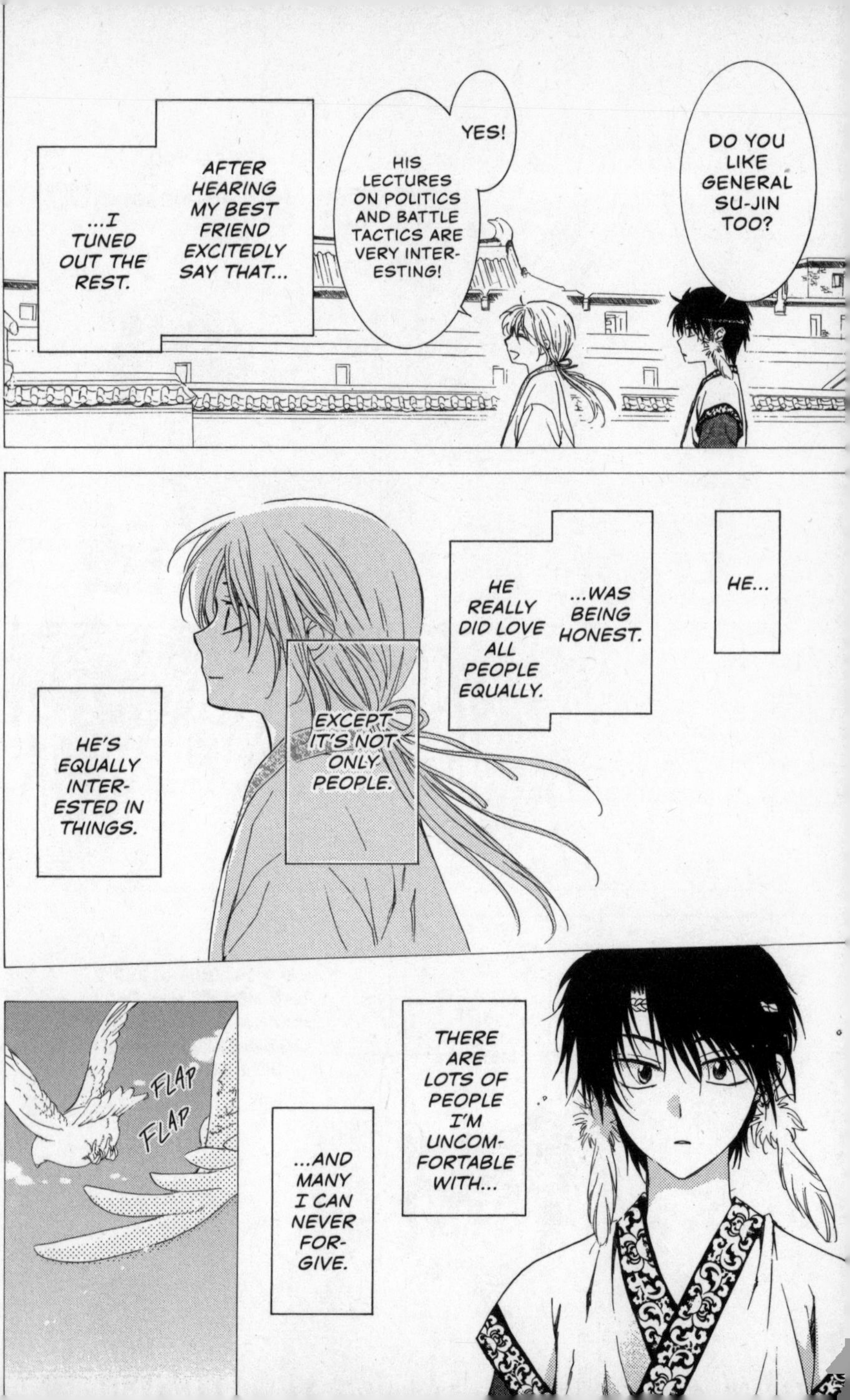
DO YOU LIKE GENERAL SU-JIN TOO?
YES! HIS LECTURES ON POLITICS AND BATTLE TACTICS ARE VERY INTERESTING!
AFTER HEARING MY BEST FRIEND EXCITEDLY SAY THAT...
...I TUNED OUT THE REST.
HE...
...WAS BEING HONEST.
HE REALLY DID LOVE ALL PEOPLE EQUALLY.
EXCEPT IT'S NOT ONLY PEOPLE.
HE'S EQUALLY INTERESTED IN THINGS.
THERE ARE LOTS OF PEOPLE I'M UNCOMFORTABLE WITH...
...AND MANY I CAN NEVER FORGIVE.
FLAP
FLAP

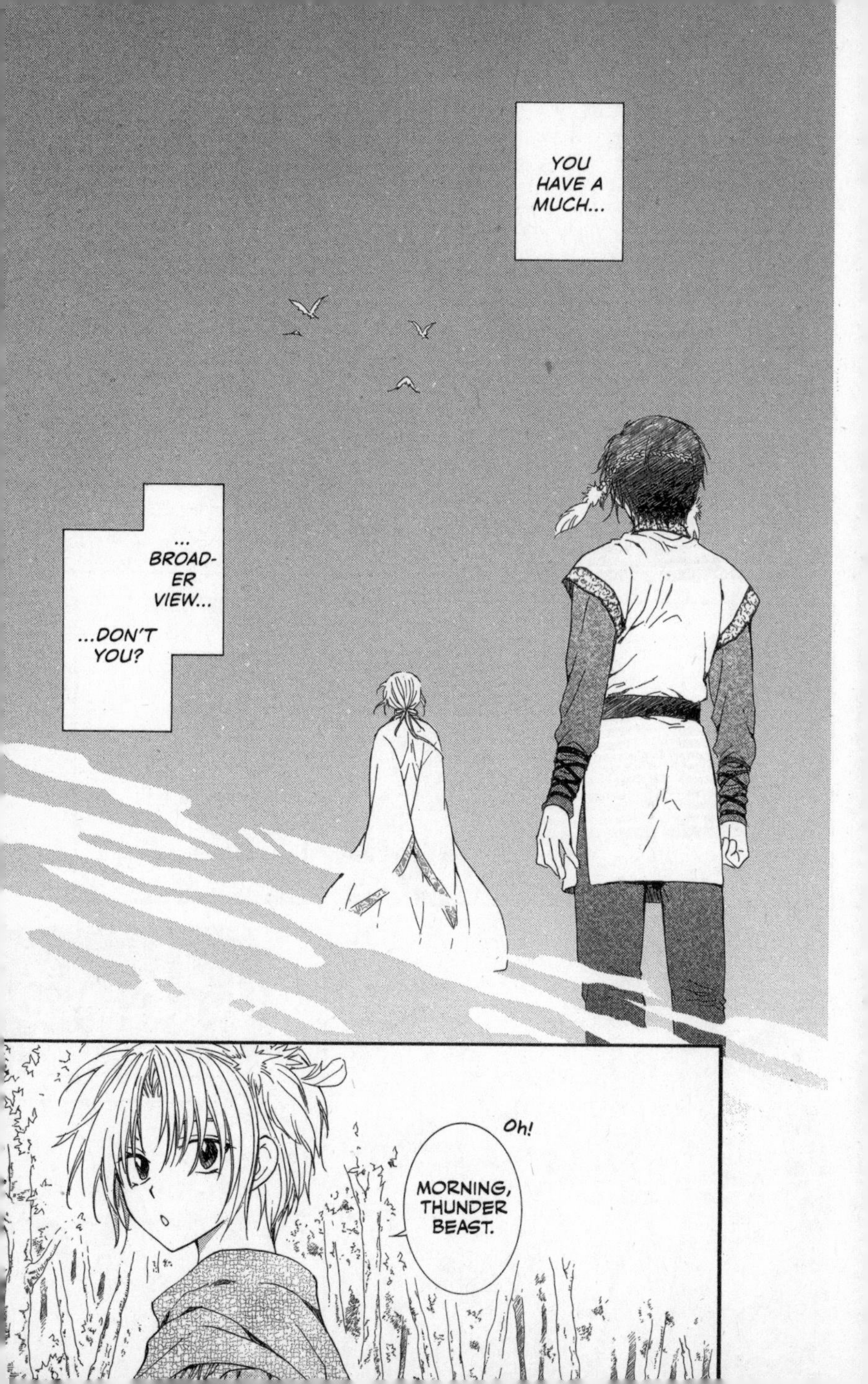
YOU HAVE A MUCH...
...BROADER VIEW...
...DON'T YOU?
Oh!
MORNING, THUNDER BEAST.

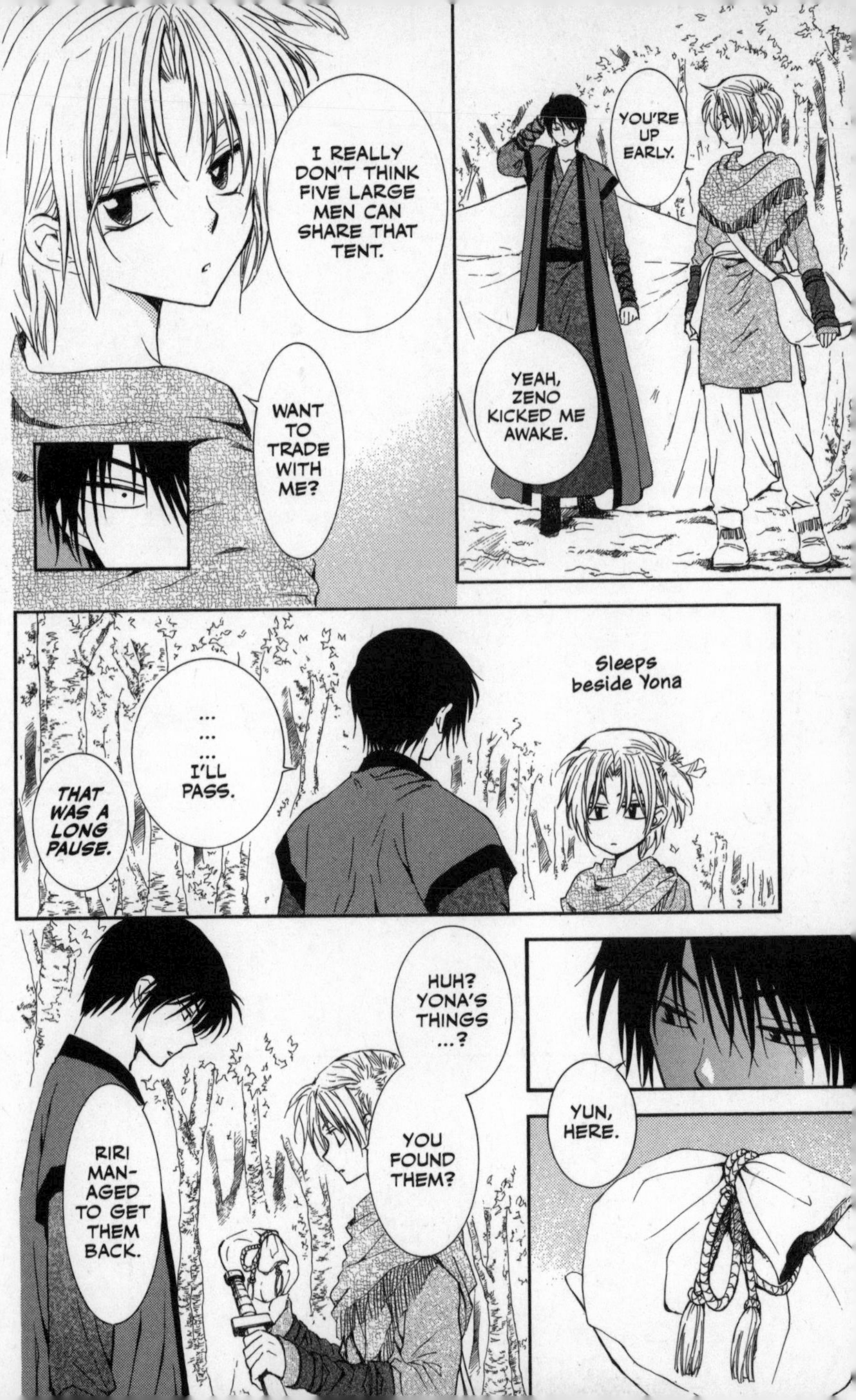
YOU'RE UP EARLY.
YEAH, ZENO KICKED ME AWAKE.
I REALLY DON'T THINK FIVE LARGE MEN CAN SHARE THAT TENT.
WANT TO TRADE WITH ME?
Sleeps beside Yona
... ... I'LL PASS.
THAT WAS A LONG PAUSE.
YUN, HERE.
HUH? YONA'S THINGS ...?
YOU FOUND THEM?
RIRI MAN-AGED TO GET THEM BACK.

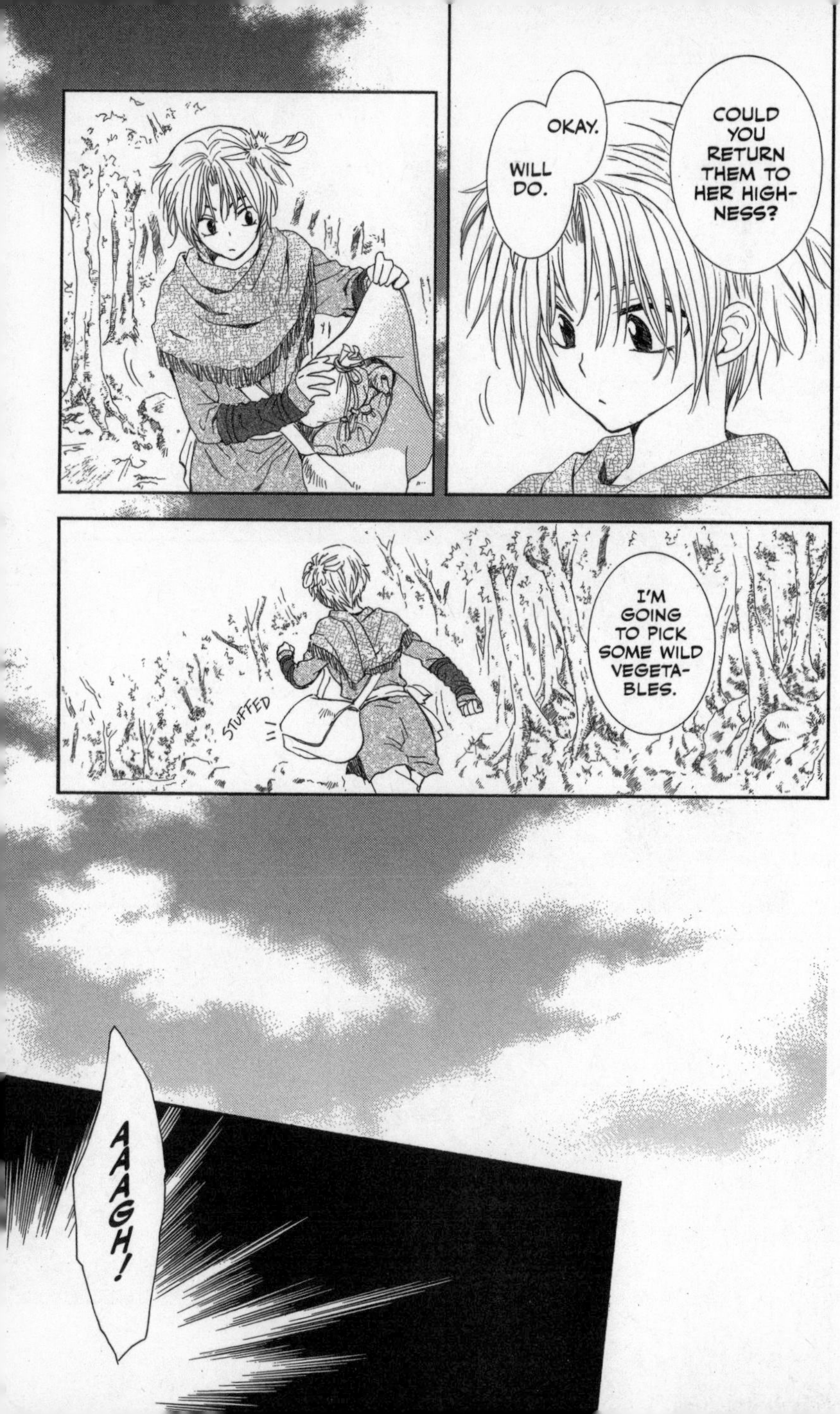
COULD YOU RETURN THEM TO HER HIGH-NESS?
OKAY.
WILL DO.
I'M GOING TO PICK SOME WILD VEGETA-BLES.
STUFFED
AAAGH!

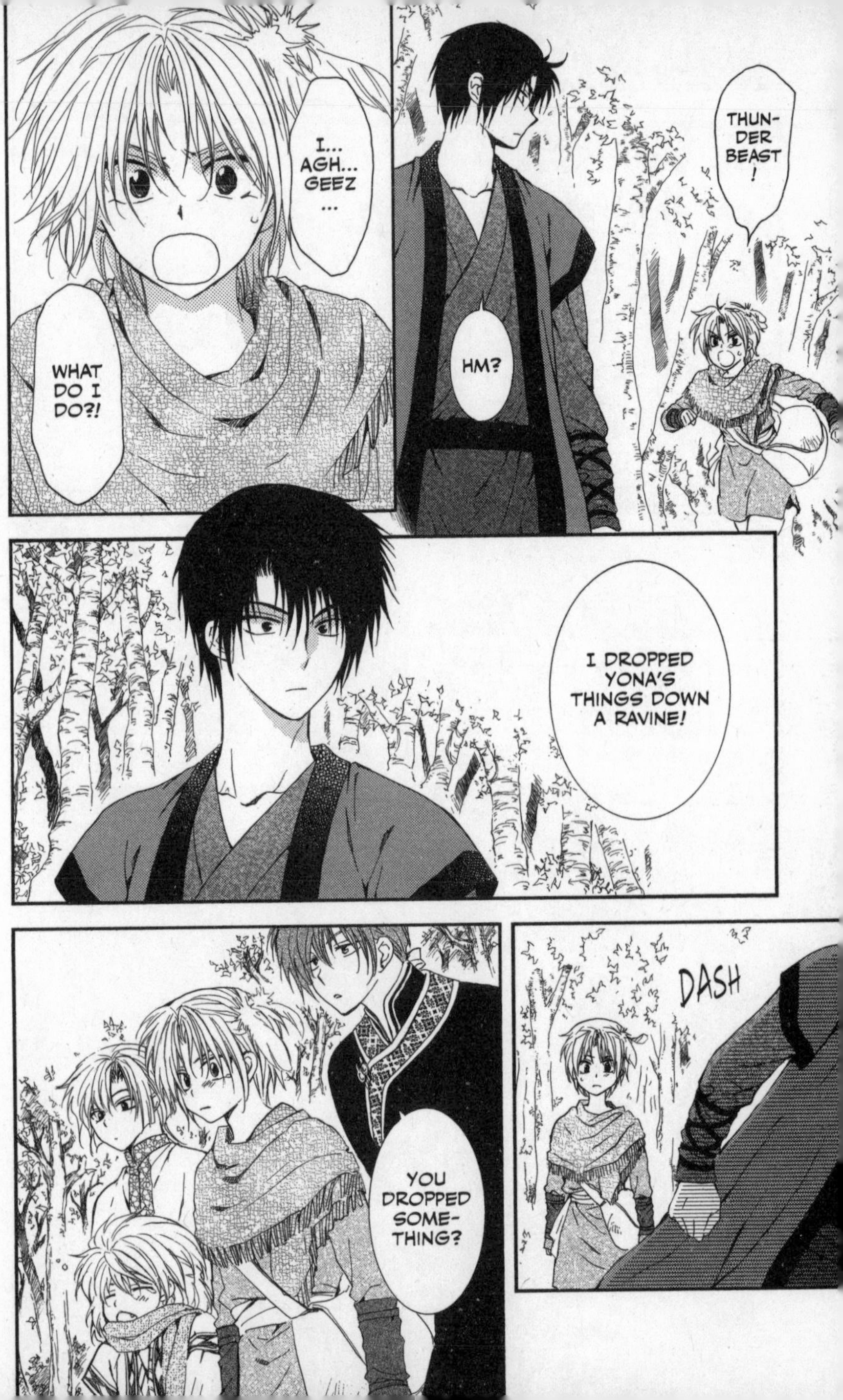
THUN-DER BEAST!
HM?
I... AGH... GEEZ...
WHAT DO I DO?!
I DROPPED YONA'S THINGS DOWN A RAVINE!
DASH
YOU DROPPED SOME-THING?

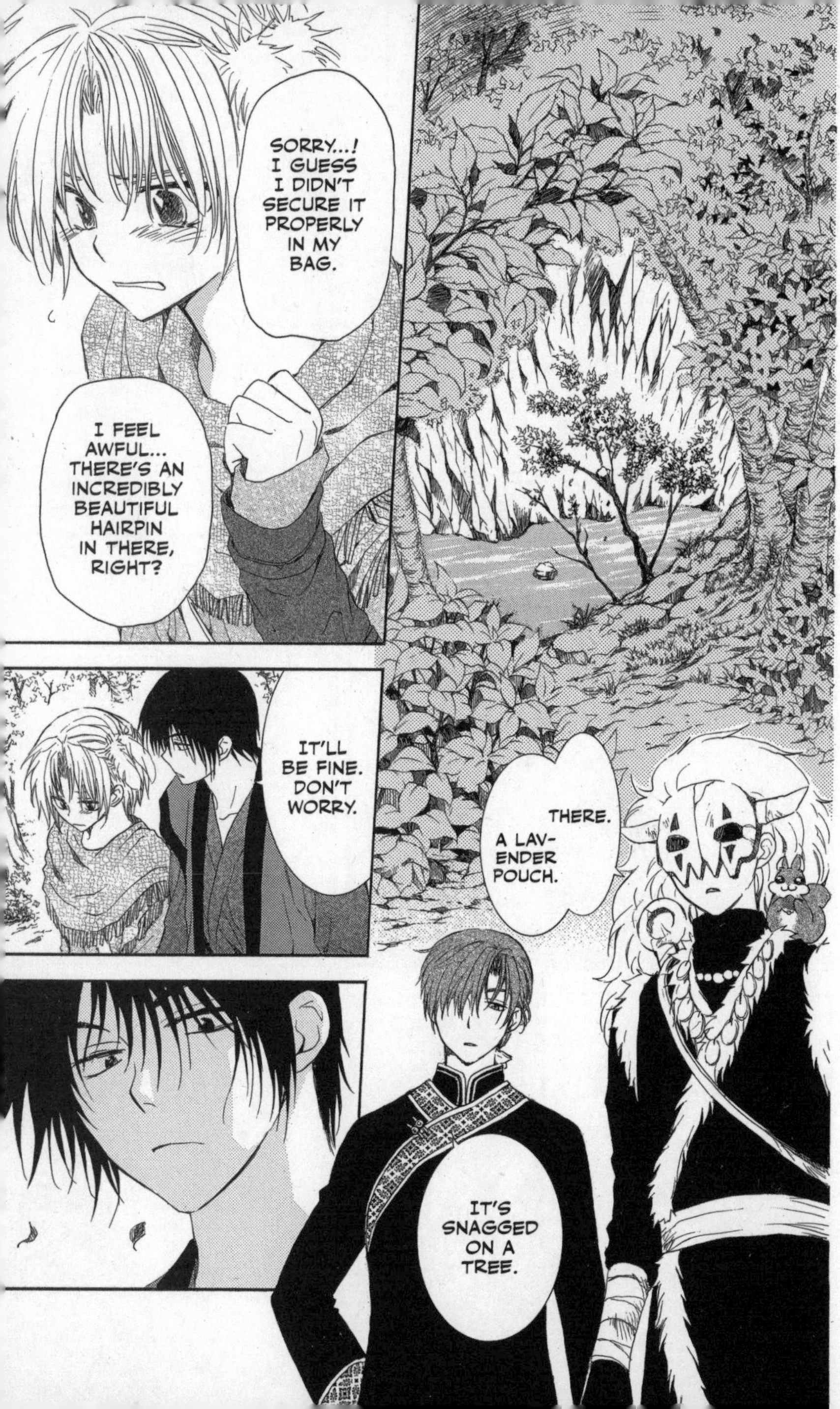
THERE. A LAV-ENDER POUCH.
IT'S SNAGGED ON A TREE.
SORRY...! I GUESS I DIDN'T SECURE IT PROPERLY IN MY BAG.
I FEEL AWFUL... THERE'S AN INCREDIBLY BEAUTIFUL HAIRPIN IN THERE, RIGHT?
IT'LL BE FINE. DON'T WORRY.

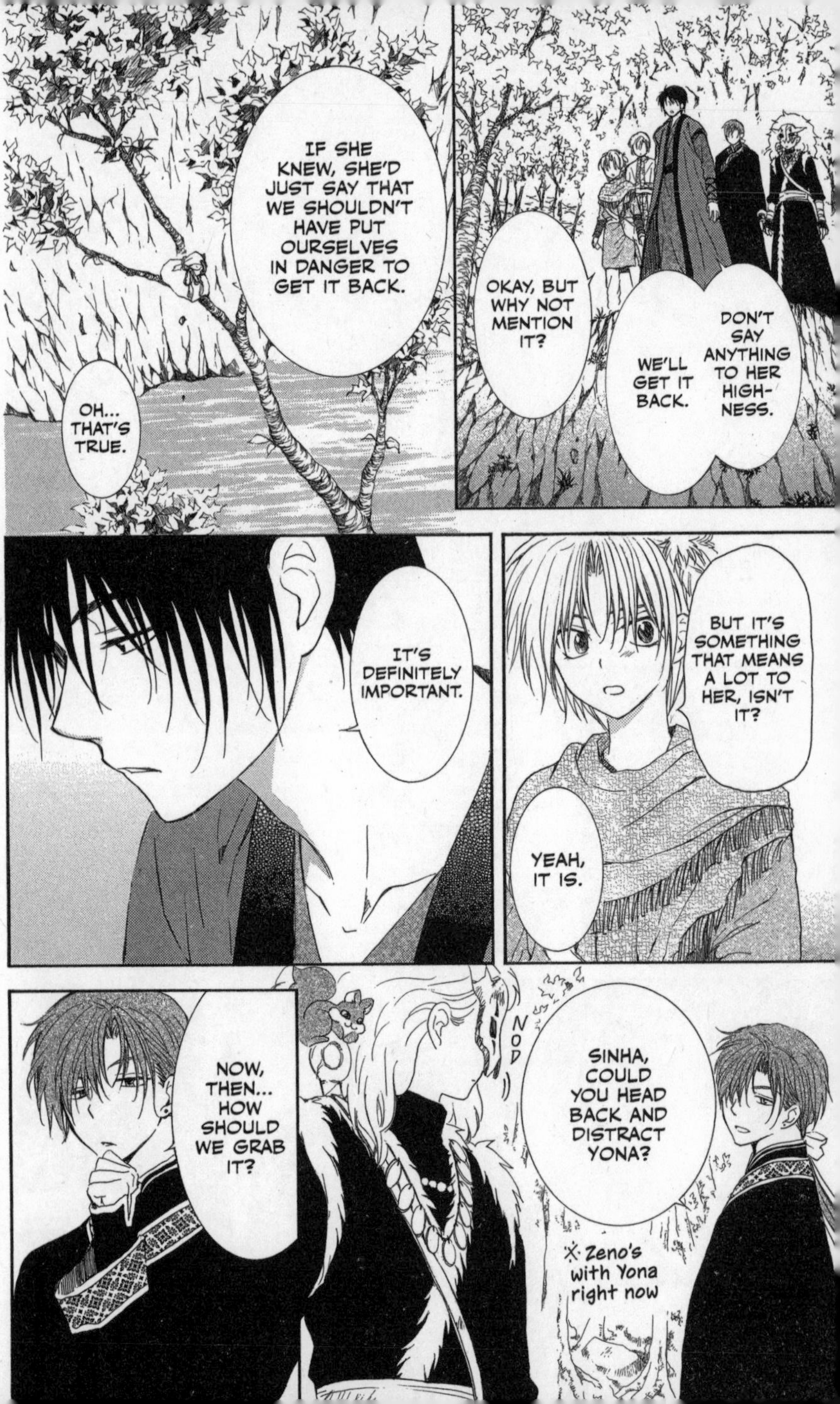
DON'T SAY ANYTHING TO HER HIGHNESS.
WE'LL GET IT BACK.
OKAY, BUT WHY NOT MENTION IT?
IF SHE KNEW, SHE'D JUST SAY THAT WE SHOULDN'T HAVE PUT OURSELVES IN DANGER TO GET IT BACK.
OH... THAT'S TRUE.
BUT IT'S SOMETHING THAT MEANS A LOT TO HER, ISN'T IT?
YEAH, IT IS.
IT'S DEFINITELY IMPORTANT.
SINHA, COULD YOU HEAD BACK AND DISTRACT YONA?
NOD
※Zeno's with Yona right now
NOW, THEN... HOW SHOULD WE GRAB IT?

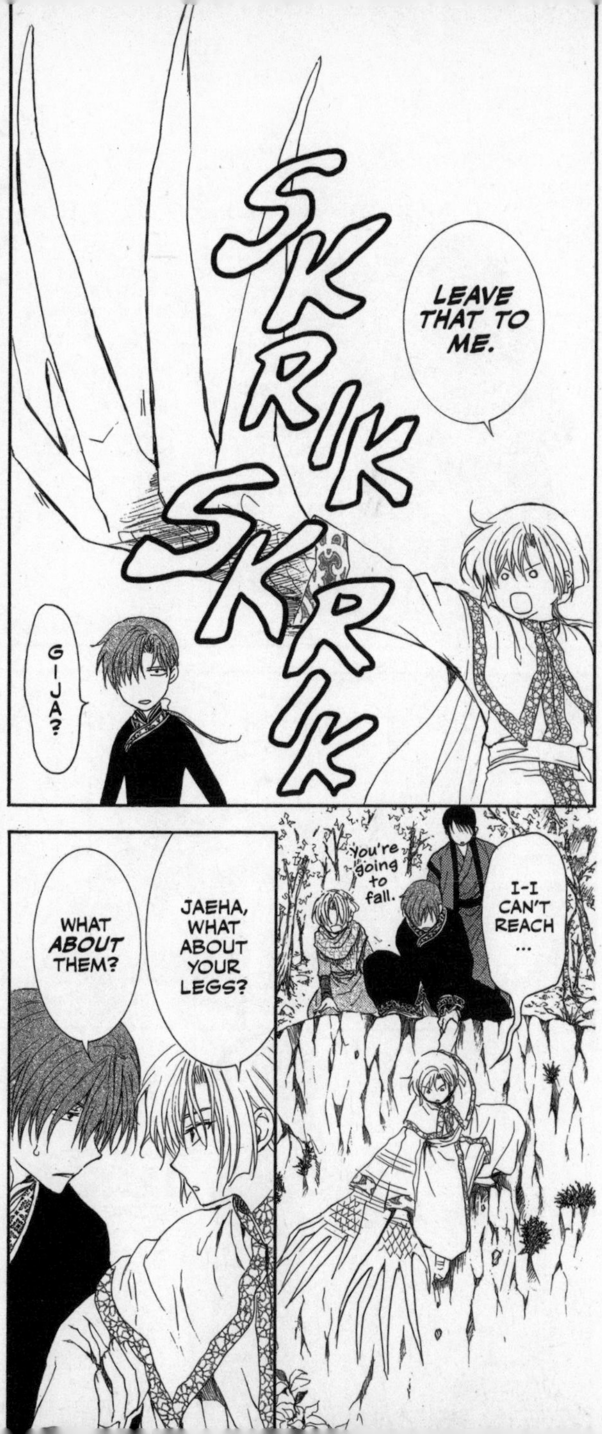
SKRIK SKRIK
LEAVE THAT TO ME.
GIJA?
I-I CAN'T REACH...
You're going to fall.
JAEHA, WHAT ABOUT YOUR LEGS?
WHAT ABOUT THEM?

I struggled with this chapter more than any other in the history of Yona. It deals with Hak's relationship with Su-won and his feelings about him... It's a complicated topic and I need to tread lightly. I spent about 20 days on my storyboard wondering how to portray it. (Storyboards usually take about five to seven days.) I like serious stories, but all this thinking and drawing serious situations makes me want to just do something ridiculous, although I can't do that at this point in the story. So I'm really glad that someone like Gija → is around.

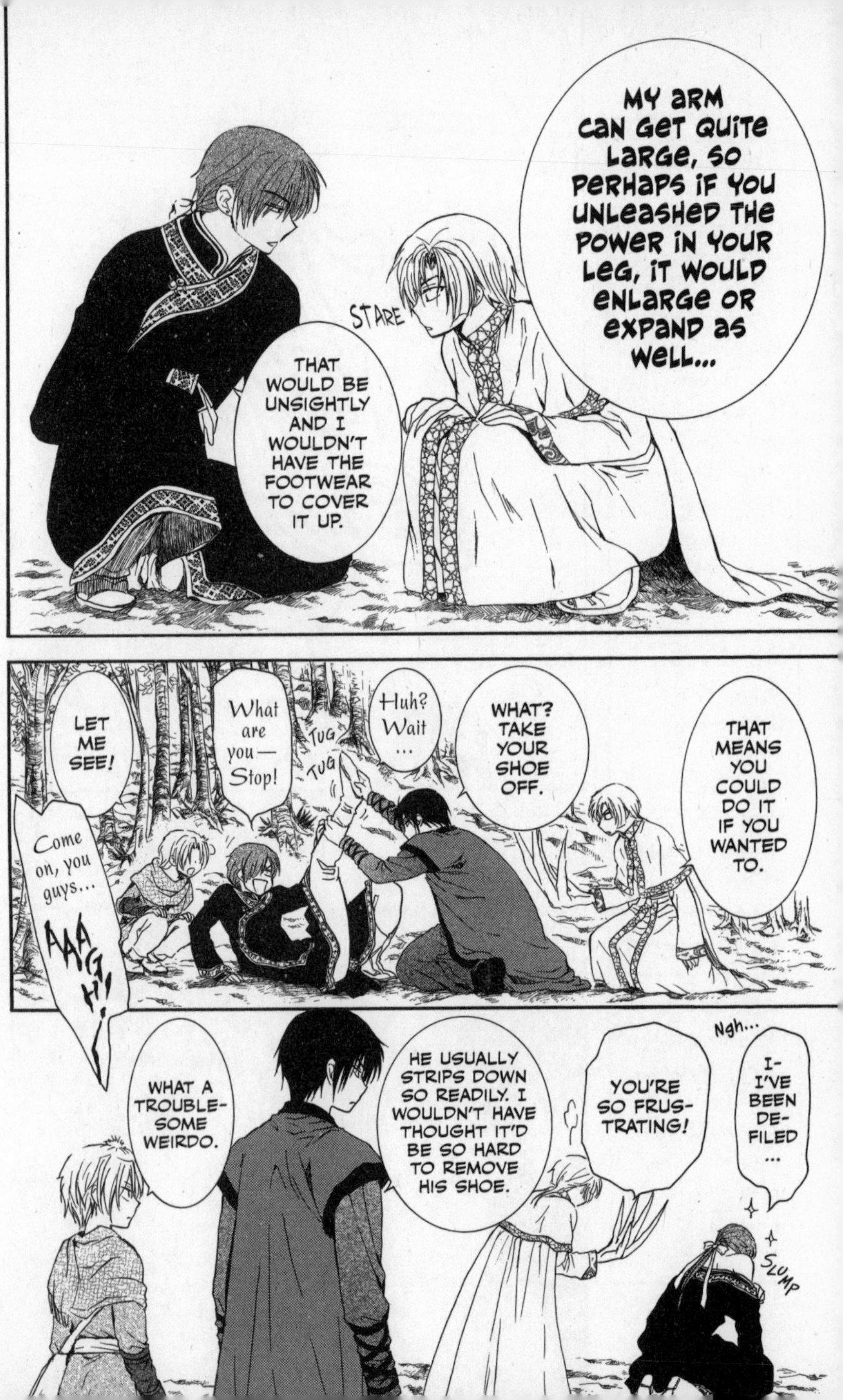
MY ARM CAN GET QUITE LARGE, SO PERHAPS IF YOU UNLEASHED THE POWER IN YOUR LEG, IT WOULD ENLARGE OR EXPAND AS WELL...
STARE
THAT WOULD BE UNSIGHTLY AND I WOULDN'T HAVE THE FOOTWEAR TO COVER IT UP.
THAT MEANS YOU COULD DO IT IF YOU WANTED TO.
WHAT? TAKE YOUR SHOE OFF.
Huh? Wait ...
TUG TUG
What are you— Stop!
LET ME SEE!
Come on, you guys...
AAAGH!!
Ngh...
I- I'VE BEEN DE-FILED ...
SLUMP
YOU'RE SO FRUS-TRATING!
HE USUALLY STRIPS DOWN SO READILY. I WOULDN'T HAVE THOUGHT IT'D BE SO HARD TO REMOVE HIS SHOE.
WHAT A TROUBLE-SOME WEIRDO.

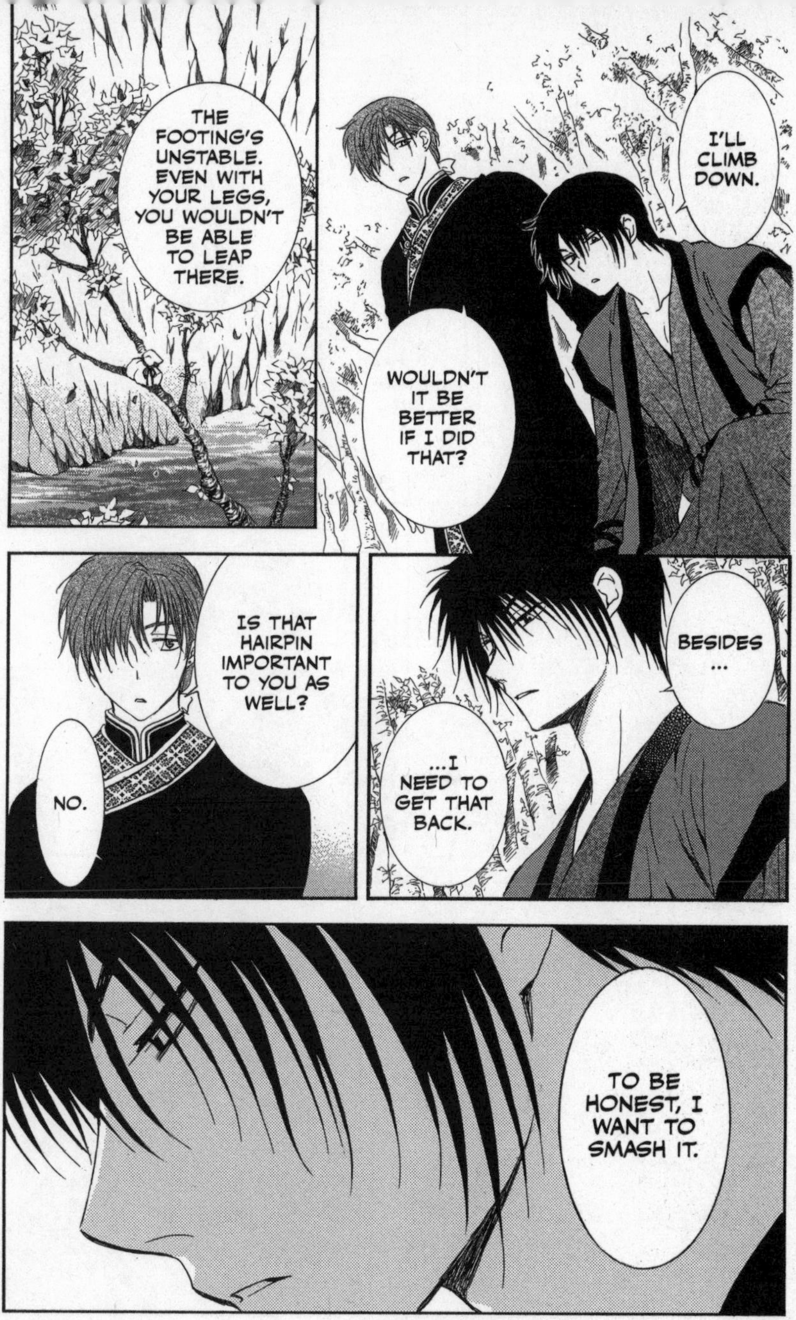
I'LL CLIMB DOWN.
WOULDN'T IT BE BETTER IF I DID THAT?
THE FOOTING'S UNSTABLE. EVEN WITH YOUR LEGS, YOU WOULDN'T BE ABLE TO LEAP THERE.
BESIDES ...
...I NEED TO GET THAT BACK.
IS THAT HAIRPIN IMPORTANT TO YOU AS WELL?
NO.
TO BE HONEST, I WANT TO SMASH IT.

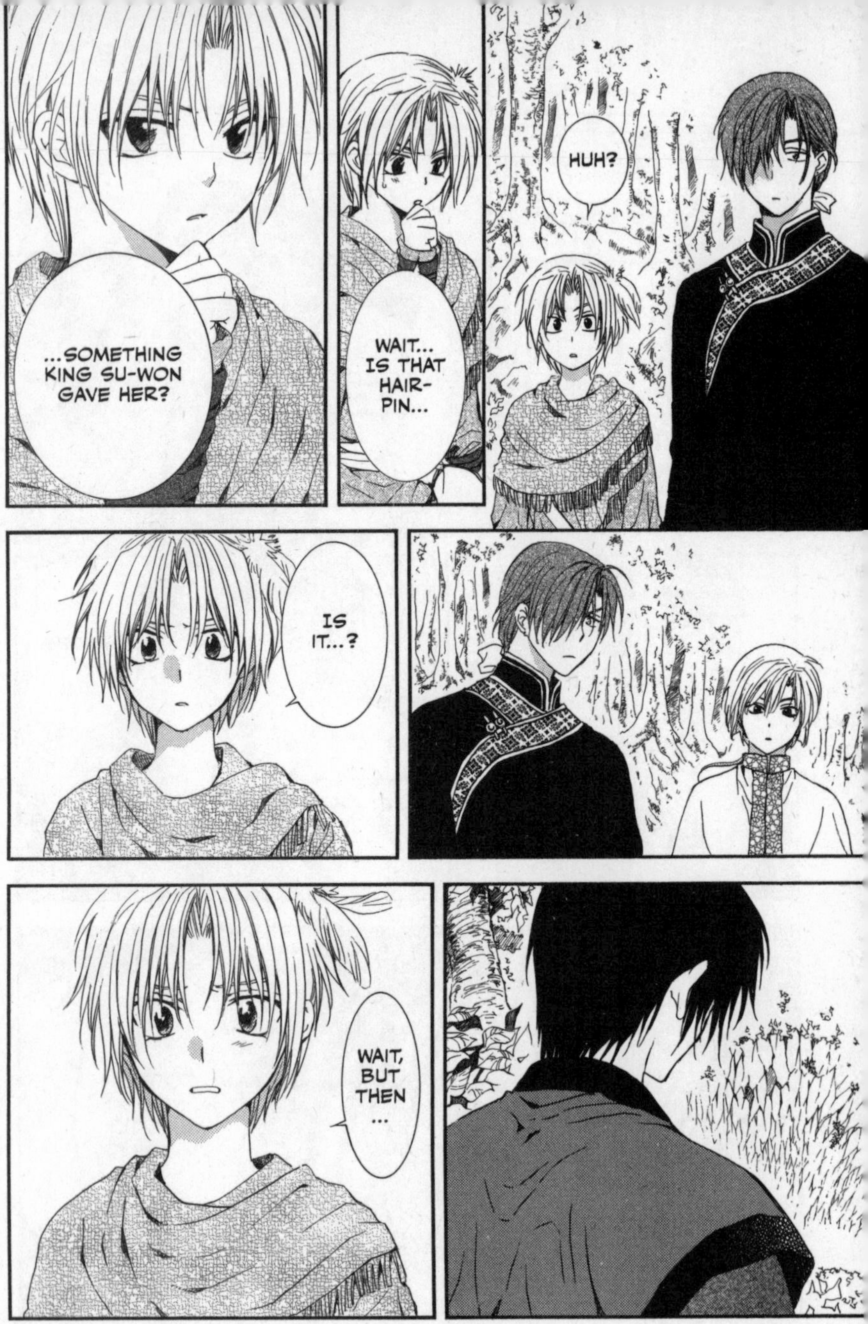
HUH?
WAIT... IS THAT HAIR-PIN...
...SOMETHING KING SU-WON GAVE HER?
IS IT...?
WAIT, BUT THEN ...

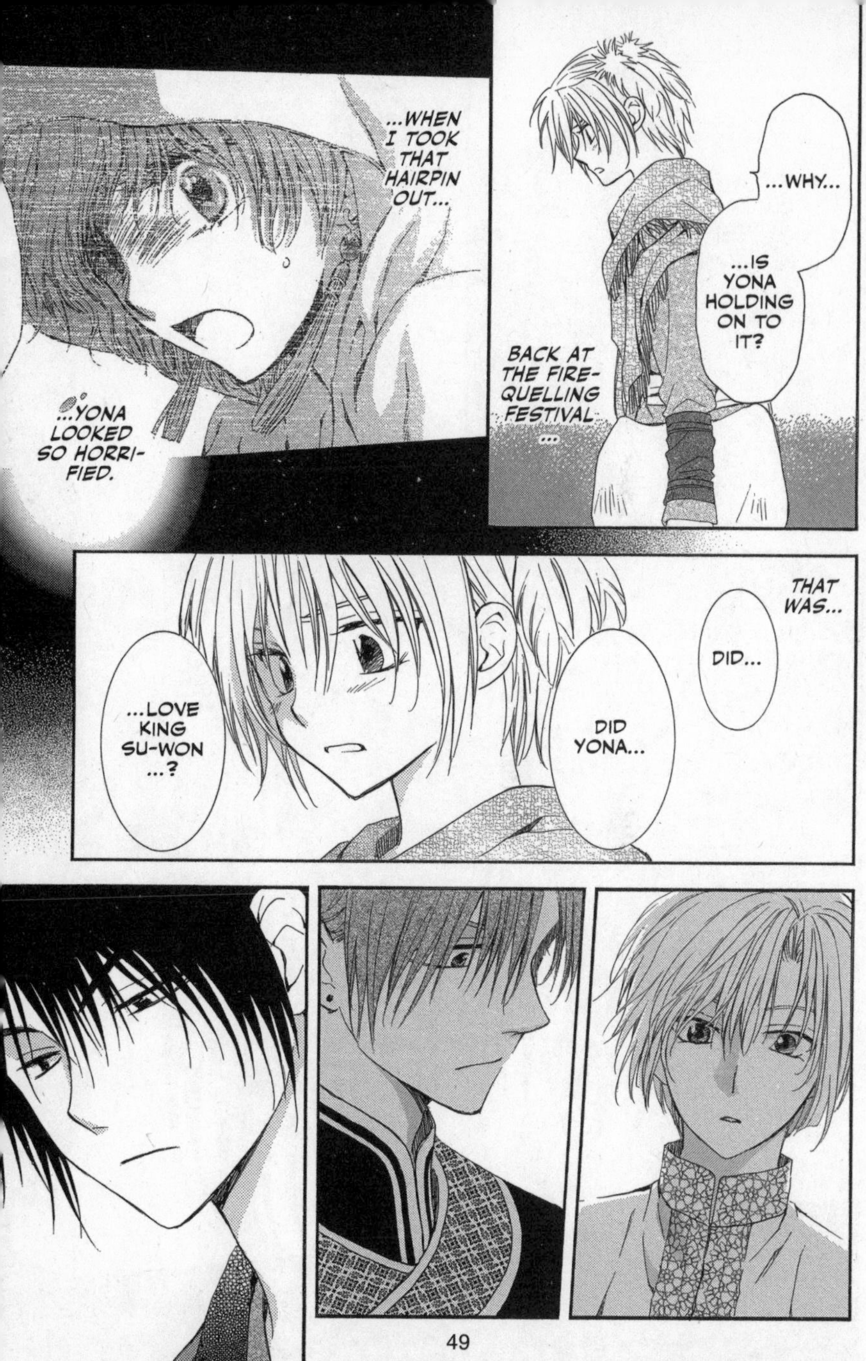
...WHY...
...IS YONA HOLDING ON TO IT?
BACK AT THE FIRE-QUELLING FESTIVAL...
...WHEN I TOOK THAT HAIRPIN OUT...
...YONA LOOKED SO HORRIFIED.
THAT WAS...
DID...
DID YONA...
...LOVE KING SU-WON ...?

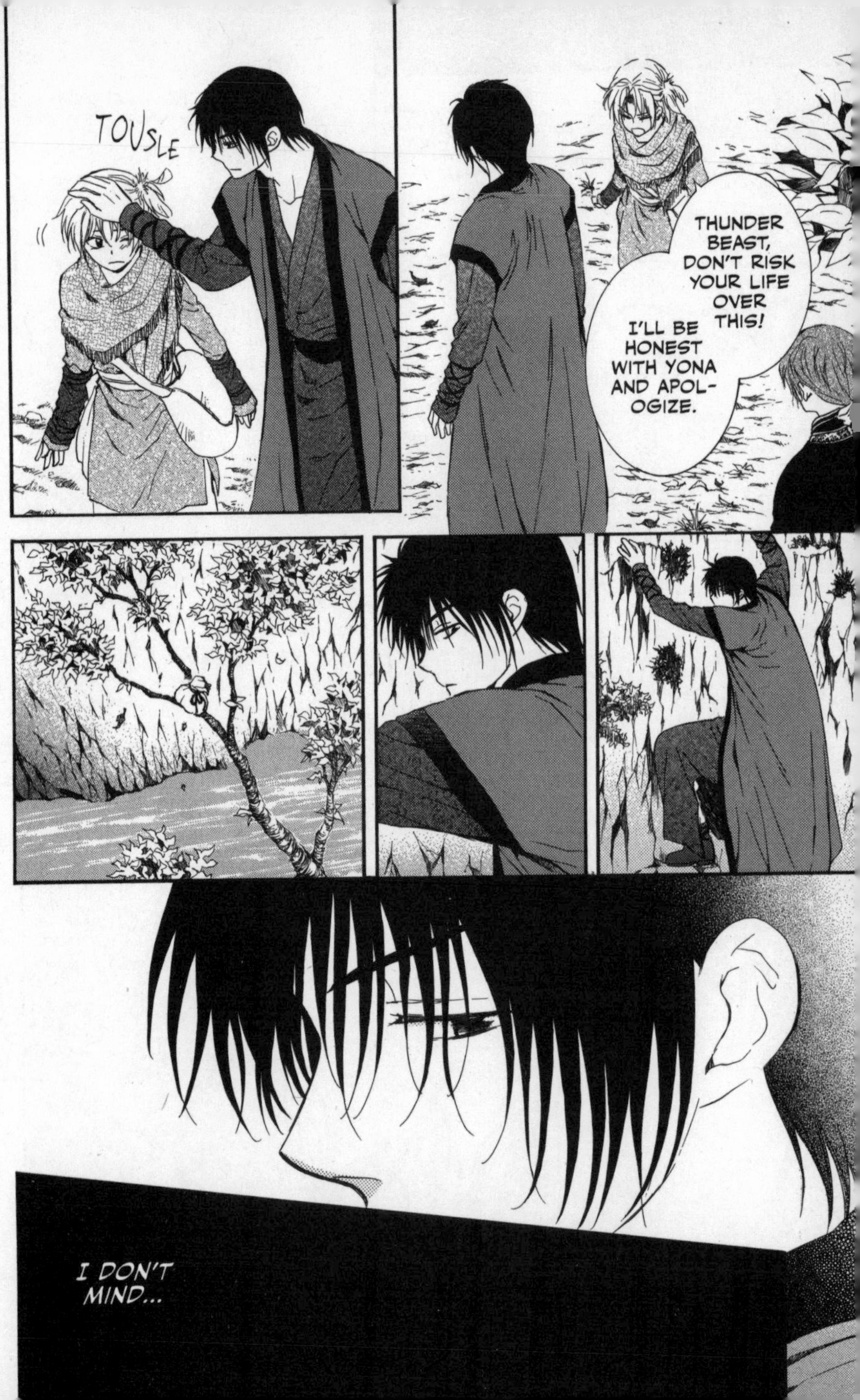
THUNDER BEAST, DON'T RISK YOUR LIFE OVER THIS! I'LL BE HONEST WITH YONA AND APOL-OGIZE.
TOUSLE
I DON'T MIND...

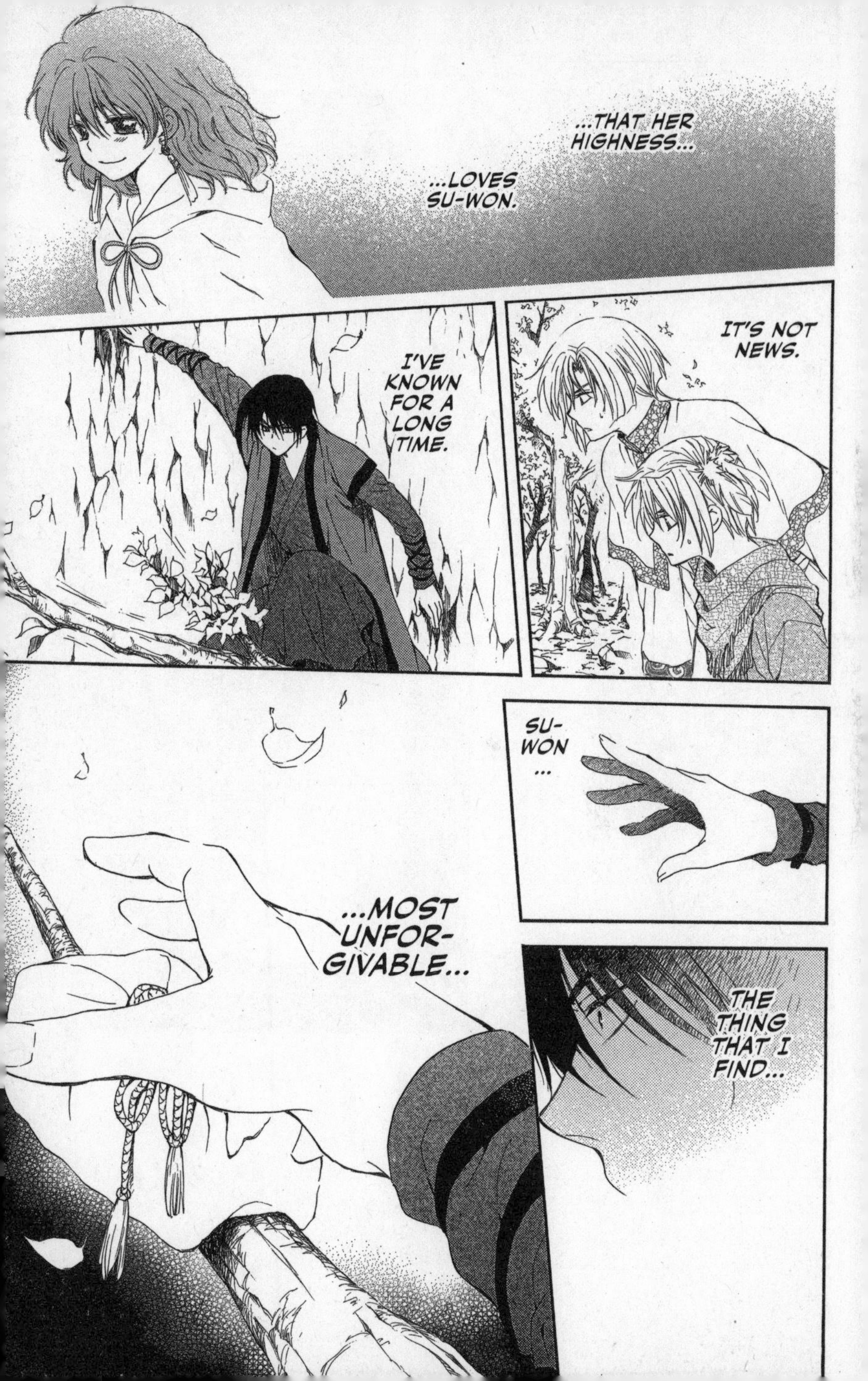
...THAT HER HIGHNESS...
...LOVES SU-WON.
IT'S NOT NEWS.
I'VE KNOWN FOR A LONG TIME.
SU-WON...
THE THING THAT I FIND...
...MOST UNFORGIVABLE...

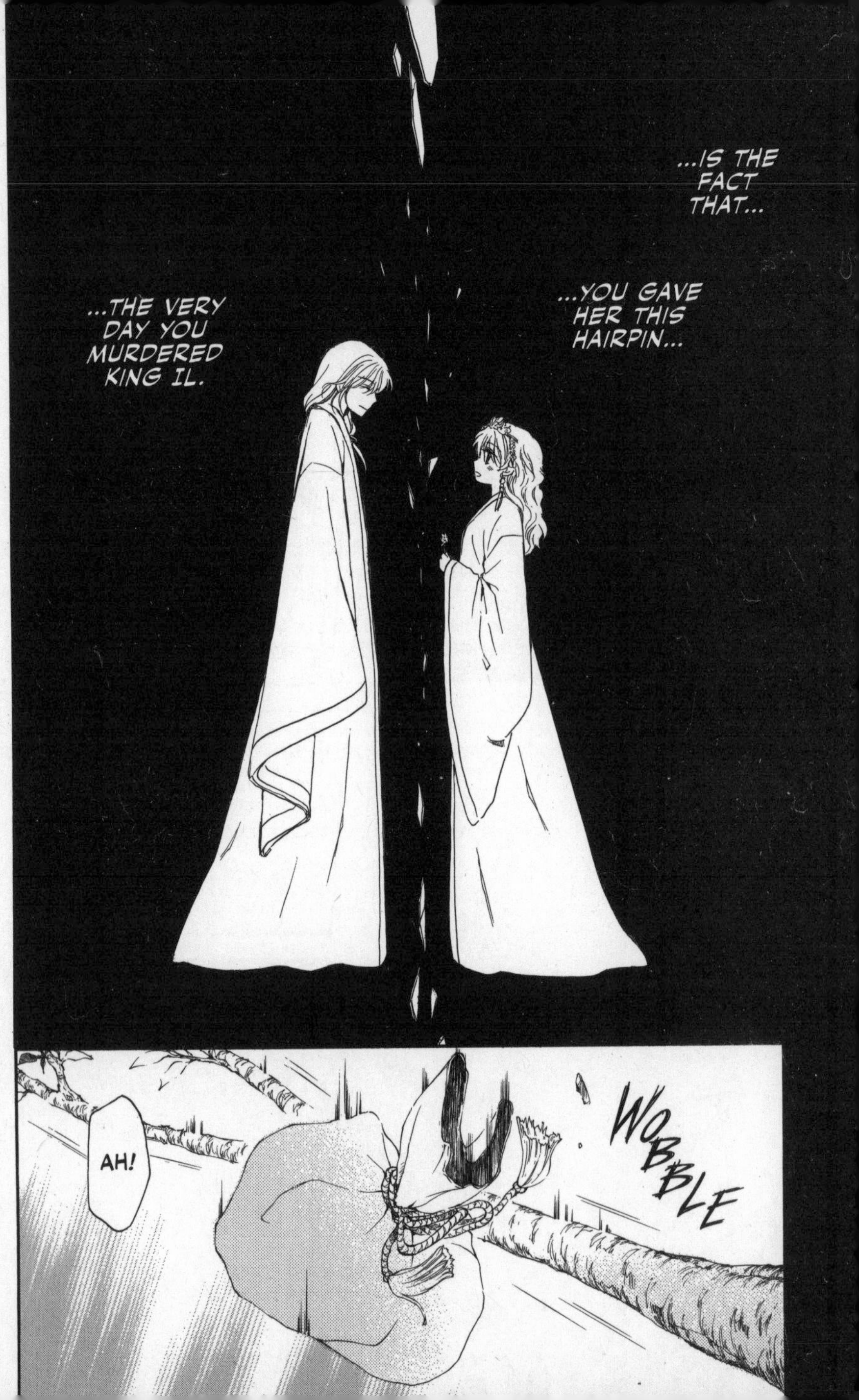
...IS THE FACT THAT...
...YOU GAVE HER THIS HAIRPIN...
...THE VERY DAY YOU MURDERED KING IL.
WOBBLE
AH!

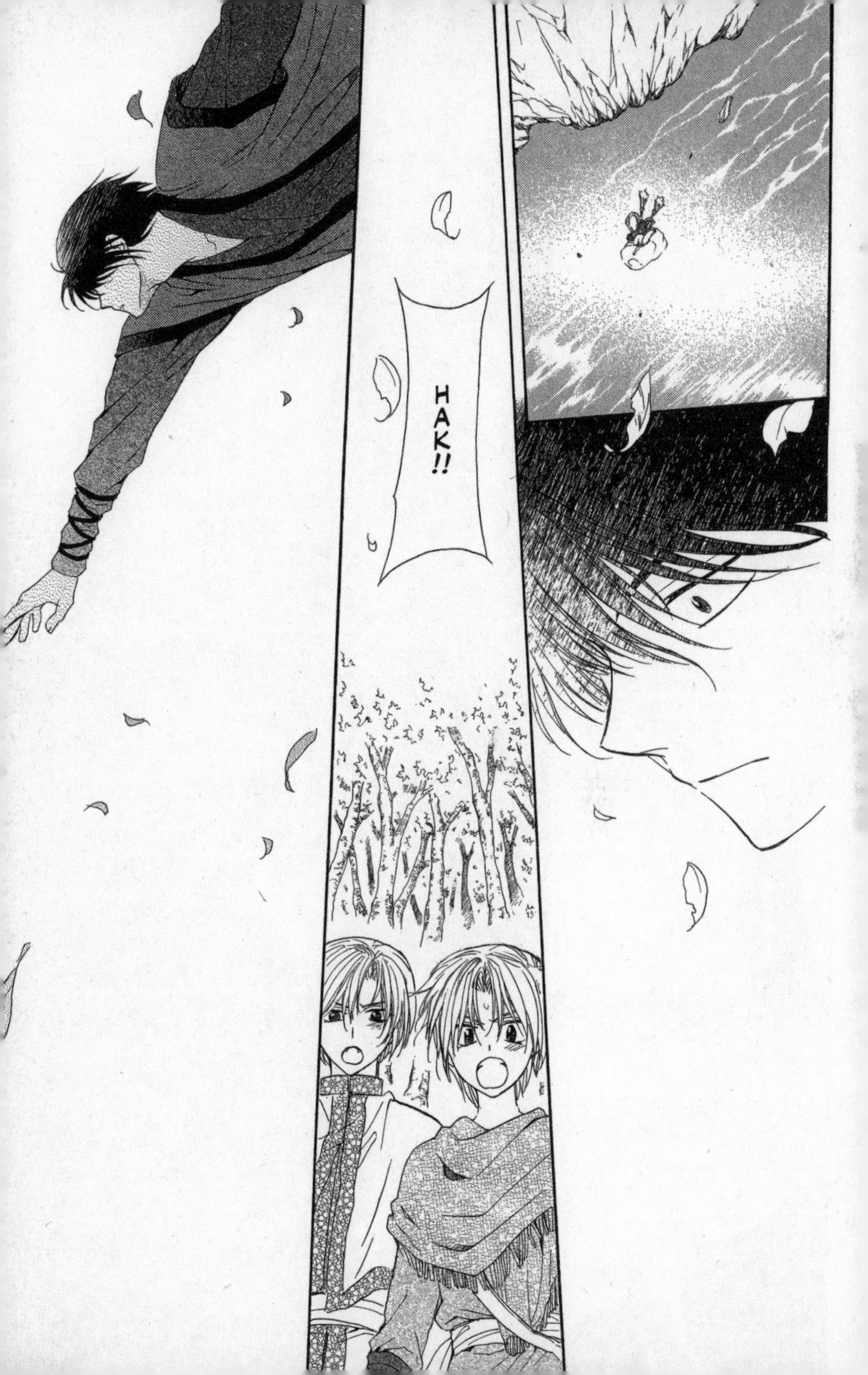
HAK!!

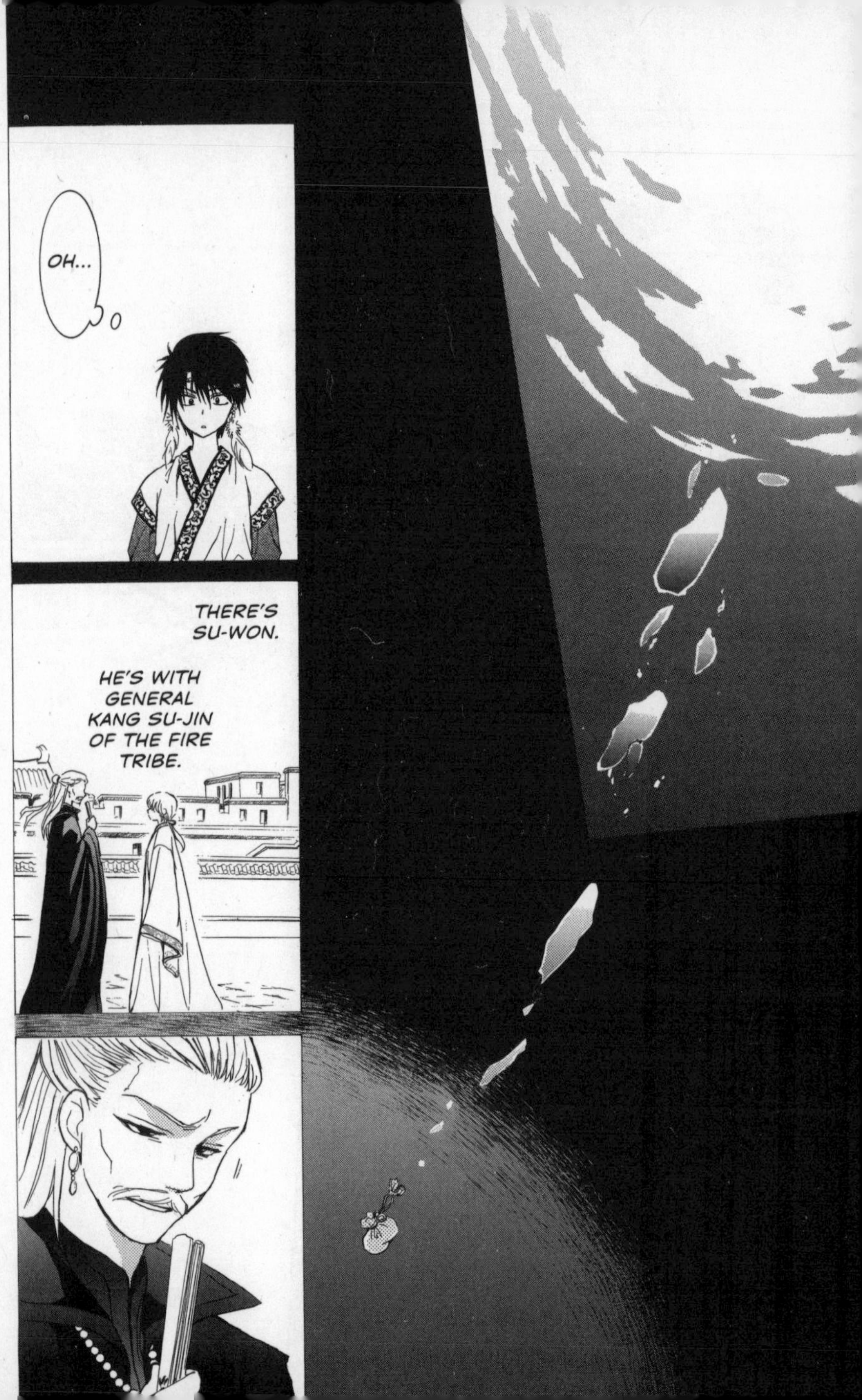
OH...
THERE'S SU-WON.
HE'S WITH GENERAL KANG SU-JIN OF THE FIRE TRIBE.

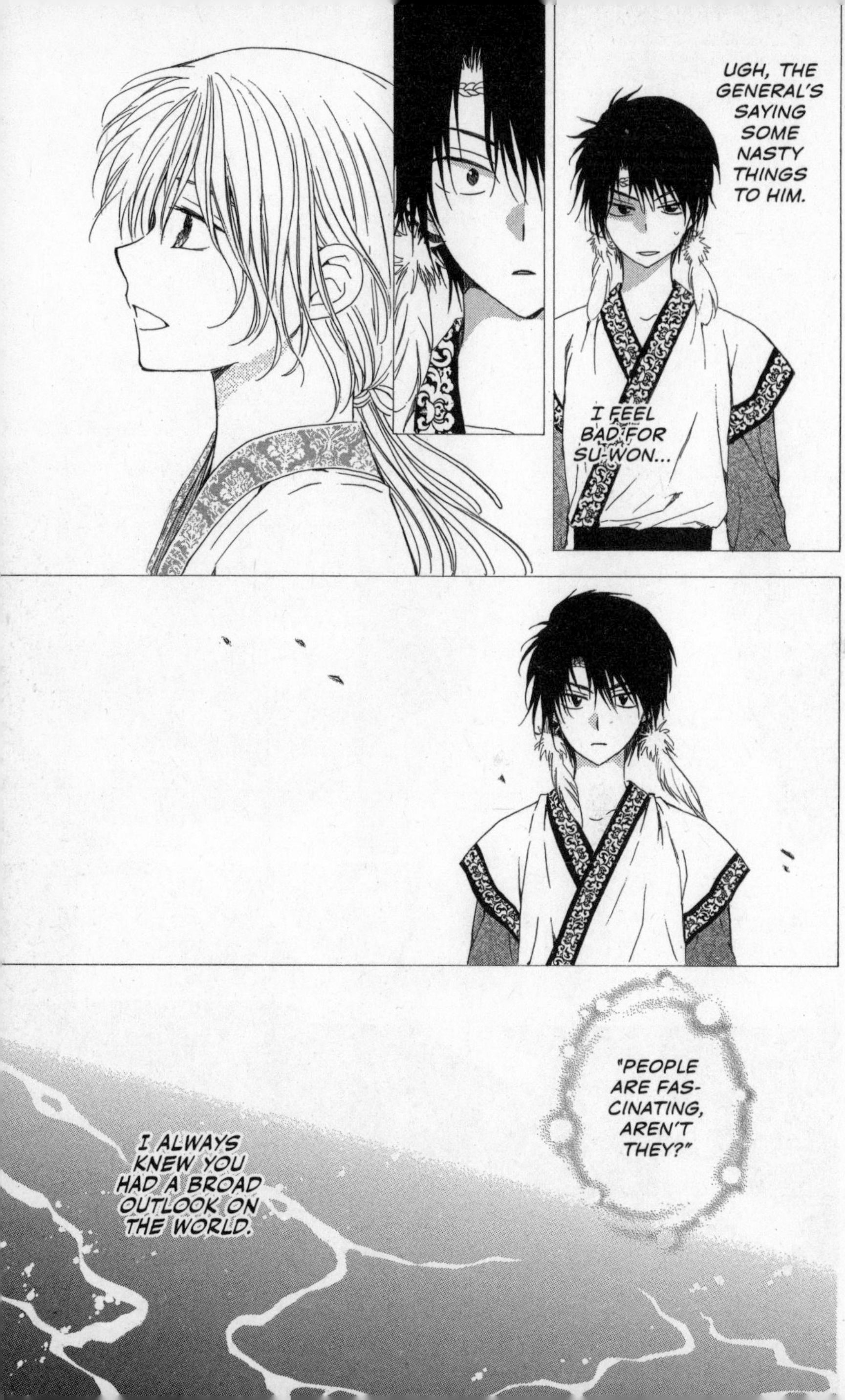
UGH, THE GENERAL'S SAYING SOME NASTY THINGS TO HIM.
I FEEL BAD FOR SU-WON...
"PEOPLE ARE FAS-CINATING, AREN'T THEY?"
I ALWAYS KNEW YOU HAD A BROAD OUTLOOK ON THE WORLD.

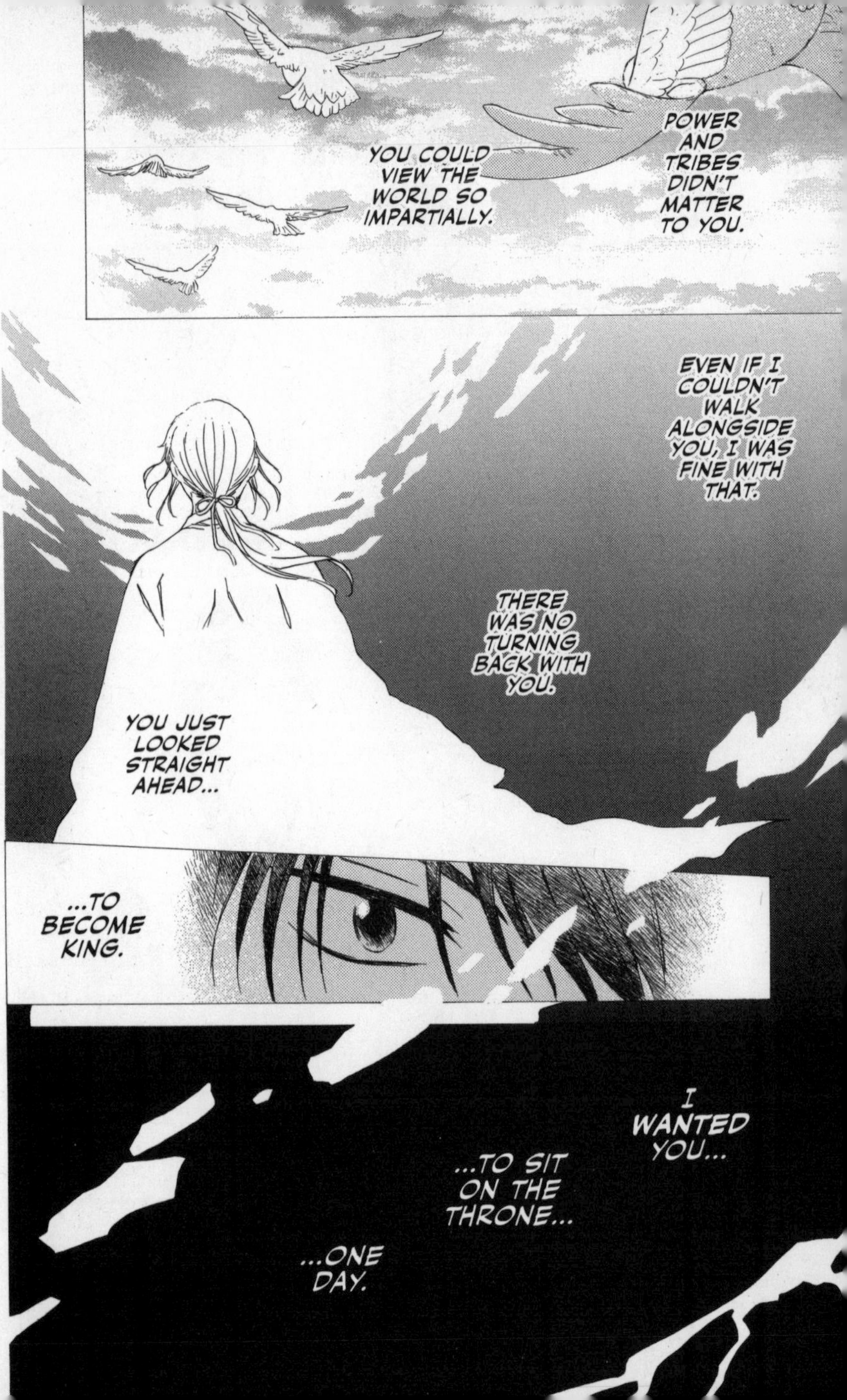
POWER AND TRIBES DIDN'T MATTER TO YOU.
YOU COULD VIEW THE WORLD SO IMPARTIALLY.
EVEN IF I COULDN'T WALK ALONGSIDE YOU, I WAS FINE WITH THAT.
THERE WAS NO TURNING BACK WITH YOU.
YOU JUST LOOKED STRAIGHT AHEAD...
...TO BECOME KING.
I WANTED YOU...
...TO SIT ON THE THRONE...
...ONE DAY.

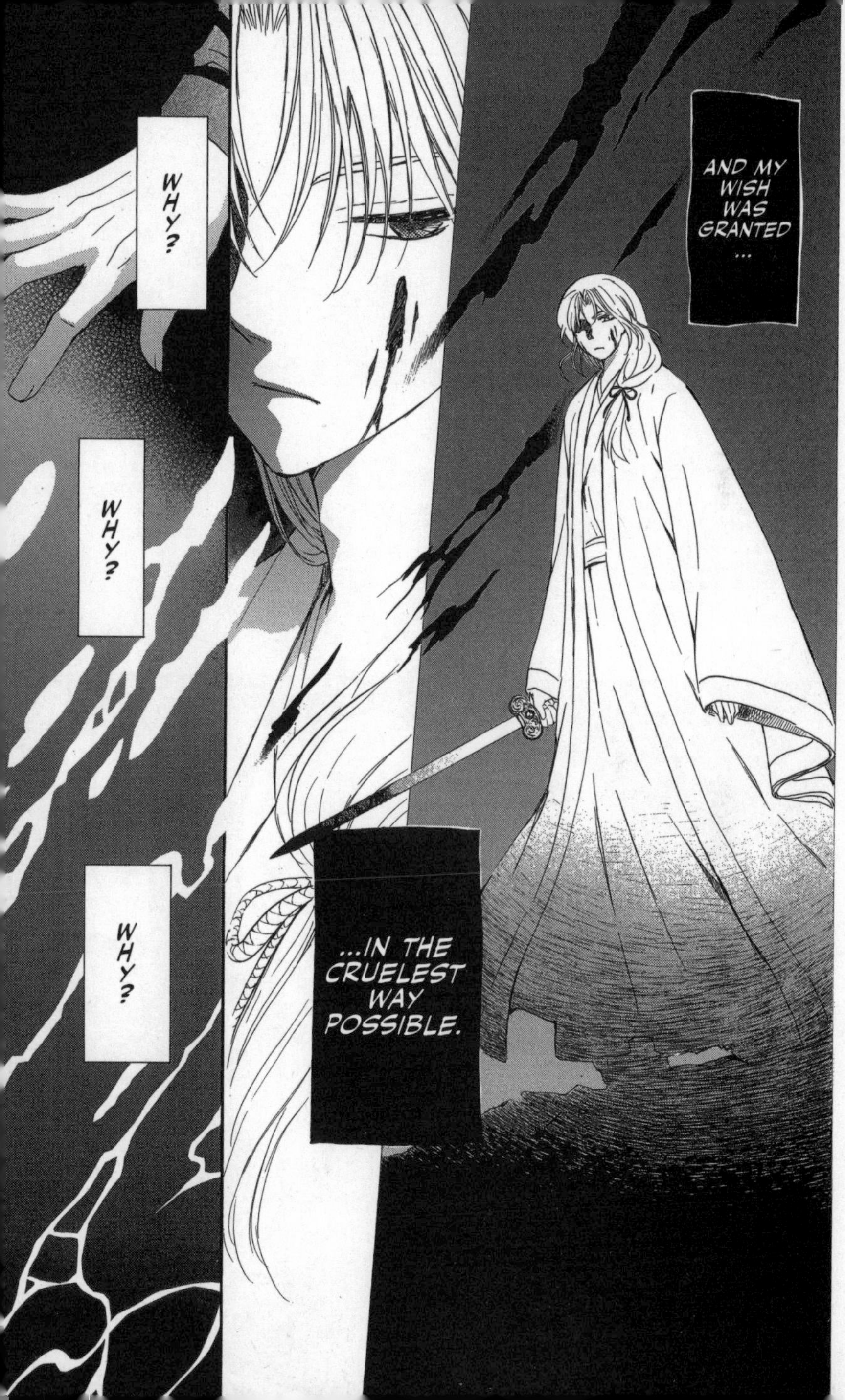
AND MY WISH WAS GRANTED ...
...IN THE CRUELEST WAY POSSIBLE.
WHY?
WHY?
WHY?

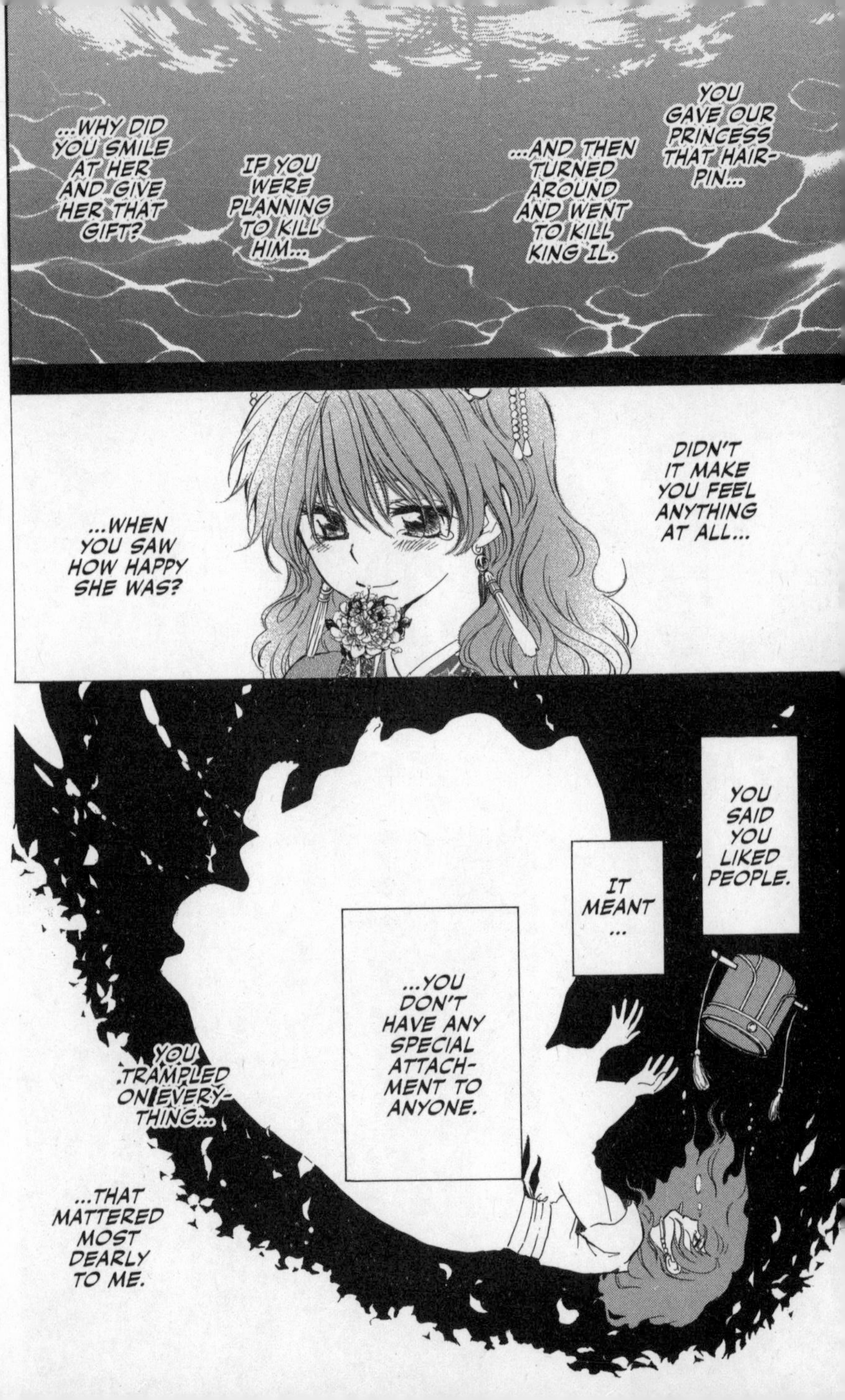
YOU GAVE OUR PRINCESS THAT HAIR-PIN...
...AND THEN TURNED AROUND AND WENT TO KILL KING IL.
IF YOU WERE PLANNING TO KILL HIM...
...WHY DID YOU SMILE AT HER AND GIVE HER THAT GIFT?
DIDN'T IT MAKE YOU FEEL ANYTHING AT ALL...
...WHEN YOU SAW HOW HAPPY SHE WAS?
YOU SAID YOU LIKED PEOPLE.
IT MEANT ...
...YOU DON'T HAVE ANY SPECIAL ATTACHMENT TO ANYONE.
YOU TRAMPLED ON EVERYTHING...
...THAT MATTERED MOST DEARLY TO ME.

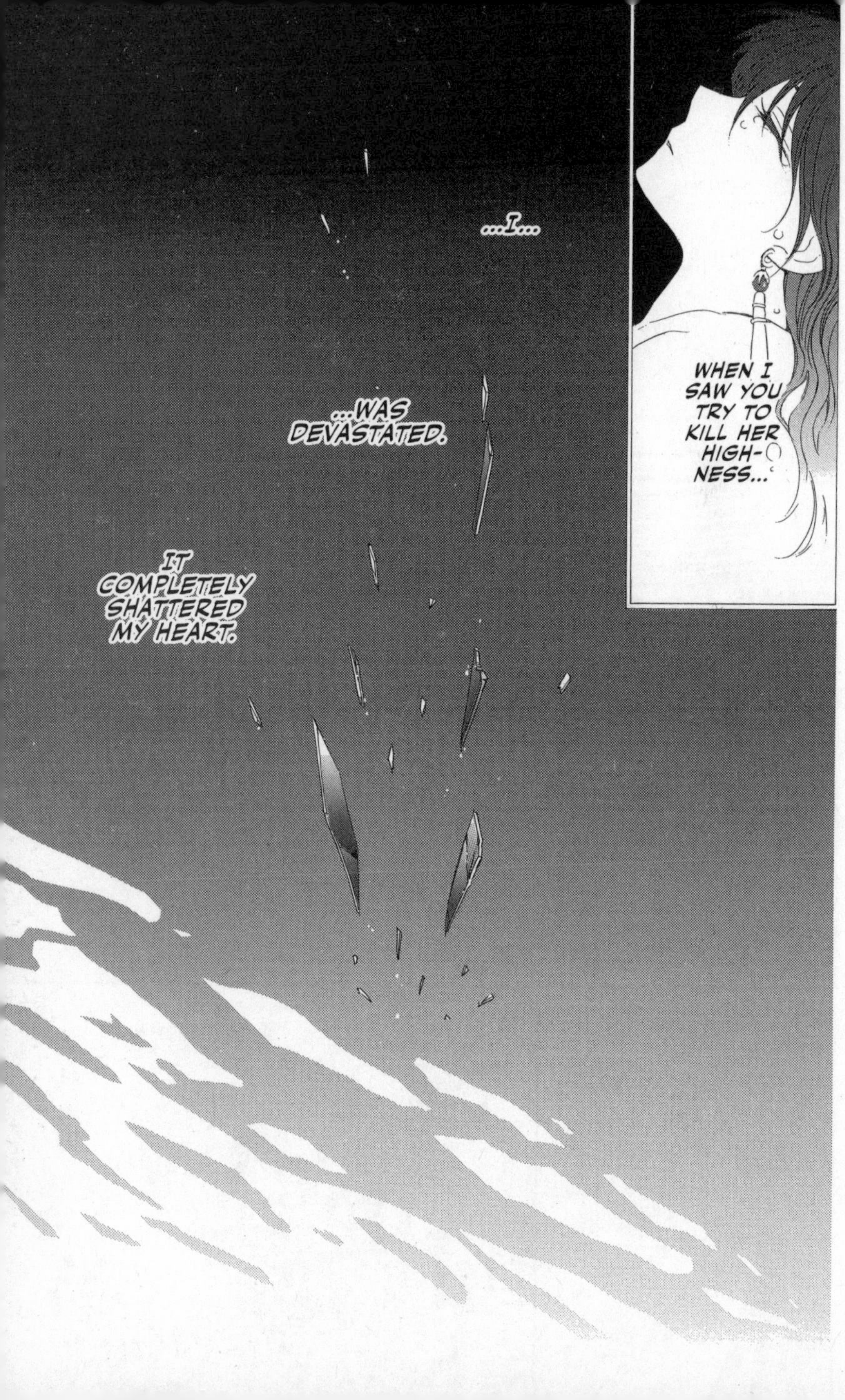
WHEN I SAW YOU TRY TO KILL HER HIGH-NESS...
...I...
...WAS DEVASTATED.
IT COMPLETELY SHATTERED MY HEART.

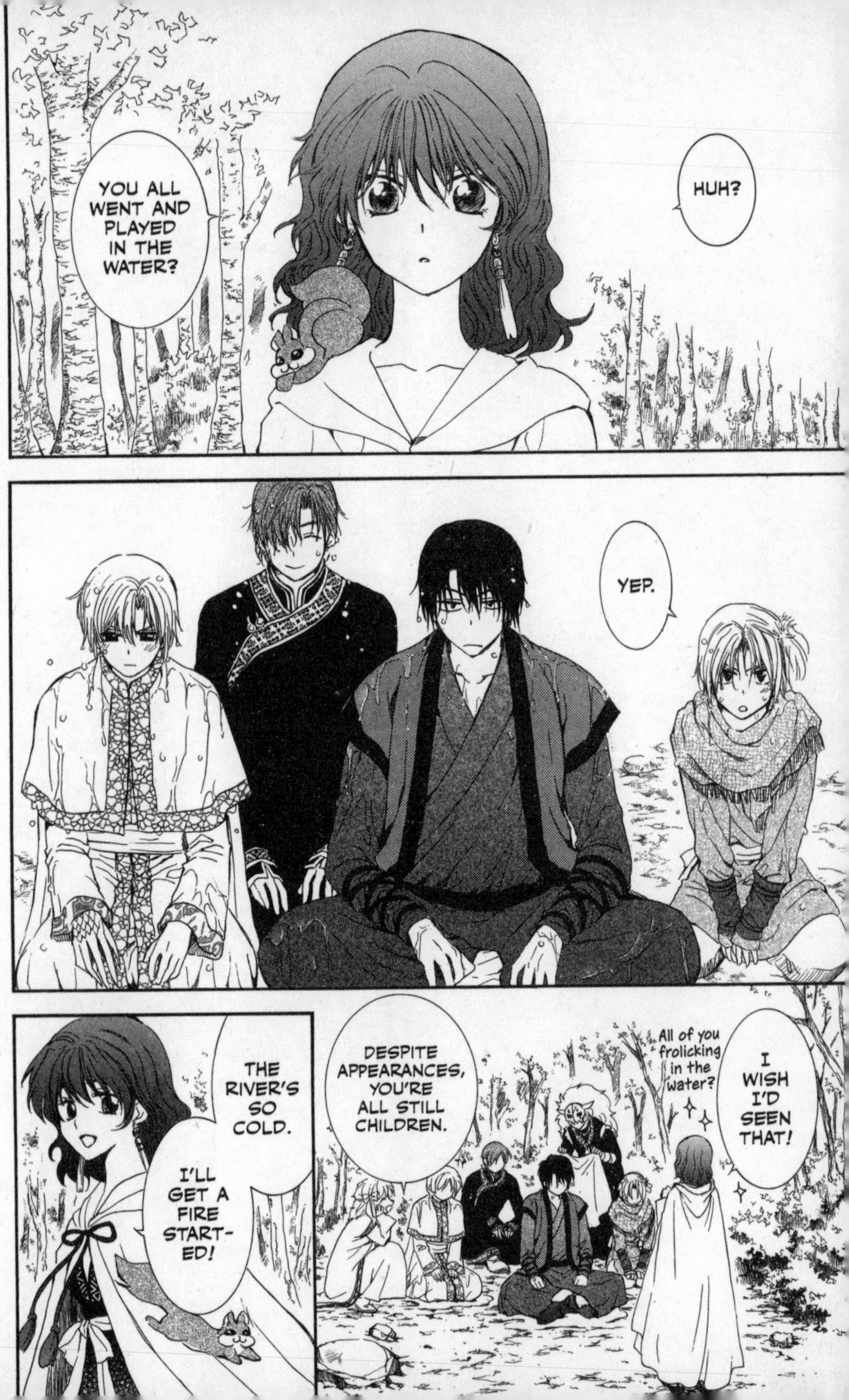
HUH?
YOU ALL WENT AND PLAYED IN THE WATER?
YEP.
I WISH I'D SEEN THAT!
All of you frolicking in the water?
DESPITE APPEARANCES, YOU'RE ALL STILL CHILDREN.
THE RIVER'S SO COLD.
I'LL GET A FIRE START-ED!

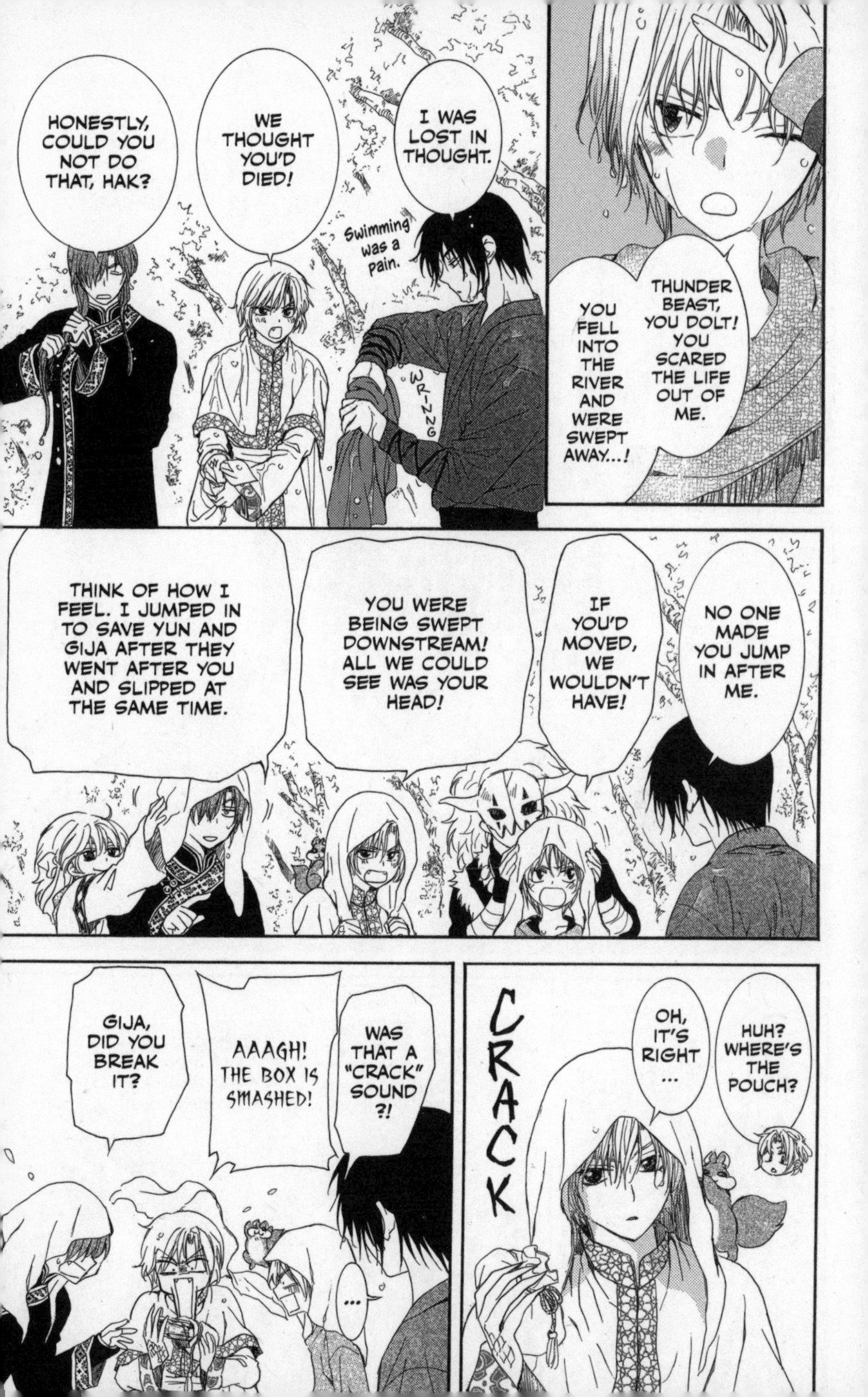
THUNDER BEAST, YOU DOLT! YOU SCARED THE LIFE OUT OF ME.
YOU FELL INTO THE RIVER AND WERE SWEPT AWAY...!
I WAS LOST IN THOUGHT.
Swimming was a pain.
WRING
WE THOUGHT YOU'D DIED!
HONESTLY, COULD YOU NOT DO THAT, HAK?
NO ONE MADE YOU JUMP IN AFTER ME.
IF YOU'D MOVED, WE WOULDN'T HAVE!
YOU WERE BEING SWEPT DOWNSTREAM! ALL WE COULD SEE WAS YOUR HEAD!
THINK OF HOW I FEEL. I JUMPED IN TO SAVE YUN AND GIJA AFTER THEY WENT AFTER YOU AND SLIPPED AT THE SAME TIME.
HUH? WHERE'S THE POUCH?
OH, IT'S RIGHT ...
CRACK
WAS THAT A "CRACK" SOUND ?!
AAAGH! THE BOX IS SMASHED!
GIJA, DID YOU BREAK IT?
...

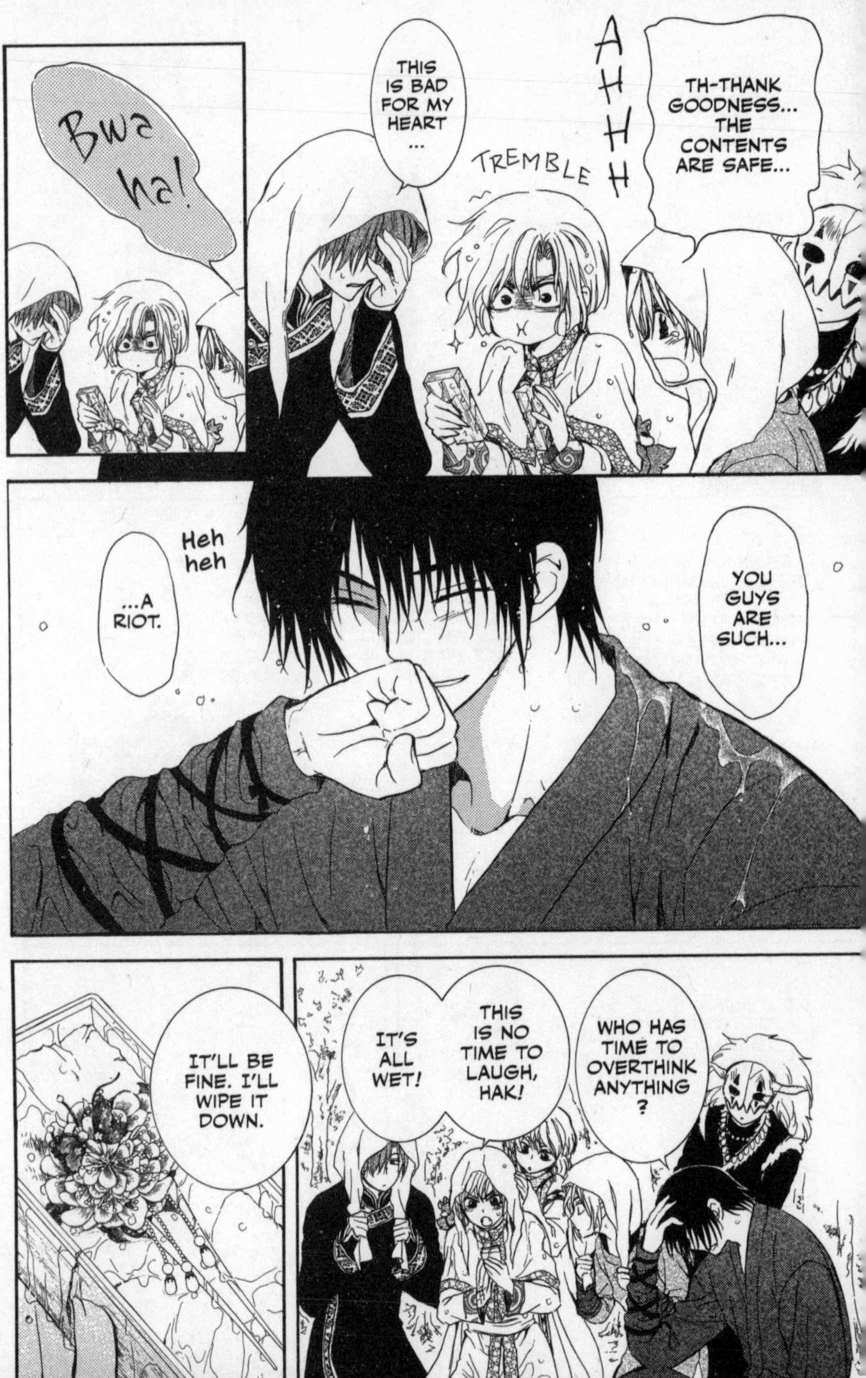
TH-THANK GOODNESS... THE CONTENTS ARE SAFE...
AHHHH
TREMBLE
THIS IS BAD FOR MY HEART ...
Bwa ha!
YOU GUYS ARE SUCH...
Heh heh
...A RIOT.
WHO HAS TIME TO OVERTHINK ANYTHING?
THIS IS NO TIME TO LAUGH, HAK!
IT'S ALL WET!
IT'LL BE FINE. I'LL WIPE IT DOWN.

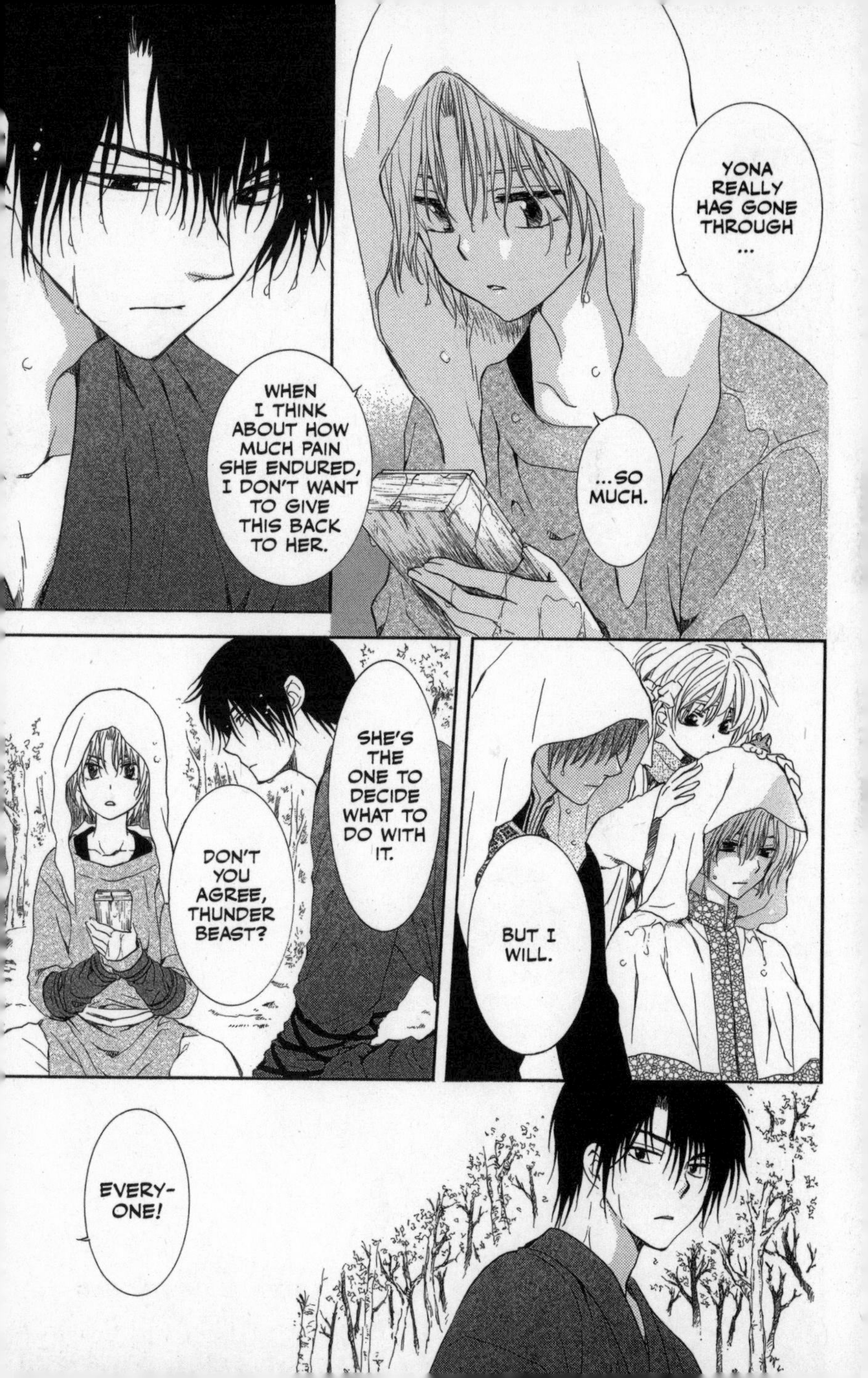
YONA REALLY HAS GONE THROUGH ...
...SO MUCH.
WHEN I THINK ABOUT HOW MUCH PAIN SHE ENDURED, I DON'T WANT TO GIVE THIS BACK TO HER.
BUT I WILL.
SHE'S THE ONE TO DECIDE WHAT TO DO WITH IT.
DON'T YOU AGREE, THUNDER BEAST?
EVERY-ONE!

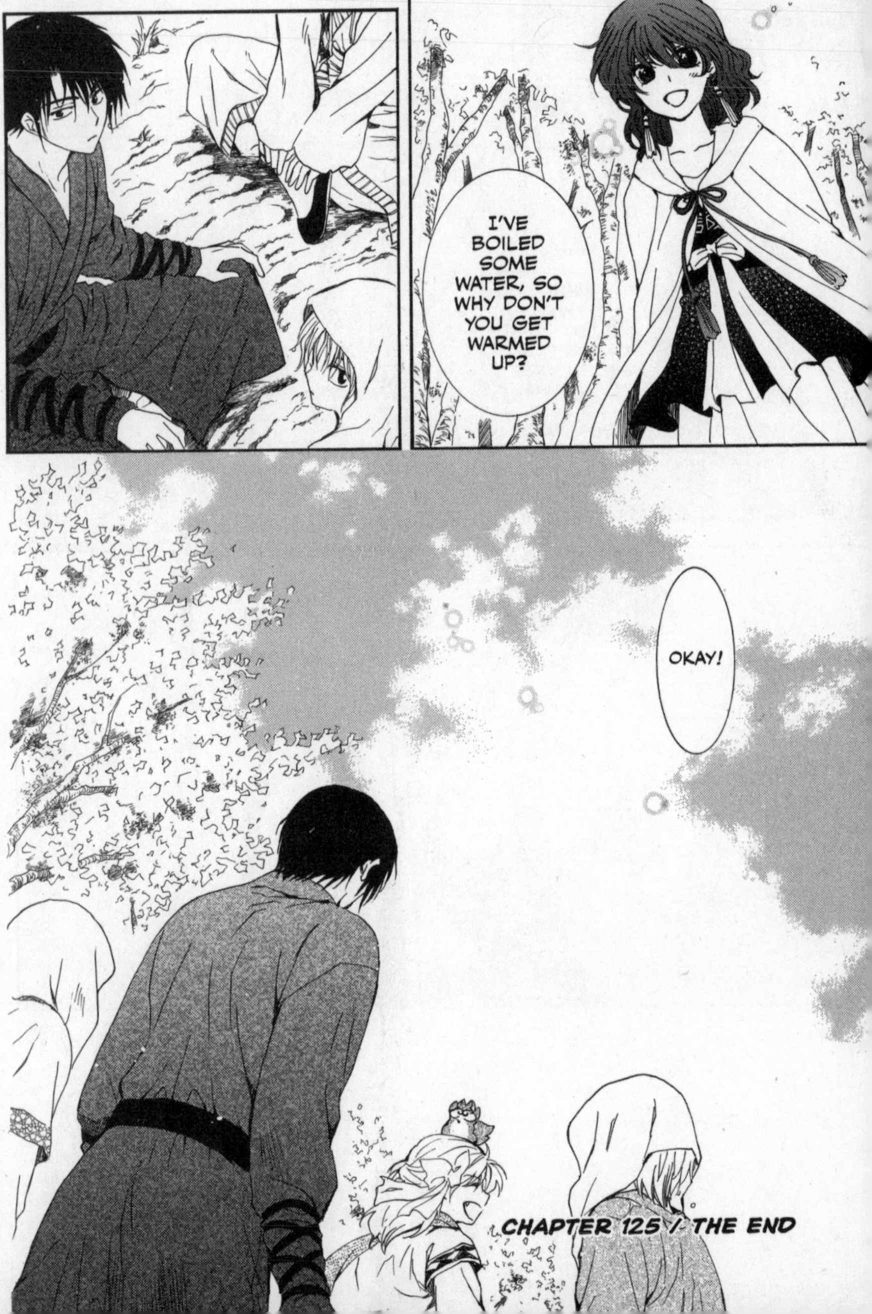
I'VE BOILED SOME WATER, SO WHY DON'T YOU GET WARMED UP?
OKAY!
CHAPTER 125 / THE END

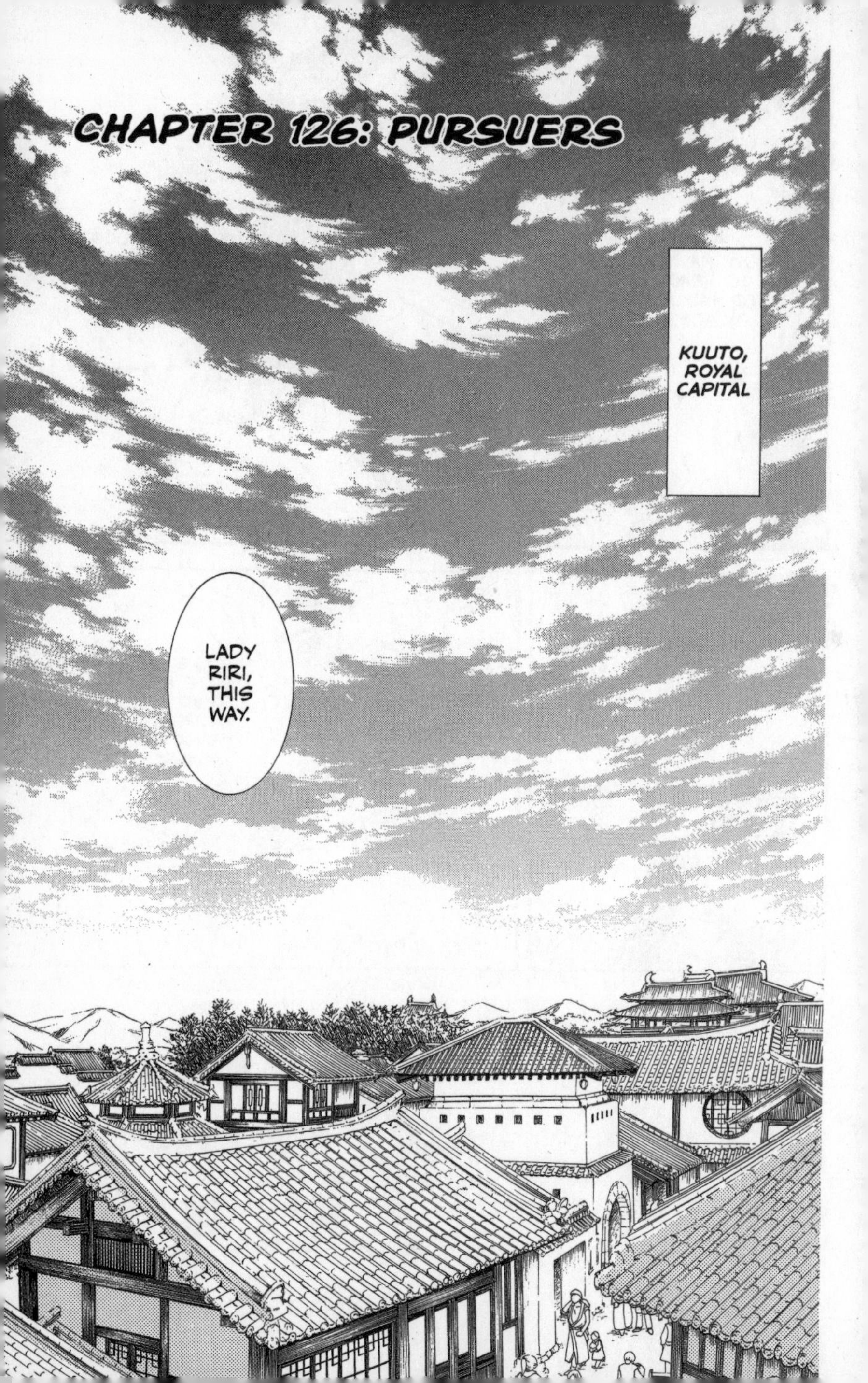
CHAPTER 126: PURSUERS
KUUTO, ROYAL CAPITAL
LADY RIRI, THIS WAY.

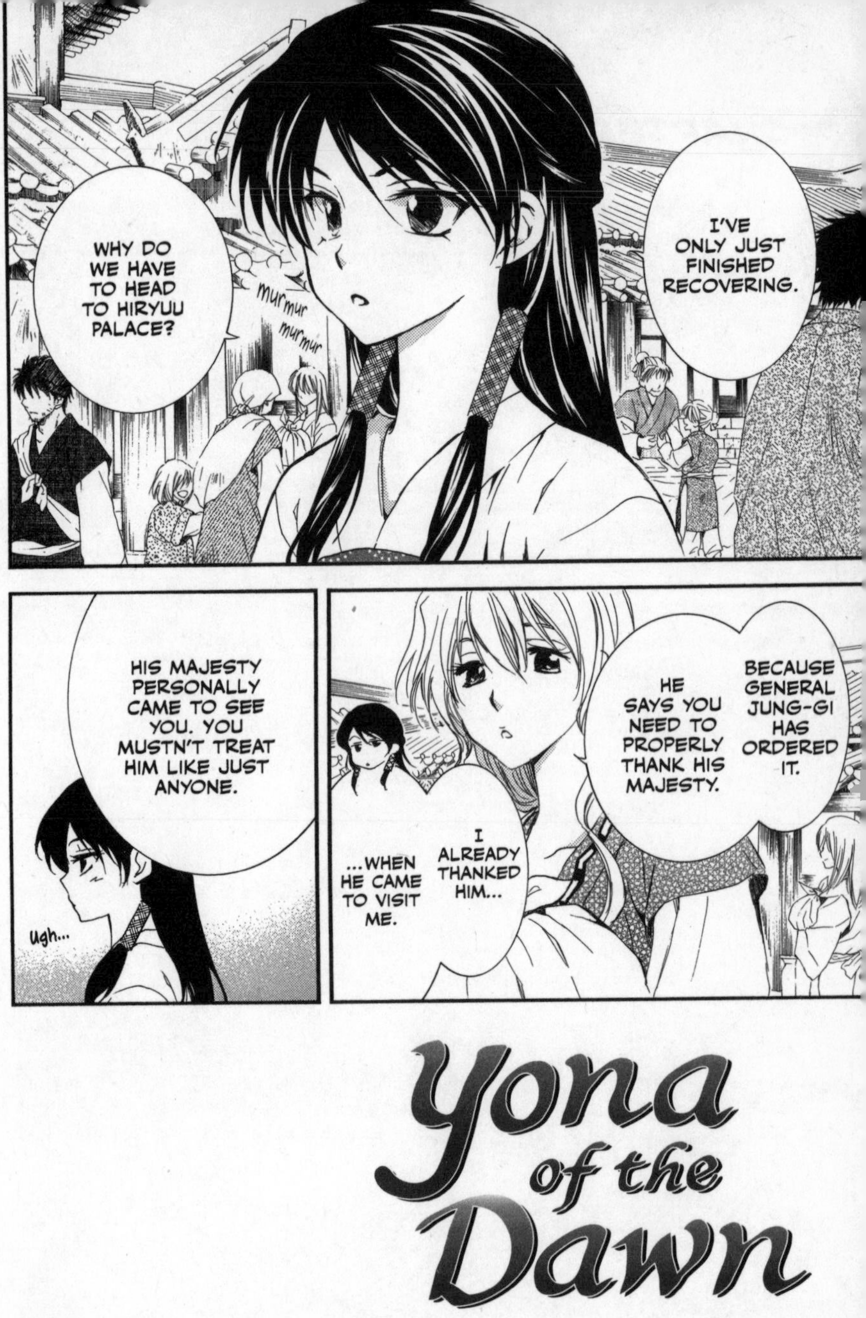
I'VE ONLY JUST FINISHED RECOVERING.
WHY DO WE HAVE TO HEAD TO HIRYUU PALACE?
murmur murmur
BECAUSE GENERAL JUNG-GI HAS ORDERED IT.
HE SAYS YOU NEED TO PROPERLY THANK HIS MAJESTY.
I ALREADY THANKED HIM...
...WHEN HE CAME TO VISIT ME.
HIS MAJESTY PERSONALLY CAME TO SEE YOU. YOU MUSTN'T TREAT HIM LIKE JUST ANYONE.
Ugh...

Yona of the Dawn

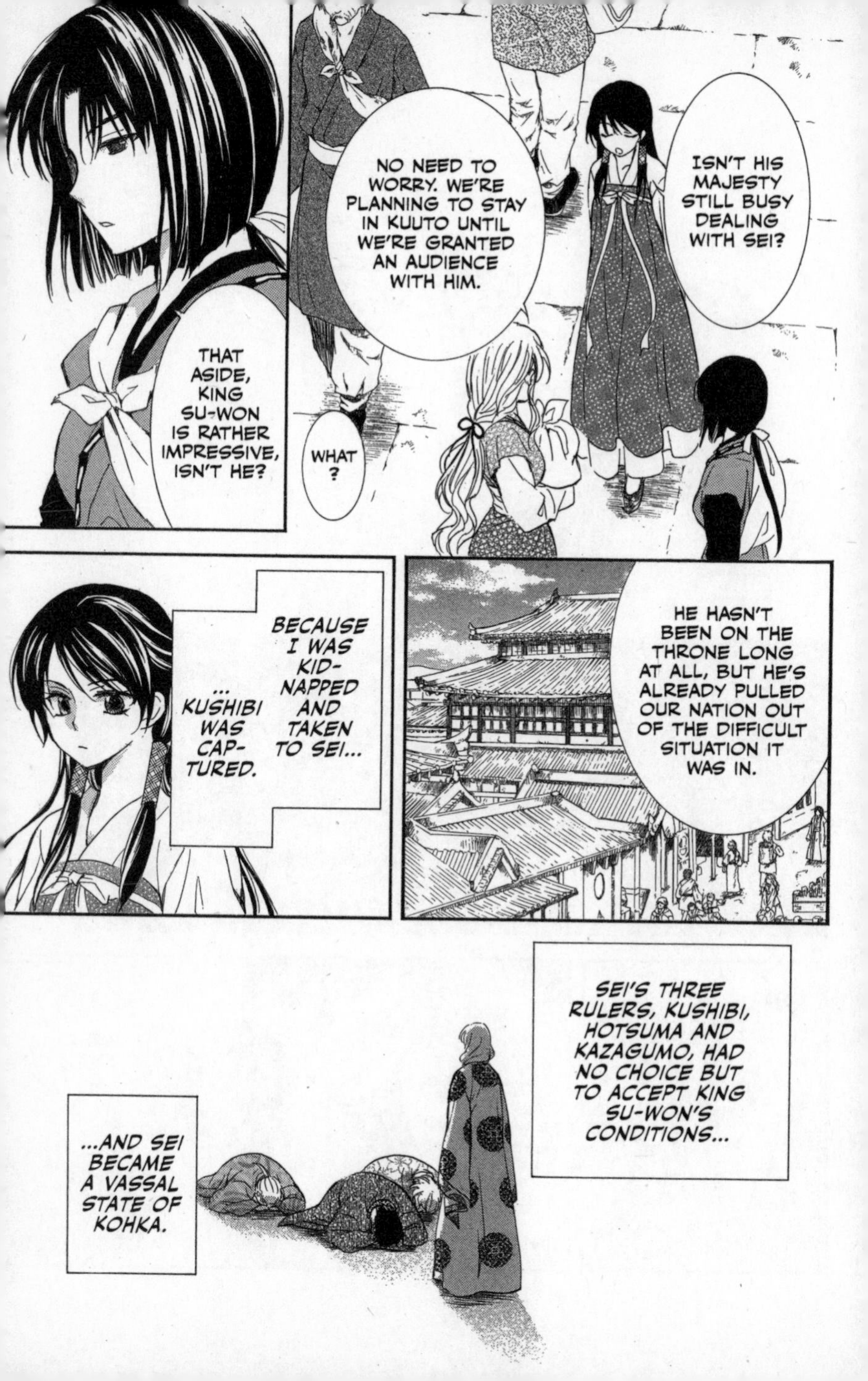
ISN'T HIS MAJESTY STILL BUSY DEALING WITH SEI?
NO NEED TO WORRY. WE'RE PLANNING TO STAY IN KUUTO UNTIL WE'RE GRANTED AN AUDIENCE WITH HIM.
WHAT?
THAT ASIDE, KING SU-WON IS RATHER IMPRESSIVE, ISN'T HE?
HE HASN'T BEEN ON THE THRONE LONG AT ALL, BUT HE'S ALREADY PULLED OUR NATION OUT OF THE DIFFICULT SITUATION IT WAS IN.
BECAUSE I WAS KID-NAPPED AND TAKEN TO SEI...
...KUSHIBI WAS CAP-TURED.
SEI'S THREE RULERS, KUSHIBI, HOTSUMA AND KAZAGUMO, HAD NO CHOICE BUT TO ACCEPT KING SU-WON'S CONDITIONS...
...AND SEI BECAME A VASSAL STATE OF KOHKA.

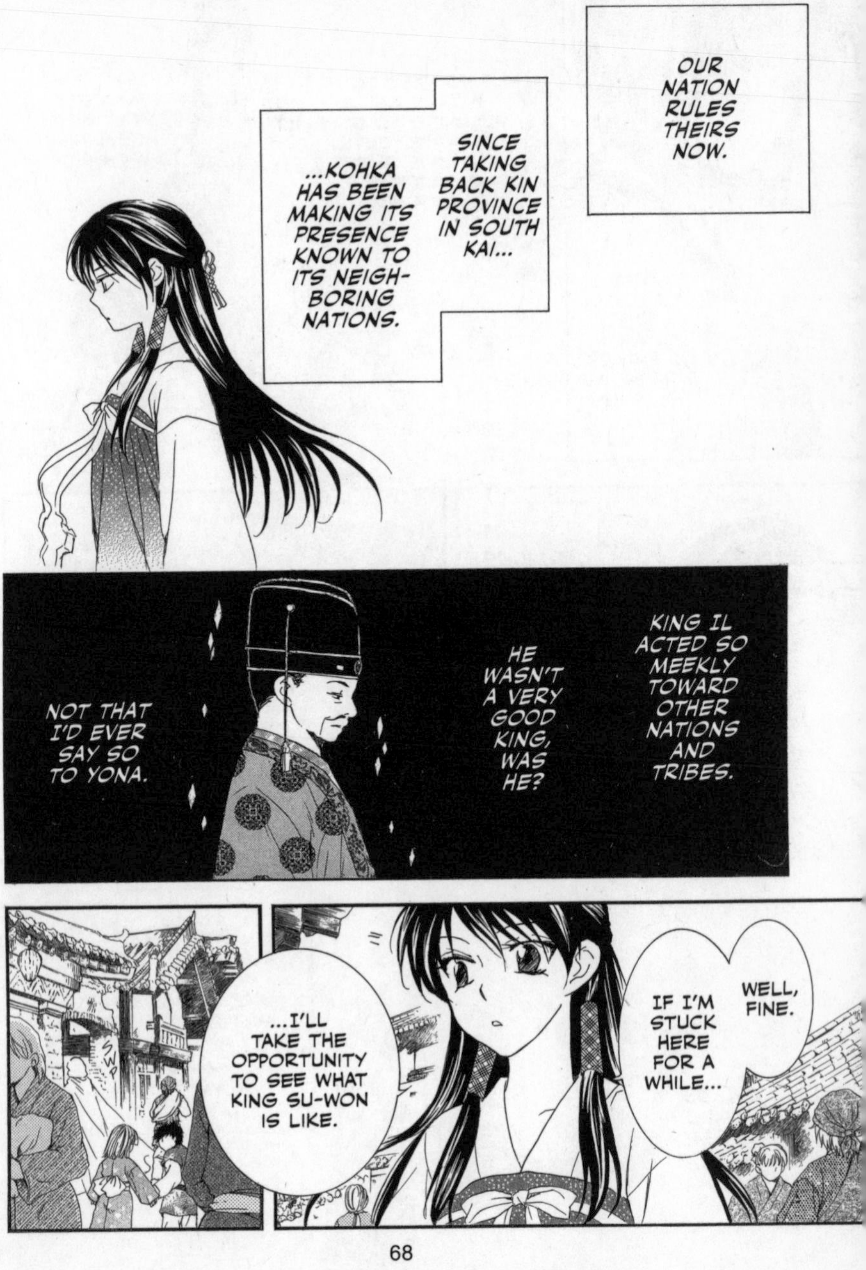
OUR NATION RULES THEIRS NOW.
SINCE TAKING BACK KIN PROVINCE IN SOUTH KAI...
...KOHKA HAS BEEN MAKING ITS PRESENCE KNOWN TO ITS NEIGH-BORING NATIONS.
KING IL ACTED SO MEEKLY TOWARD OTHER NATIONS AND TRIBES.
HE WASN'T A VERY GOOD KING, WAS HE?
NOT THAT I'D EVER SAY SO TO YONA.
WELL, FINE.
IF I'M STUCK HERE FOR A WHILE...
...I'LL TAKE THE OPPORTUNITY TO SEE WHAT KING SU-WON IS LIKE.
SWP

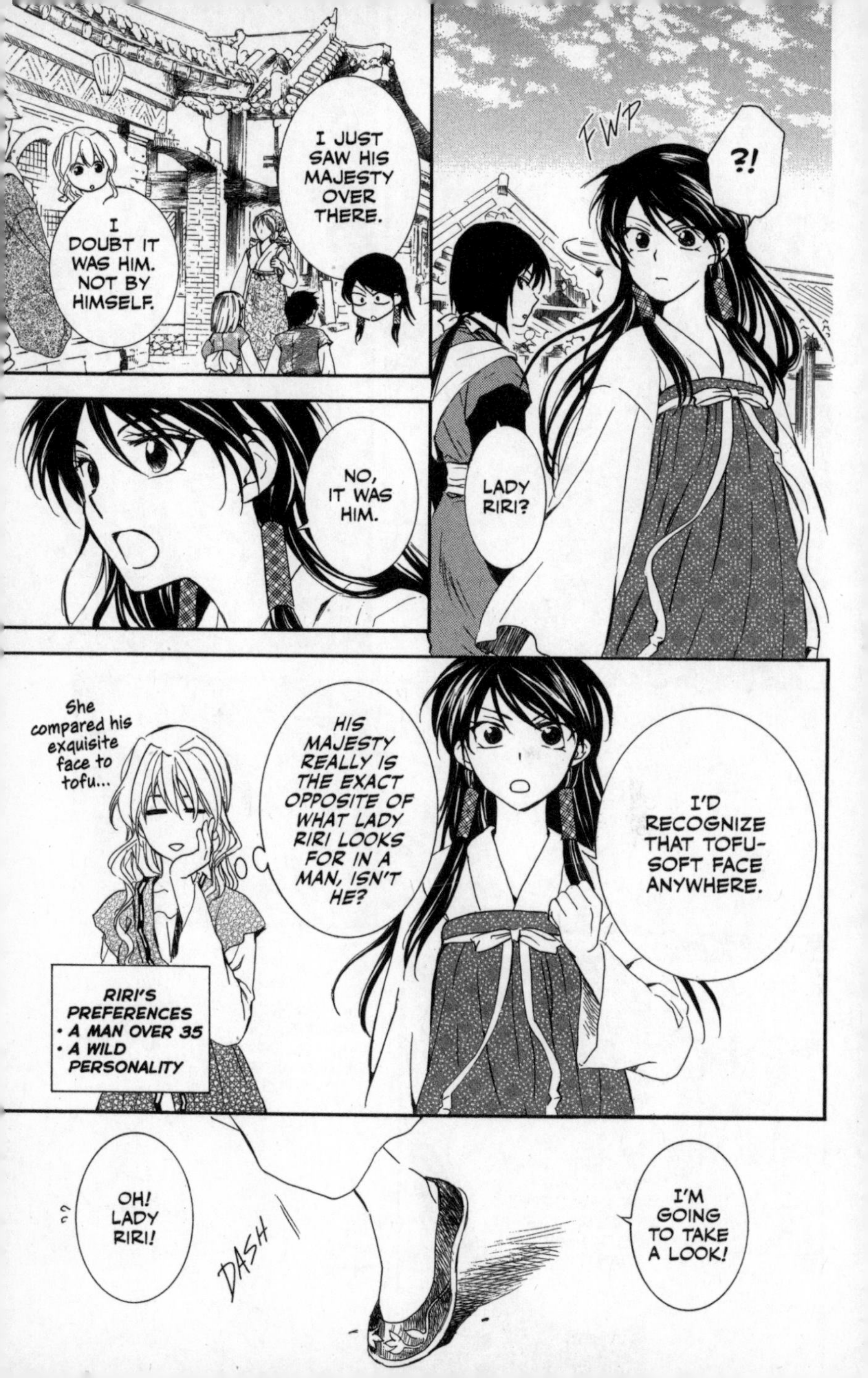
LADY RIRI?
FWP
?!
I JUST SAW HIS MAJESTY OVER THERE.
I DOUBT IT WAS HIM. NOT BY HIMSELF.
NO, IT WAS HIM.
I'D RECOGNIZE THAT TOFU-SOFT FACE ANYWHERE.
HIS MAJESTY REALLY IS THE EXACT OPPOSITE OF WHAT LADY RIRI LOOKS FOR IN A MAN, ISN'T HE?
She compared his exquisite face to tofu...
RIRI'S PREFERENCES
• A MAN OVER 35
• A WILD PERSONALITY
I'M GOING TO TAKE A LOOK!
DASH
OH! LADY RIRI!

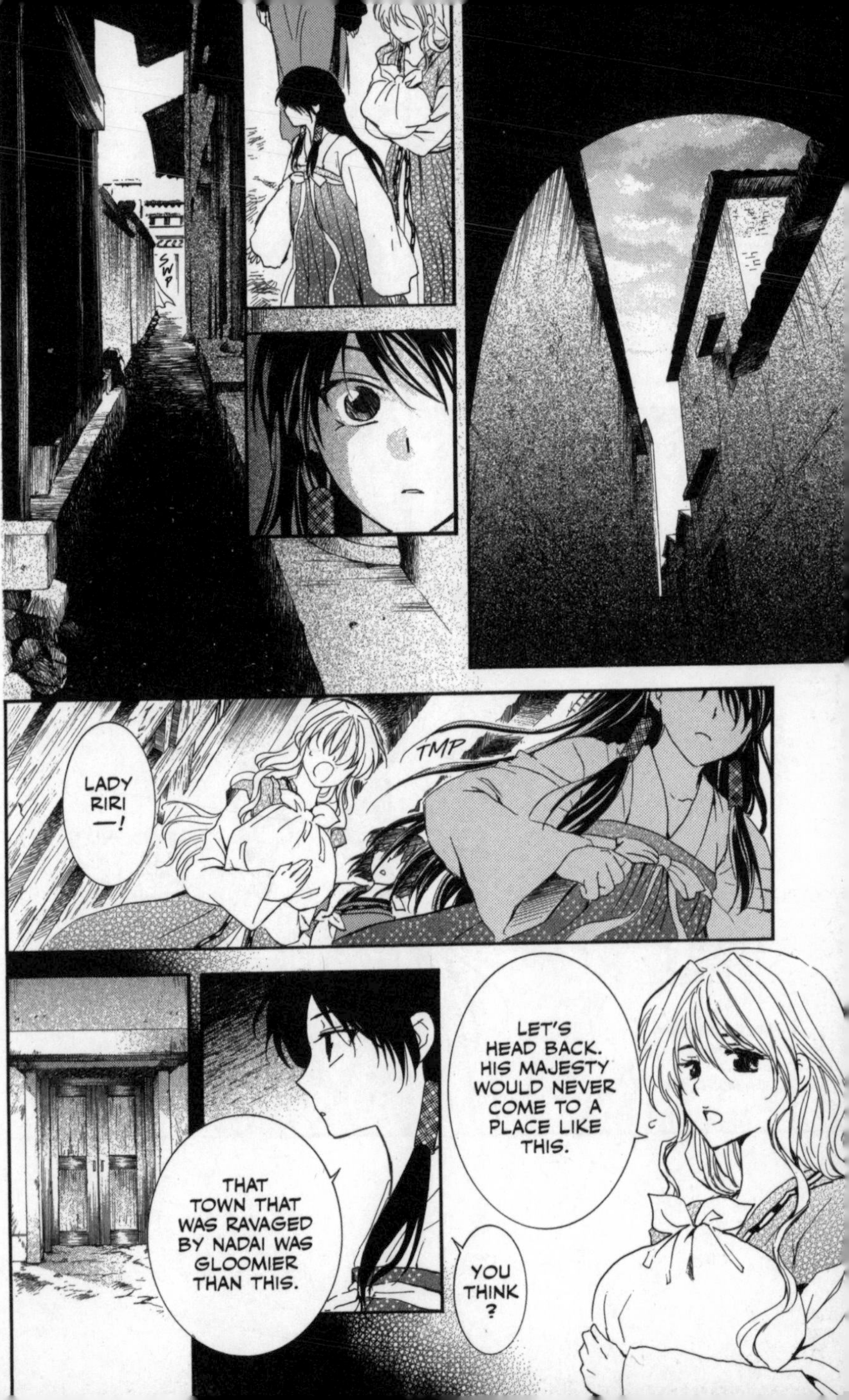
SWP
TMP
LADY RIRI—!
LET'S HEAD BACK. HIS MAJESTY WOULD NEVER COME TO A PLACE LIKE THIS.
YOU THINK?
THAT TOWN THAT WAS RAVAGED BY NADAI WAS GLOOMIER THAN THIS.

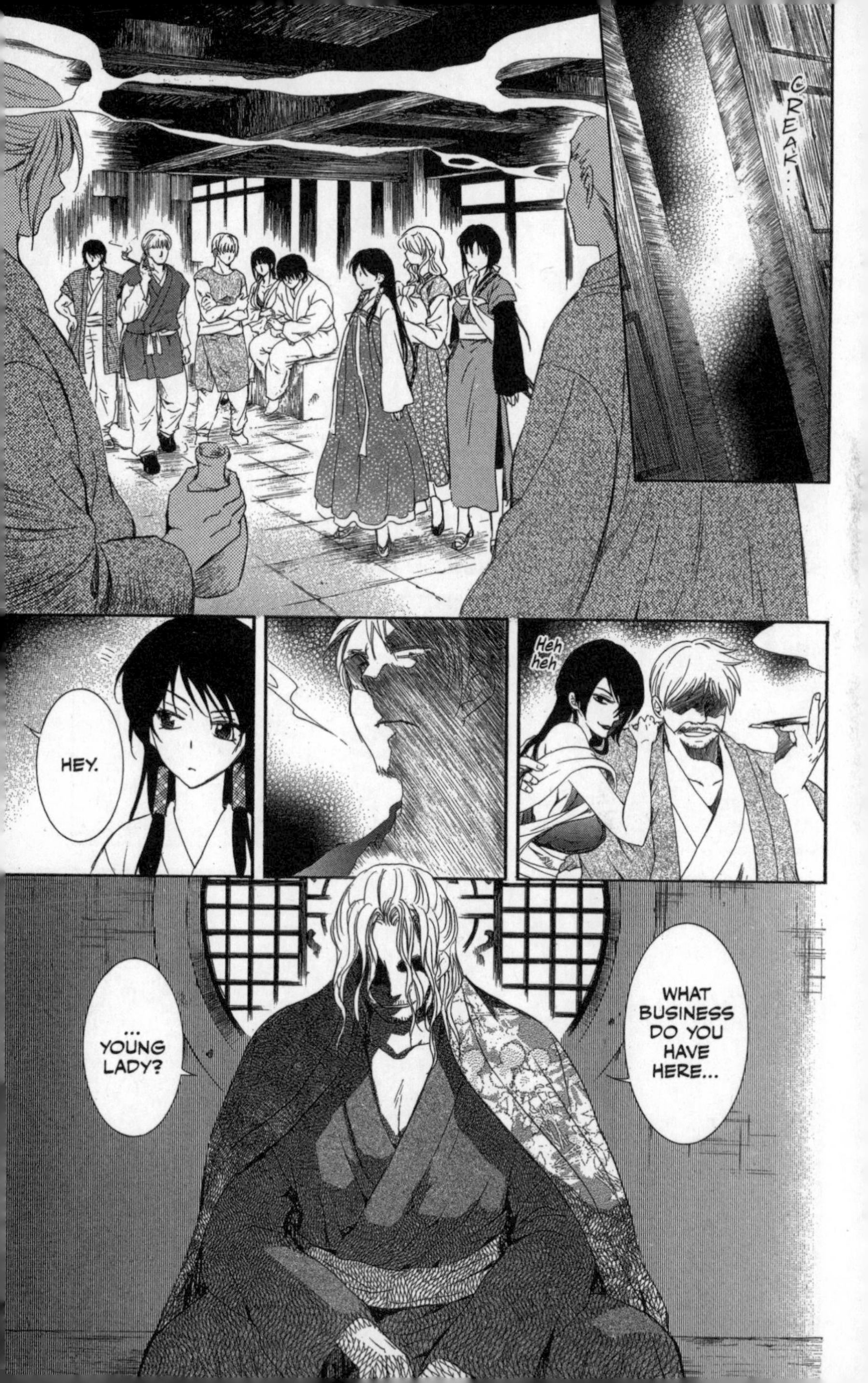
CREAK...
Heh heh
HEY.
WHAT BUSINESS DO YOU HAVE HERE...
...YOUNG LADY?

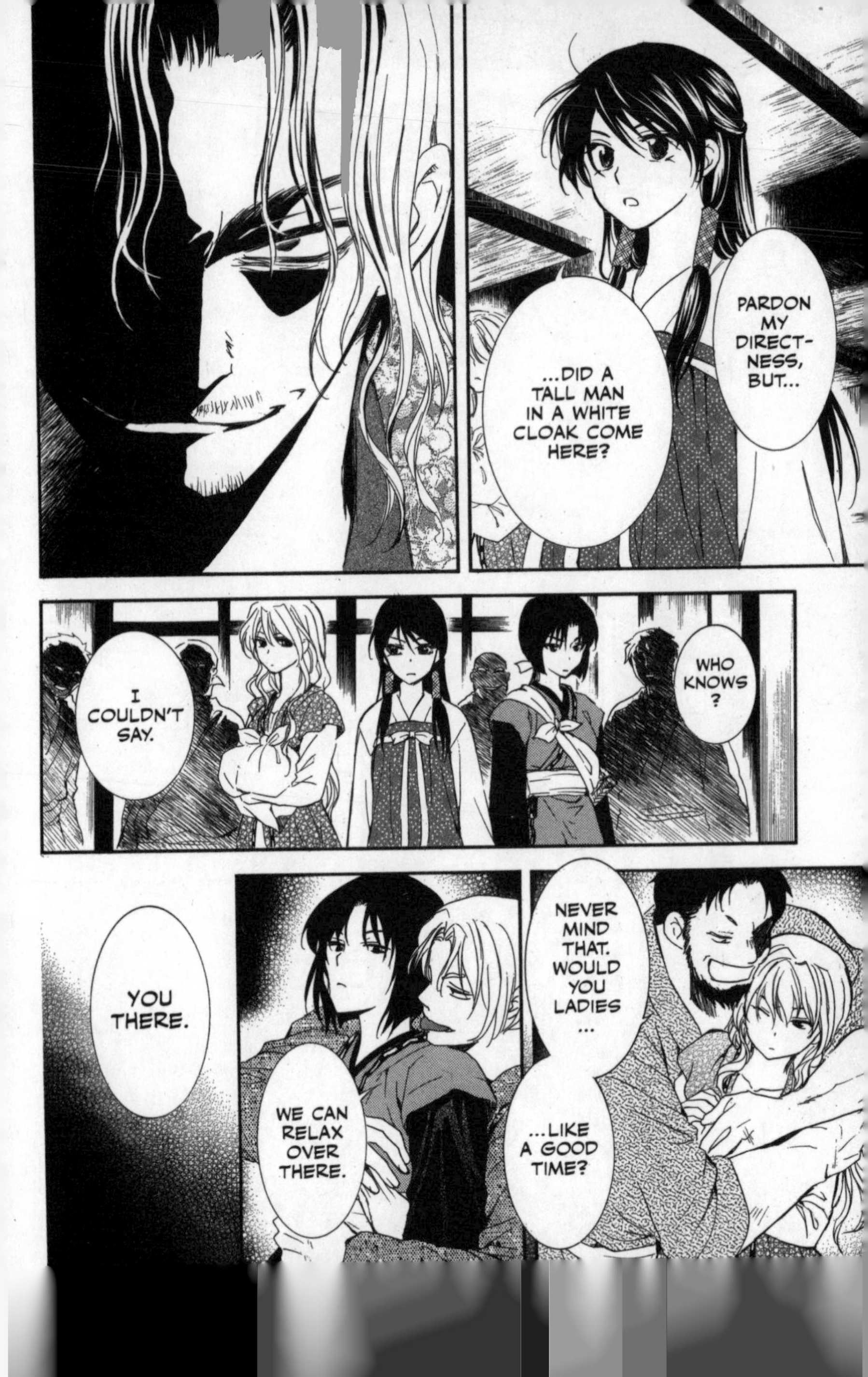
PARDON MY DIRECTNESS, BUT...
...DID A TALL MAN IN A WHITE CLOAK COME HERE?
WHO KNOWS?
I COULDN'T SAY.
NEVER MIND THAT. WOULD YOU LADIES...
...LIKE A GOOD TIME?
YOU THERE.
WE CAN RELAX OVER THERE.

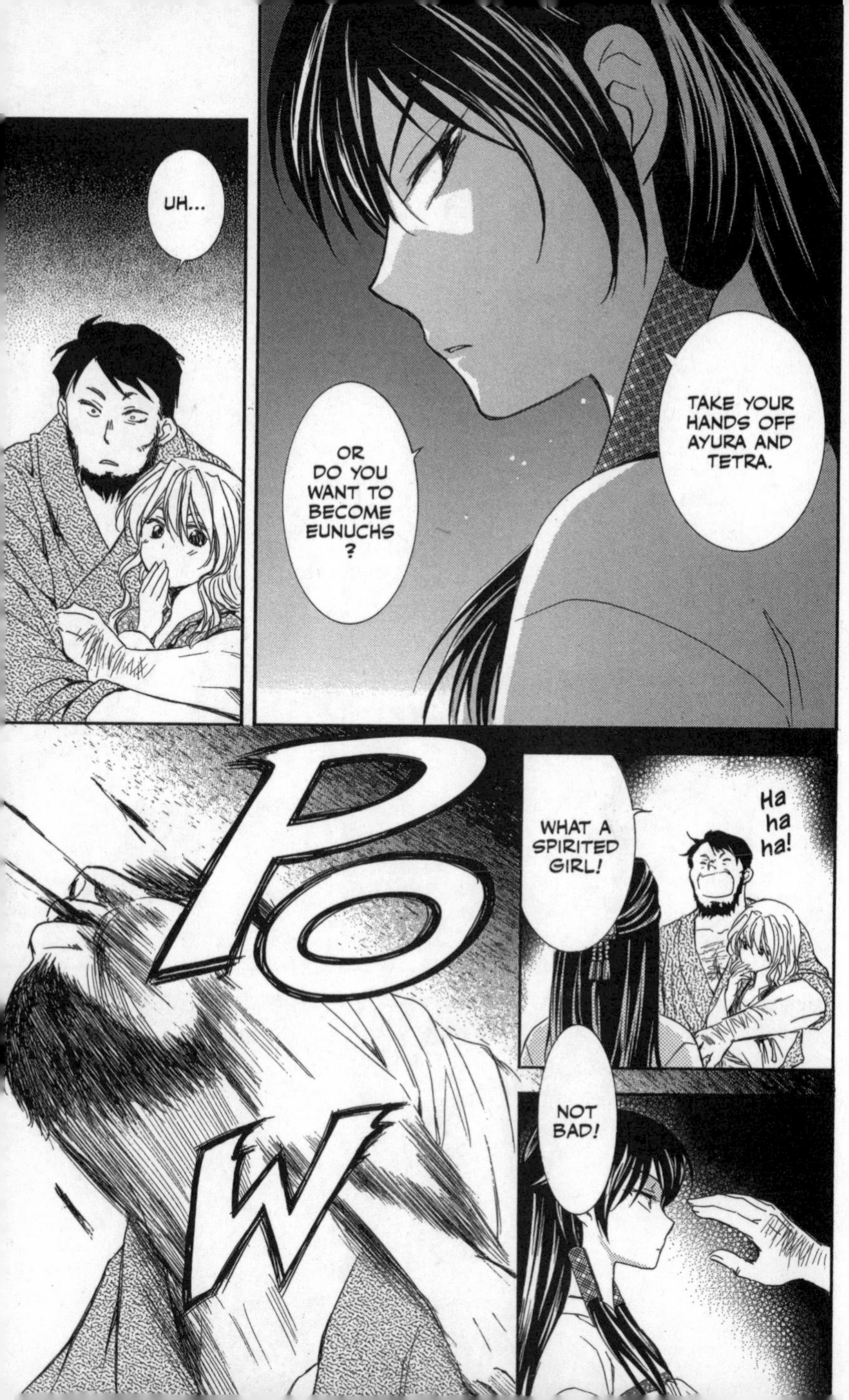
TAKE YOUR HANDS OFF AYURA AND TETRA.
OR DO YOU WANT TO BECOME EUNUCHS?
UH...
Ha ha ha!
WHAT A SPIRITED GIRL!
NOT BAD!
POW

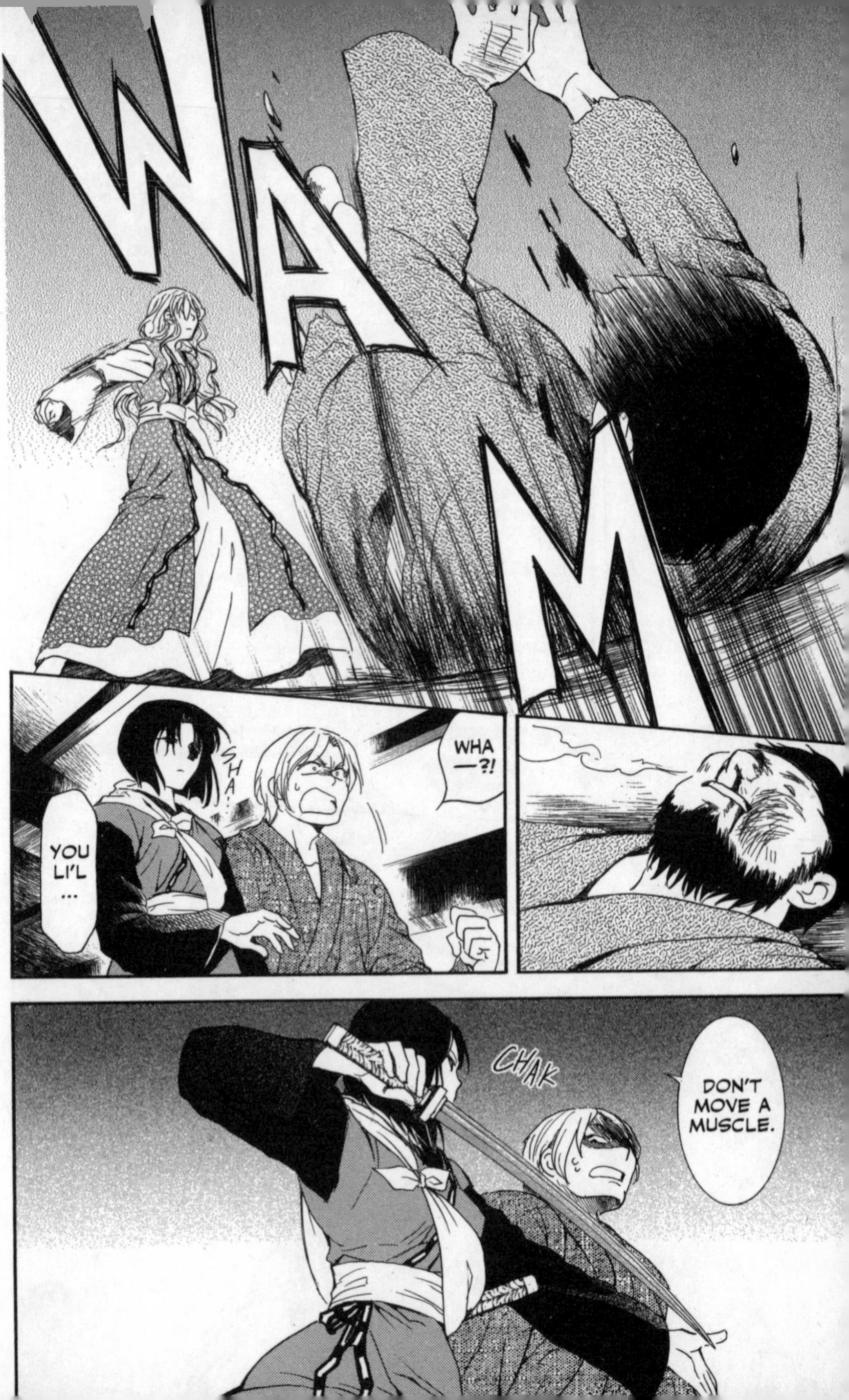
WAM
WHA—?!
SHA!
YOU LI'L ...
CHAK
DON'T MOVE A MUSCLE.

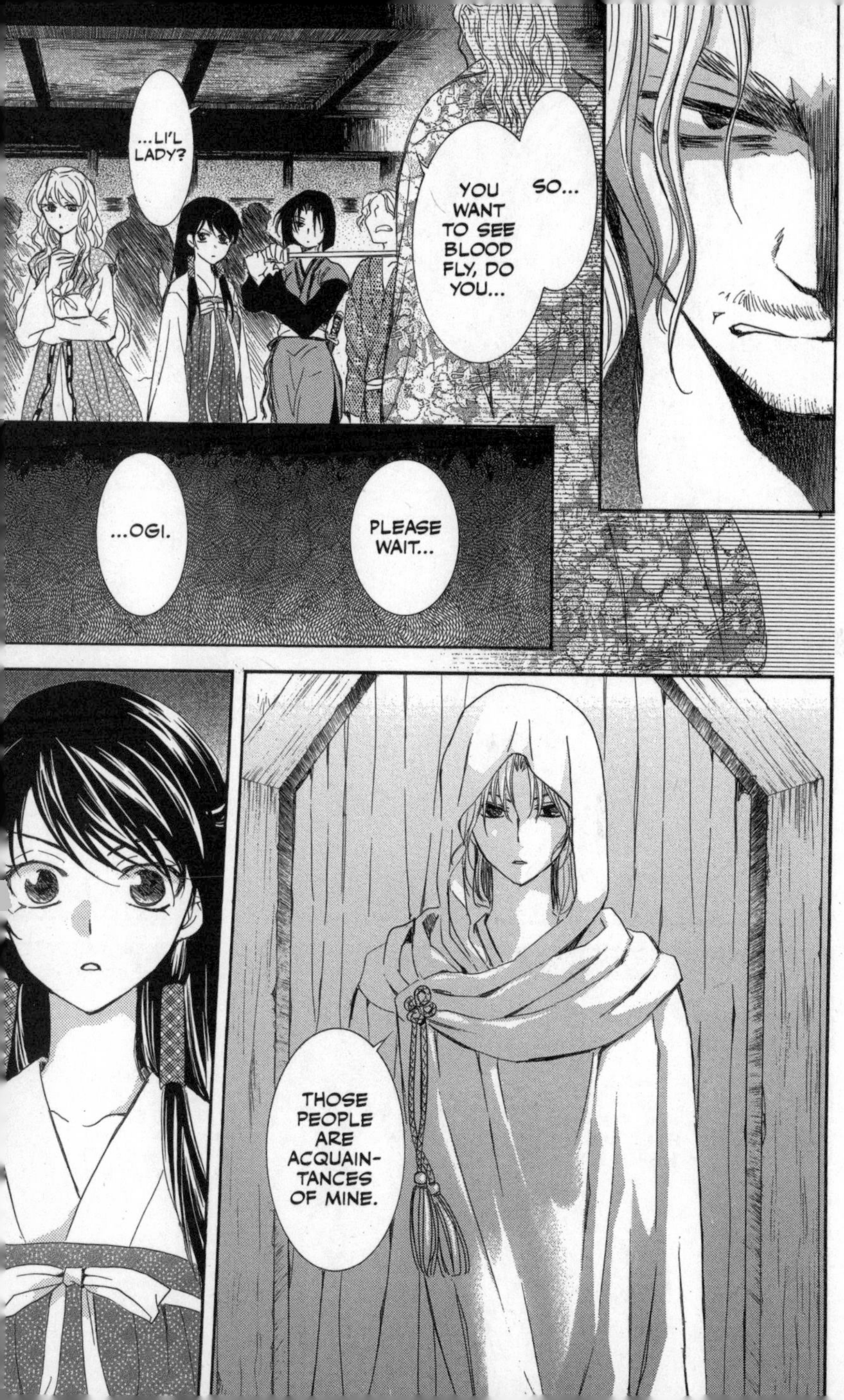
SO... YOU WANT TO SEE BLOOD FLY, DO YOU...
...LI'L LADY?
PLEASE WAIT...
...OGI.
THOSE PEOPLE ARE ACQUAIN-TANCES OF MINE.

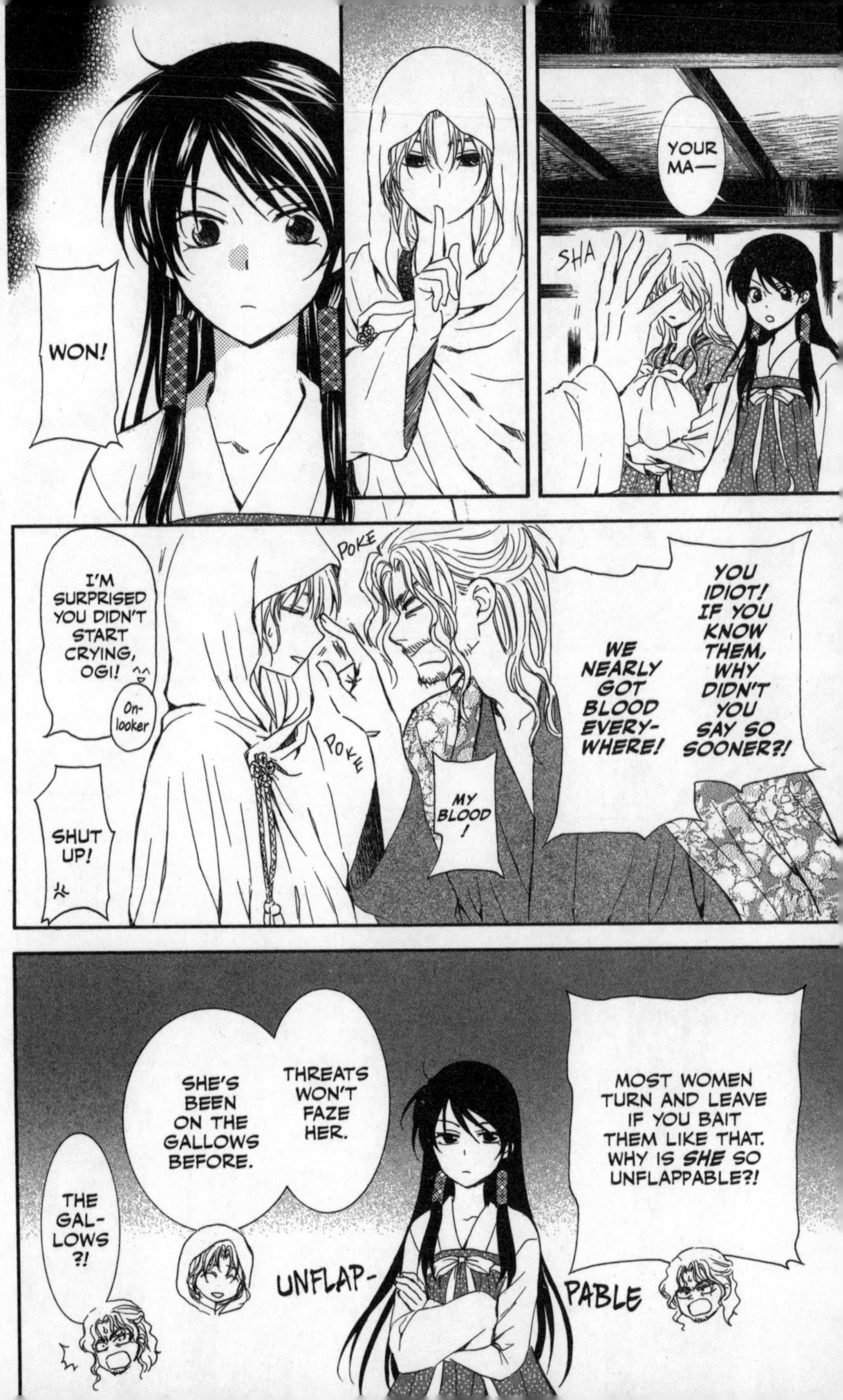
YOUR MA—
SHA
WON!
YOU IDIOT! IF YOU KNOW THEM, WHY DIDN'T YOU SAY SO SOONER?!
WE NEARLY GOT BLOOD EVERY-WHERE!
MY BLOOD!
POKE
POKE
I'M SURPRISED YOU DIDN'T START CRYING, OGI!
On-looker
SHUT UP!
MOST WOMEN TURN AND LEAVE IF YOU BAIT THEM LIKE THAT. WHY IS *SHE* SO UNFLAPPABLE?!
THREATS WON'T FAZE HER.
SHE'S BEEN ON THE GALLOWS BEFORE.
PABLE
UNFLAP-
THE GAL-LOWS?!

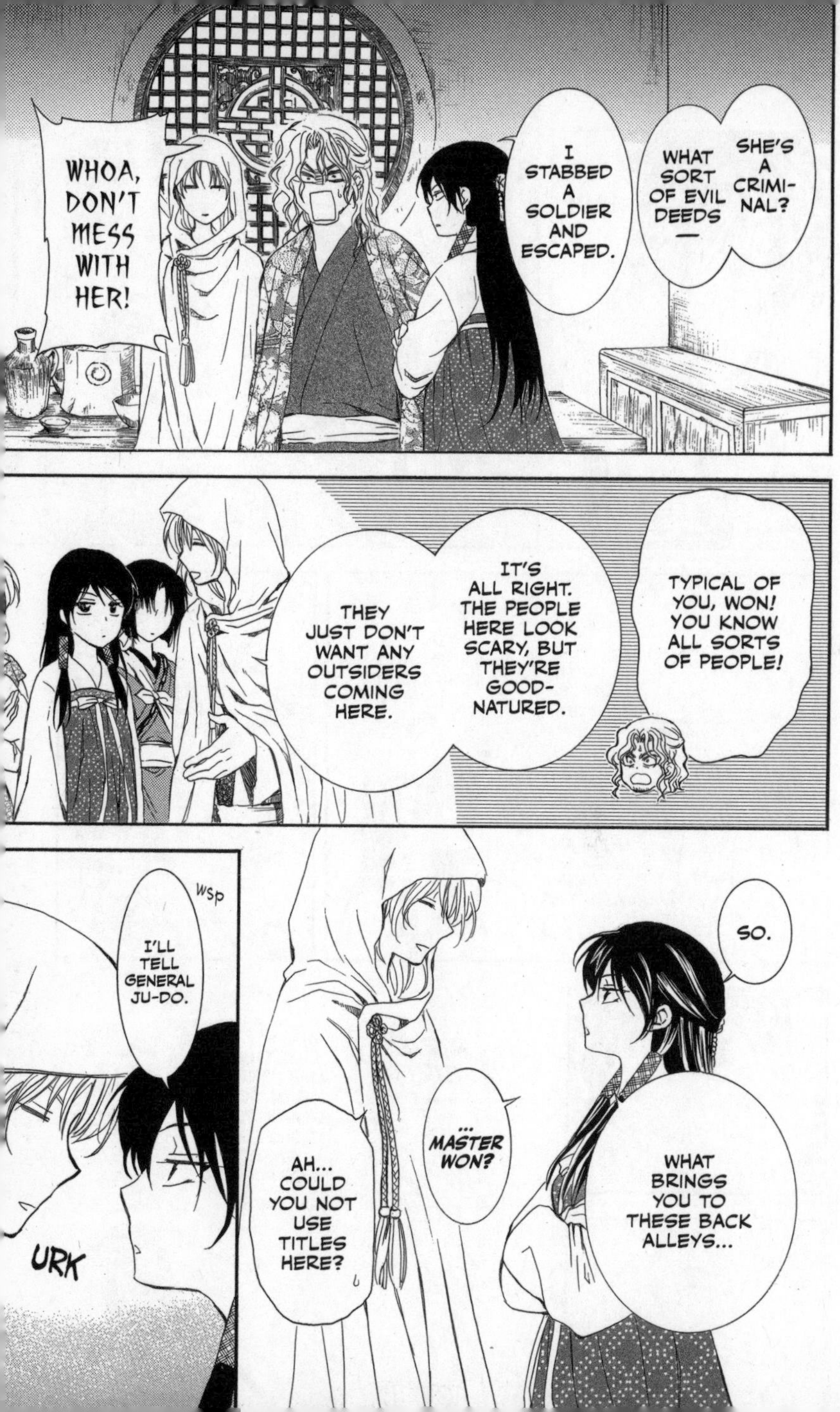
SHE'S A CRIMI-NAL?
WHAT SORT OF EVIL DEEDS —
I STABBED A SOLDIER AND ESCAPED.
WHOA, DON'T MESS WITH HER!
TYPICAL OF YOU, WON! YOU KNOW ALL SORTS OF PEOPLE!
IT'S ALL RIGHT. THE PEOPLE HERE LOOK SCARY, BUT THEY'RE GOOD-NATURED.
THEY JUST DON'T WANT ANY OUTSIDERS COMING HERE.
SO.
WHAT BRINGS YOU TO THESE BACK ALLEYS...
...MASTER WON?
AH... COULD YOU NOT USE TITLES HERE?
WSP
I'LL TELL GENERAL JU-DO.
URK

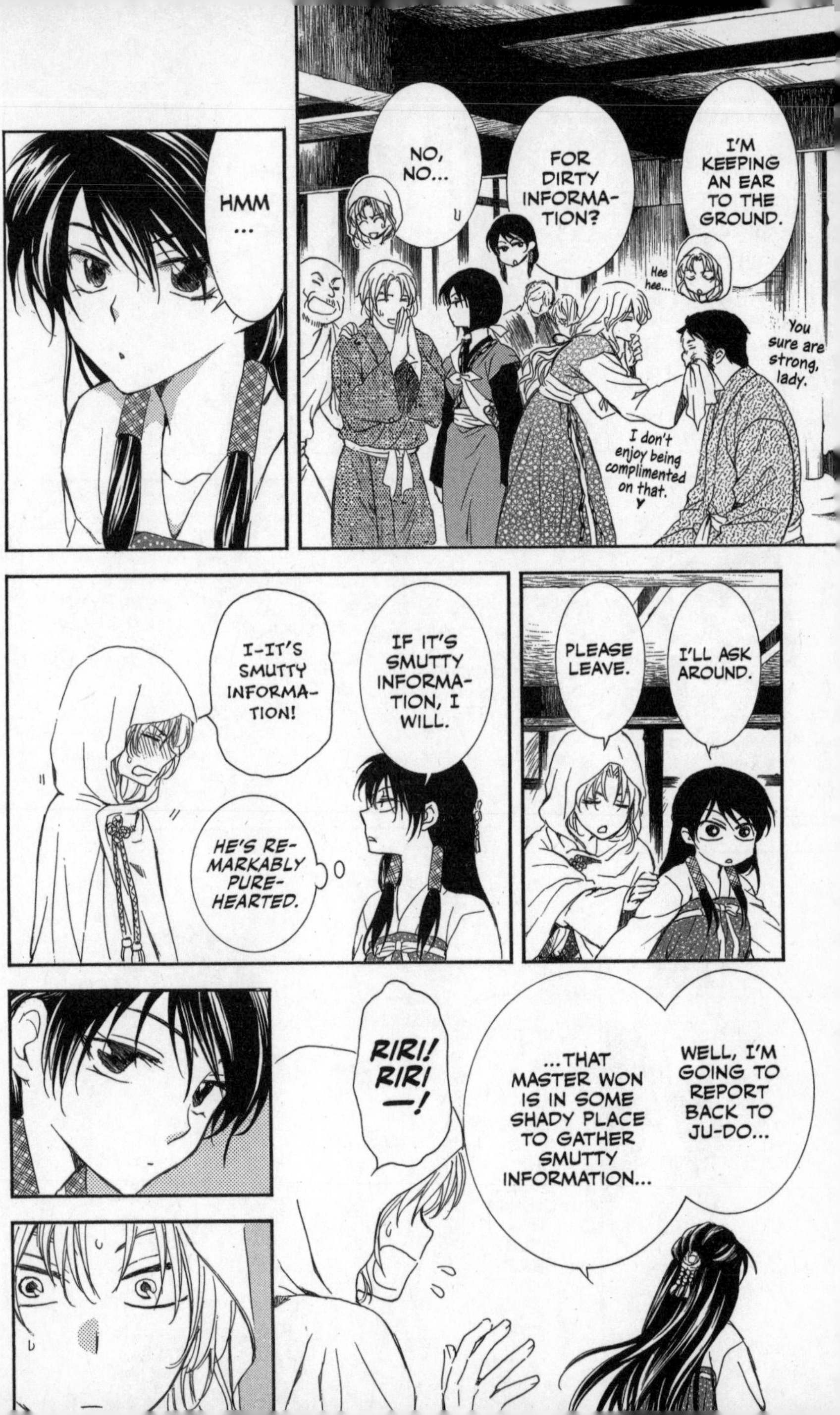
I'M KEEPING AN EAR TO THE GROUND.
You sure are strong, lady.
Hee hee...
FOR DIRTY INFORMATION?
I don't enjoy being complimented on that.
NO, NO...
HMM ...
I'LL ASK AROUND.
PLEASE LEAVE.
IF IT'S SMUTTY INFORMATION, I WILL.
I-IT'S SMUTTY INFORMATION!
HE'S REMARKABLY PURE-HEARTED.
WELL, I'M GOING TO REPORT BACK TO JU-DO...
...THAT MASTER WON IS IN SOME SHADY PLACE TO GATHER SMUTTY INFORMATION...
RIRI! RIRI—!

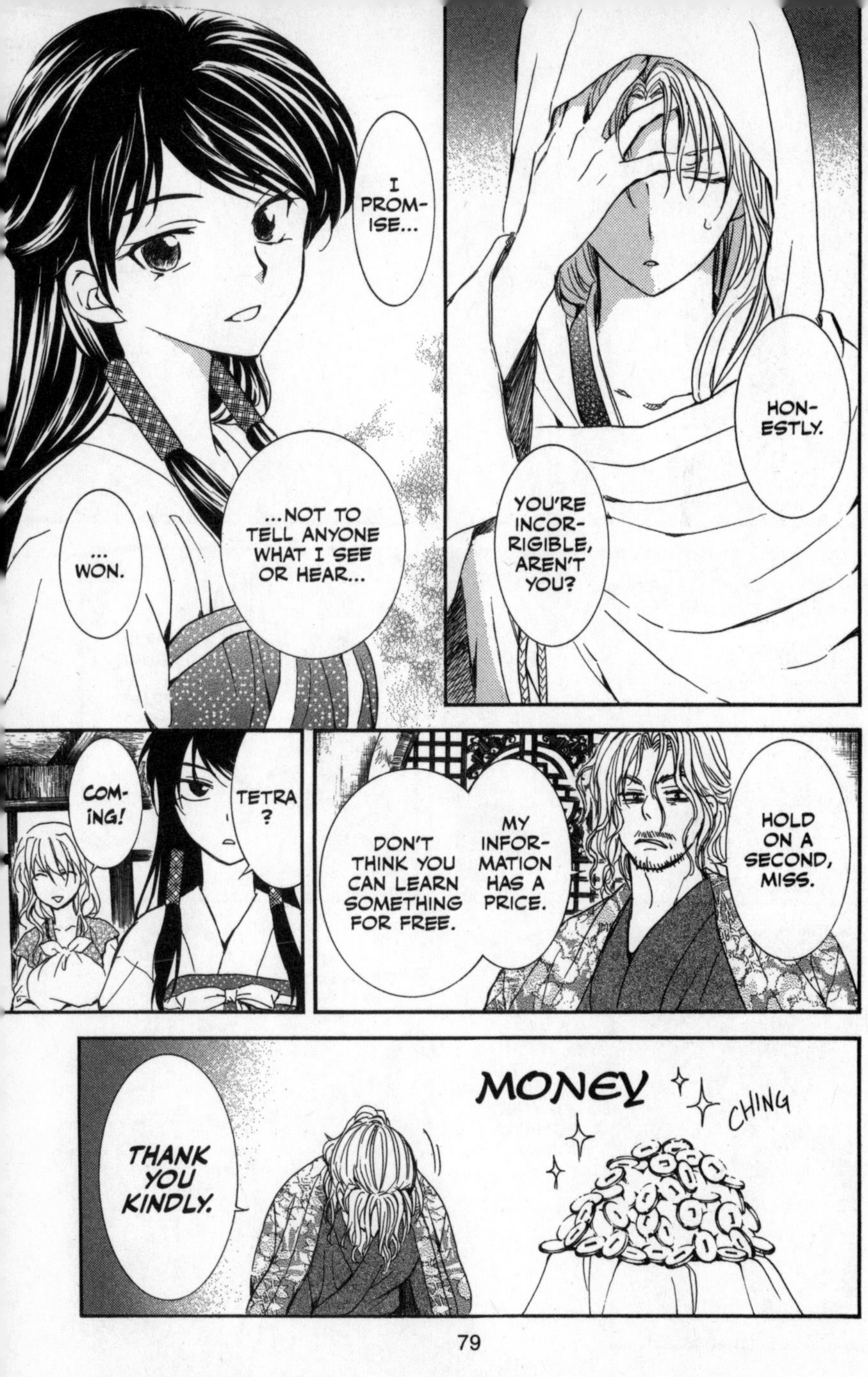
HON-ESTLY.
YOU'RE INCOR-RIGIBLE, AREN'T YOU?
I PROM-ISE...
...NOT TO TELL ANYONE WHAT I SEE OR HEAR...
... WON.
HOLD ON A SECOND, MISS.
MY INFOR-MATION HAS A PRICE.
DON'T THINK YOU CAN LEARN SOMETHING FOR FREE.
TETRA ?
COM-ING!
MONEY
CHING
THANK YOU KINDLY.

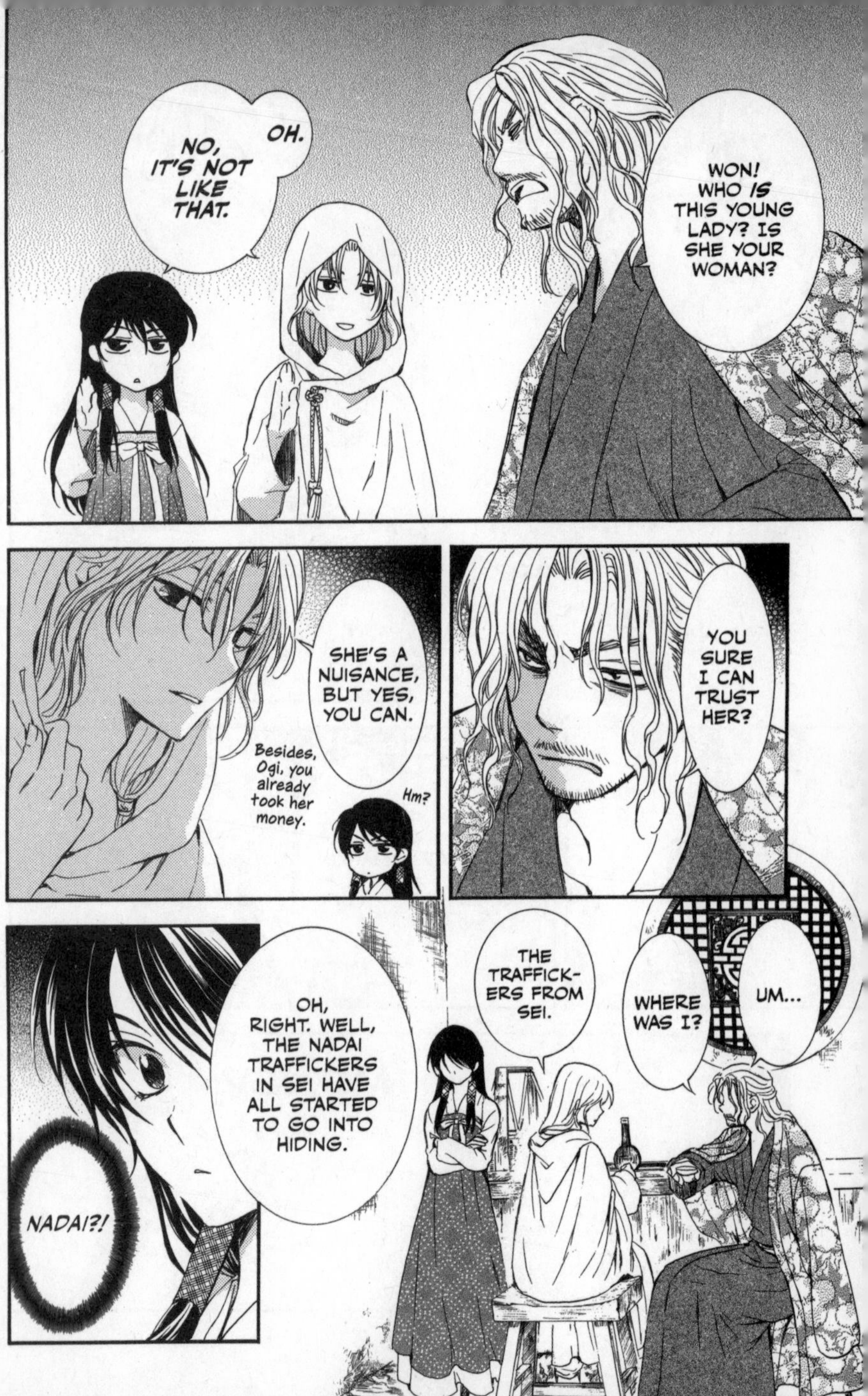
WON! WHO IS THIS YOUNG LADY? IS SHE YOUR WOMAN?
OH.
NO, IT'S NOT LIKE THAT.
YOU SURE I CAN TRUST HER?
SHE'S A NUISANCE, BUT YES, YOU CAN.
Besides, Ogi, you already took her money.
Hm?
UM...
WHERE WAS I?
THE TRAFFICKERS FROM SEI.
OH, RIGHT. WELL, THE NADAI TRAFFICKERS IN SEI HAVE ALL STARTED TO GO INTO HIDING.
NADAI?!

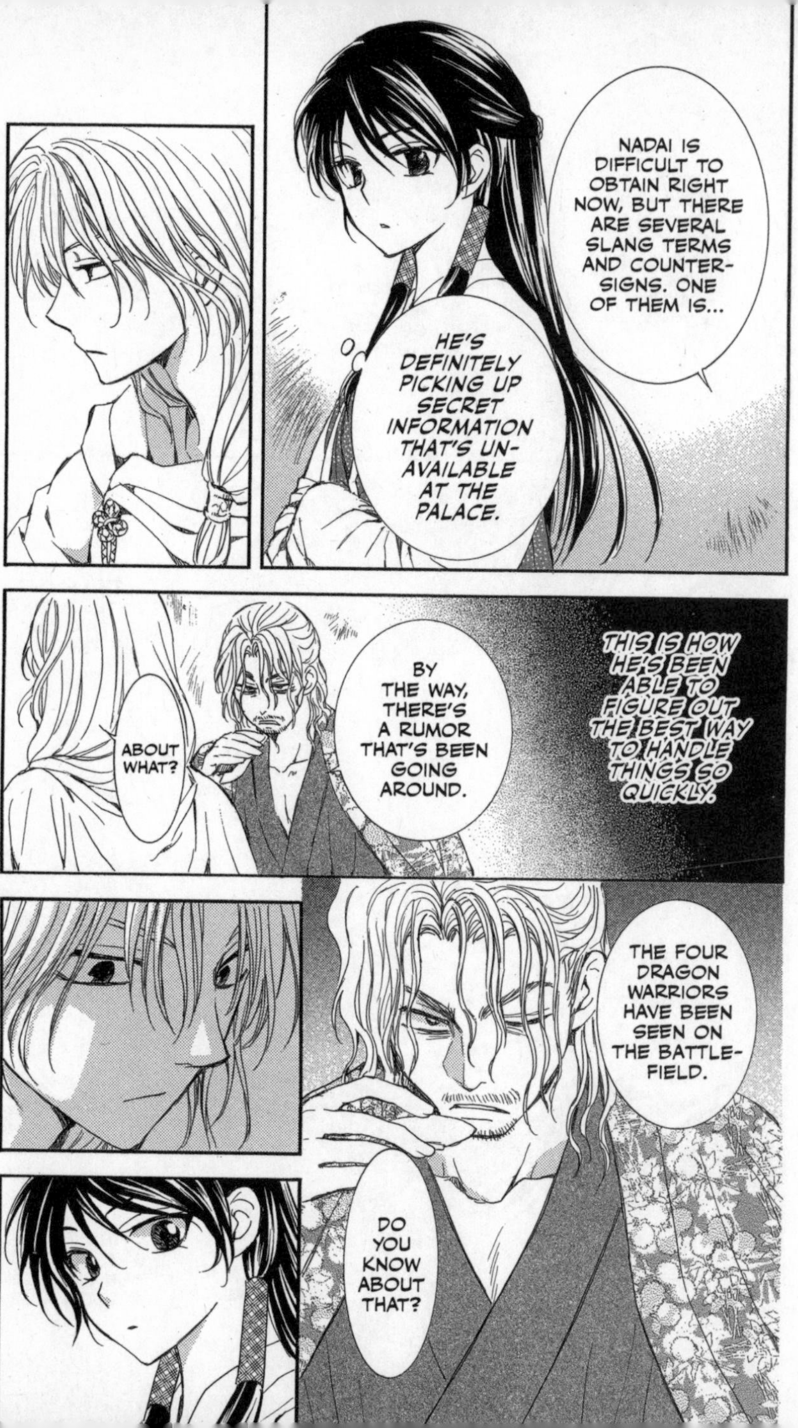
NADAI IS DIFFICULT TO OBTAIN RIGHT NOW, BUT THERE ARE SEVERAL SLANG TERMS AND COUNTER-SIGNS. ONE OF THEM IS...
HE'S DEFINITELY PICKING UP SECRET INFORMATION THAT'S UN-AVAILABLE AT THE PALACE.
THIS IS HOW HE'S BEEN ABLE TO FIGURE OUT THE BEST WAY TO HANDLE THINGS SO QUICKLY.
BY THE WAY, THERE'S A RUMOR THAT'S BEEN GOING AROUND.
ABOUT WHAT?
THE FOUR DRAGON WARRIORS HAVE BEEN SEEN ON THE BATTLE-FIELD.
DO YOU KNOW ABOUT THAT?

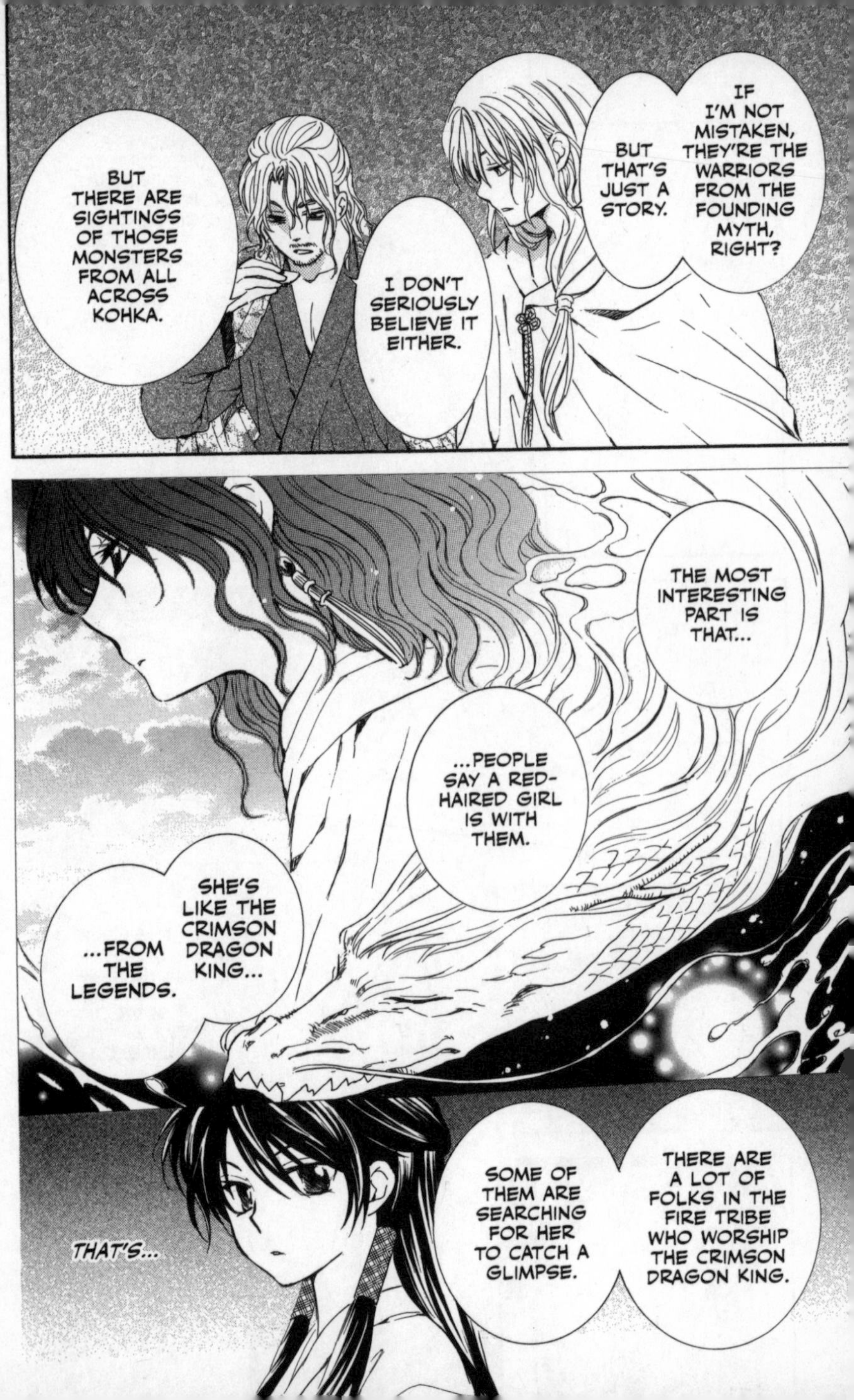
IF I'M NOT MISTAKEN, THEY'RE THE WARRIORS FROM THE FOUNDING MYTH, RIGHT?
BUT THAT'S JUST A STORY.
I DON'T SERIOUSLY BELIEVE IT EITHER.
BUT THERE ARE SIGHTINGS OF THOSE MONSTERS FROM ALL ACROSS KOHKA.
THE MOST INTERESTING PART IS THAT...
...PEOPLE SAY A RED-HAIRED GIRL IS WITH THEM.
SHE'S LIKE THE CRIMSON DRAGON KING...
...FROM THE LEGENDS.
THERE ARE A LOT OF FOLKS IN THE FIRE TRIBE WHO WORSHIP THE CRIMSON DRAGON KING.
SOME OF THEM ARE SEARCHING FOR HER TO CATCH A GLIMPSE.
THAT'S...

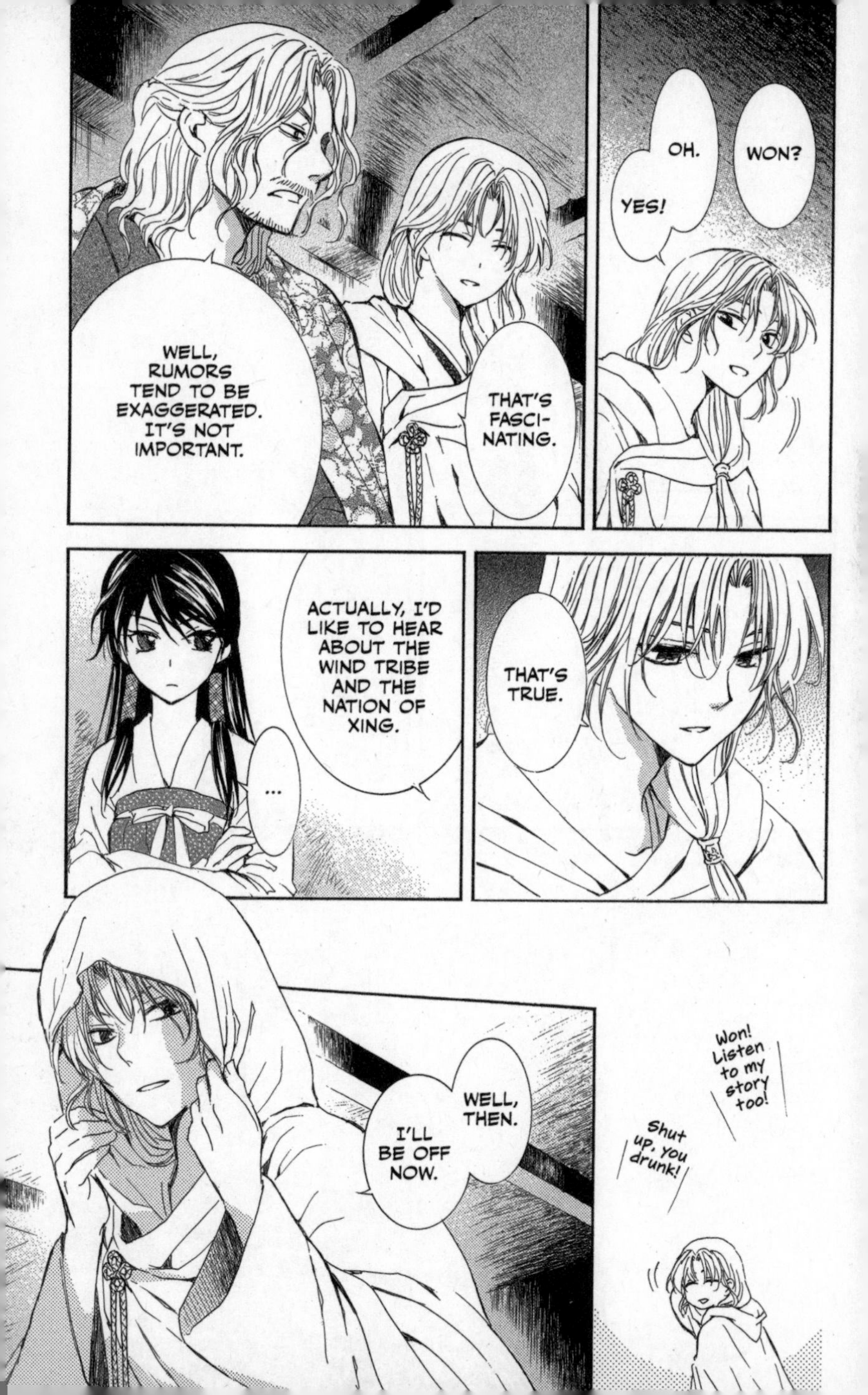
WON?
OH.
YES!
THAT'S FASCI-NATING.
WELL, RUMORS TEND TO BE EXAGGERATED. IT'S NOT IMPORTANT.
THAT'S TRUE.
ACTUALLY, I'D LIKE TO HEAR ABOUT THE WIND TRIBE AND THE NATION OF XING.
...
Won! Listen to my story too!
Shut up, you drunk!
WELL, THEN.
I'LL BE OFF NOW.

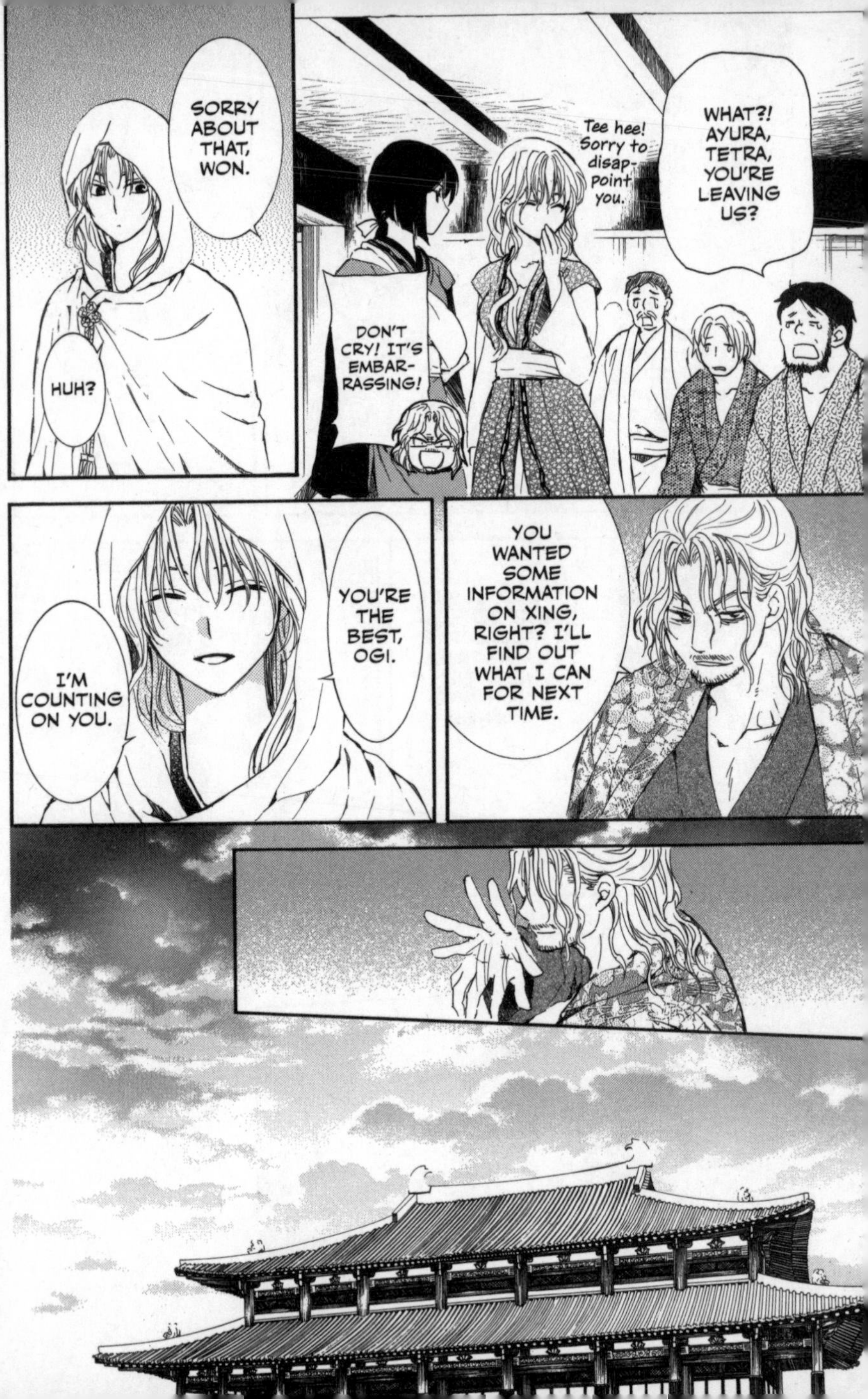

WHAT?! AYURA, TETRA, YOU'RE LEAVING US?
Tee hee! Sorry to disap-point you.
DON'T CRY! IT'S EMBAR-RASSING!
SORRY ABOUT THAT, WON.
HUH?
YOU WANTED SOME INFORMATION ON XING, RIGHT? I'LL FIND OUT WHAT I CAN FOR NEXT TIME.
YOU'RE THE BEST, OGI.
I'M COUNTING ON YOU.

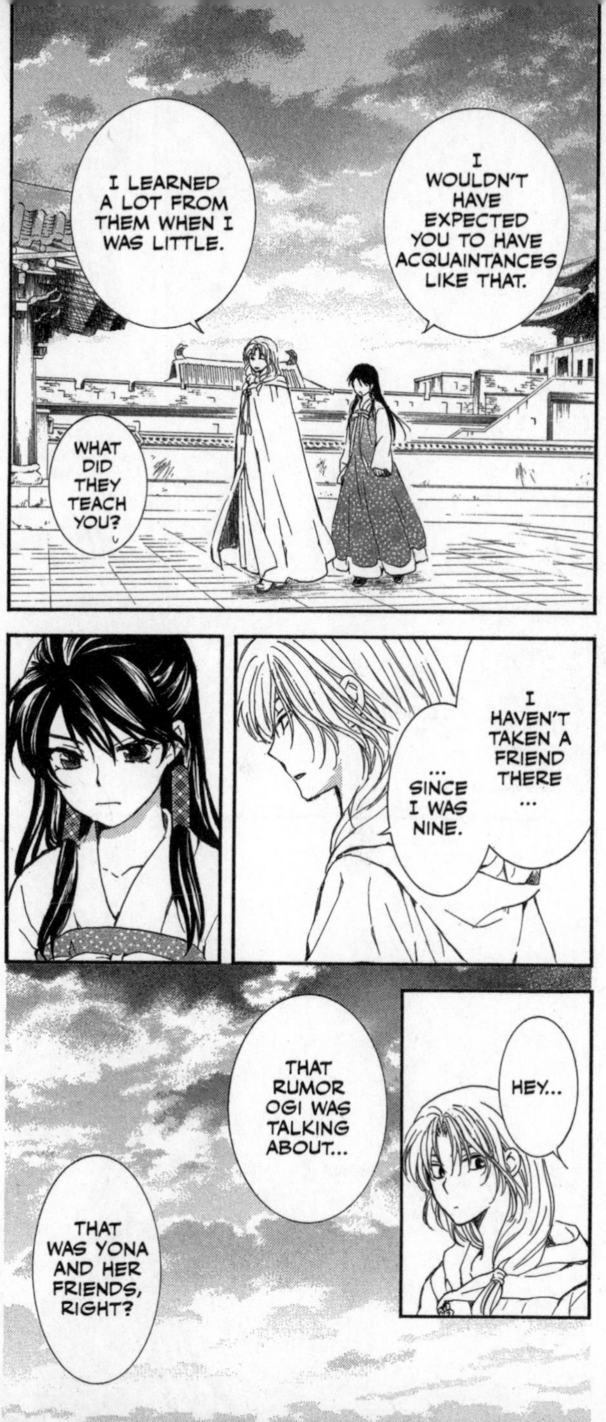
I WOULDN'T HAVE EXPECTED YOU TO HAVE ACQUAINTANCES LIKE THAT.
I LEARNED A LOT FROM THEM WHEN I WAS LITTLE.
WHAT DID THEY TEACH YOU?
I HAVEN'T TAKEN A FRIEND THERE...
...SINCE I WAS NINE.
HEY...
THAT RUMOR OGI WAS TALKING ABOUT...
THAT WAS YONA AND HER FRIENDS, RIGHT?

In the Nation of Sei arc, Riri was punched, stomped on, had her hair pulled (by a powerful soldier), and nearly wound up being executed. That was quite a dark experience she had. In chapter 120, she told the people who were about to be executed with her to fight. I think that's what makes her different from Yona. Yona takes it upon herself to protect people, but Riri thinks that if you don't like a situation, you should stand up and fight back. Her sense of justice is stronger than Yona's. Until this point, Yona felt that Riri was a friend she needed to protect, but after the Nation of Sei arc, I think Riri has become a close friend she can respect.

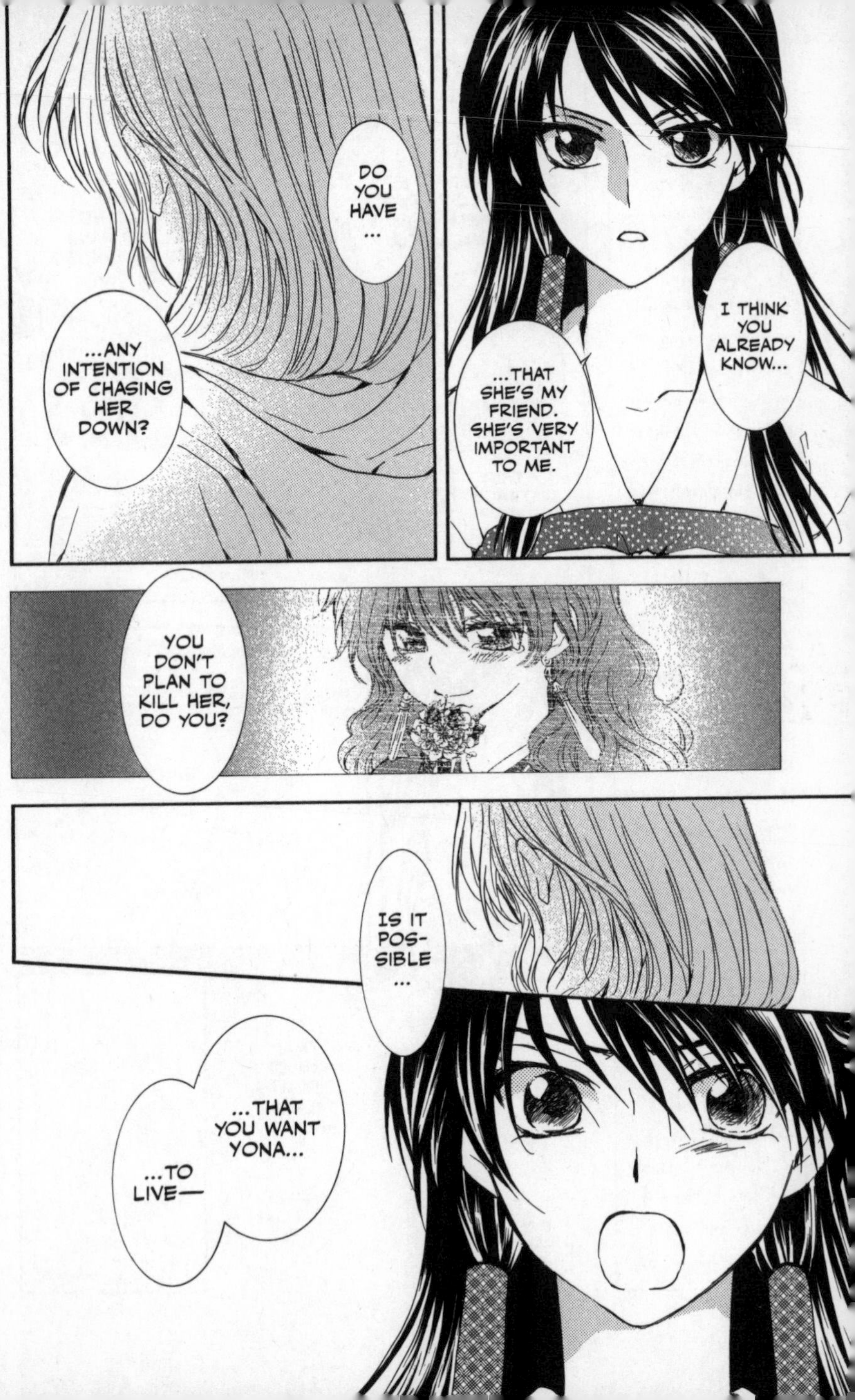
I THINK YOU ALREADY KNOW...
...THAT SHE'S MY FRIEND. SHE'S VERY IMPORTANT TO ME.
DO YOU HAVE ...
...ANY INTENTION OF CHASING HER DOWN?
YOU DON'T PLAN TO KILL HER, DO YOU?
IS IT POS-SIBLE ...
...THAT YOU WANT YONA...
...TO LIVE—

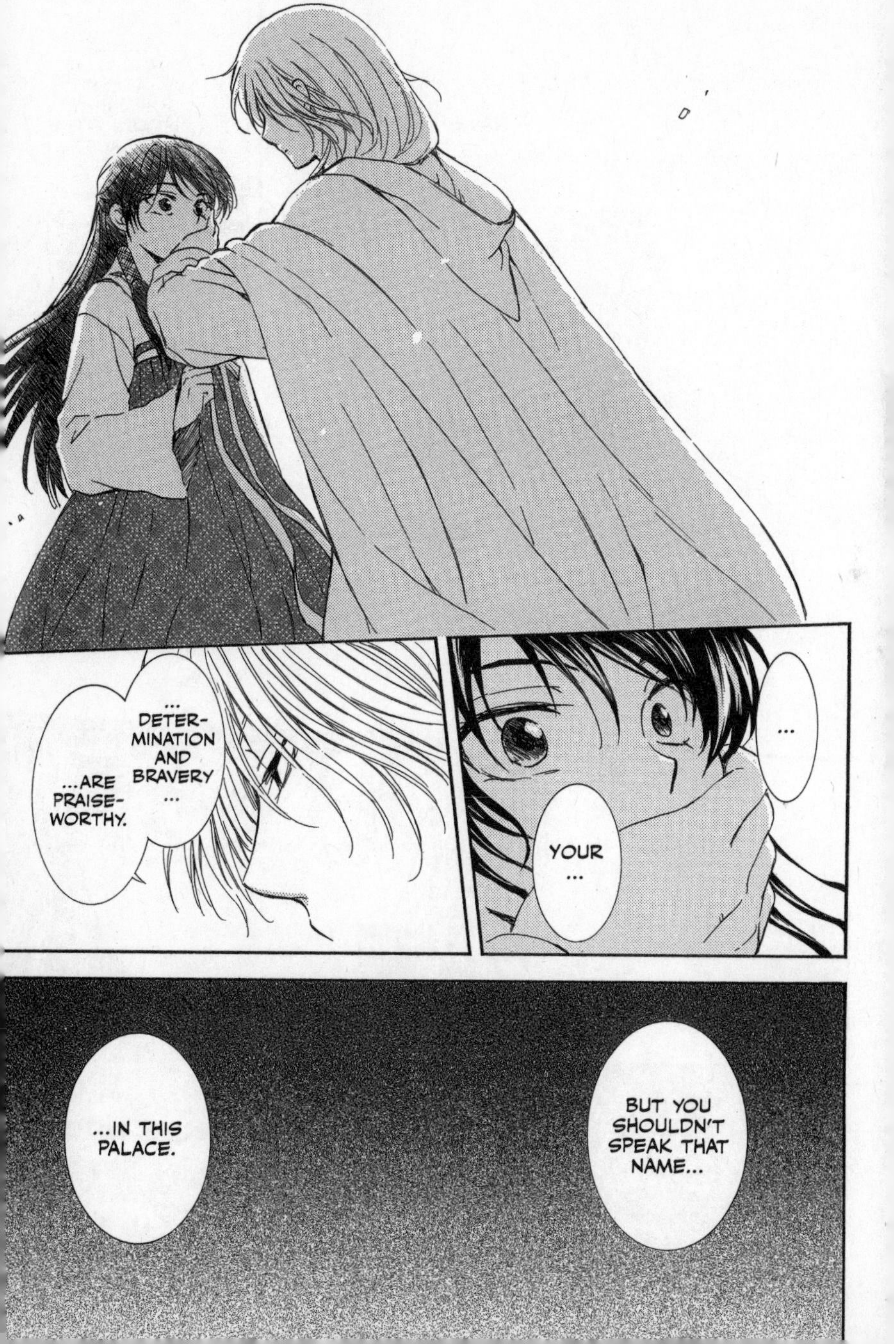
...
YOUR ...
... DETERMINATION AND BRAVERY ...
...ARE PRAISEWORTHY.
BUT YOU SHOULDN'T SPEAK THAT NAME...
...IN THIS PALACE.

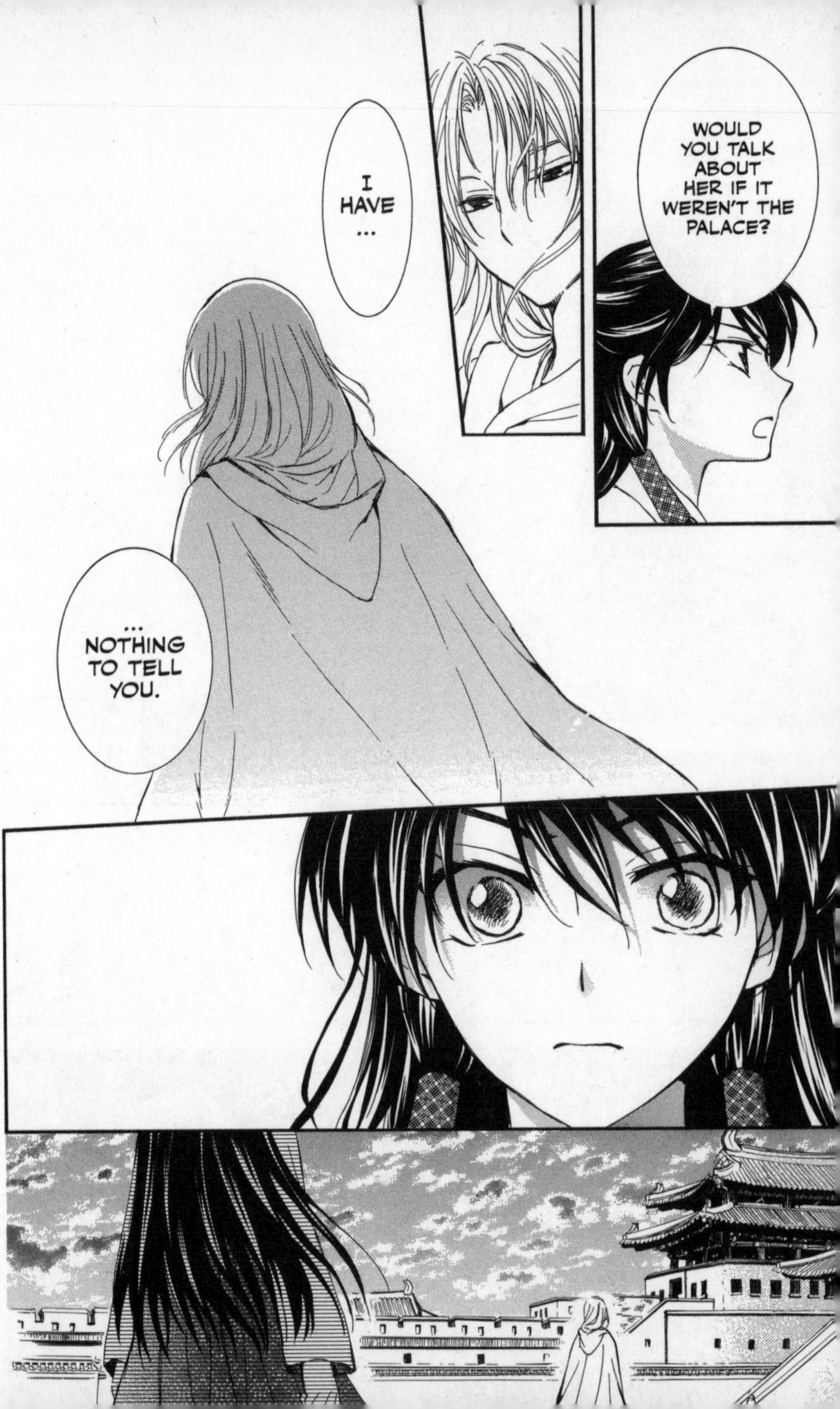
WOULD YOU TALK ABOUT HER IF IT WEREN'T THE PALACE?
I HAVE ...
... NOTHING TO TELL YOU.

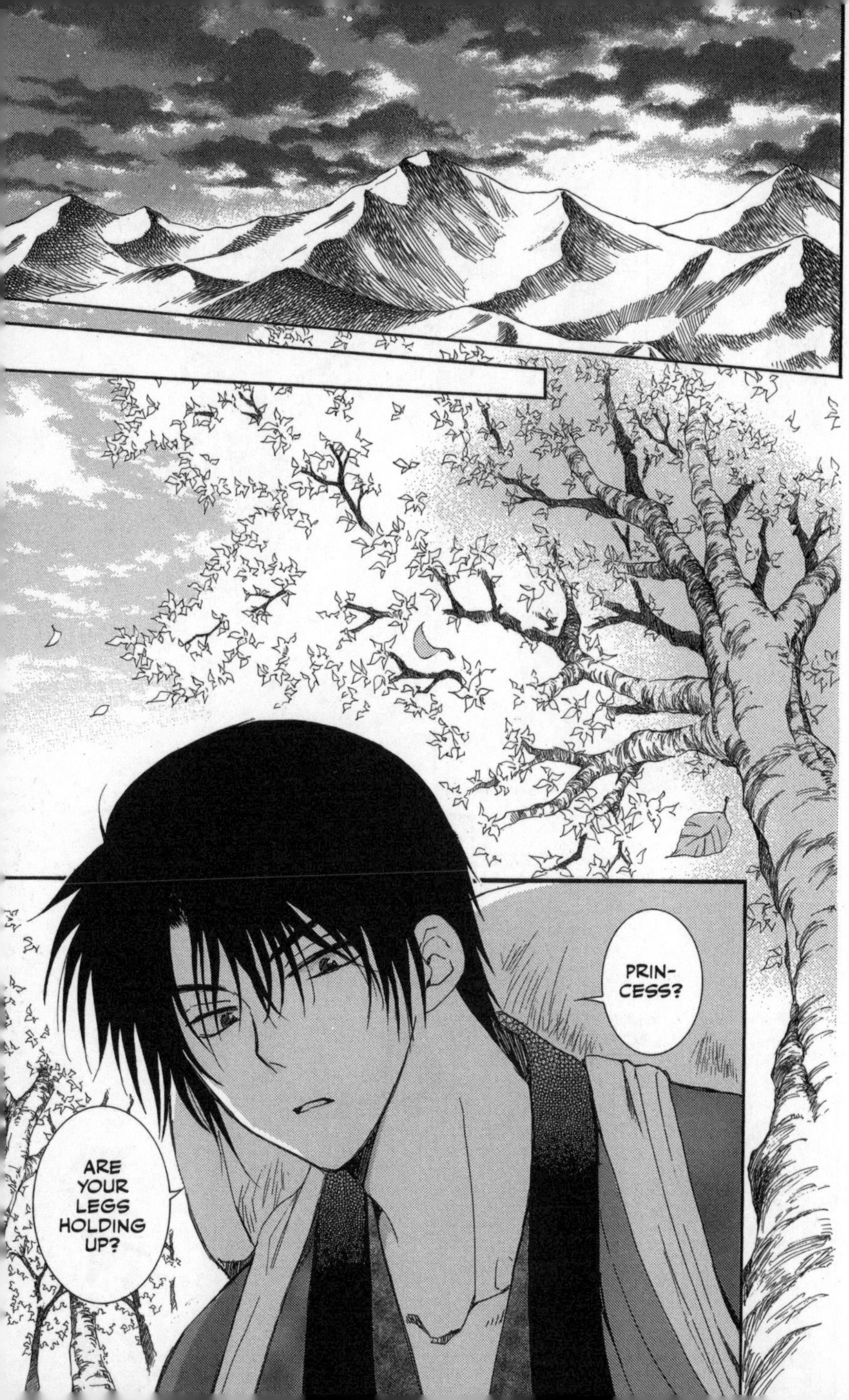
PRIN-
CESS?
ARE YOUR LEGS HOLDING UP?

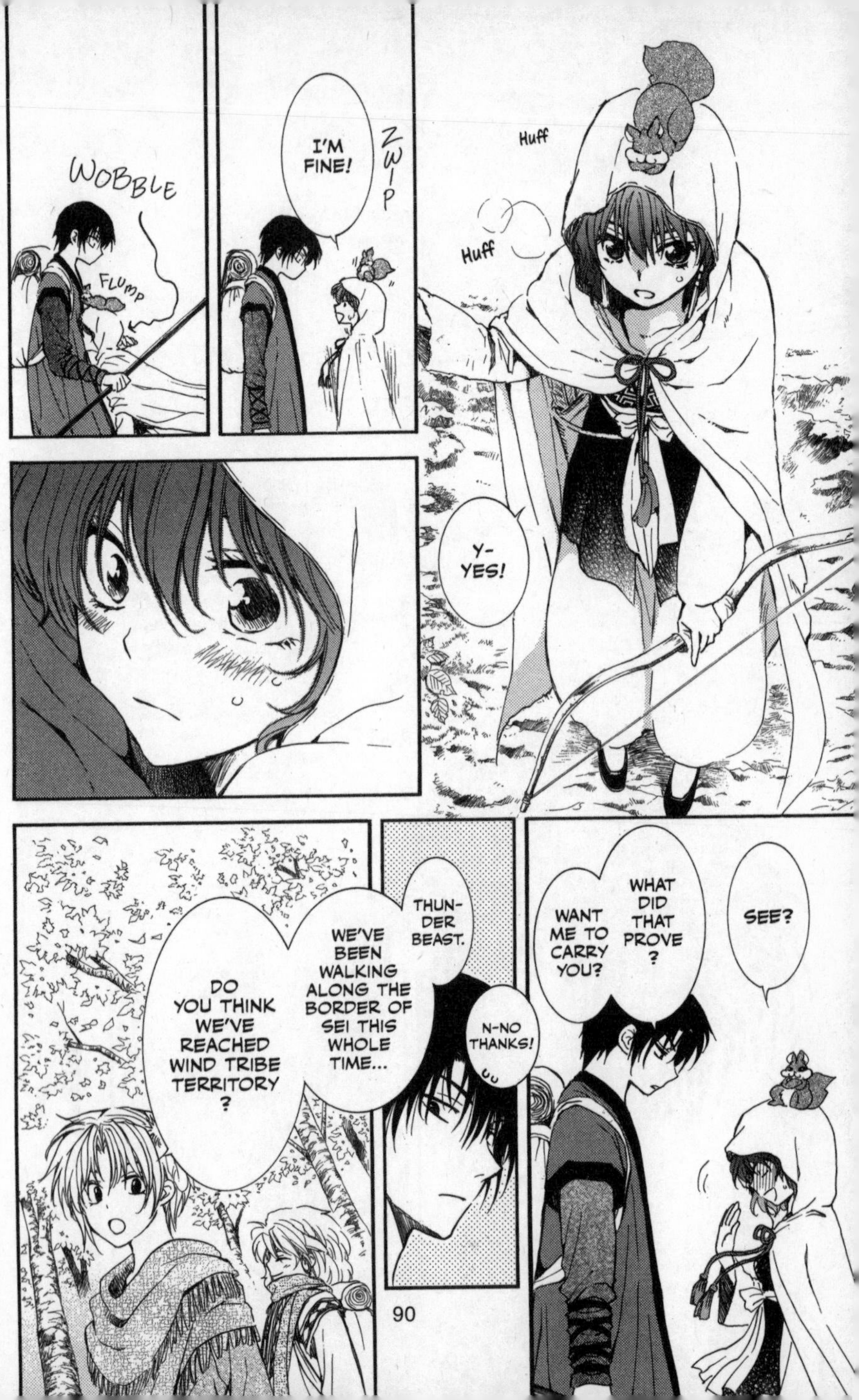
Huff
Huff
Y-YES!
I'M FINE!
ZWIP
WOBBLE
FLUMP
SEE?
WHAT DID THAT PROVE?
WANT ME TO CARRY YOU?
N-NO THANKS!
THUNDER BEAST.
WE'VE BEEN WALKING ALONG THE BORDER OF SEI THIS WHOLE TIME...
DO YOU THINK WE'VE REACHED WIND TRIBE TERRITORY?

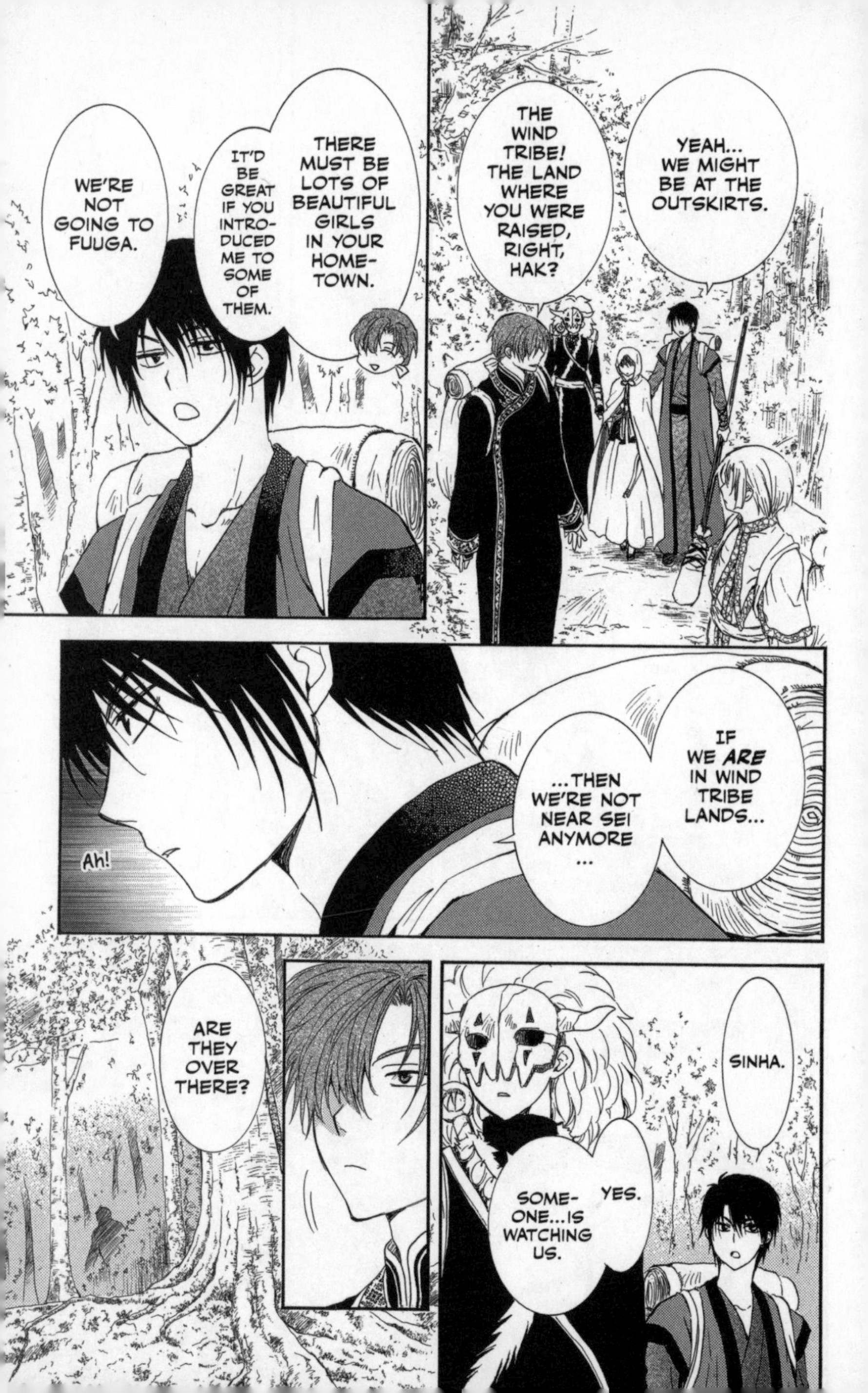
YEAH... WE MIGHT BE AT THE OUTSKIRTS.
THE WIND TRIBE! THE LAND WHERE YOU WERE RAISED, RIGHT, HAK?
THERE MUST BE LOTS OF BEAUTIFUL GIRLS IN YOUR HOME-TOWN.
IT'D BE GREAT IF YOU INTRO-DUCED ME TO SOME OF THEM.
WE'RE NOT GOING TO FUUGA.
IF WE *ARE* IN WIND TRIBE LANDS...
...THEN WE'RE NOT NEAR SEI ANYMORE ...
Ah!
SINHA.
YES.
SOME-ONE...IS WATCHING US.
ARE THEY OVER THERE?

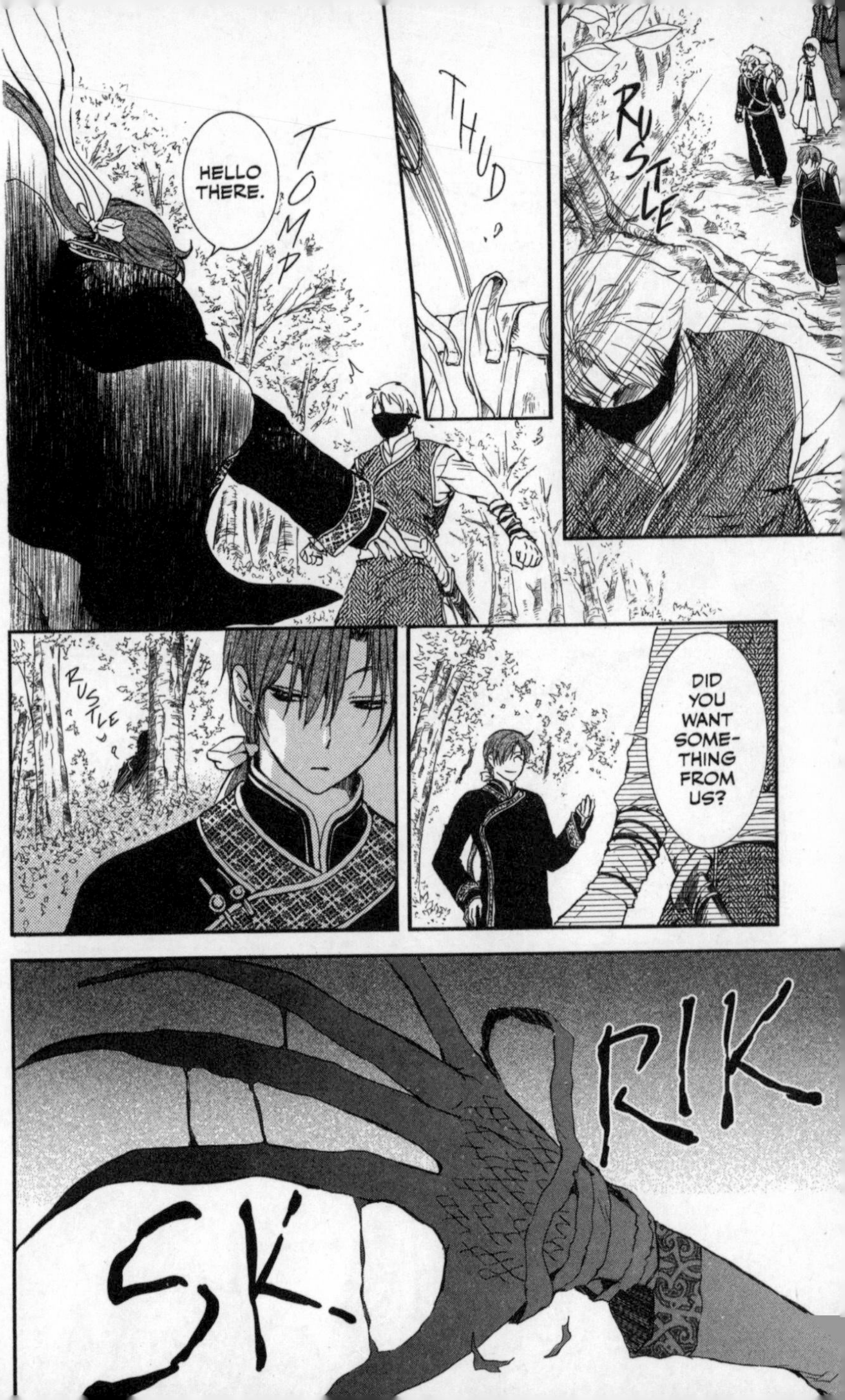
RUSTLE
THUD
HELLO THERE.
TOMP TOMP
DID YOU WANT SOMETHING FROM US?
RUSTLE
RIK
SK-

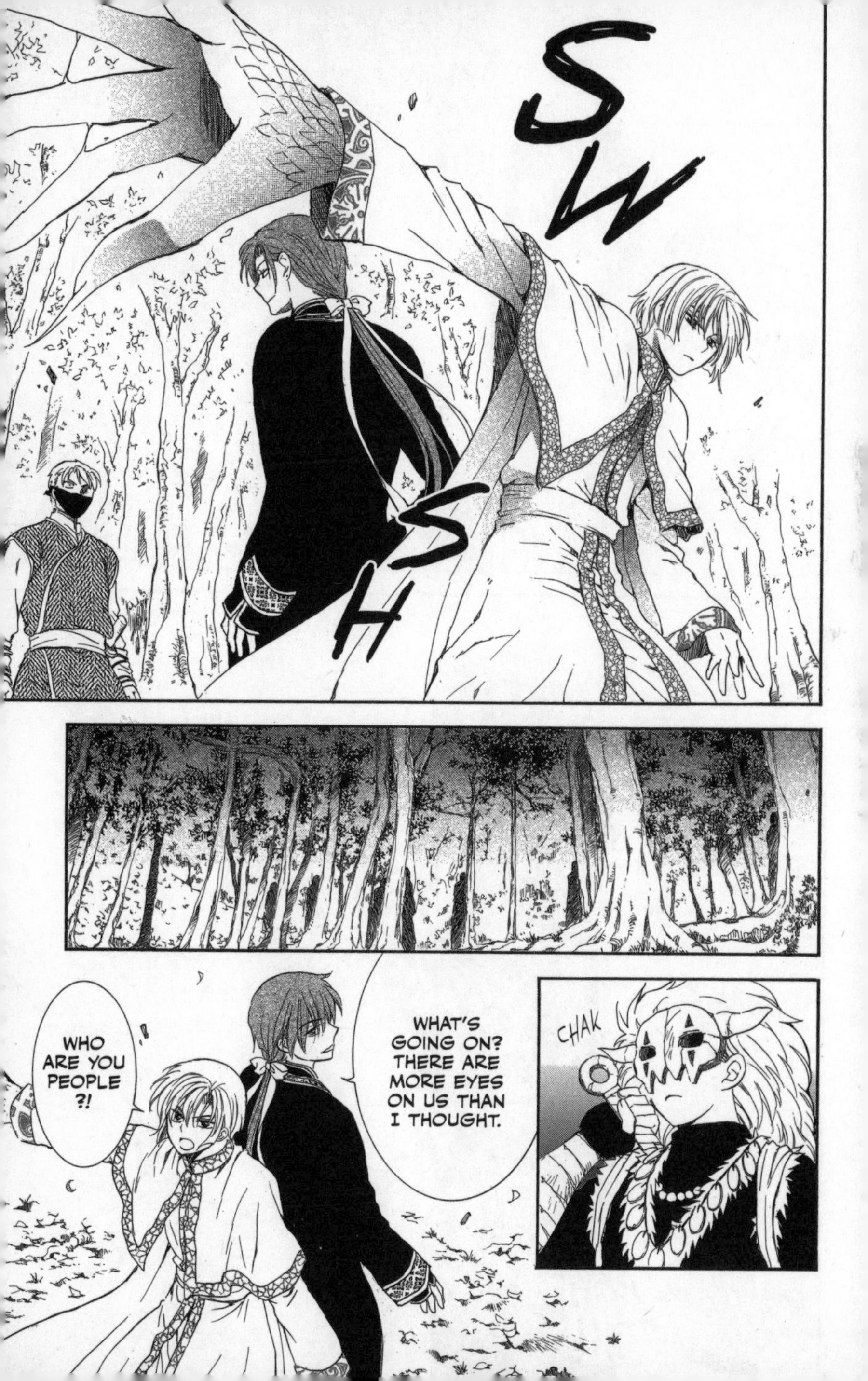
SWSH
CHAK
WHAT'S GOING ON? THERE ARE MORE EYES ON US THAN I THOUGHT.
WHO ARE YOU PEOPLE ?!

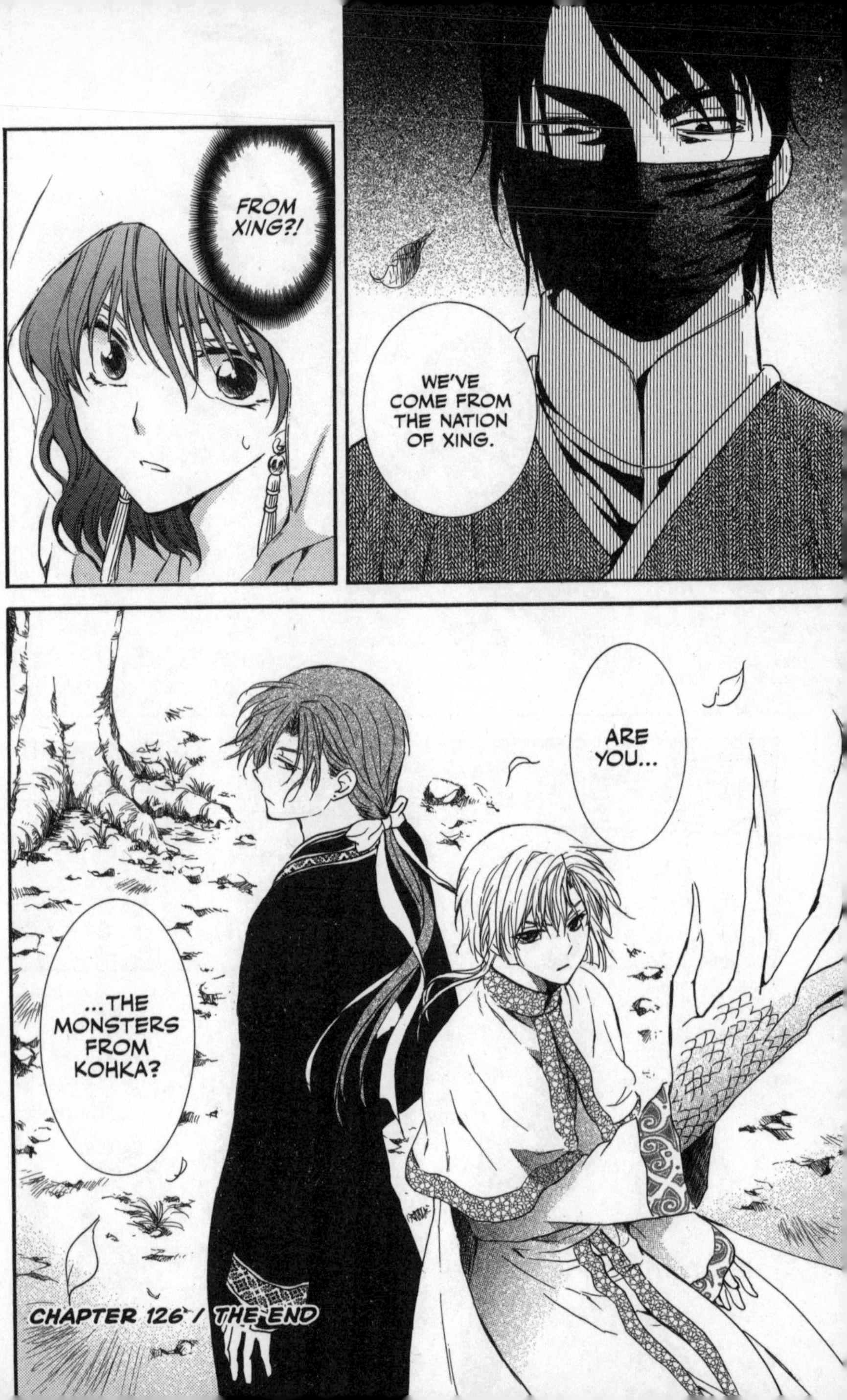
WE'VE COME FROM THE NATION OF XING.
FROM XING?!
ARE YOU...
...THE MONSTERS FROM KOHKA?
CHAPTER 126 / THE END

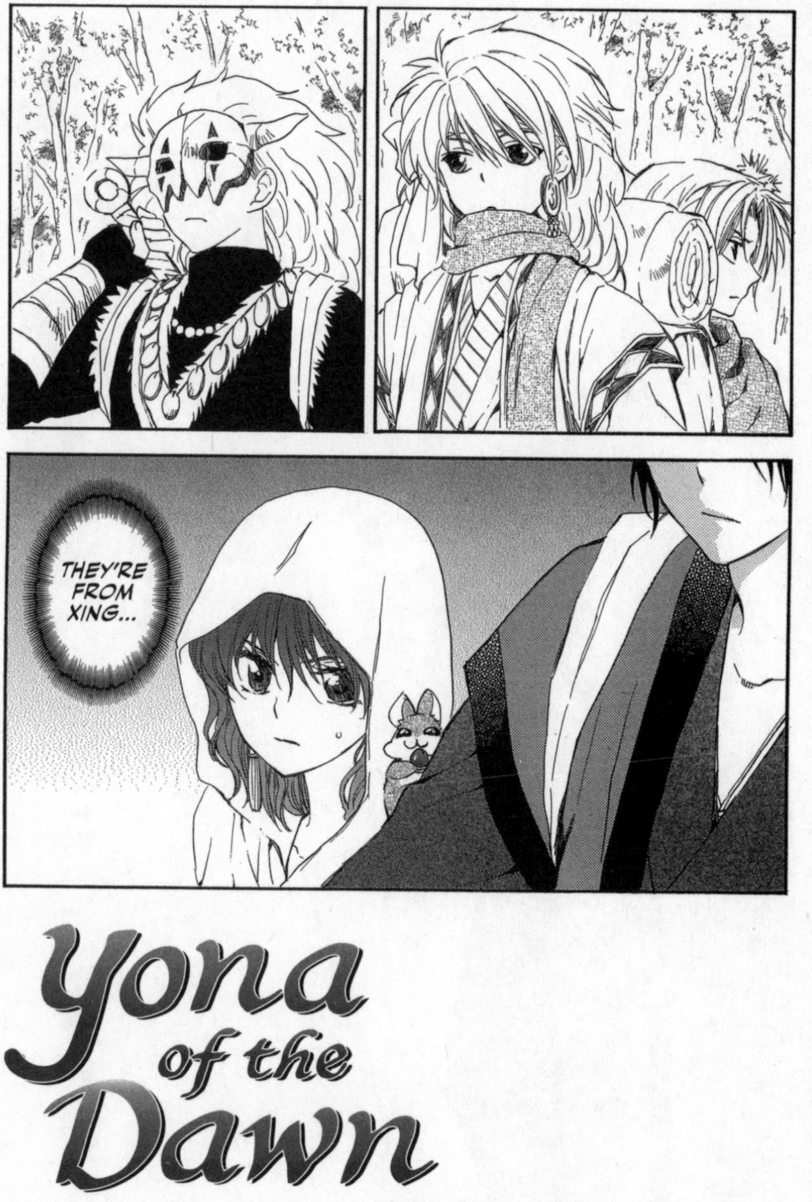
THEY'RE FROM XING...

Yona of the Dawn

CHAPTER 127: THE PRINCESS OF XING

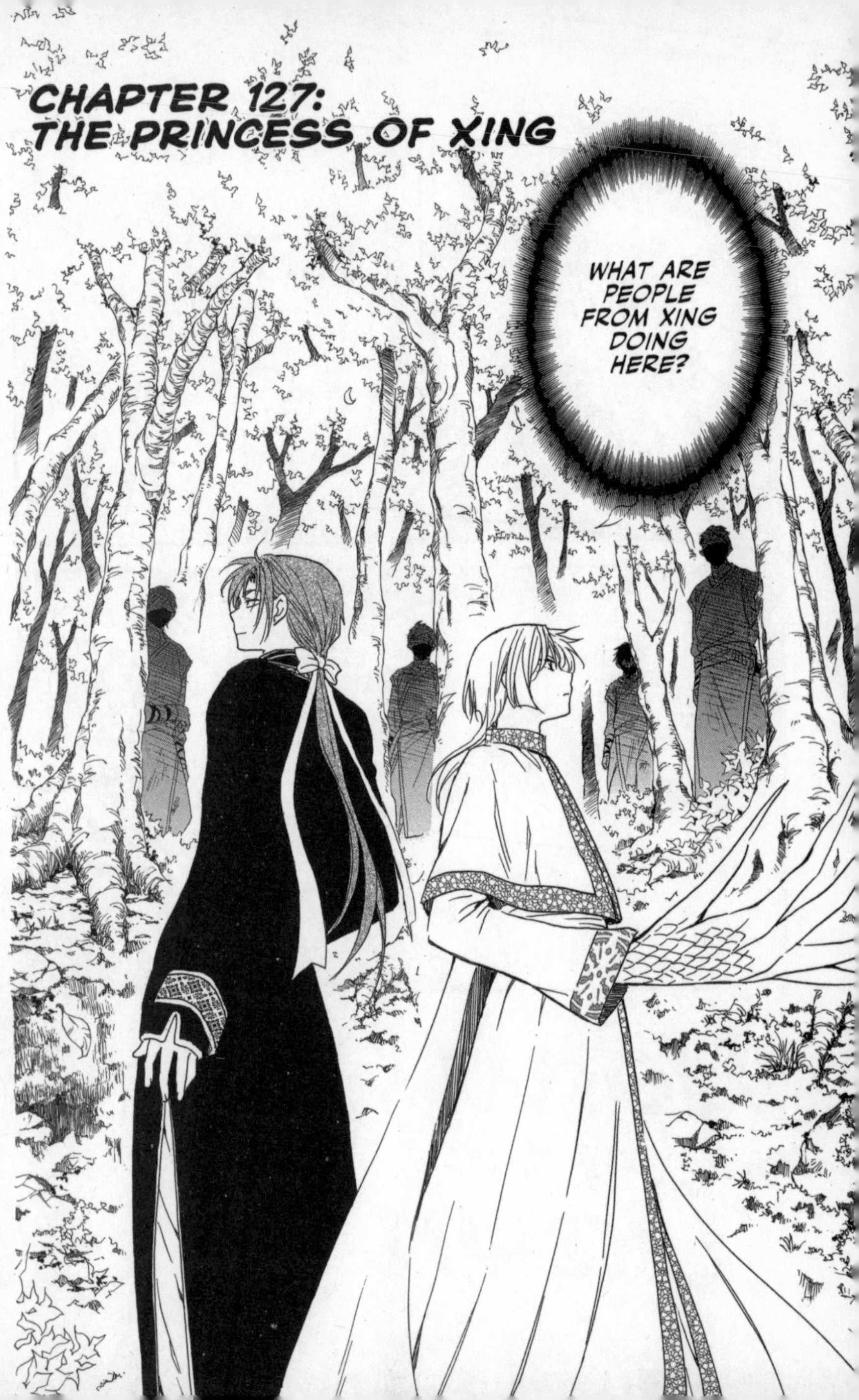
WHAT ARE PEOPLE FROM XING DOING HERE?

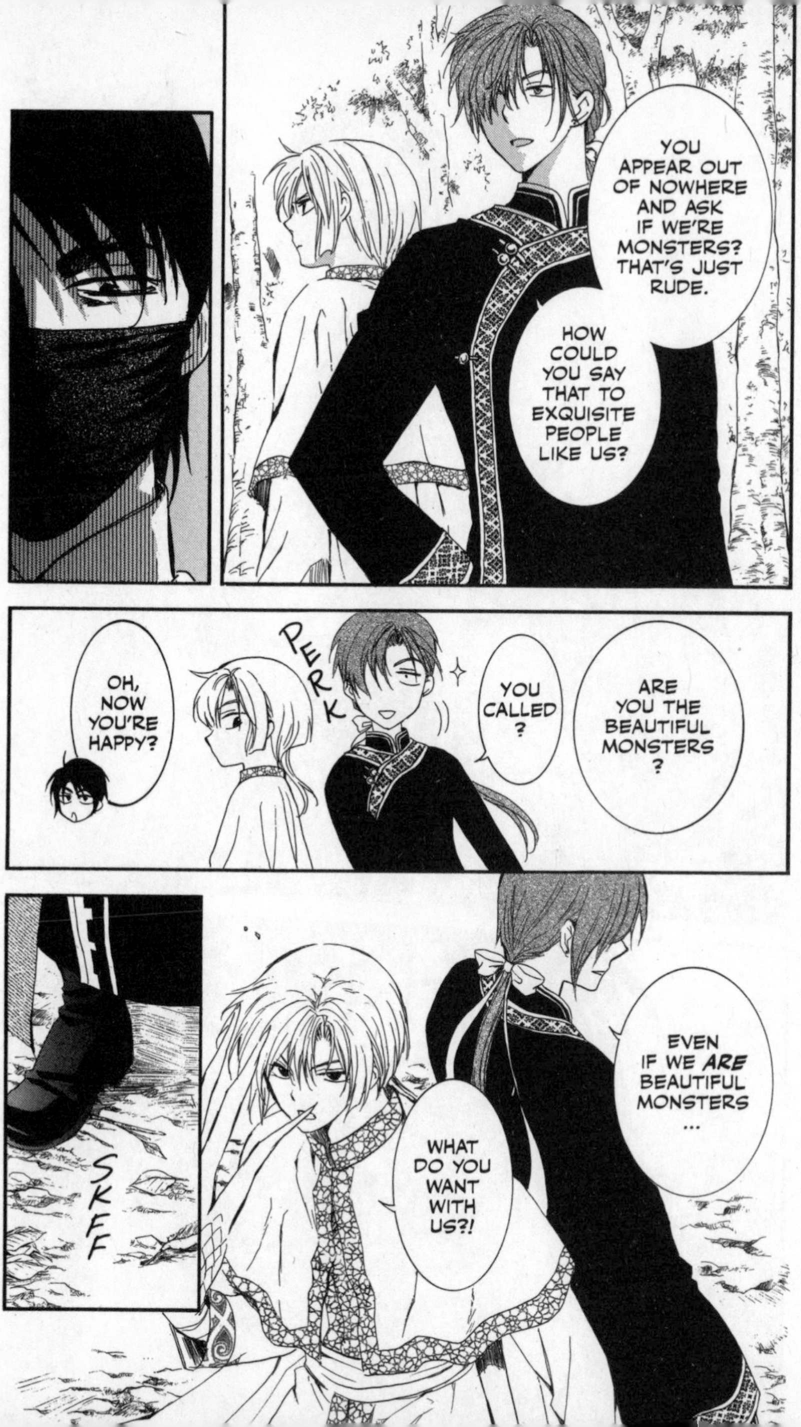
YOU APPEAR OUT OF NOWHERE AND ASK IF WE'RE MONSTERS? THAT'S JUST RUDE.
HOW COULD YOU SAY THAT TO EXQUISITE PEOPLE LIKE US?
ARE YOU THE BEAUTIFUL MONSTERS?
YOU CALLED?
PERK
OH, NOW YOU'RE HAPPY?
EVEN IF WE *ARE* BEAUTIFUL MONSTERS...
WHAT DO YOU WANT WITH US?!
SKFF

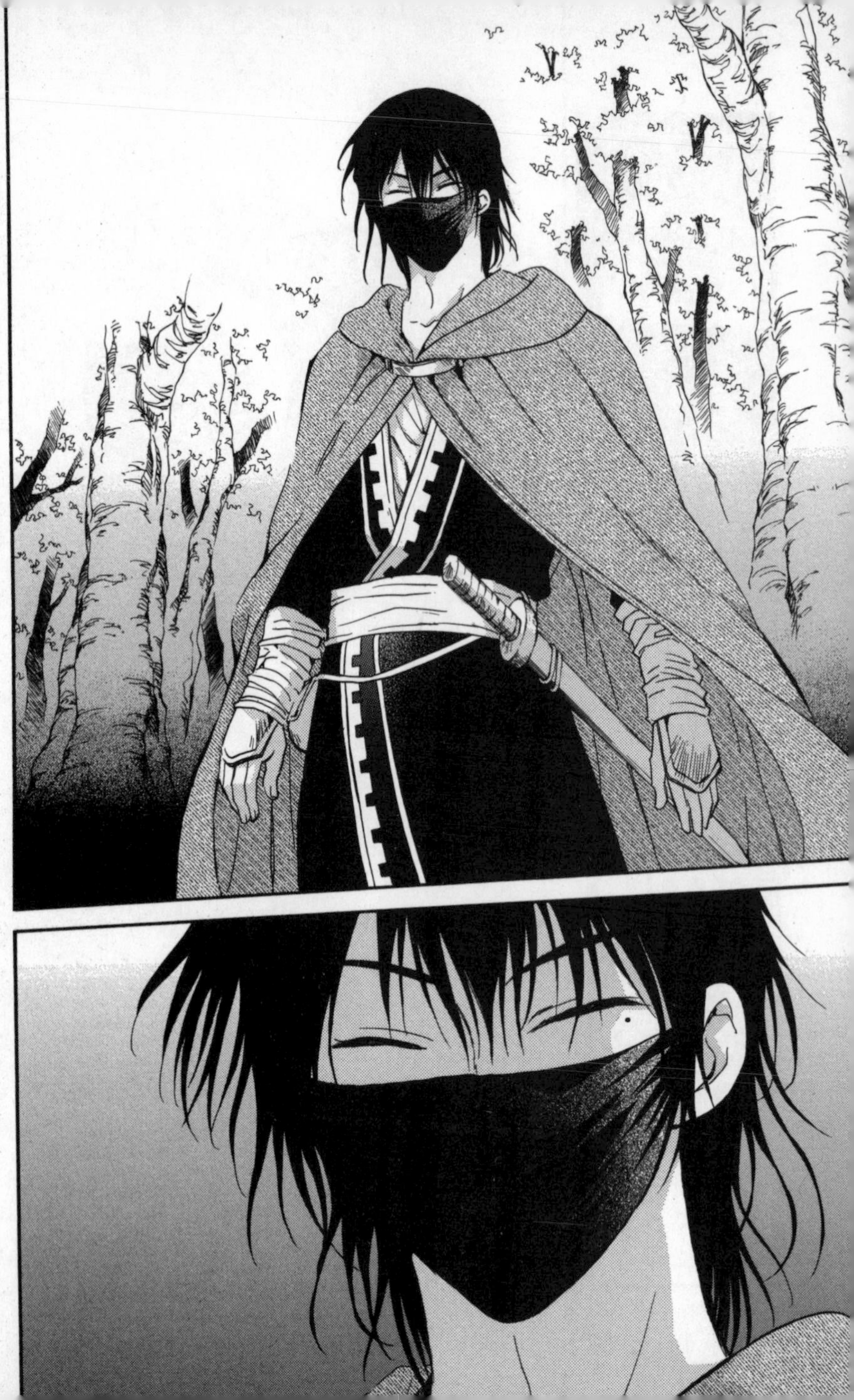

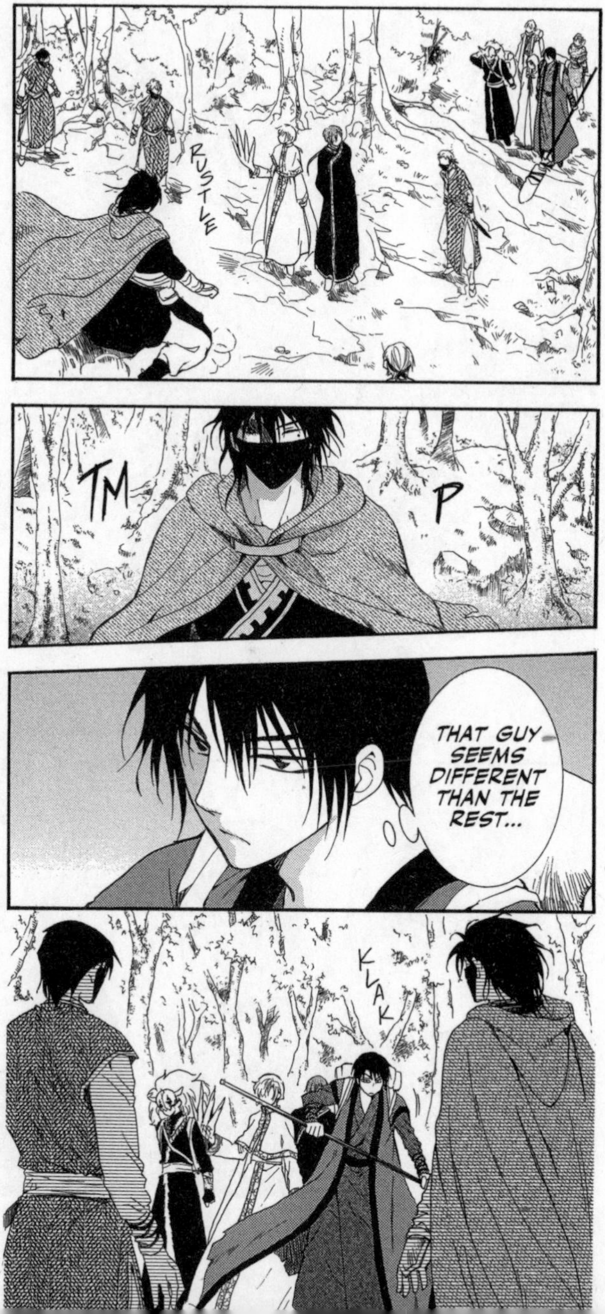
RUSTLE
TMP
THAT GUY SEEMS DIFFERENT THAN THE REST...
KLAK

We're heading into a new arc. There are so many characters I can't remember them all. Sorry! But since we're already at volume 22, I suppose it might be a normal number of characters for this kind of story.

Now, on to a different topic... In the bonus chapter in volume 21, Hak picked up the cup that Yona used. Some readers claimed that they'd indirectly kissed! (*Heh.*) They're right. But for the Happy Hungry Bunch, every day is a struggle to survive. Sharing drinks and food is so common that Hak and Yona never think twice about it. (*Heh.*)

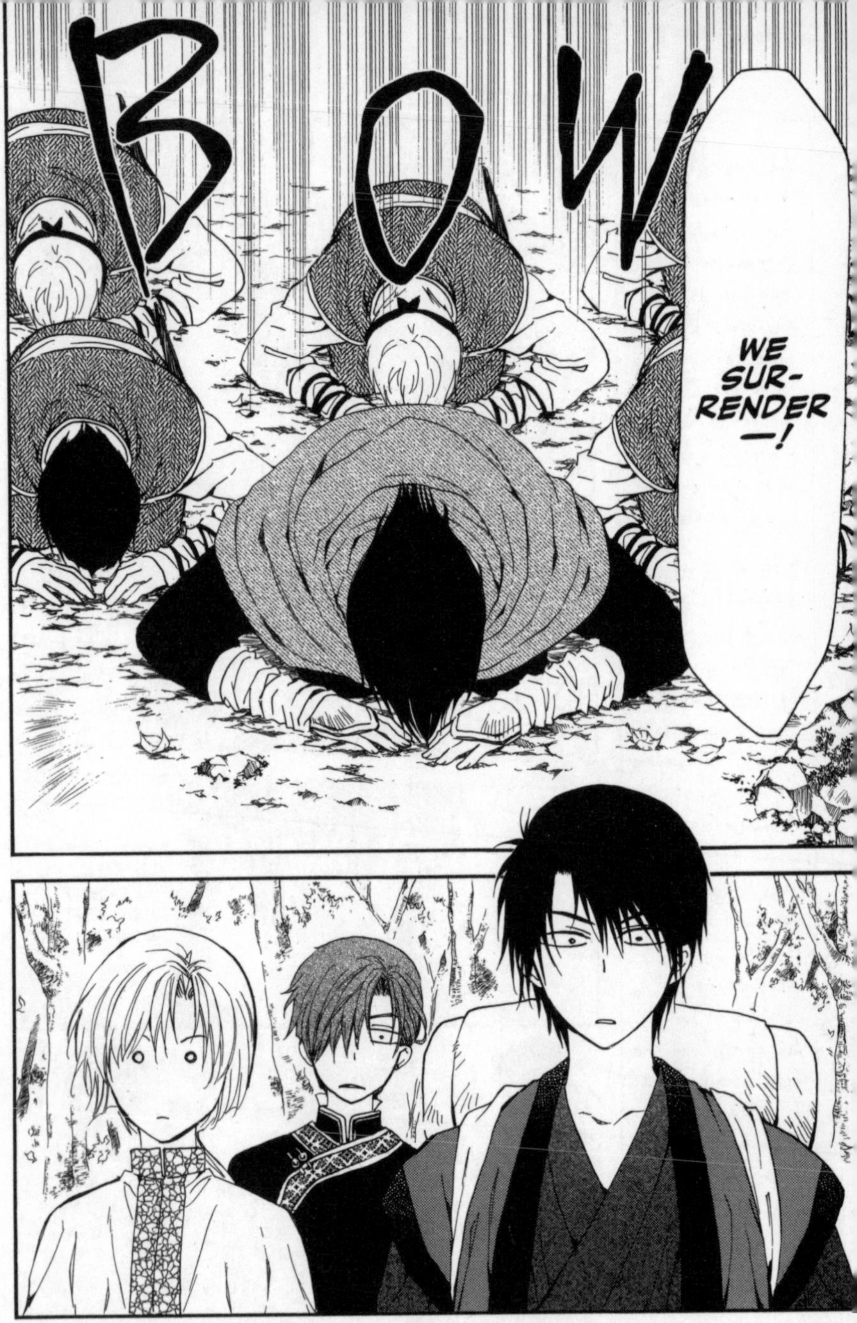
BOW
WE SUR-RENDER—!

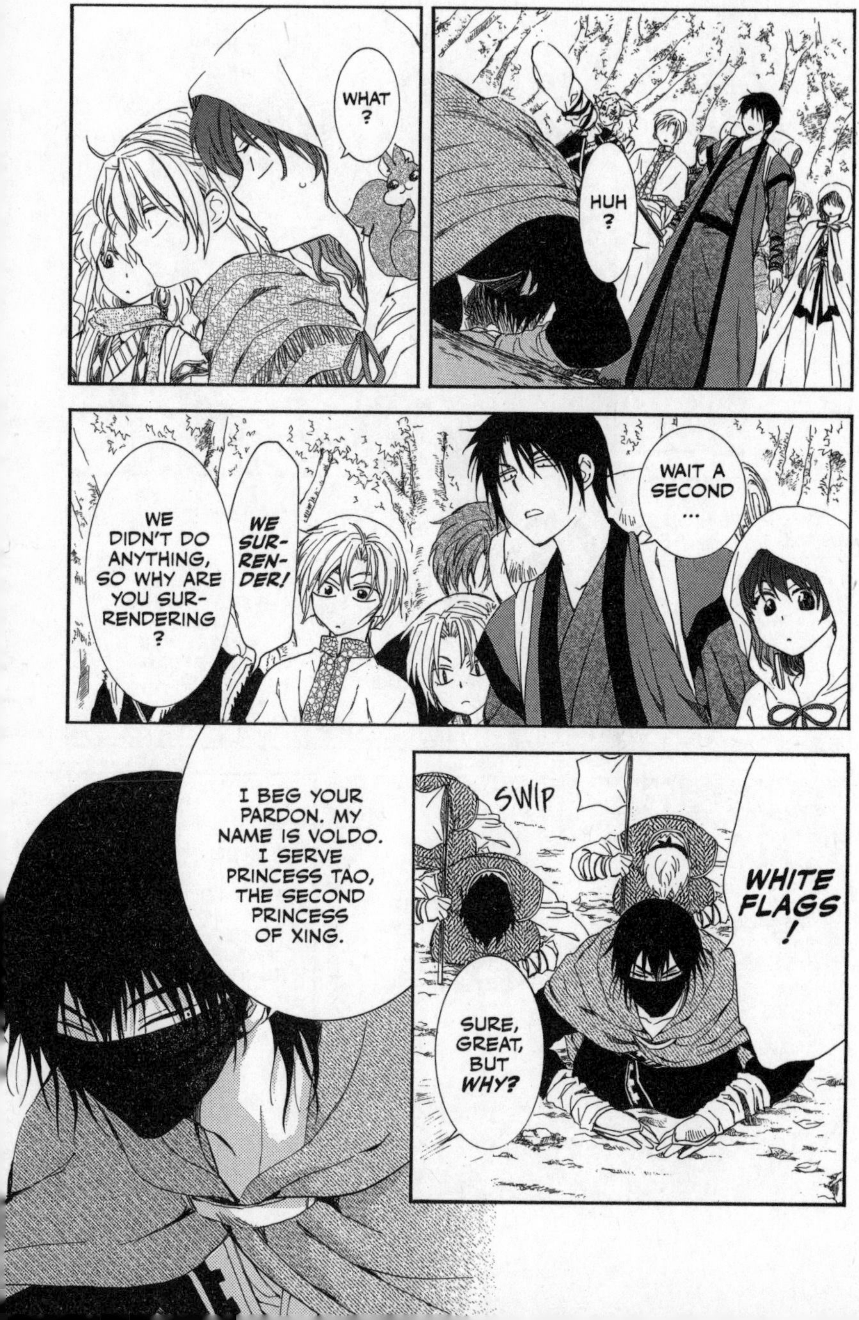
HUH?
WHAT?
WAIT A SECOND...
WE SURRENDER!
WE DIDN'T DO ANYTHING, SO WHY ARE YOU SURRENDERING?
WHITE FLAGS!
SWIP
SURE, GREAT, BUT WHY?
I BEG YOUR PARDON. MY NAME IS VOLDO. I SERVE PRINCESS TAO, THE SECOND PRINCESS OF XING.

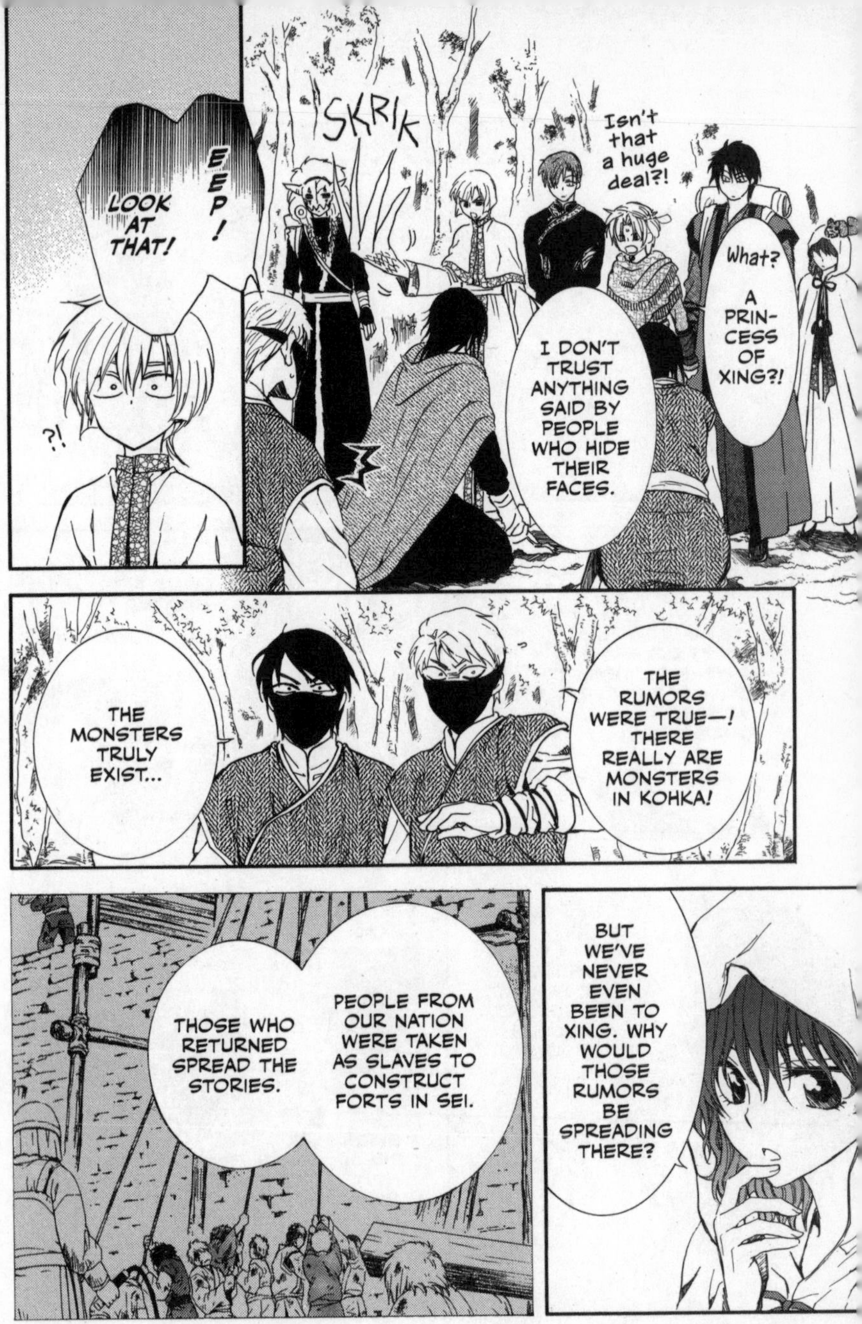
What? A PRINCESS OF XING?!
Isn't that a huge deal?!
SKRIK
I DON'T TRUST ANYTHING SAID BY PEOPLE WHO HIDE THEIR FACES.
EEP!
LOOK AT THAT!
?!
THE RUMORS WERE TRUE—! THERE REALLY ARE MONSTERS IN KOHKA!
THE MONSTERS TRULY EXIST...
BUT WE'VE NEVER EVEN BEEN TO XING. WHY WOULD THOSE RUMORS BE SPREADING THERE?
PEOPLE FROM OUR NATION WERE TAKEN AS SLAVES TO CONSTRUCT FORTS IN SEI.
THOSE WHO RETURNED SPREAD THE STORIES.

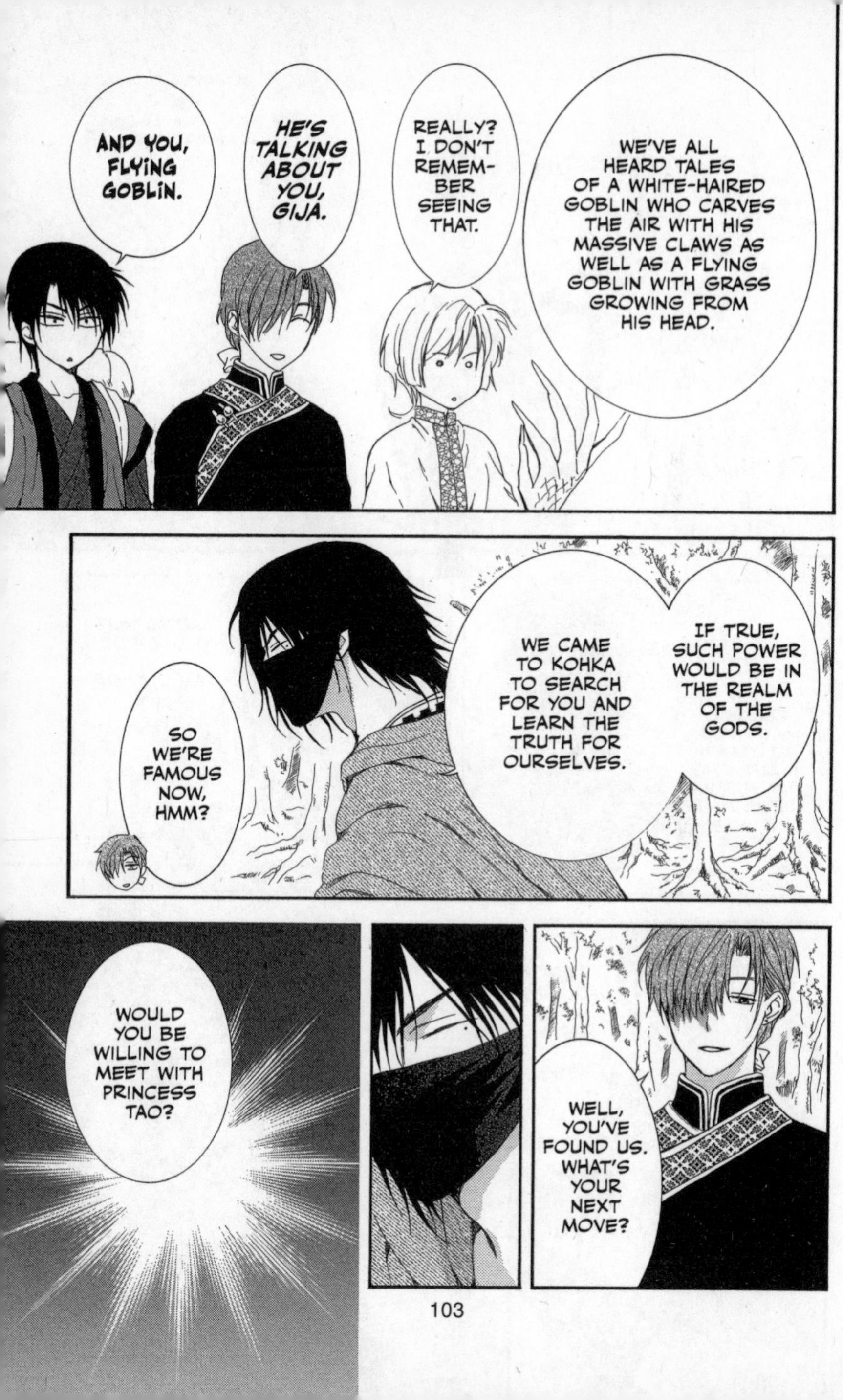
WE'VE ALL HEARD TALES OF A WHITE-HAIRED GOBLIN WHO CARVES THE AIR WITH HIS MASSIVE CLAWS AS WELL AS A FLYING GOBLIN WITH GRASS GROWING FROM HIS HEAD.
REALLY? I DON'T REMEMBER SEEING THAT.
HE'S TALKING ABOUT YOU, GIJA.
AND YOU, FLYING GOBLIN.
IF TRUE, SUCH POWER WOULD BE IN THE REALM OF THE GODS.
WE CAME TO KOHKA TO SEARCH FOR YOU AND LEARN THE TRUTH FOR OURSELVES.
SO WE'RE FAMOUS NOW, HMM?
WELL, YOU'VE FOUND US. WHAT'S YOUR NEXT MOVE?
WOULD YOU BE WILLING TO MEET WITH PRINCESS TAO?

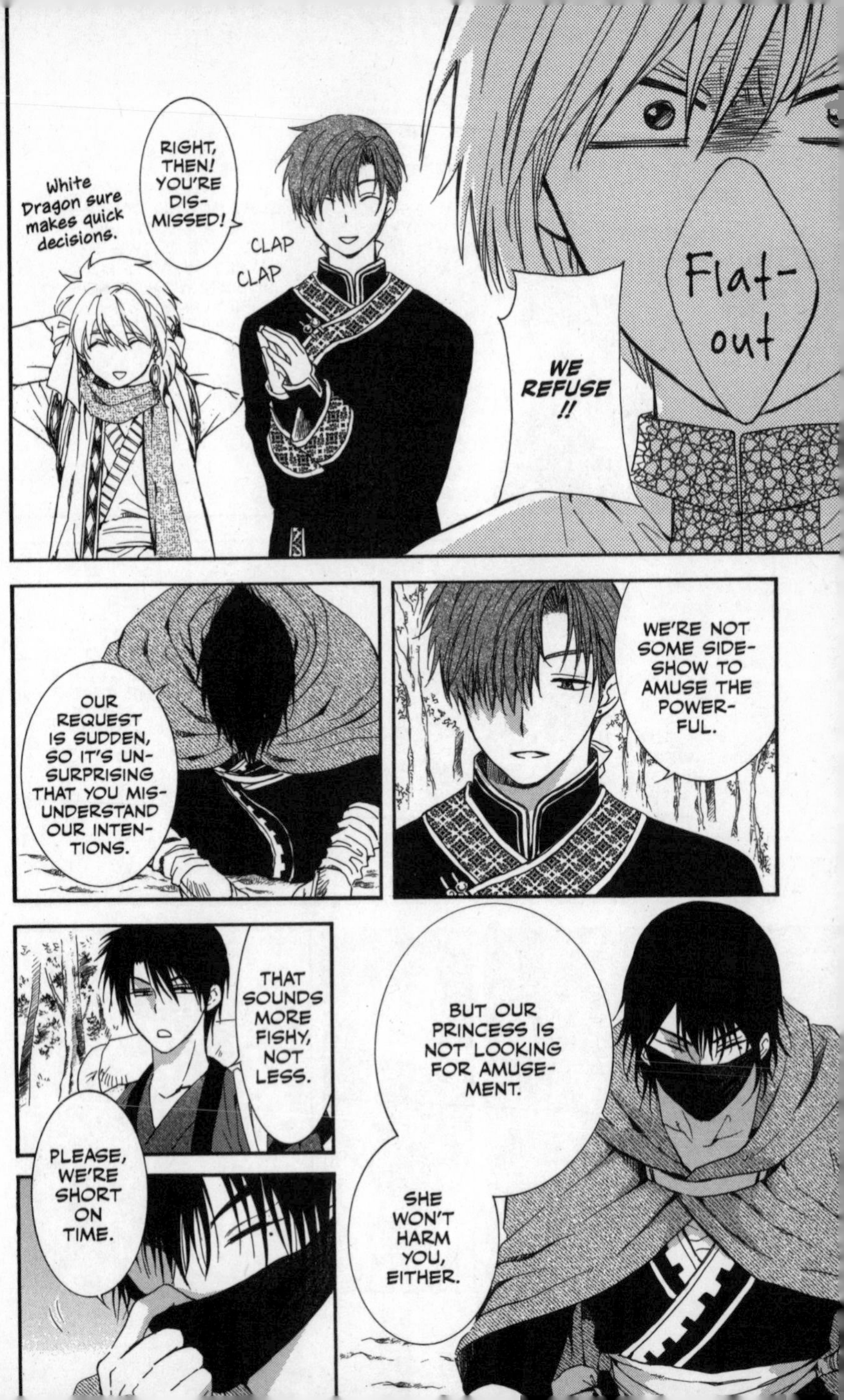
Flat-out
WE REFUSE !!
RIGHT, THEN! YOU'RE DIS-MISSED!
CLAP
CLAP
White Dragon sure makes quick decisions.
WE'RE NOT SOME SIDE-SHOW TO AMUSE THE POWER-FUL.
OUR REQUEST IS SUDDEN, SO IT'S UN-SURPRISING THAT YOU MIS-UNDERSTAND OUR INTEN-TIONS.
BUT OUR PRINCESS IS NOT LOOKING FOR AMUSE-MENT.
SHE WON'T HARM YOU, EITHER.
THAT SOUNDS MORE FISHY, NOT LESS.
PLEASE, WE'RE SHORT ON TIME.

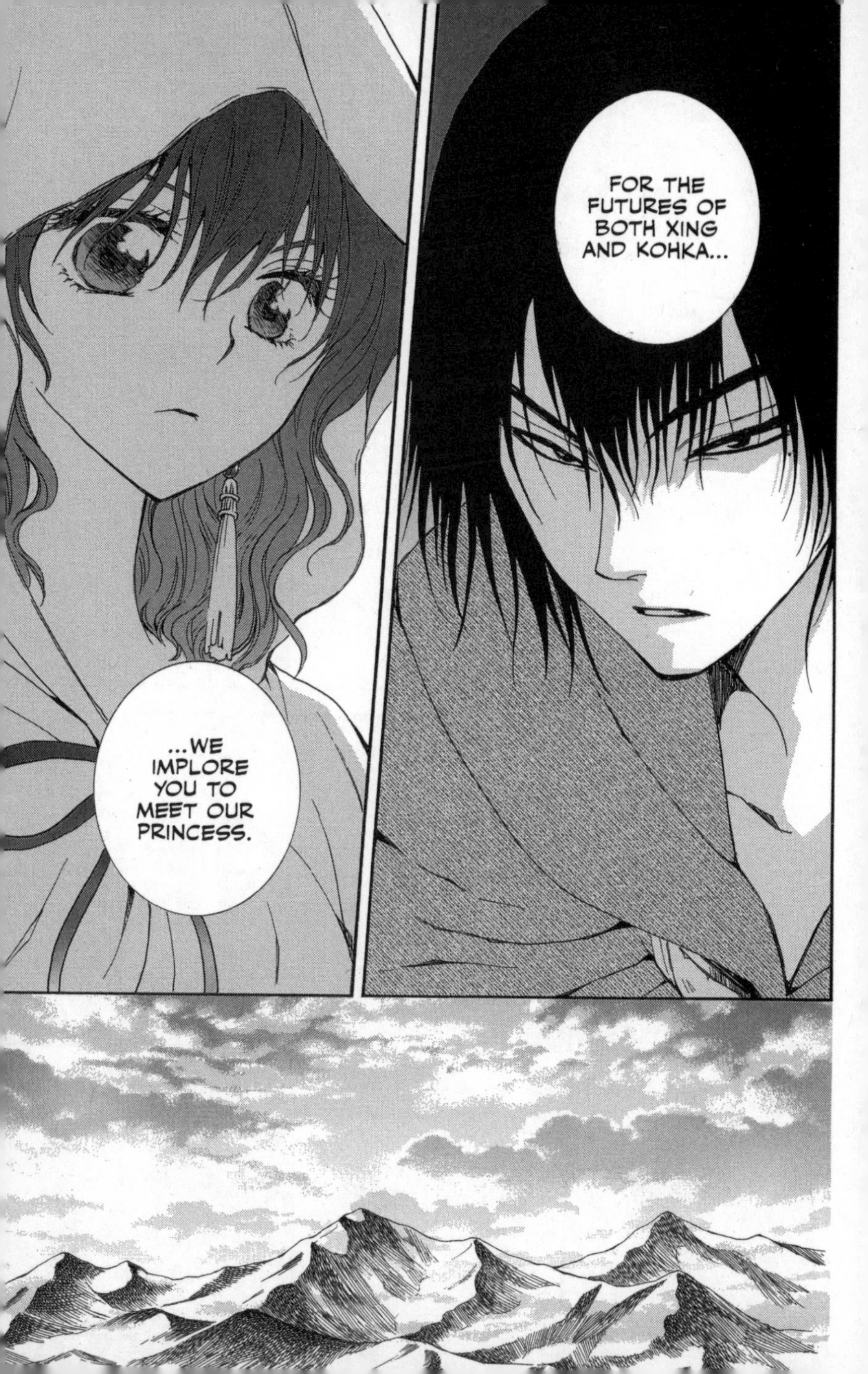
FOR THE FUTURES OF BOTH XING AND KOHKA...
...WE IMPLORE YOU TO MEET OUR PRINCESS.

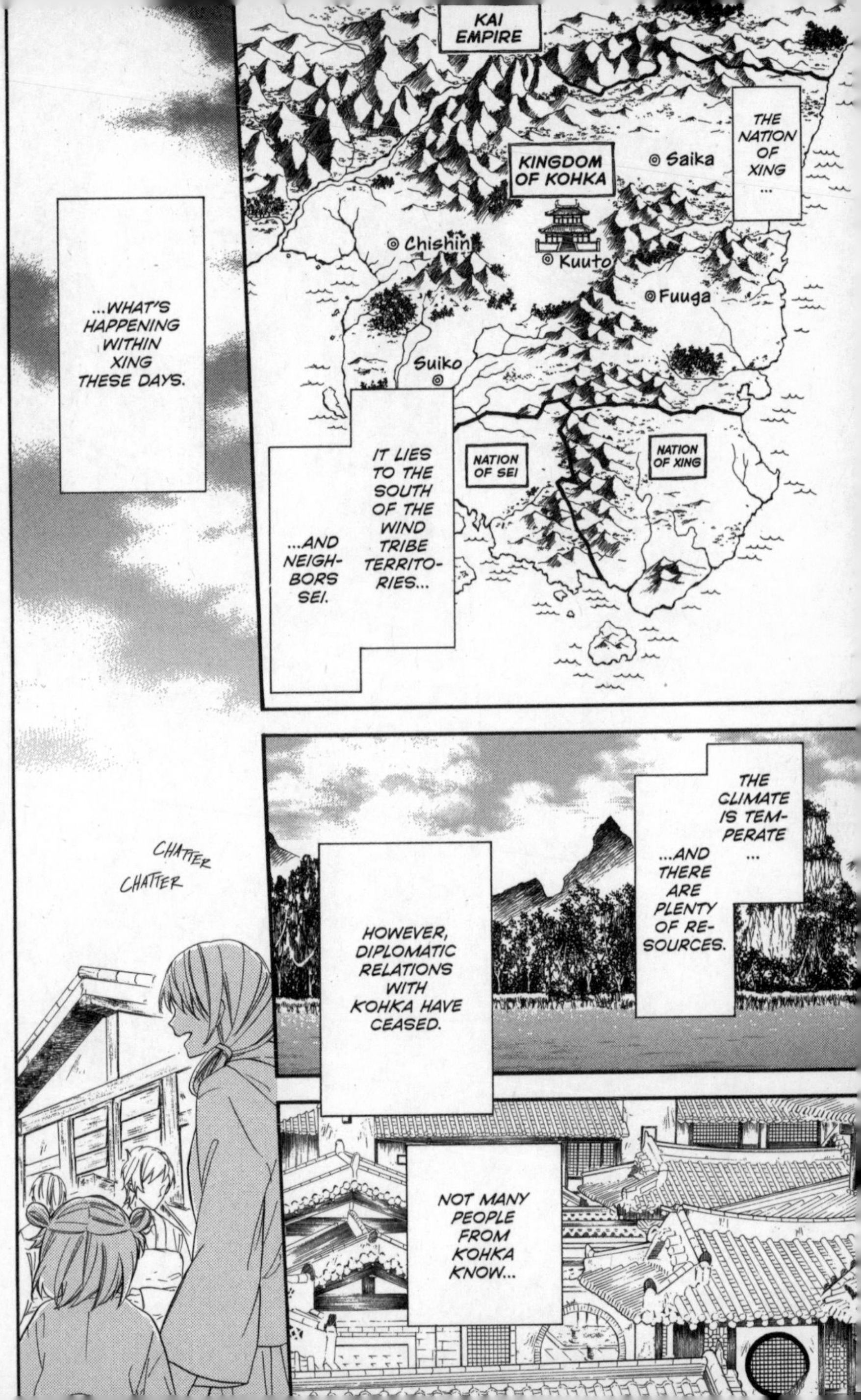
THE NATION OF XING...
KAI EMPIRE
KINGDOM OF KOHKA
Saika
Chishin
Kuuto
Fuuga
Suiko
NATION OF SEI
NATION OF XING
IT LIES TO THE SOUTH OF THE WIND TRIBE TERRITORIES...
...AND NEIGHBORS SEI.
THE CLIMATE IS TEMPERATE...
...AND THERE ARE PLENTY OF RESOURCES.
HOWEVER, DIPLOMATIC RELATIONS WITH KOHKA HAVE CEASED.
NOT MANY PEOPLE FROM KOHKA KNOW...
...WHAT'S HAPPENING WITHIN XING THESE DAYS.
CHATTER
CHATTER

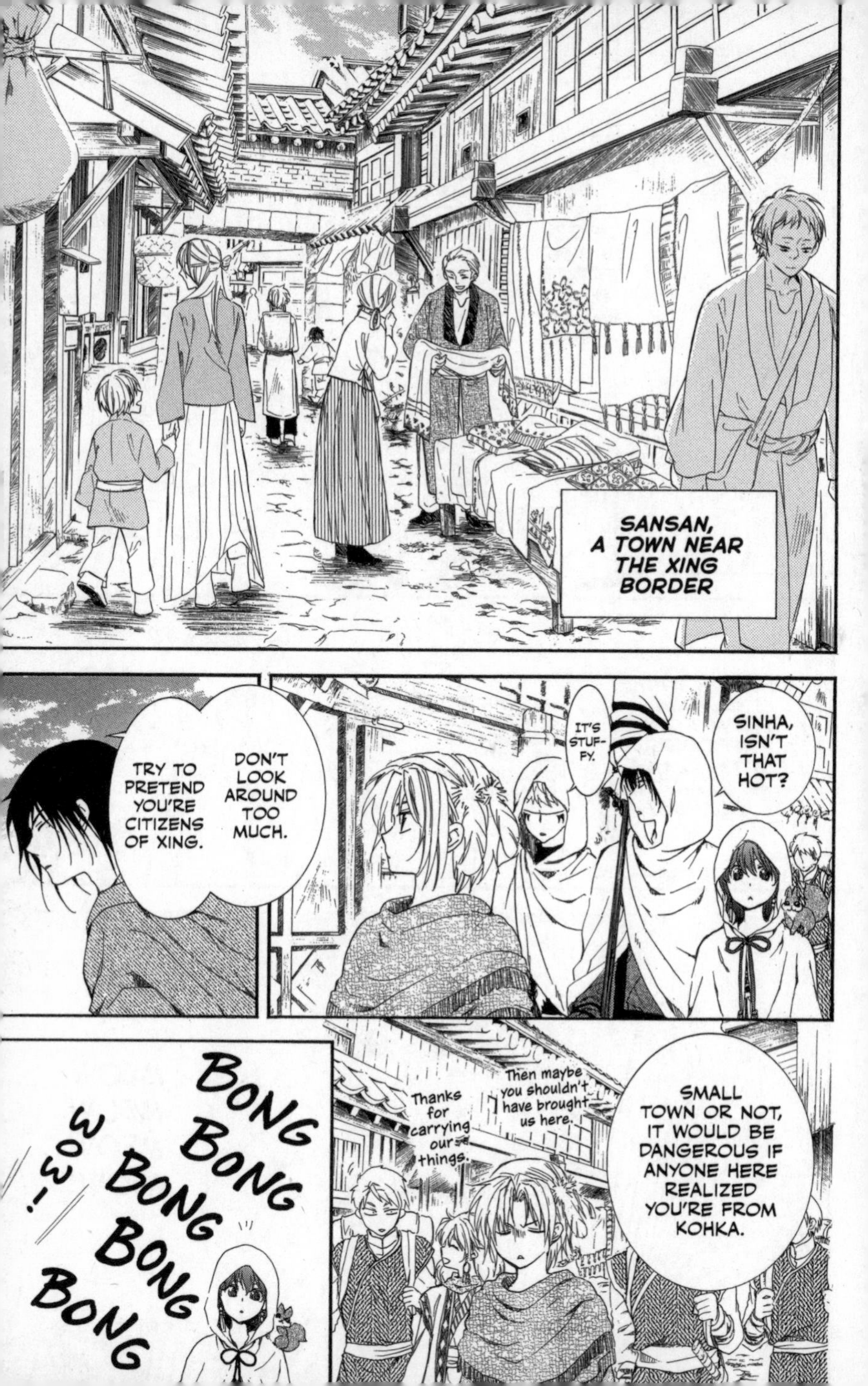
SANSAN, A TOWN NEAR THE XING BORDER
SINHA, ISN'T THAT HOT?
IT'S STUFF-FY.
DON'T LOOK AROUND TOO MUCH.
TRY TO PRETEND YOU'RE CITIZENS OF XING.
SMALL TOWN OR NOT, IT WOULD BE DANGEROUS IF ANYONE HERE REALIZED YOU'RE FROM KOHKA.
Then maybe you shouldn't have brought us here.
Thanks for carrying our things.
BONG BONG BONG BONG BONG
WOW!

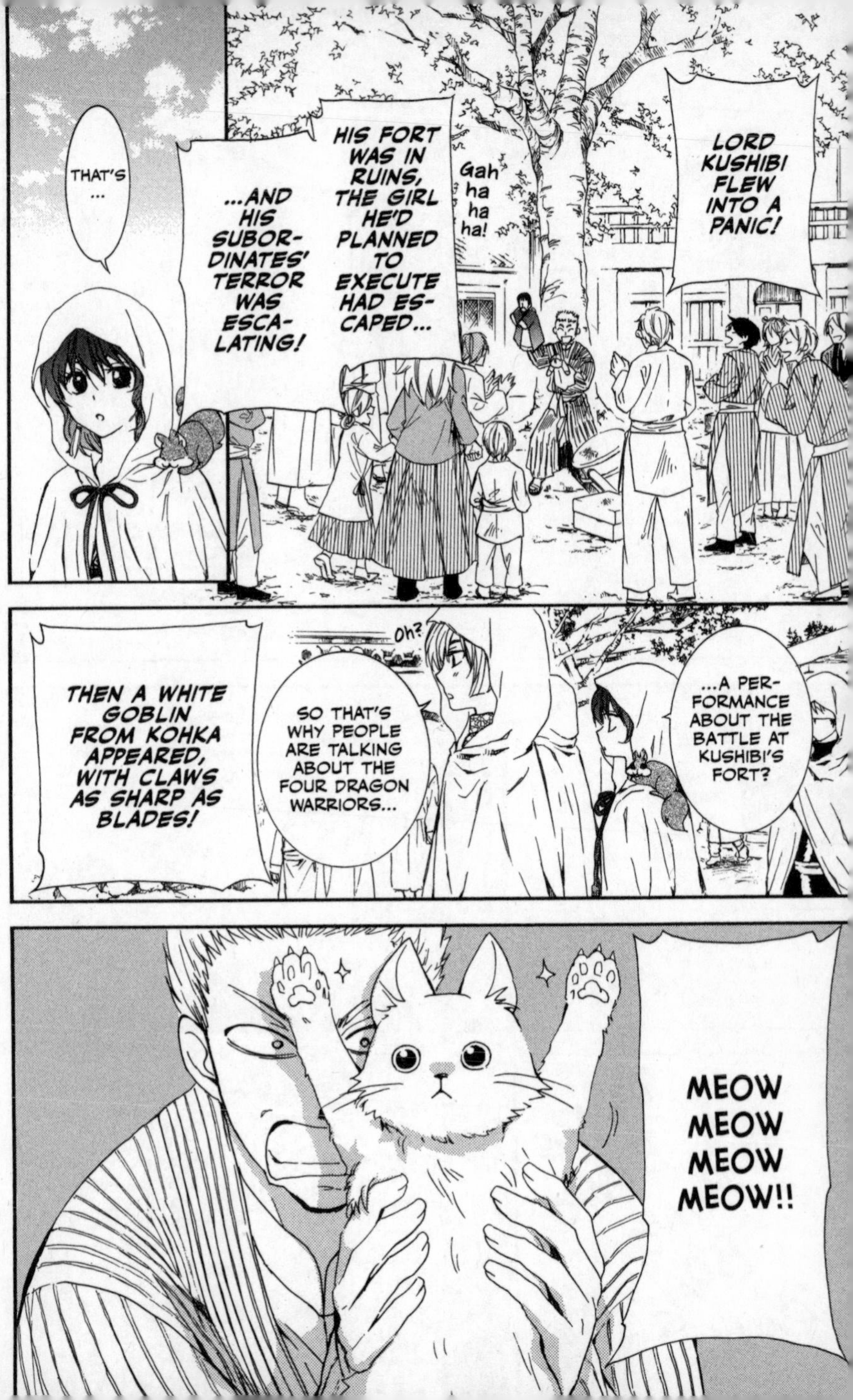
LORD KUSHIBI FLEW INTO A PANIC!
Gah ha ha ha!
HIS FORT WAS IN RUINS, THE GIRL HE'D PLANNED TO EXECUTE HAD ESCAPED...
...AND HIS SUBORDINATES' TERROR WAS ESCALATING!
THAT'S ...
...A PERFORMANCE ABOUT THE BATTLE AT KUSHIBI'S FORT?
Oh?
SO THAT'S WHY PEOPLE ARE TALKING ABOUT THE FOUR DRAGON WARRIORS...
THEN A WHITE GOBLIN FROM KOHKA APPEARED, WITH CLAWS AS SHARP AS BLADES!
MEOW MEOW MEOW MEOW!!

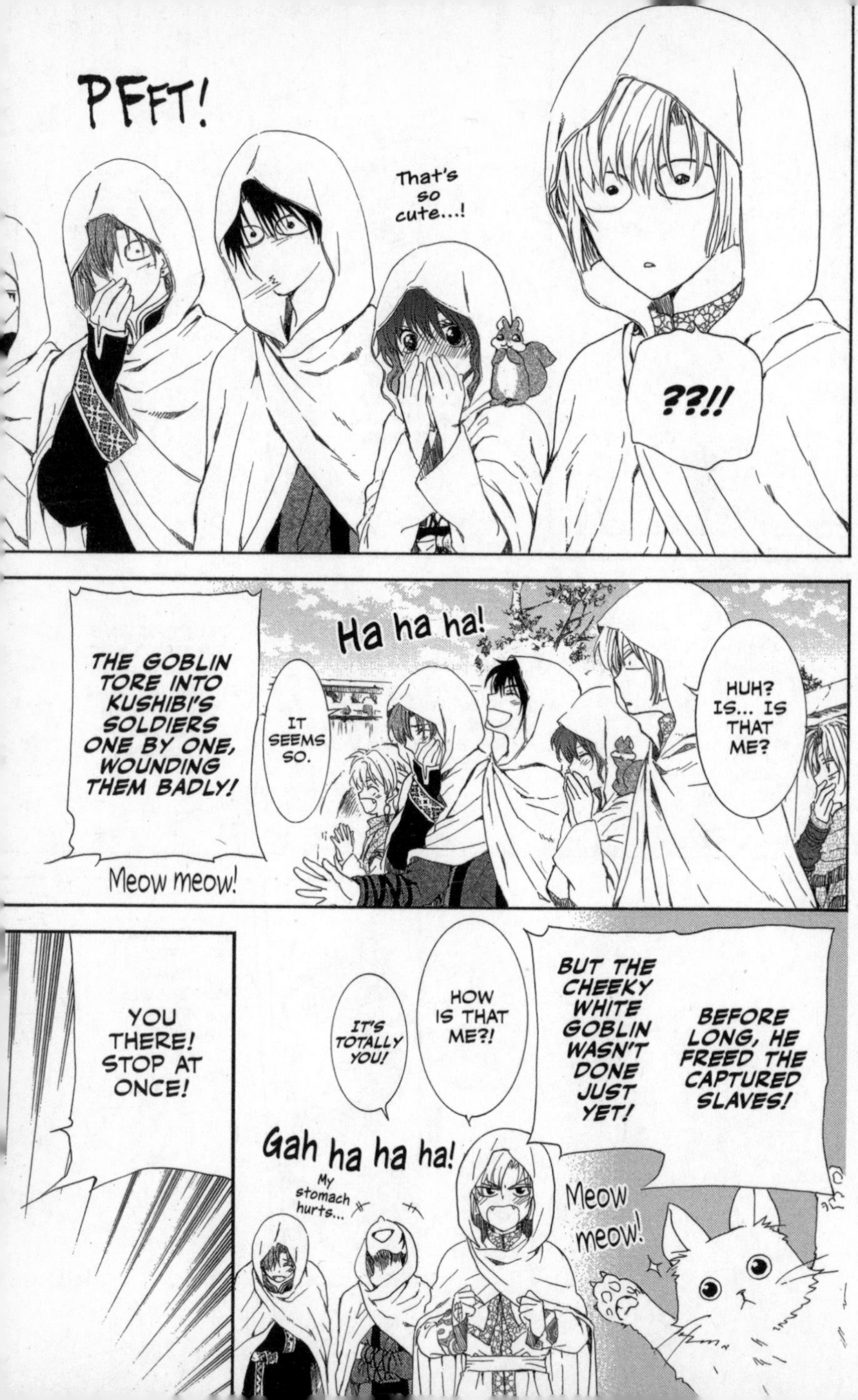
??!!
That's so cute...!
PFFT!
HUH? IS... IS THAT ME?
Ha ha ha!
IT SEEMS SO.
THE GOBLIN TORE INTO KUSHIBI'S SOLDIERS ONE BY ONE, WOUNDING THEM BADLY!
Meow meow!
BEFORE LONG, HE FREED THE CAPTURED SLAVES!
BUT THE CHEEKY WHITE GOBLIN WASN'T DONE JUST YET!
HOW IS THAT ME?!
IT'S TOTALLY YOU!
Gah ha ha ha!
My stomach hurts...
Meow meow!
YOU THERE! STOP AT ONCE!

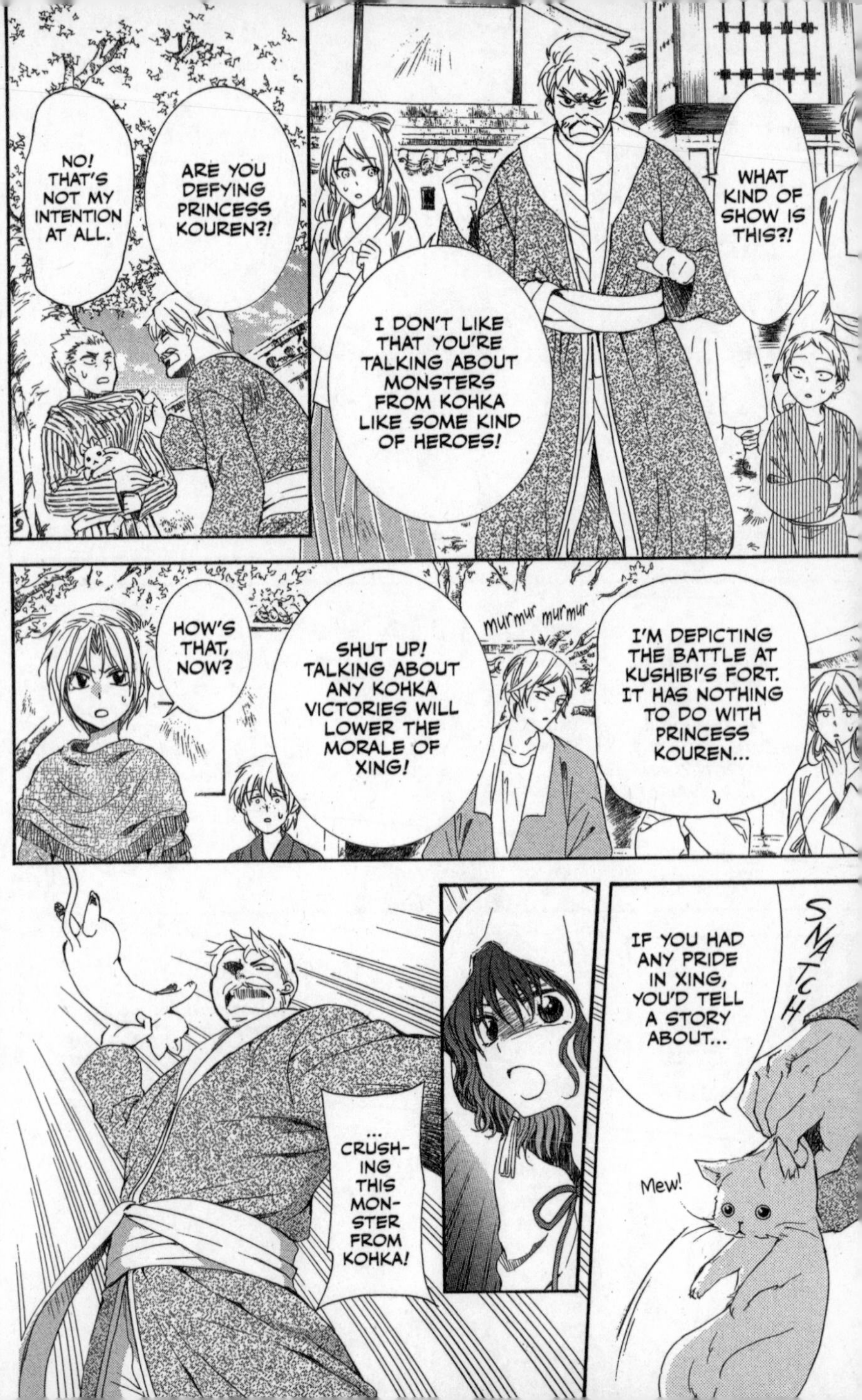
WHAT KIND OF SHOW IS THIS?!
I DON'T LIKE THAT YOU'RE TALKING ABOUT MONSTERS FROM KOHKA LIKE SOME KIND OF HEROES!
ARE YOU DEFYING PRINCESS KOUREN?!
NO! THAT'S NOT MY INTENTION AT ALL.
I'M DEPICTING THE BATTLE AT KUSHIBI'S FORT. IT HAS NOTHING TO DO WITH PRINCESS KOUREN...
murmur murmur
SHUT UP! TALKING ABOUT ANY KOHKA VICTORIES WILL LOWER THE MORALE OF XING!
HOW'S THAT, NOW?
SNATCH
IF YOU HAD ANY PRIDE IN XING, YOU'D TELL A STORY ABOUT...
Mew!
...CRUSHING THIS MONSTER FROM KOHKA!

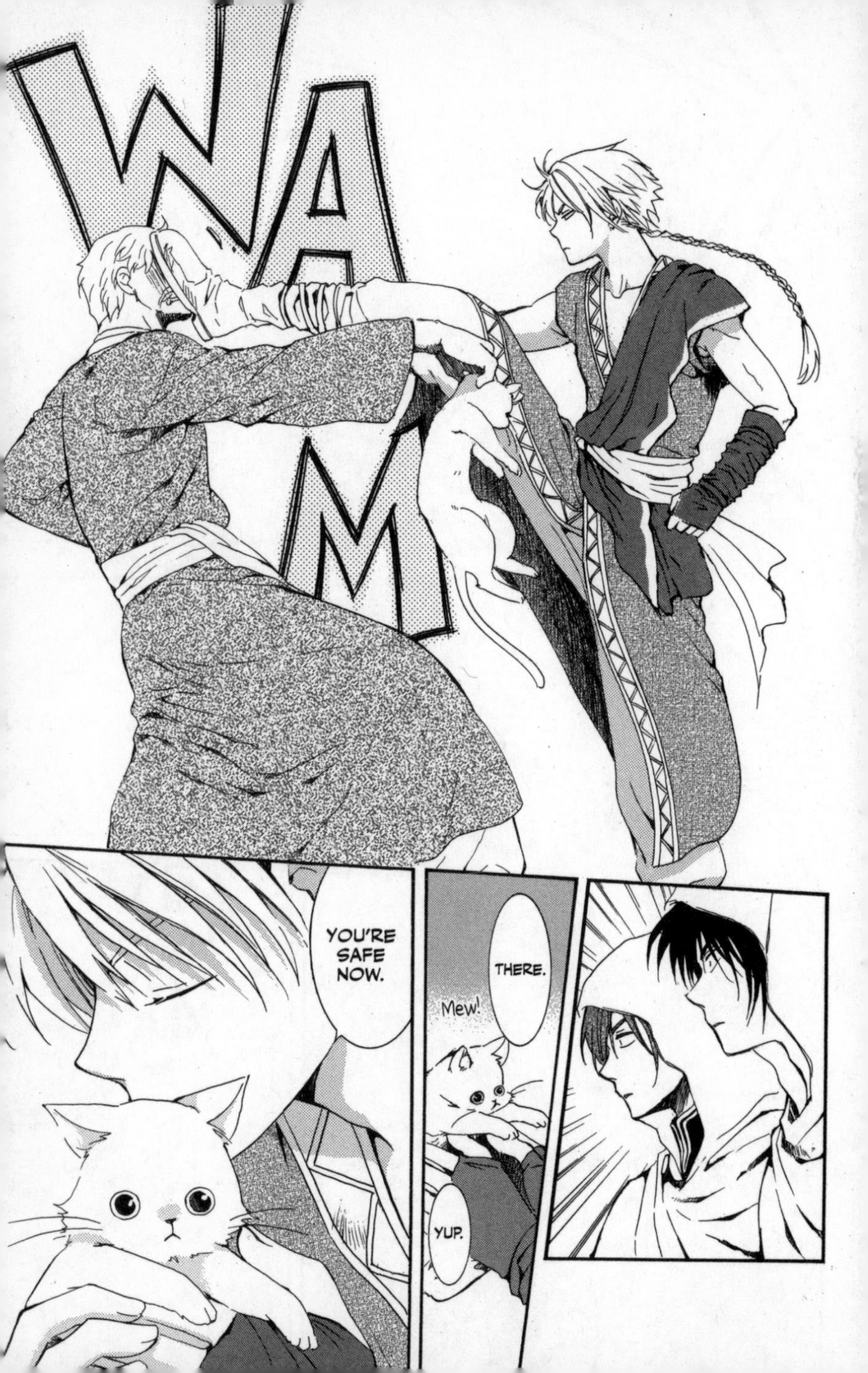
WAMM
THERE.
Mew!
YUP.
YOU'RE SAFE NOW.

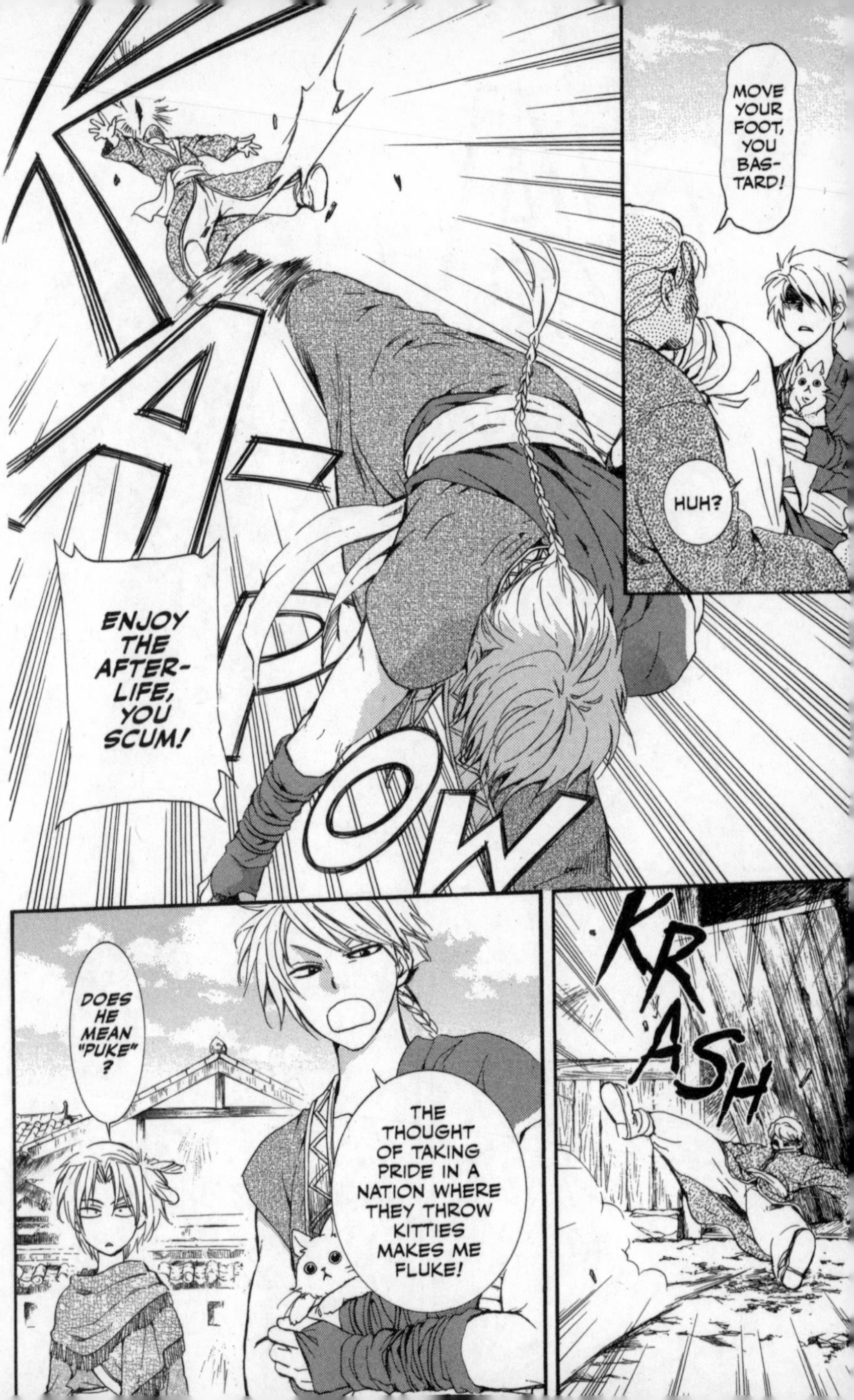
MOVE YOUR FOOT, YOU BAS-TARD!
HUH?
KA-POW
ENJOY THE AFTER-LIFE, YOU SCUM!
KRASH
THE THOUGHT OF TAKING PRIDE IN A NATION WHERE THEY THROW KITTIES MAKES ME FLUKE!
DOES HE MEAN "PUKE"?

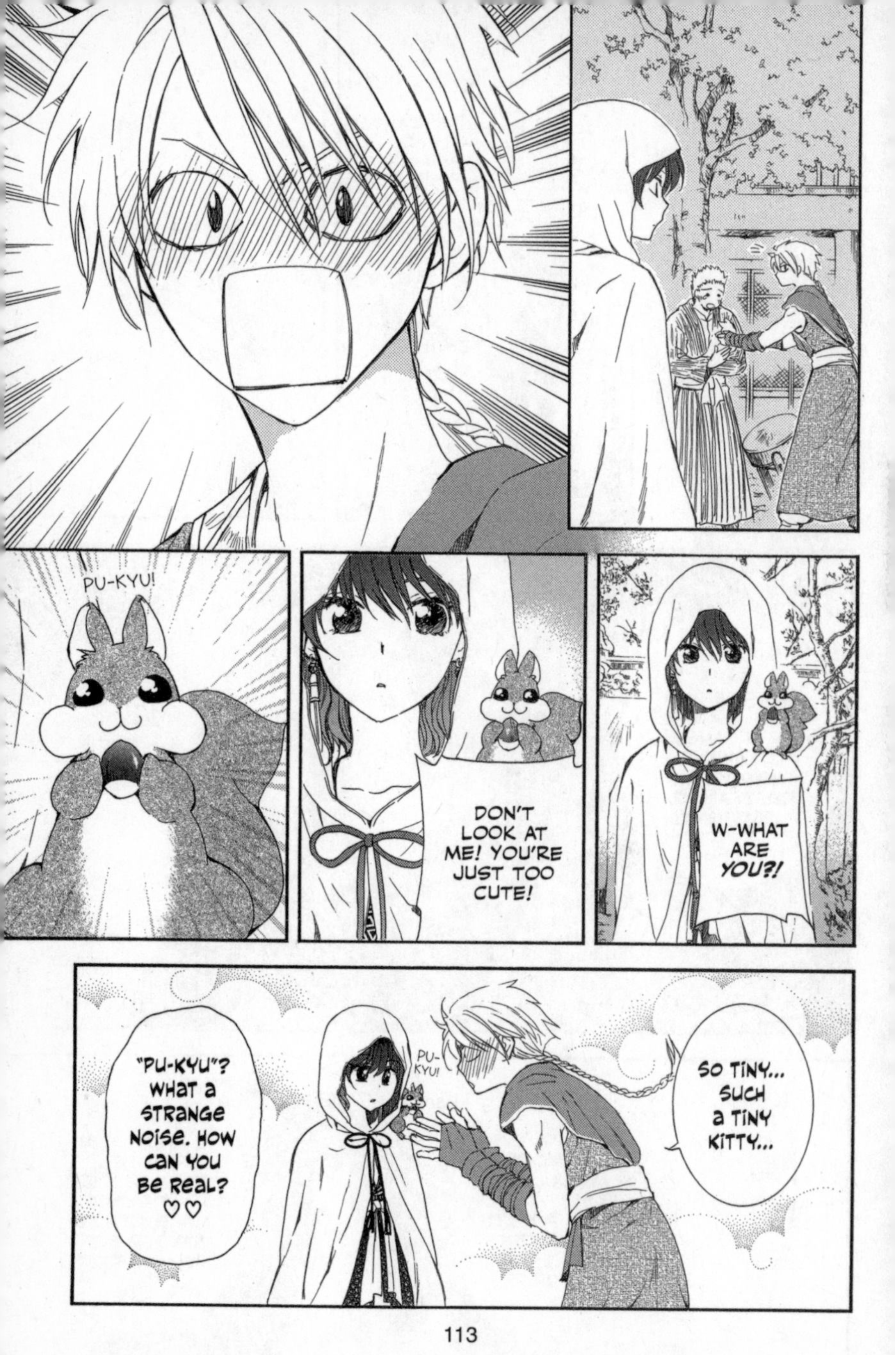
W-WHAT ARE YOU?!
DON'T LOOK AT ME! YOU'RE JUST TOO CUTE!
PU-KYU!
SO TINY... SUCH A TINY KITTY...
PU-KYU!
"PU-KYU"? WHAT A STRANGE NOISE. HOW CAN YOU BE REAL? ♡♡

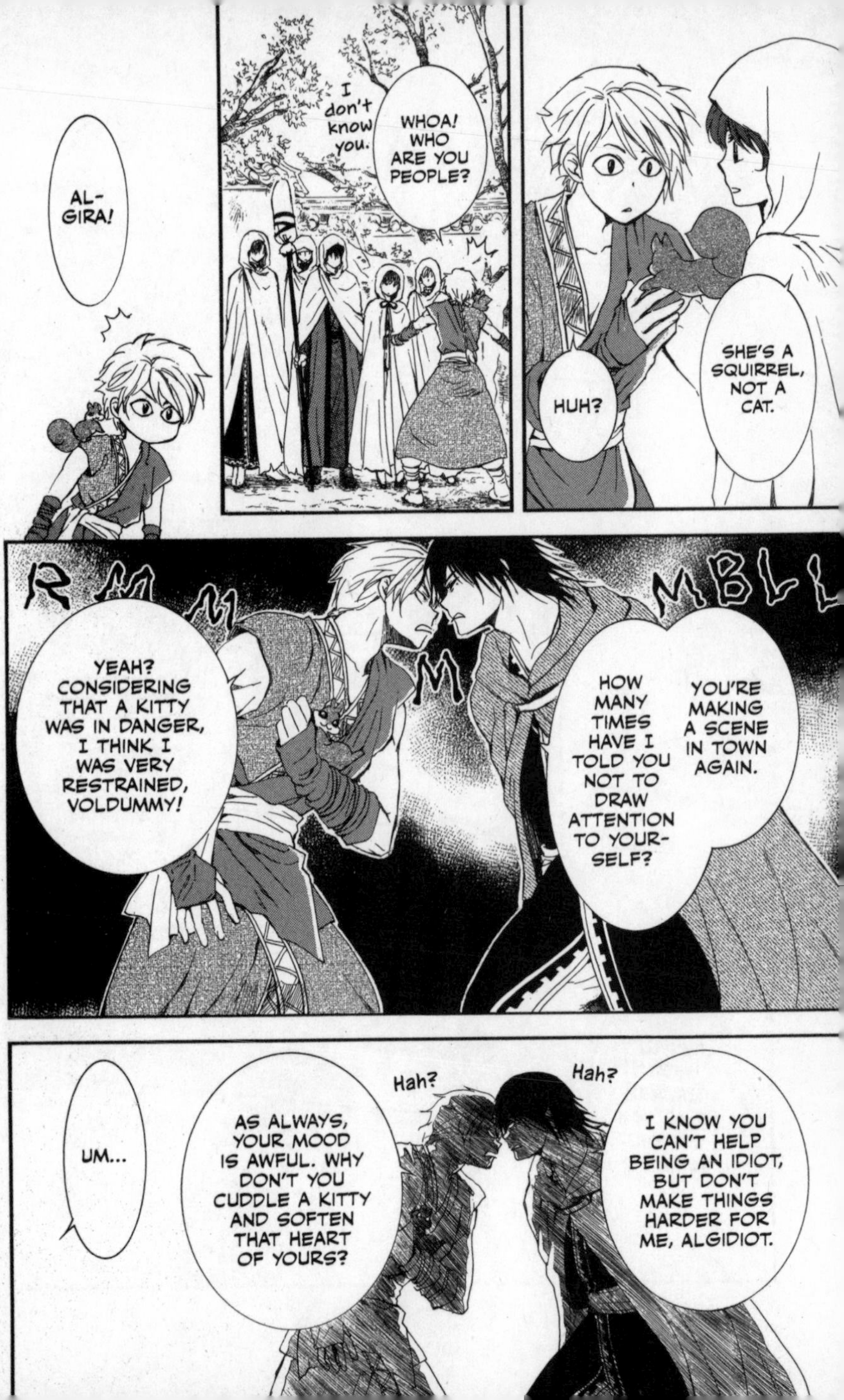
SHE'S A SQUIRREL, NOT A CAT.
HUH?
WHOA! WHO ARE YOU PEOPLE?
I don't know you.
AL-GIRA!
RMMMMBLL
YOU'RE MAKING A SCENE IN TOWN AGAIN.
HOW MANY TIMES HAVE I TOLD YOU NOT TO DRAW ATTENTION TO YOURSELF?
YEAH? CONSIDERING THAT A KITTY WAS IN DANGER, I THINK I WAS VERY RESTRAINED, VOLDUMMY!
Hah?
I KNOW YOU CAN'T HELP BEING AN IDIOT, BUT DON'T MAKE THINGS HARDER FOR ME, ALGIDIOT.
Hah?
AS ALWAYS, YOUR MOOD IS AWFUL. WHY DON'T YOU CUDDLE A KITTY AND SOFTEN THAT HEART OF YOURS?
UM...

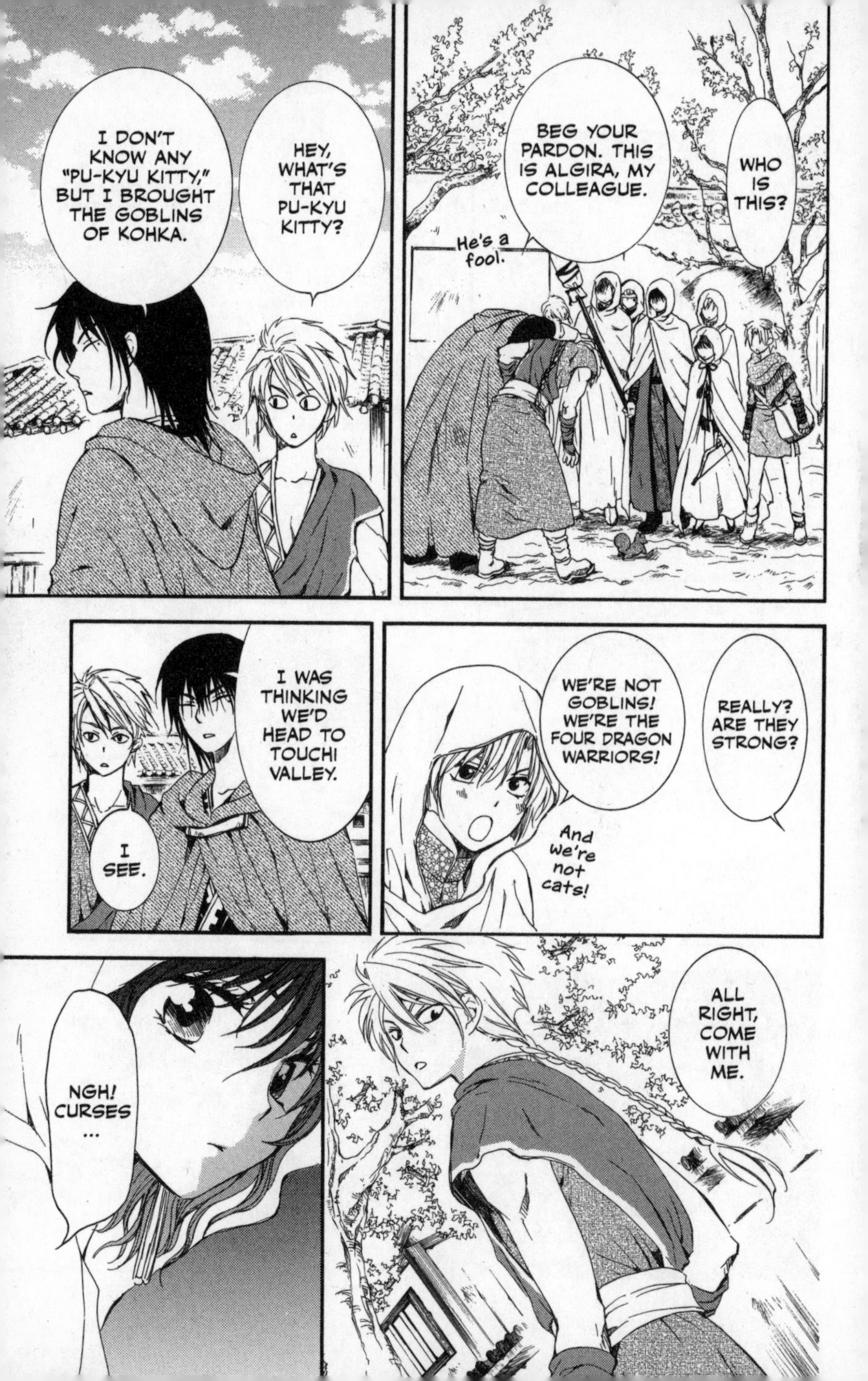
WHO IS THIS?
BEG YOUR PARDON. THIS IS ALGIRA, MY COLLEAGUE.
He's a fool.
HEY, WHAT'S THAT PU-KYU KITTY?
I DON'T KNOW ANY "PU-KYU KITTY," BUT I BROUGHT THE GOBLINS OF KOHKA.
REALLY? ARE THEY STRONG?
WE'RE NOT GOBLINS! WE'RE THE FOUR DRAGON WARRIORS!
And we're not cats!
I WAS THINKING WE'D HEAD TO TOUCHI VALLEY.
I SEE.
ALL RIGHT, COME WITH ME.
NGH! CURSES ...

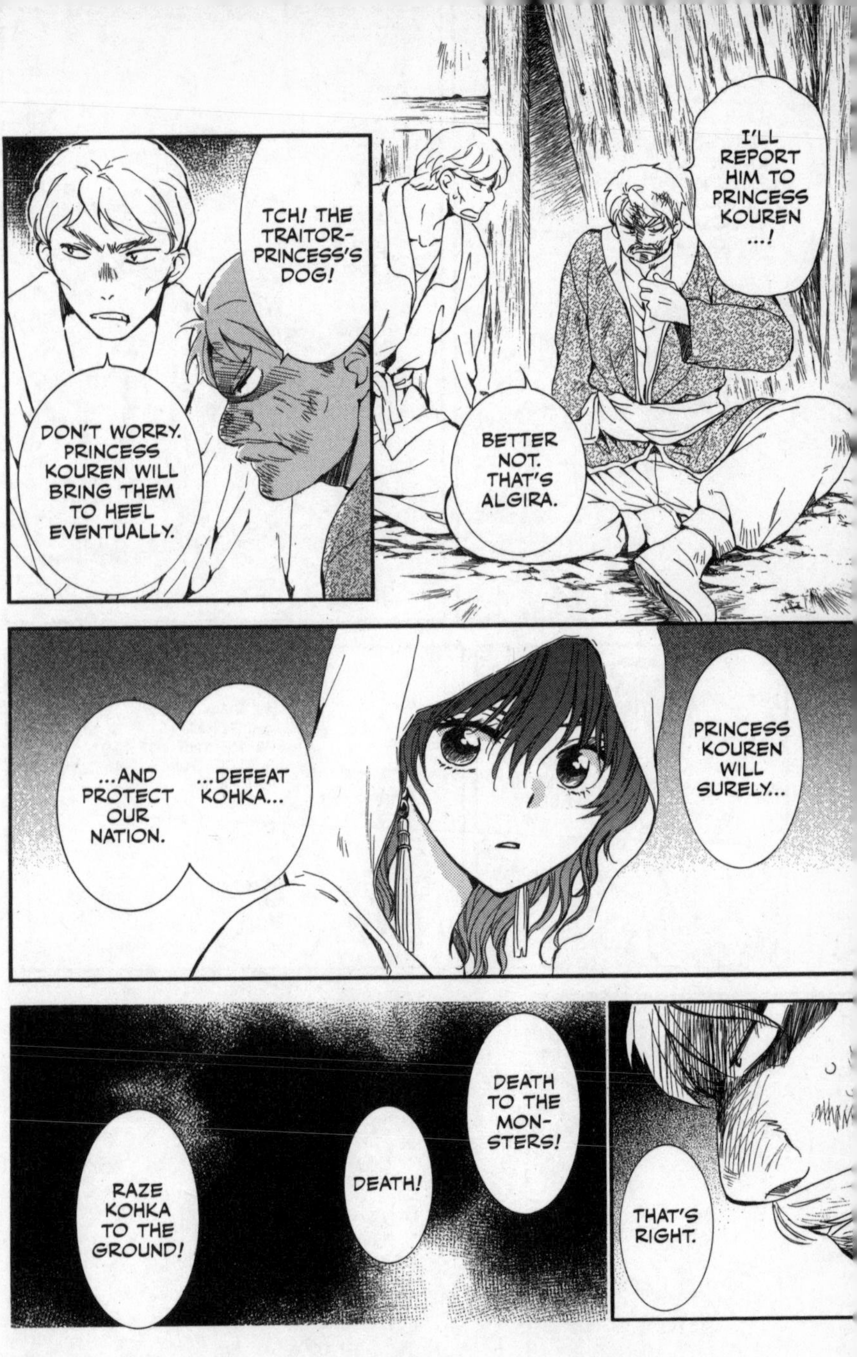
I'LL REPORT HIM TO PRINCESS KOUREN ...!
BETTER NOT. THAT'S ALGIRA.
TCH! THE TRAITOR-PRINCESS'S DOG!
DON'T WORRY. PRINCESS KOUREN WILL BRING THEM TO HEEL EVENTUALLY.
PRINCESS KOUREN WILL SURELY...
...DEFEAT KOHKA...
...AND PROTECT OUR NATION.
THAT'S RIGHT.
DEATH TO THE MON-STERS!
DEATH!
RAZE KOHKA TO THE GROUND!

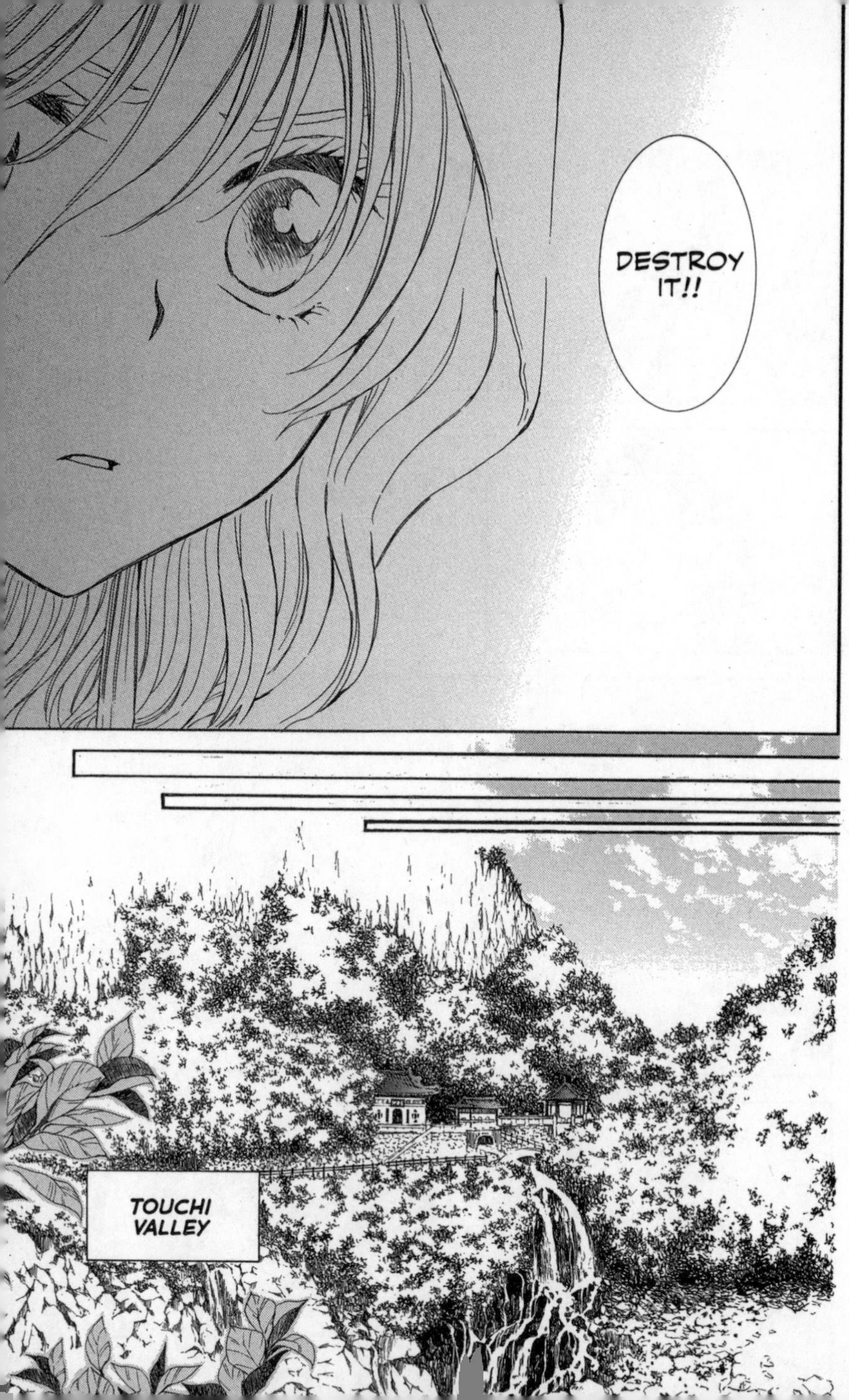
DESTROY IT!!
TOUCHI VALLEY

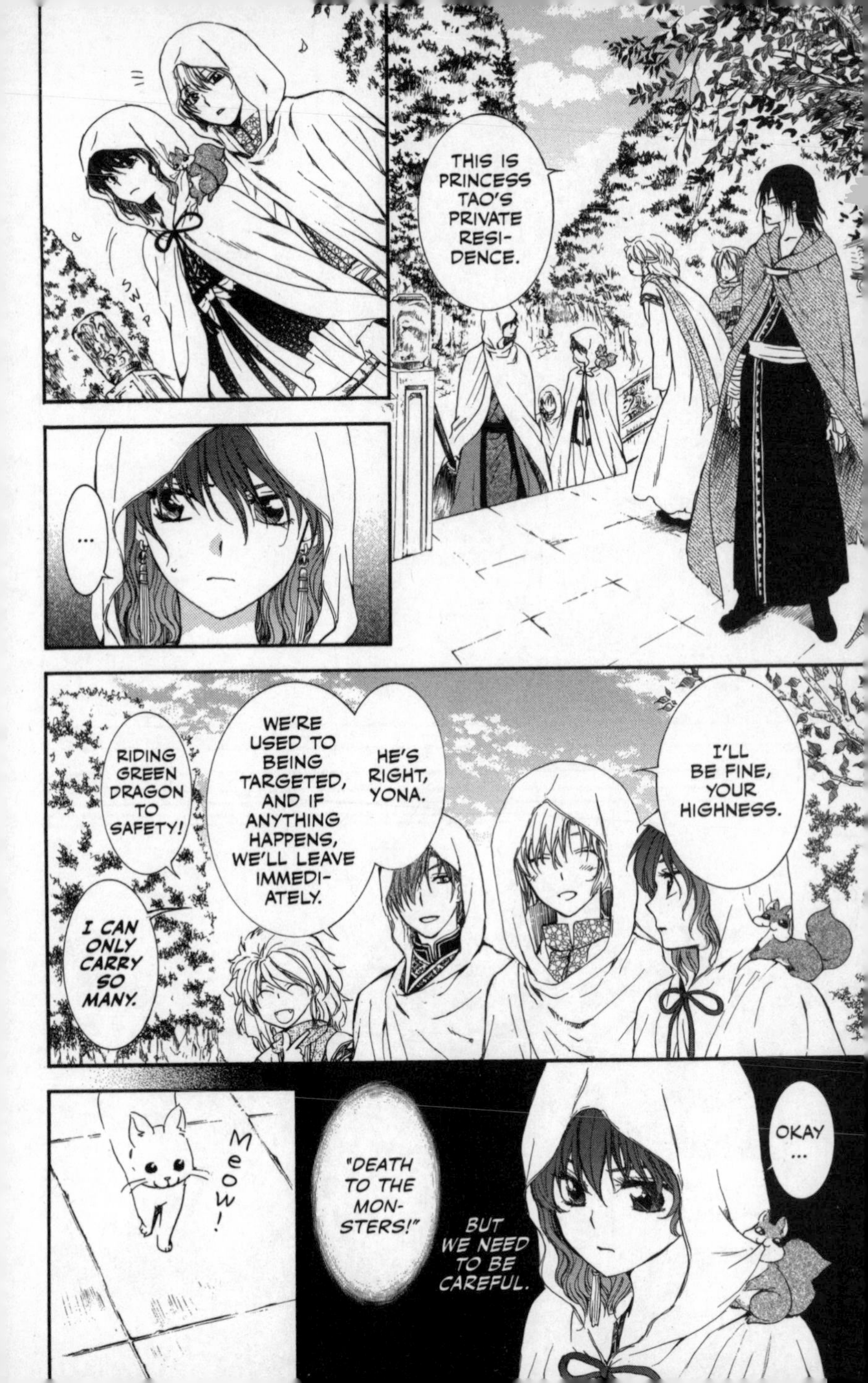

THIS IS PRINCESS TAO'S PRIVATE RESI-DENCE.
SWIP
...
I'LL BE FINE, YOUR HIGHNESS.
HE'S RIGHT, YONA.
WE'RE USED TO BEING TARGETED, AND IF ANYTHING HAPPENS, WE'LL LEAVE IMMEDI-ATELY.
RIDING GREEN DRAGON TO SAFETY!
I CAN ONLY CARRY SO MANY.
OKAY...
BUT WE NEED TO BE CAREFUL.
"DEATH TO THE MON-STERS!"
Meow!

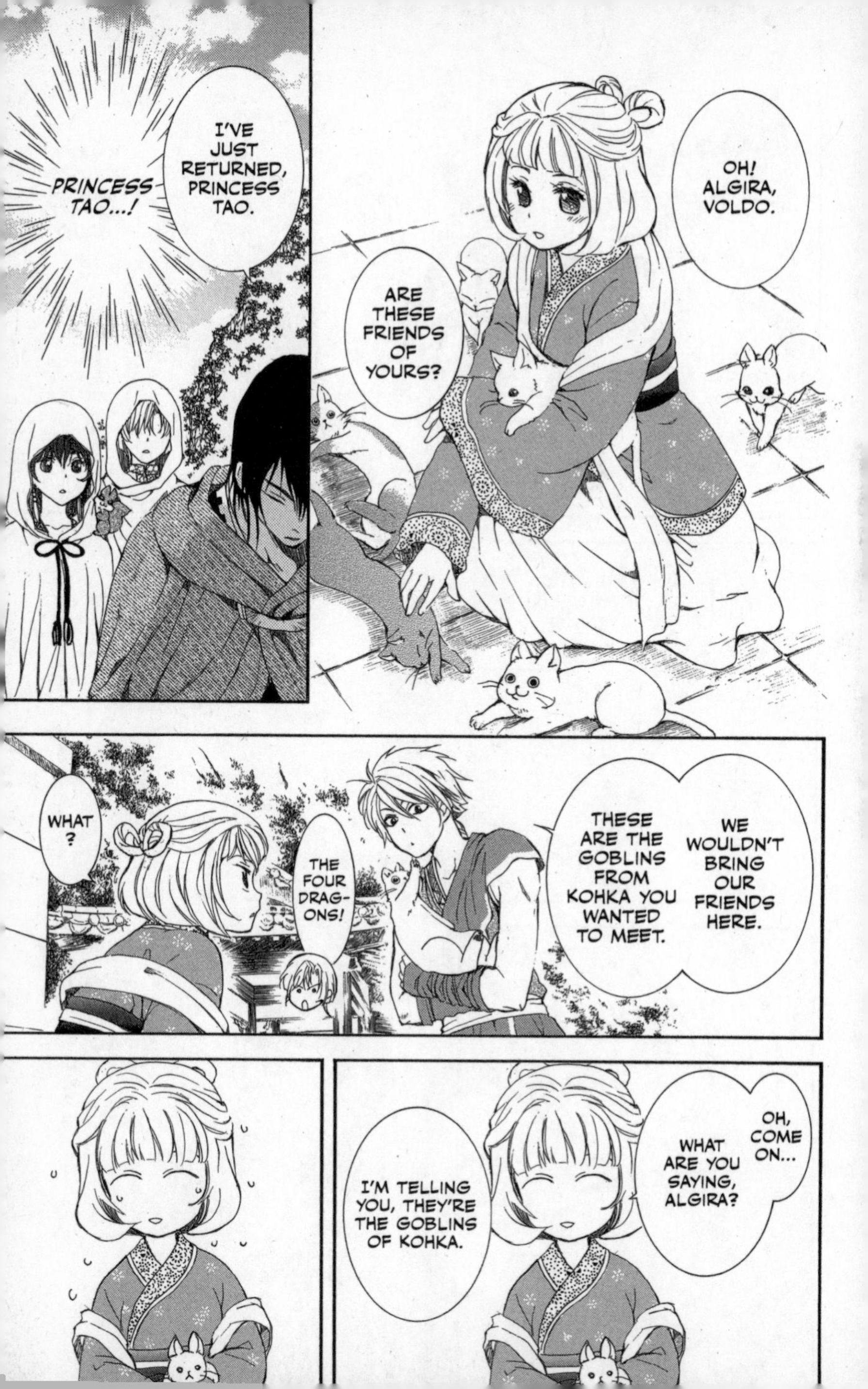
OH! ALGIRA, VOLDO.
ARE THESE FRIENDS OF YOURS?
I'VE JUST RETURNED, PRINCESS TAO.
PRINCESS TAO...!
WE WOULDN'T BRING OUR FRIENDS HERE.
THESE ARE THE GOBLINS FROM KOHKA YOU WANTED TO MEET.
THE FOUR DRAGONS!
WHAT?
OH, COME ON...
WHAT ARE YOU SAYING, ALGIRA?
I'M TELLING YOU, THEY'RE THE GOBLINS OF KOHKA.

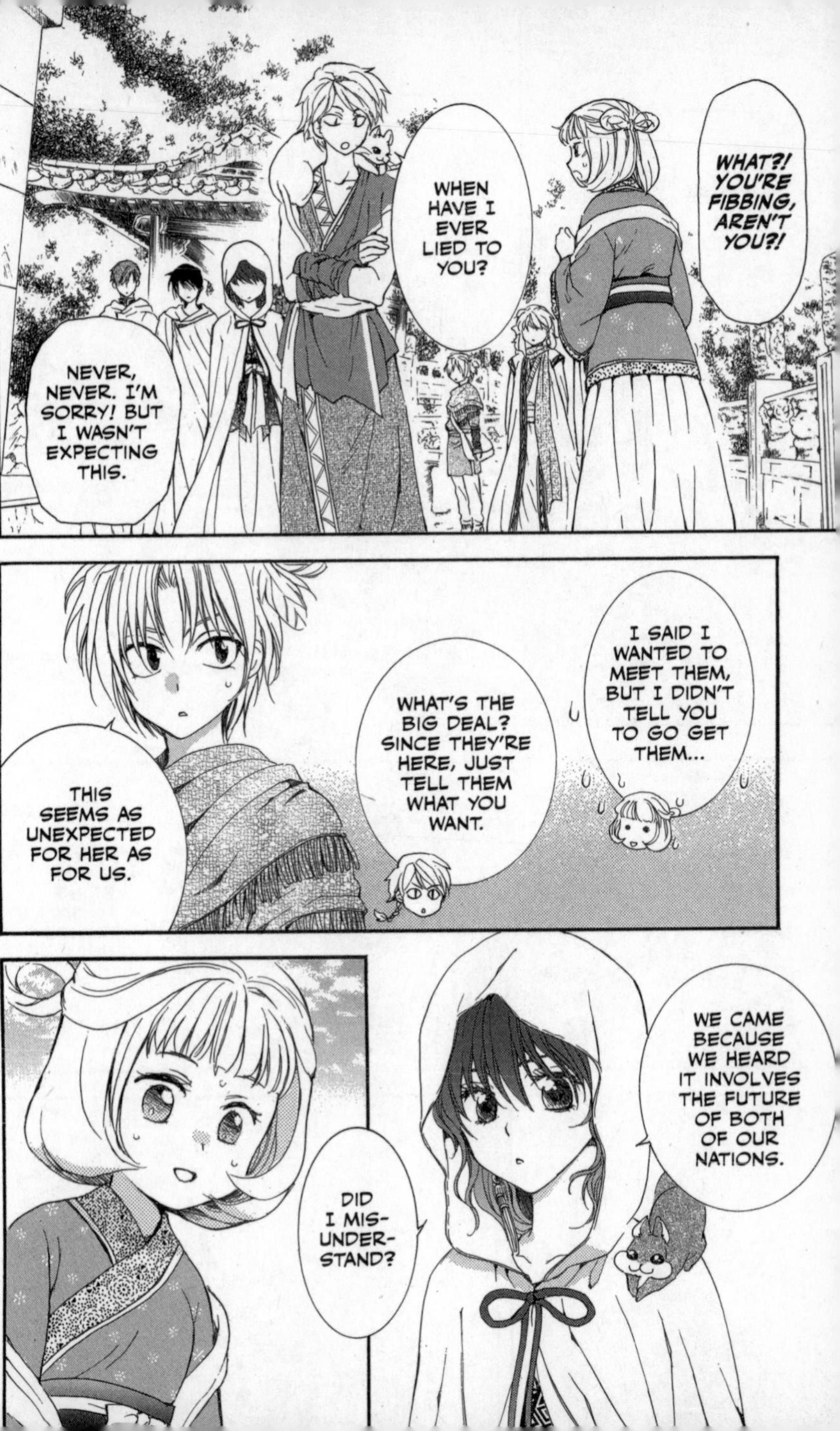
WHAT?! YOU'RE FIBBING, AREN'T YOU?!
WHEN HAVE I EVER LIED TO YOU?
NEVER, NEVER. I'M SORRY! BUT I WASN'T EXPECTING THIS.
I SAID I WANTED TO MEET THEM, BUT I DIDN'T TELL YOU TO GO GET THEM...
WHAT'S THE BIG DEAL? SINCE THEY'RE HERE, JUST TELL THEM WHAT YOU WANT.
THIS SEEMS AS UNEXPECTED FOR HER AS FOR US.
WE CAME BECAUSE WE HEARD IT INVOLVES THE FUTURE OF BOTH OF OUR NATIONS.
DID I MIS-UNDER-STAND?

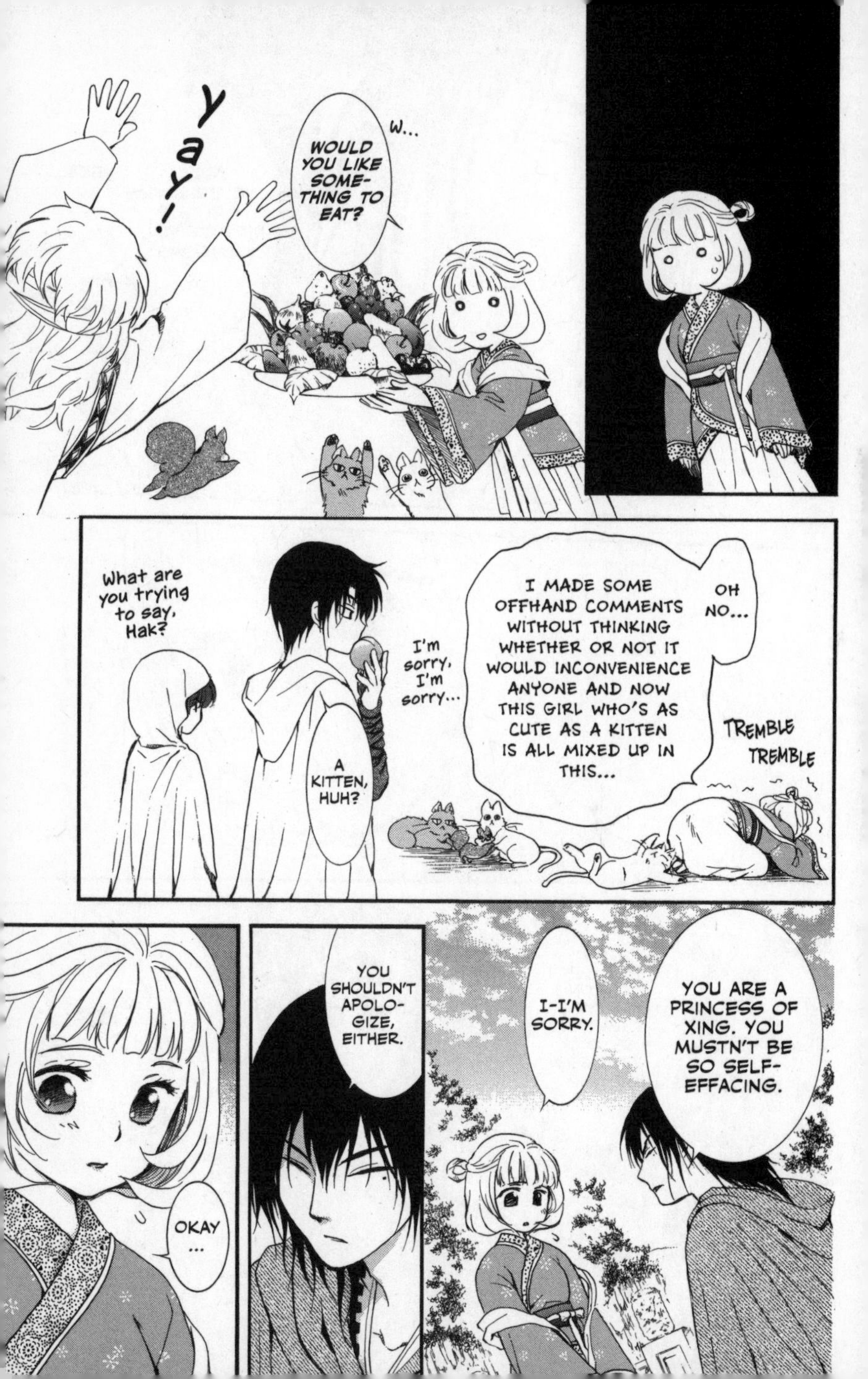
W...
WOULD YOU LIKE SOMETHING TO EAT?
yay!
OH NO...
I MADE SOME OFFHAND COMMENTS WITHOUT THINKING WHETHER OR NOT IT WOULD INCONVENIENCE ANYONE AND NOW THIS GIRL WHO'S AS CUTE AS A KITTEN IS ALL MIXED UP IN THIS...
TREMBLE TREMBLE
I'm sorry, I'm sorry...
A KITTEN, HUH?
What are you trying to say, Hak?
YOU ARE A PRINCESS OF XING. YOU MUSTN'T BE SO SELF-EFFACING.
I-I'M SORRY.
YOU SHOULDN'T APOLOGIZE, EITHER.
OKAY ...

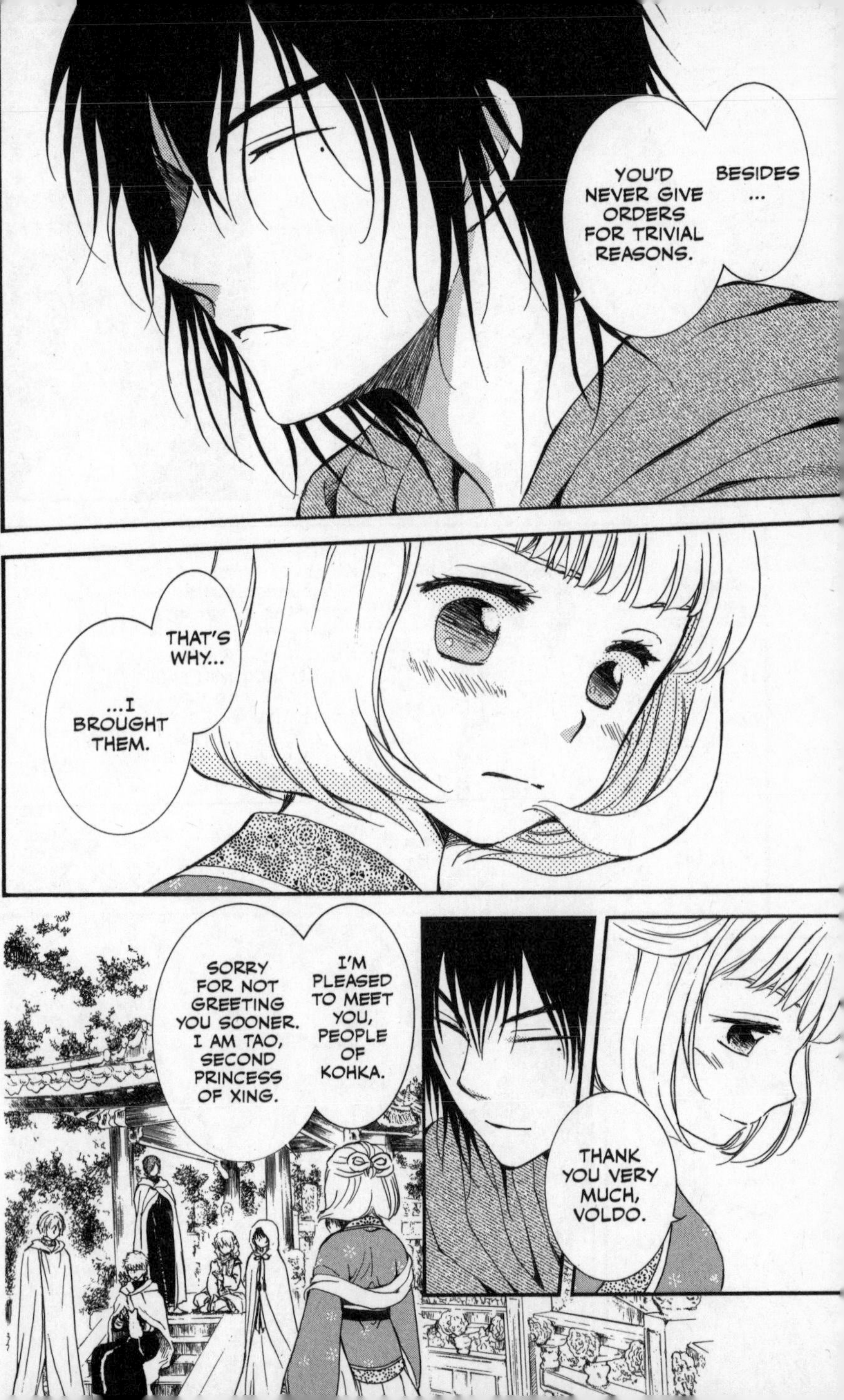
BESIDES ...
YOU'D NEVER GIVE ORDERS FOR TRIVIAL REASONS.
THAT'S WHY...
...I BROUGHT THEM.
THANK YOU VERY MUCH, VOLDO.
I'M PLEASED TO MEET YOU, PEOPLE OF KOHKA.
SORRY FOR NOT GREETING YOU SOONER. I AM TAO, SECOND PRINCESS OF XING.

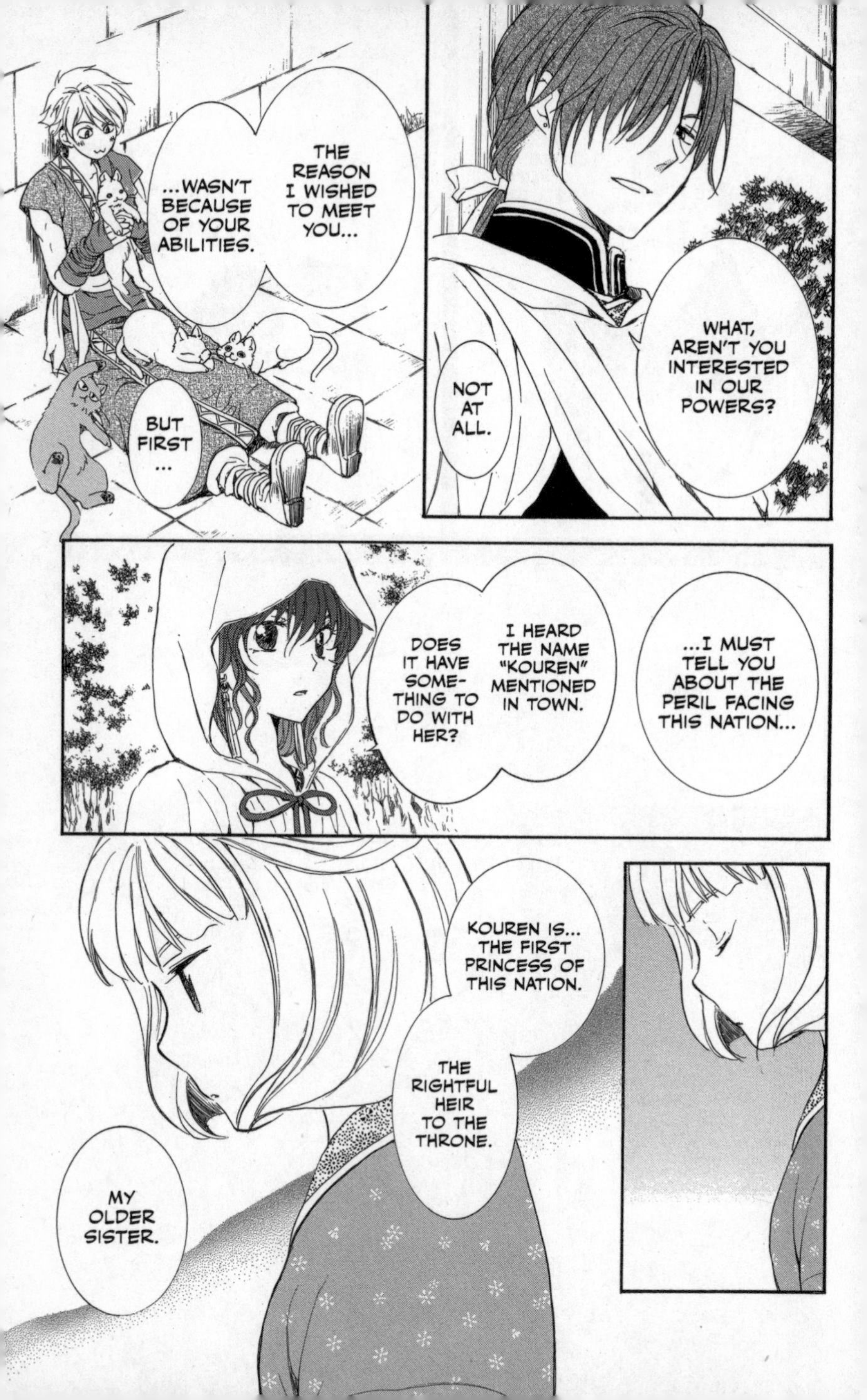
WHAT, AREN'T YOU INTERESTED IN OUR POWERS?
NOT AT ALL.
THE REASON I WISHED TO MEET YOU...
...WASN'T BECAUSE OF YOUR ABILITIES.
BUT FIRST...
...I MUST TELL YOU ABOUT THE PERIL FACING THIS NATION...
I HEARD THE NAME "KOUREN" MENTIONED IN TOWN.
DOES IT HAVE SOME-THING TO DO WITH HER?
KOUREN IS... THE FIRST PRINCESS OF THIS NATION.
THE RIGHTFUL HEIR TO THE THRONE.
MY OLDER SISTER.

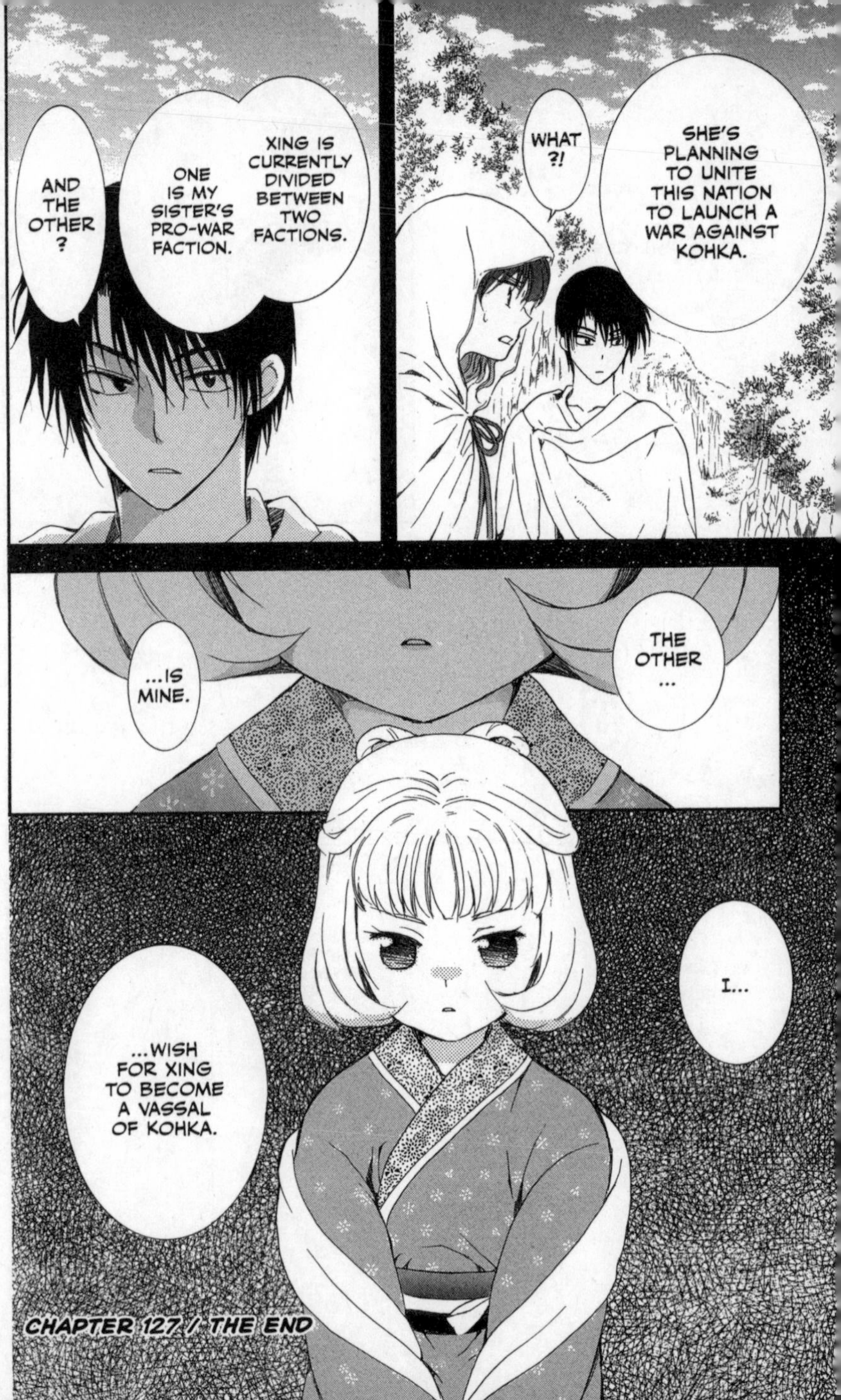
SHE'S PLANNING TO UNITE THIS NATION TO LAUNCH A WAR AGAINST KOHKA.
WHAT ?!
XING IS CURRENTLY DIVIDED BETWEEN TWO FACTIONS.
ONE IS MY SISTER'S PRO-WAR FACTION.
AND THE OTHER ?
THE OTHER ...
...IS MINE.
I...
...WISH FOR XING TO BECOME A VASSAL OF KOHKA.
CHAPTER 127 / THE END

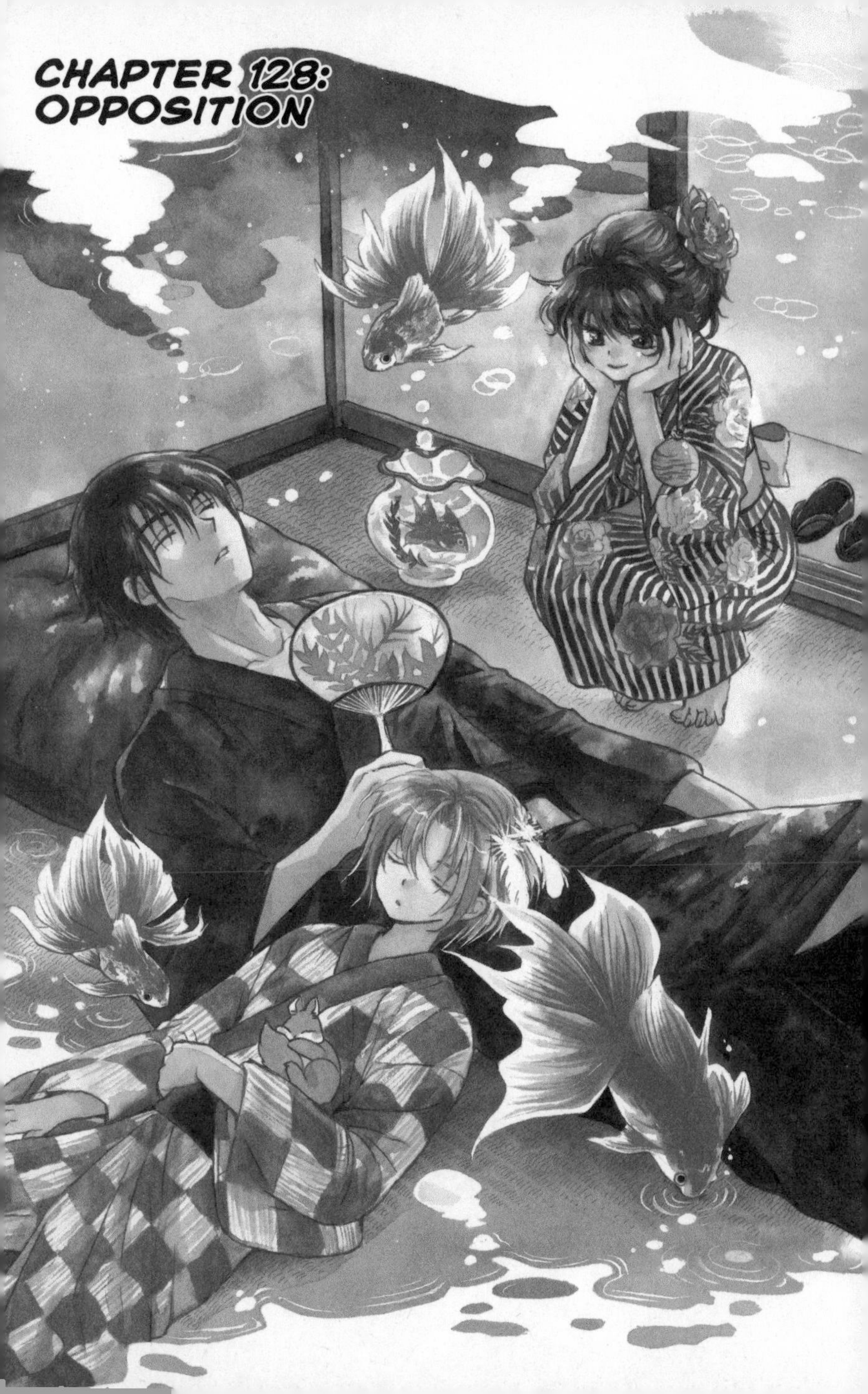
CHAPTER 128:
OPPOSITION

This is something I drew when I was struggling with the extra chapter in the drama CD that came with *Hana to Yume*. On Twitter, it was Gija instead of Tae-jun, but I thought that Tae-jun would be more familiar with struggles.

The drama CD was very well received, so my struggles were worth it.

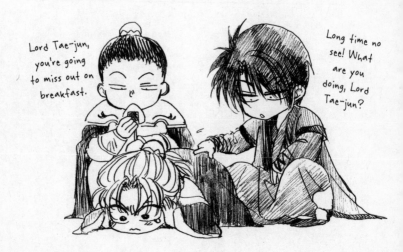

Long time no see! What are you doing, Lord Tae-jun?
Lord Tae-jun, you're going to miss out on breakfast.

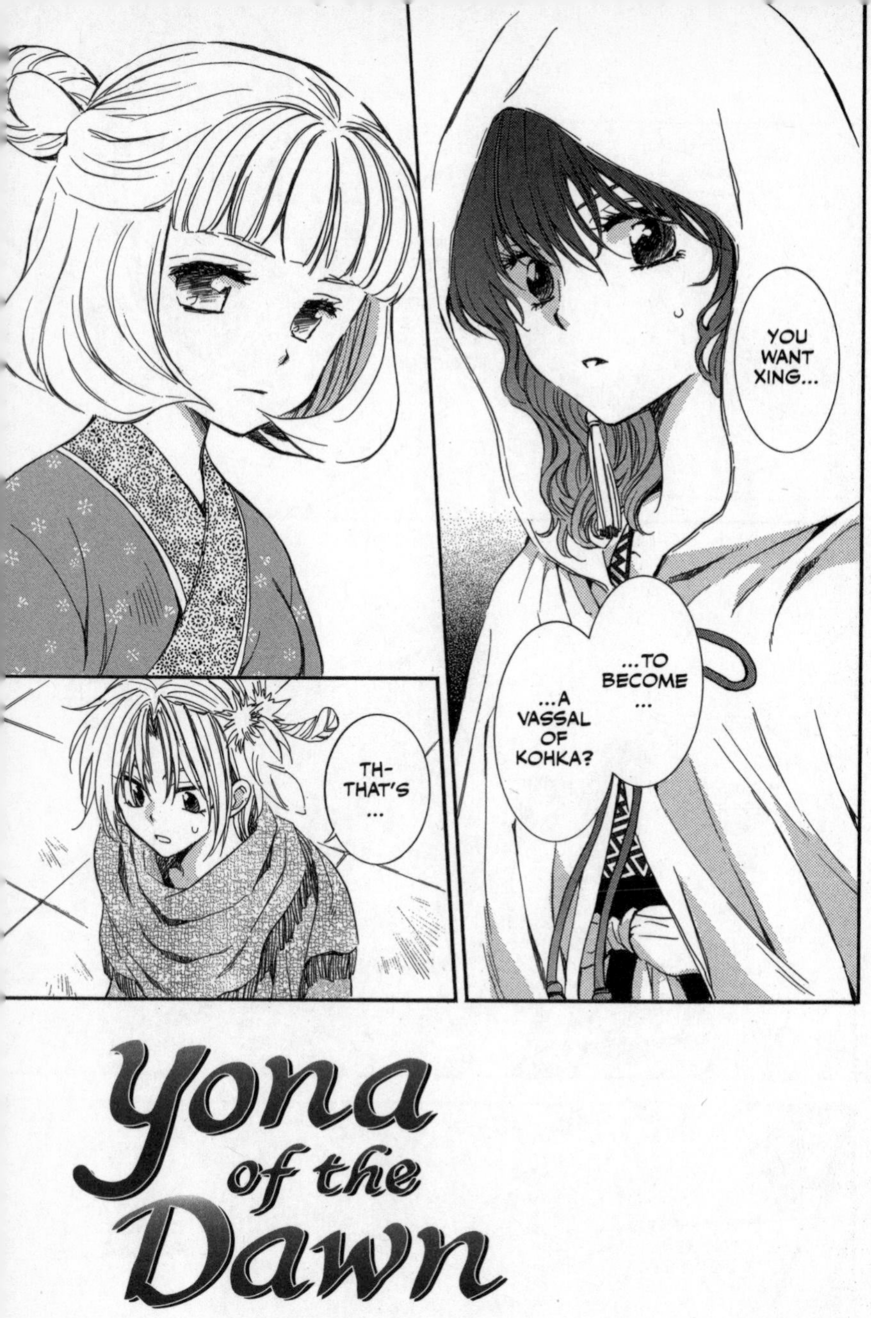
YOU WANT XING...
...TO BECOME ...
...A VASSAL OF KOHKA?
TH- THAT'S ...

Yona of the Dawn

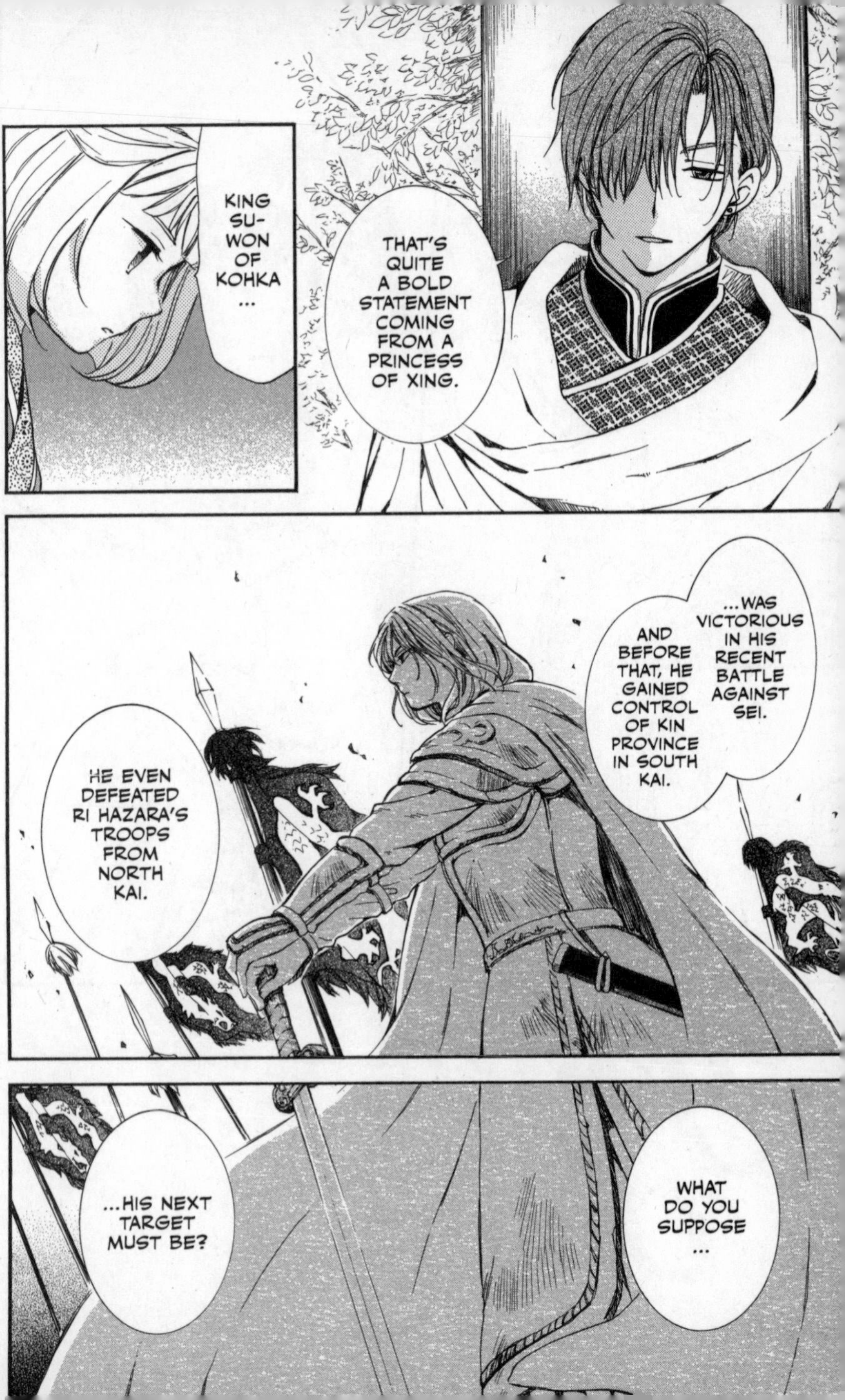
THAT'S QUITE A BOLD STATEMENT COMING FROM A PRINCESS OF XING.
KING SU-WON OF KOHKA ...
...WAS VICTORIOUS IN HIS RECENT BATTLE AGAINST SEI.
AND BEFORE THAT, HE GAINED CONTROL OF KIN PROVINCE IN SOUTH KAI.
HE EVEN DEFEATED RI HAZARA'S TROOPS FROM NORTH KAI.
WHAT DO YOU SUPPOSE ...
...HIS NEXT TARGET MUST BE?

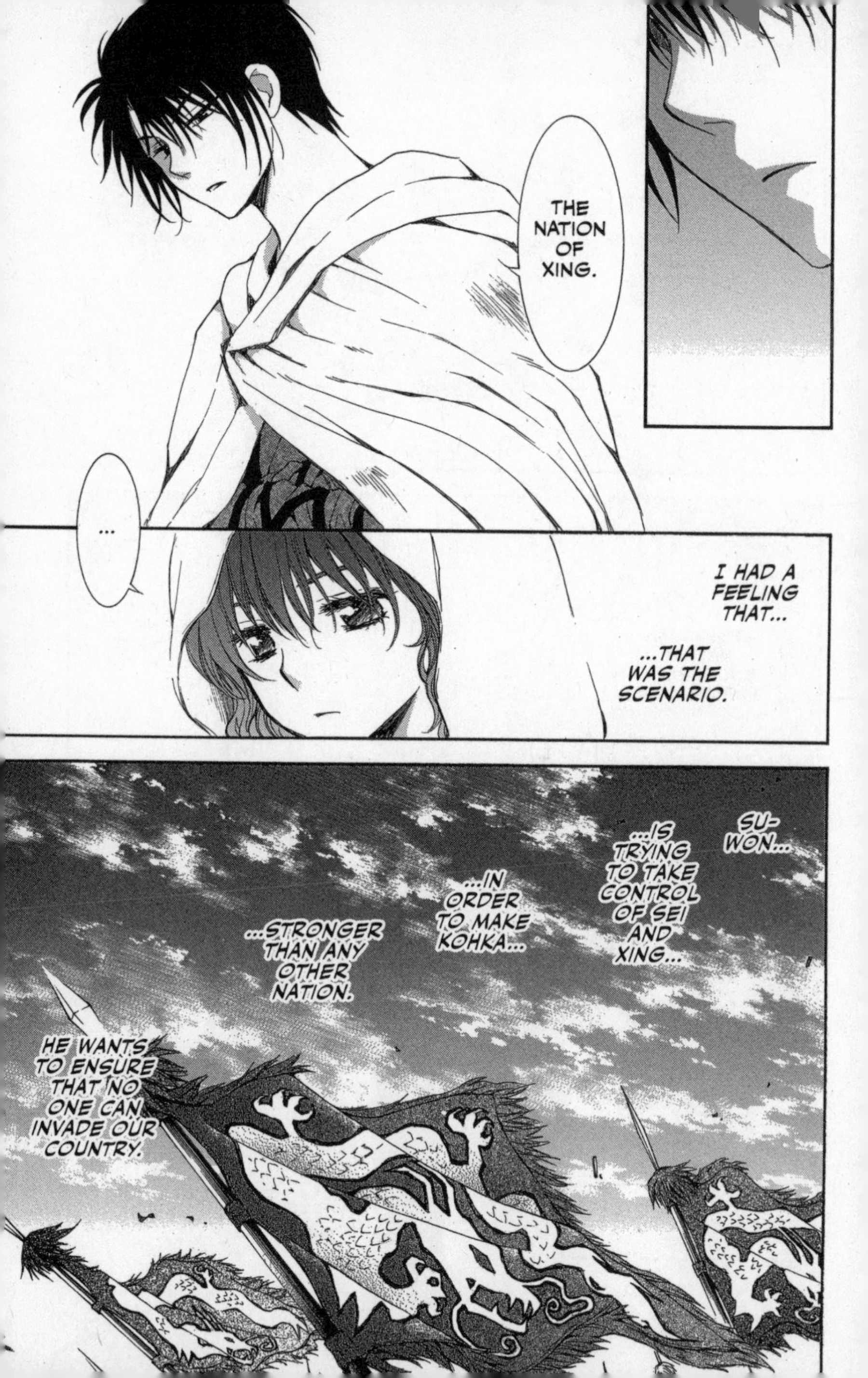
THE NATION OF XING.
...
I HAD A FEELING THAT...
...THAT WAS THE SCENARIO.
SU-WON...
...IS TRYING TO TAKE CONTROL OF SEI AND XING...
...IN ORDER TO MAKE KOHKA...
...STRONGER THAN ANY OTHER NATION.
HE WANTS TO ENSURE THAT NO ONE CAN INVADE OUR COUNTRY.

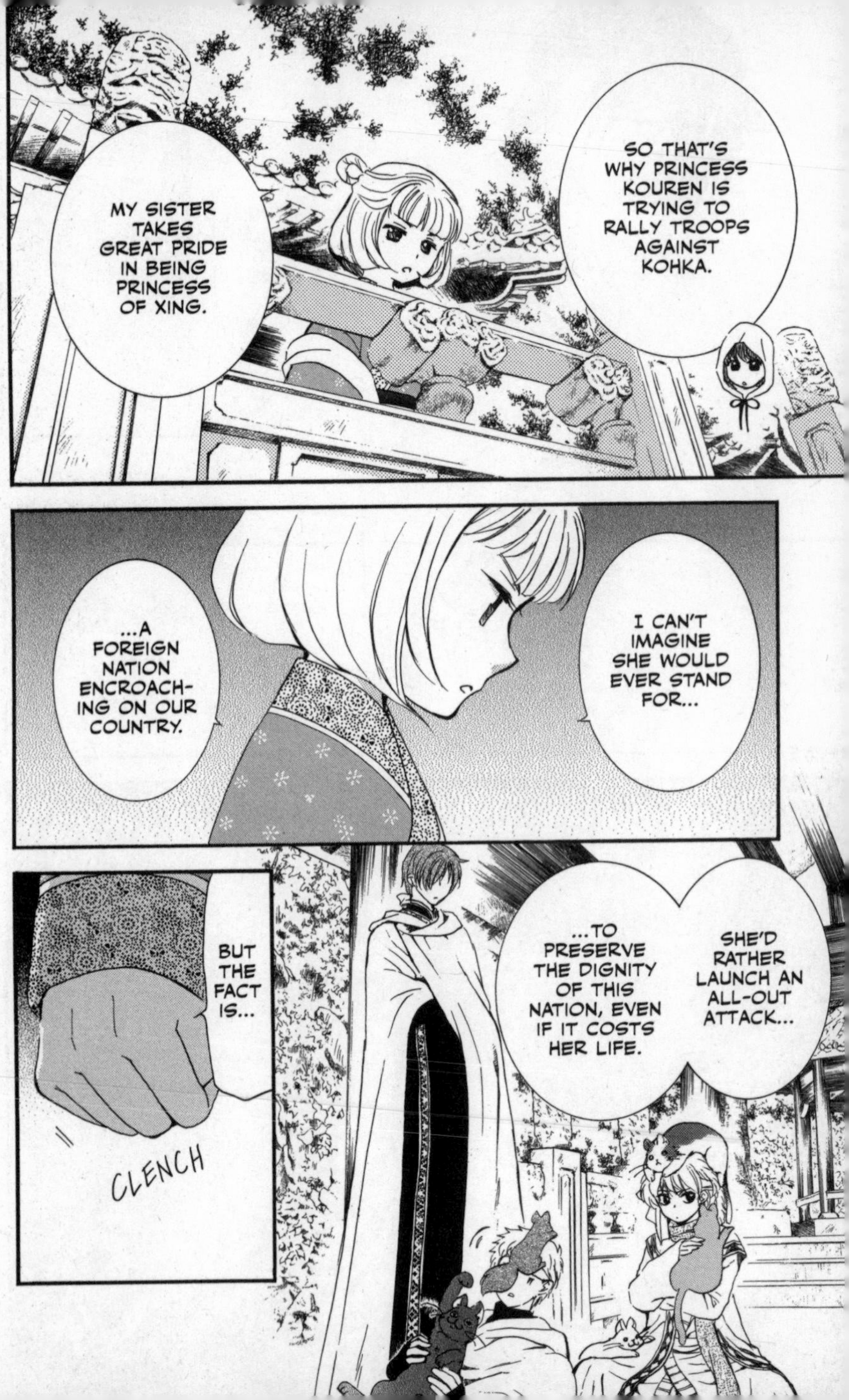
SO THAT'S WHY PRINCESS KOUREN IS TRYING TO RALLY TROOPS AGAINST KOHKA.
MY SISTER TAKES GREAT PRIDE IN BEING PRINCESS OF XING.
I CAN'T IMAGINE SHE WOULD EVER STAND FOR...
...A FOREIGN NATION ENCROACHING ON OUR COUNTRY.
SHE'D RATHER LAUNCH AN ALL-OUT ATTACK...
...TO PRESERVE THE DIGNITY OF THIS NATION, EVEN IF IT COSTS HER LIFE.
BUT THE FACT IS...
CLENCH

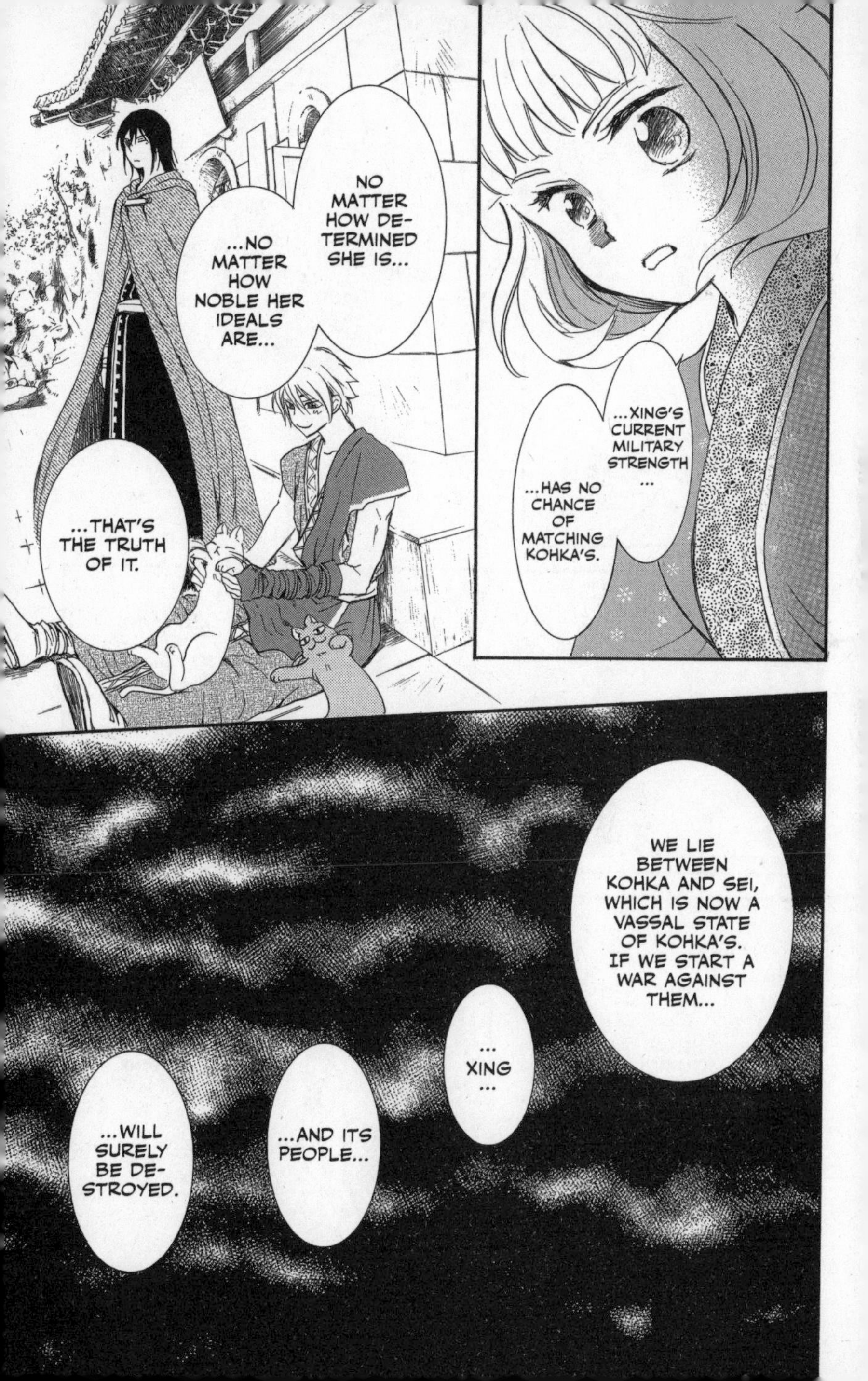
...XING'S CURRENT MILITARY STRENGTH ...
...HAS NO CHANCE OF MATCHING KOHKA'S.
NO MATTER HOW DETERMINED SHE IS...
...NO MATTER HOW NOBLE HER IDEALS ARE...
...THAT'S THE TRUTH OF IT.
WE LIE BETWEEN KOHKA AND SEI, WHICH IS NOW A VASSAL STATE OF KOHKA'S. IF WE START A WAR AGAINST THEM...
... XING ...
...AND ITS PEOPLE...
...WILL SURELY BE DESTROYED.

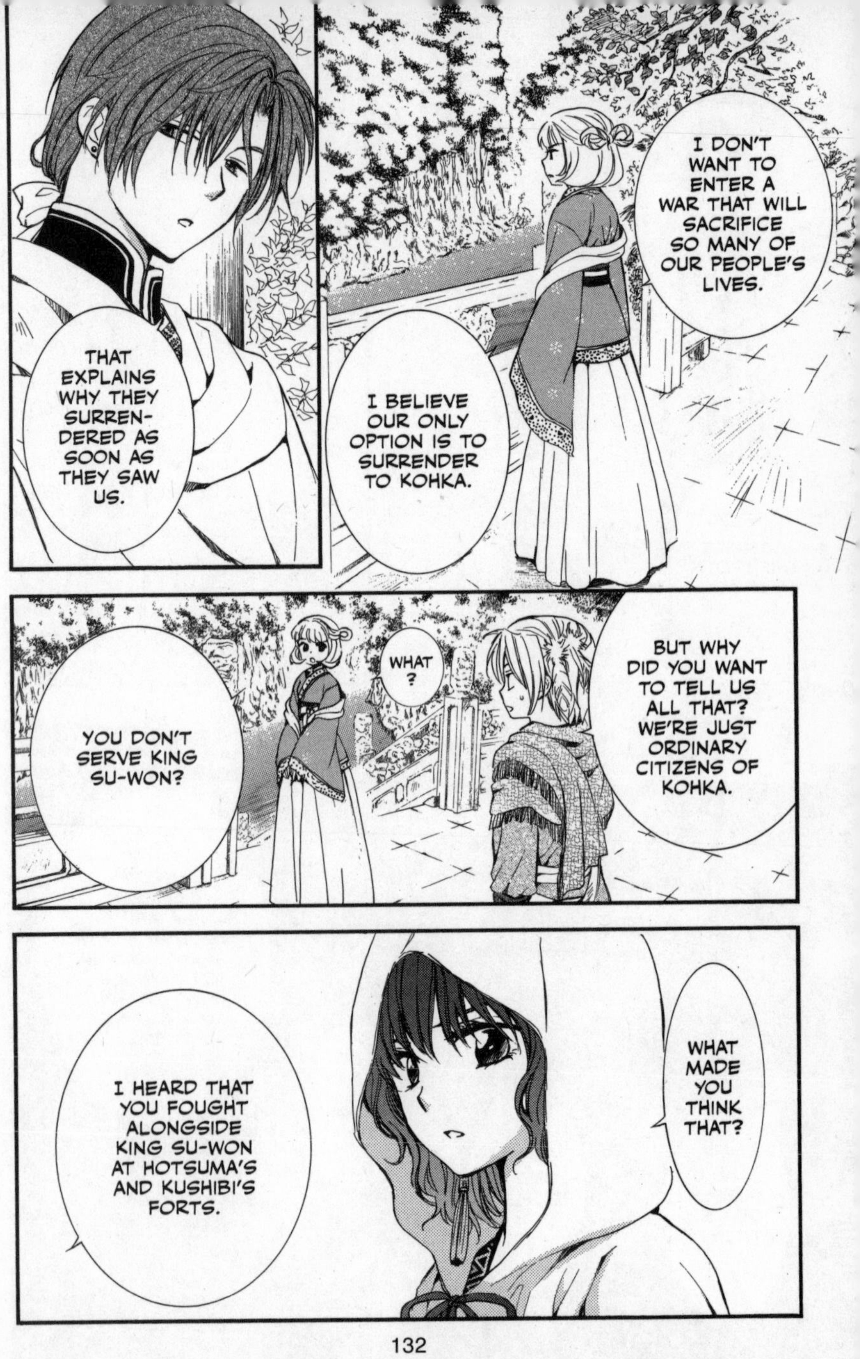
I DON'T WANT TO ENTER A WAR THAT WILL SACRIFICE SO MANY OF OUR PEOPLE'S LIVES.
I BELIEVE OUR ONLY OPTION IS TO SURRENDER TO KOHKA.
THAT EXPLAINS WHY THEY SURREN-DERED AS SOON AS THEY SAW US.
BUT WHY DID YOU WANT TO TELL US ALL THAT? WE'RE JUST ORDINARY CITIZENS OF KOHKA.
WHAT?
YOU DON'T SERVE KING SU-WON?
WHAT MADE YOU THINK THAT?
I HEARD THAT YOU FOUGHT ALONGSIDE KING SU-WON AT HOTSUMA'S AND KUSHIBI'S FORTS.

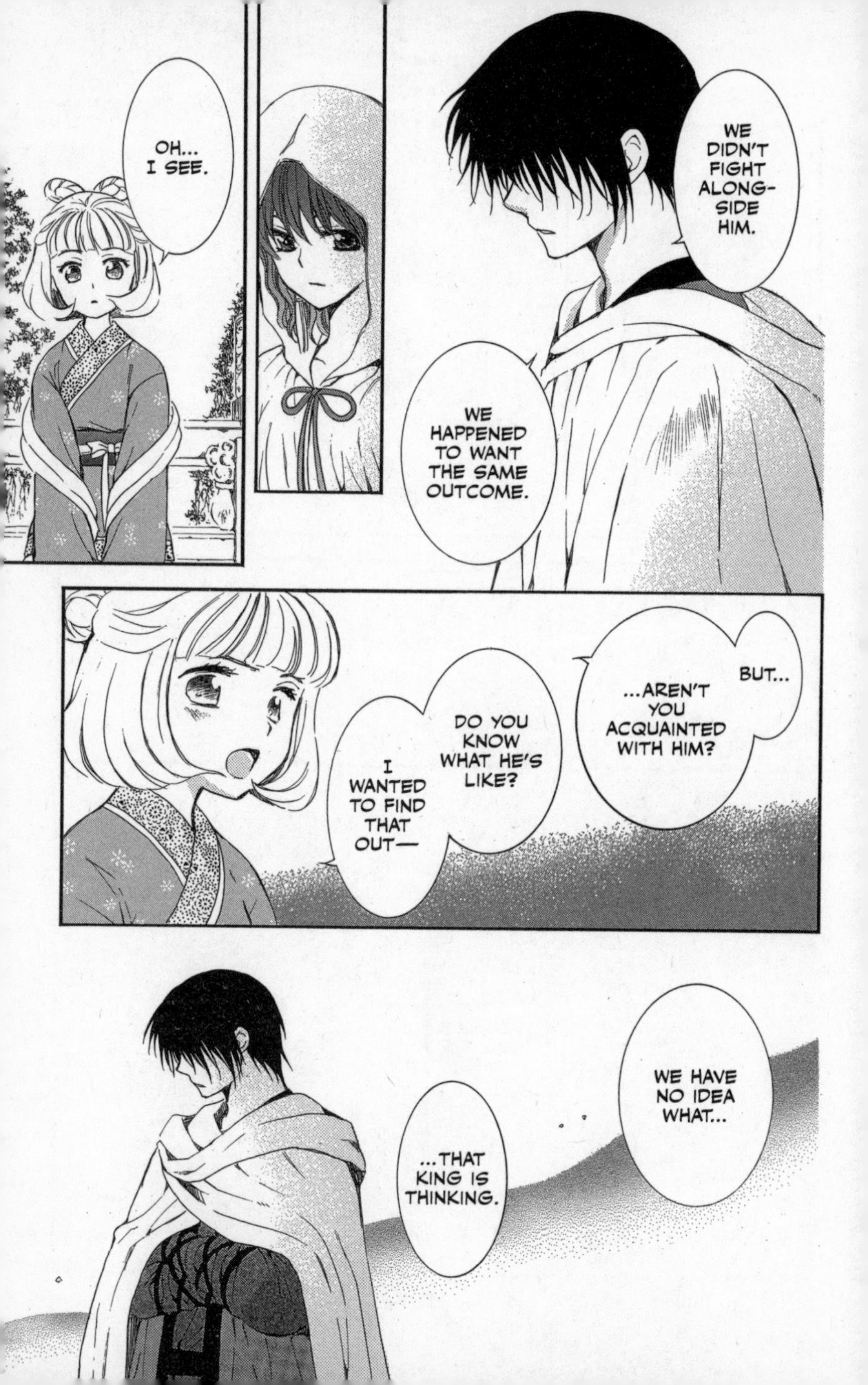
WE DIDN'T FIGHT ALONG-SIDE HIM.
WE HAPPENED TO WANT THE SAME OUTCOME.
OH... I SEE.
BUT...
...AREN'T YOU ACQUAINTED WITH HIM?
DO YOU KNOW WHAT HE'S LIKE?
I WANTED TO FIND THAT OUT—
WE HAVE NO IDEA WHAT...
...THAT KING IS THINKING.

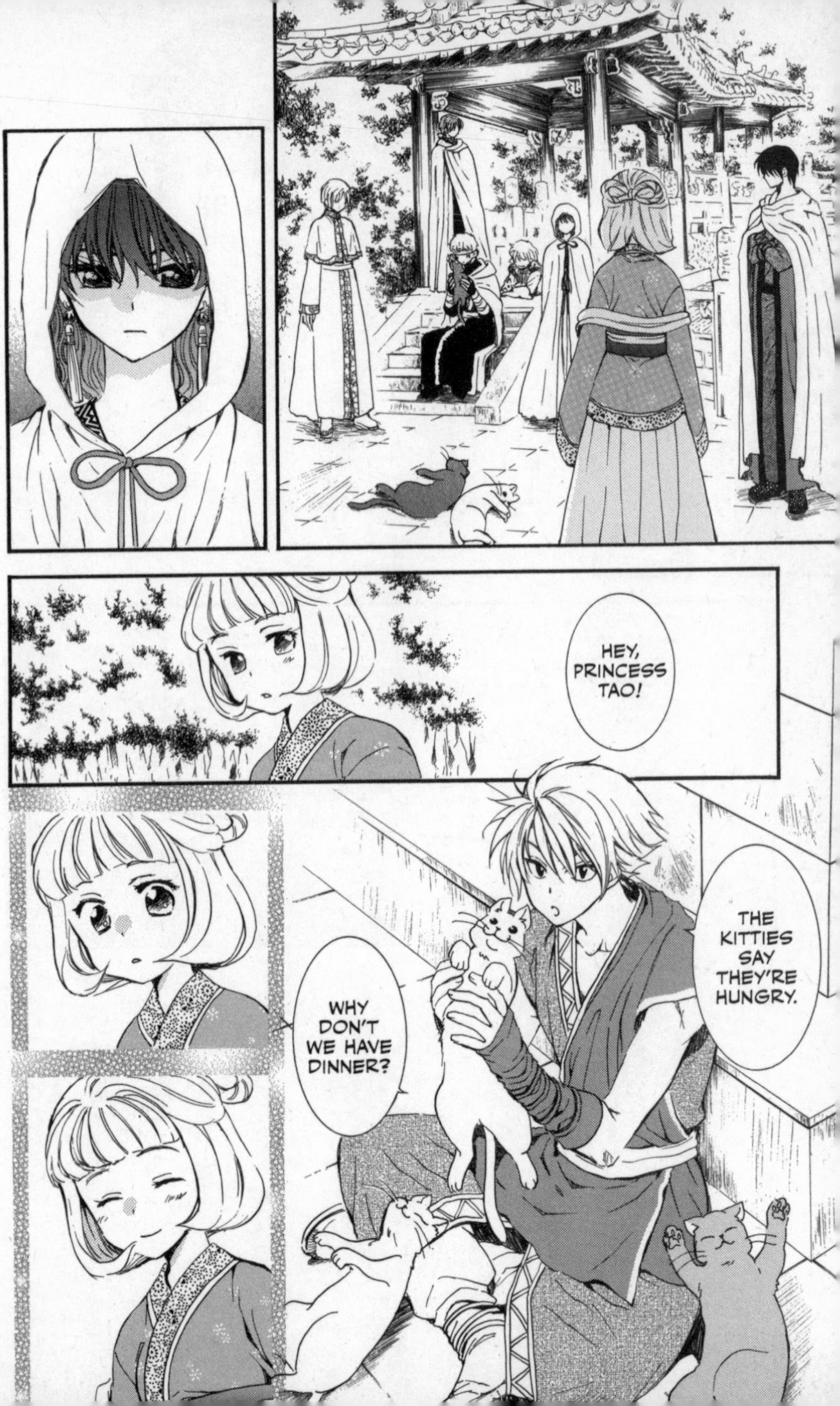
HEY, PRINCESS TAO!
THE KITTIES SAY THEY'RE HUNGRY.
WHY DON'T WE HAVE DINNER?

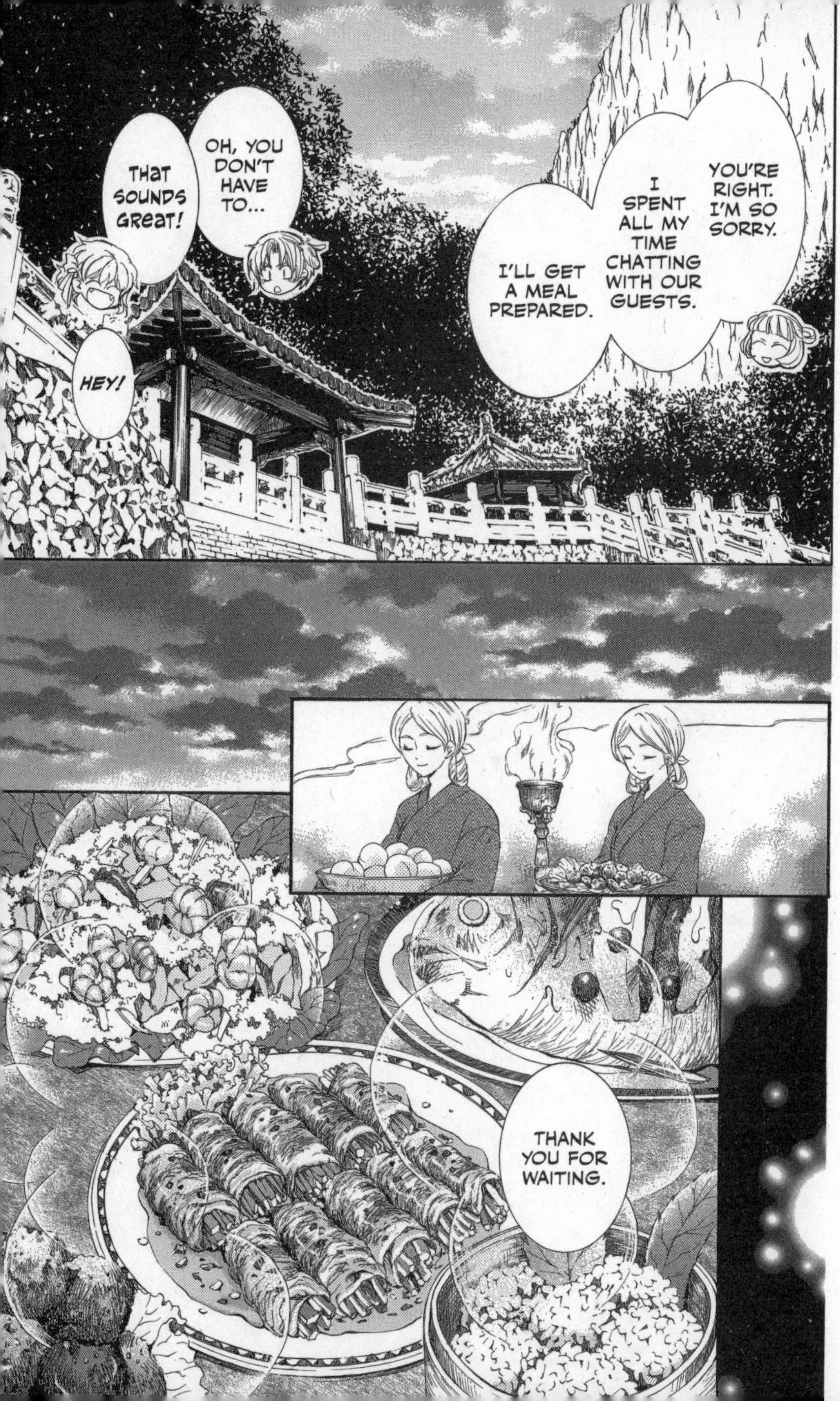
YOU'RE RIGHT. I'M SO SORRY.
I SPENT ALL MY TIME CHATTING WITH OUR GUESTS.
I'LL GET A MEAL PREPARED.
OH, YOU DON'T HAVE TO...
THAT SOUNDS GREAT!
HEY!
THANK YOU FOR WAITING.

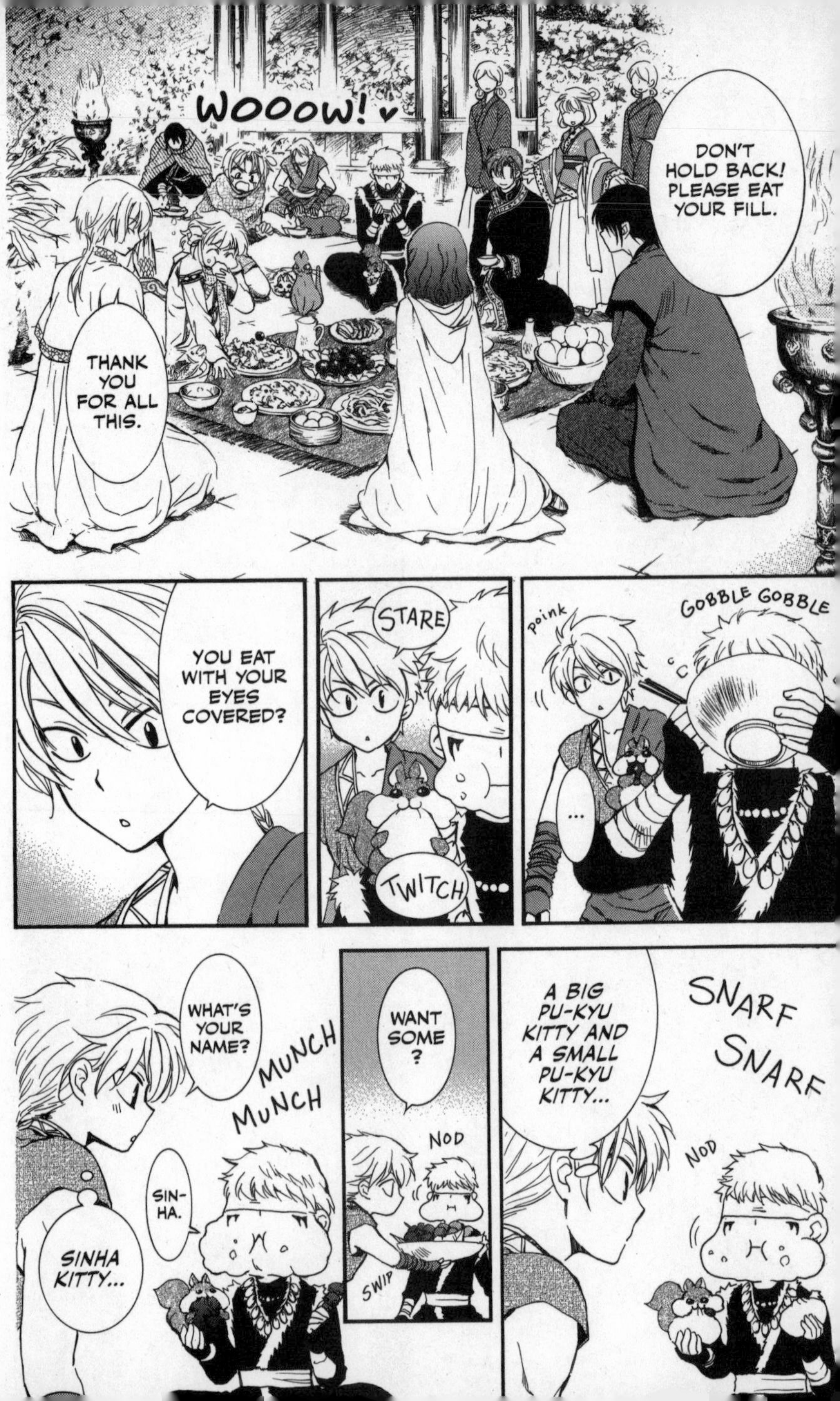
DON'T HOLD BACK! PLEASE EAT YOUR FILL.
WOOOW! ♥
THANK YOU FOR ALL THIS.
GOBBLE GOBBLE
poink
...
STARE
TWITCH
YOU EAT WITH YOUR EYES COVERED?
SNARF SNARF
A BIG PU-KYU KITTY AND A SMALL PU-KYU KITTY...
NOD
WANT SOME?
NOD
SWIP
WHAT'S YOUR NAME?
MUNCH MUNCH
SIN-HA.
SINHA KITTY...

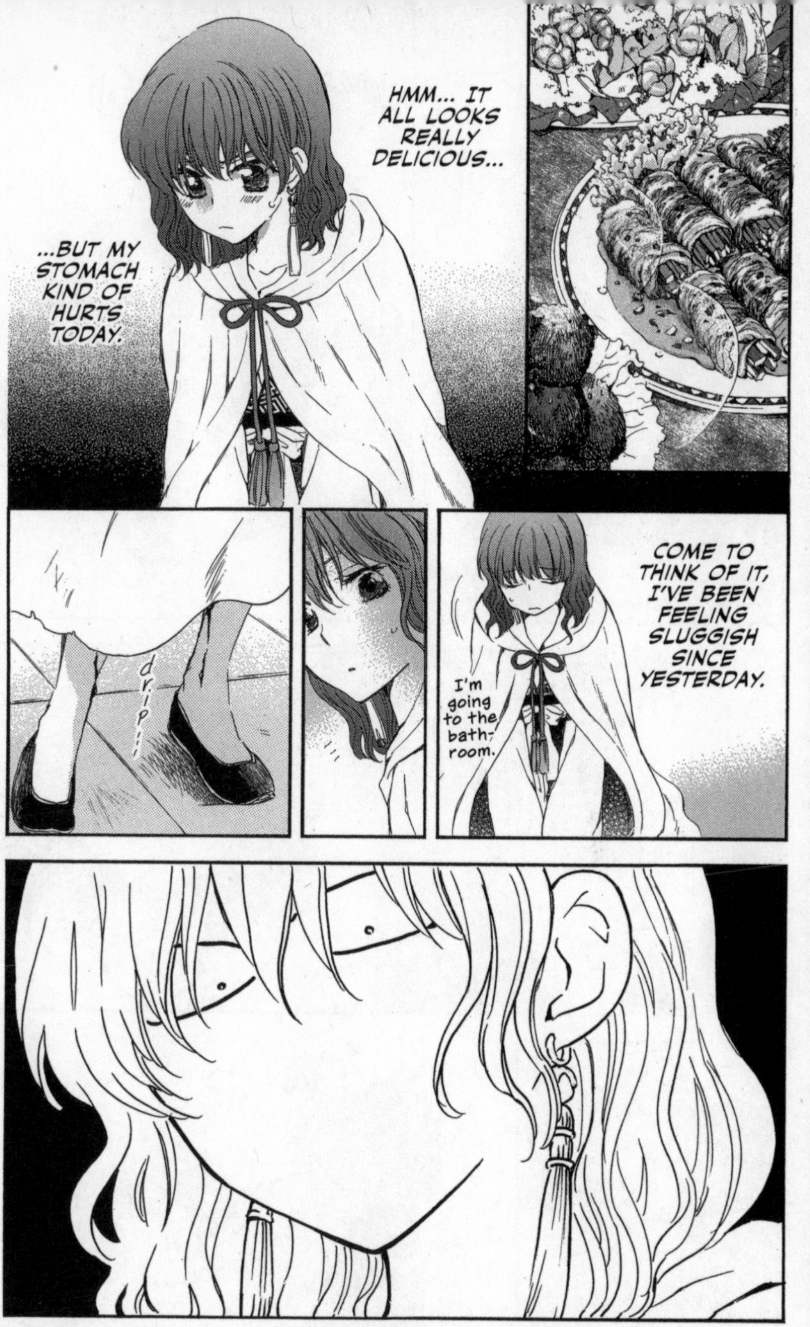
HMM... IT ALL LOOKS REALLY DELICIOUS...
...BUT MY STOMACH KIND OF HURTS TODAY.
COME TO THINK OF IT, I'VE BEEN FEELING SLUGGISH SINCE YESTERDAY.
I'm going to the bath-room.
drip...

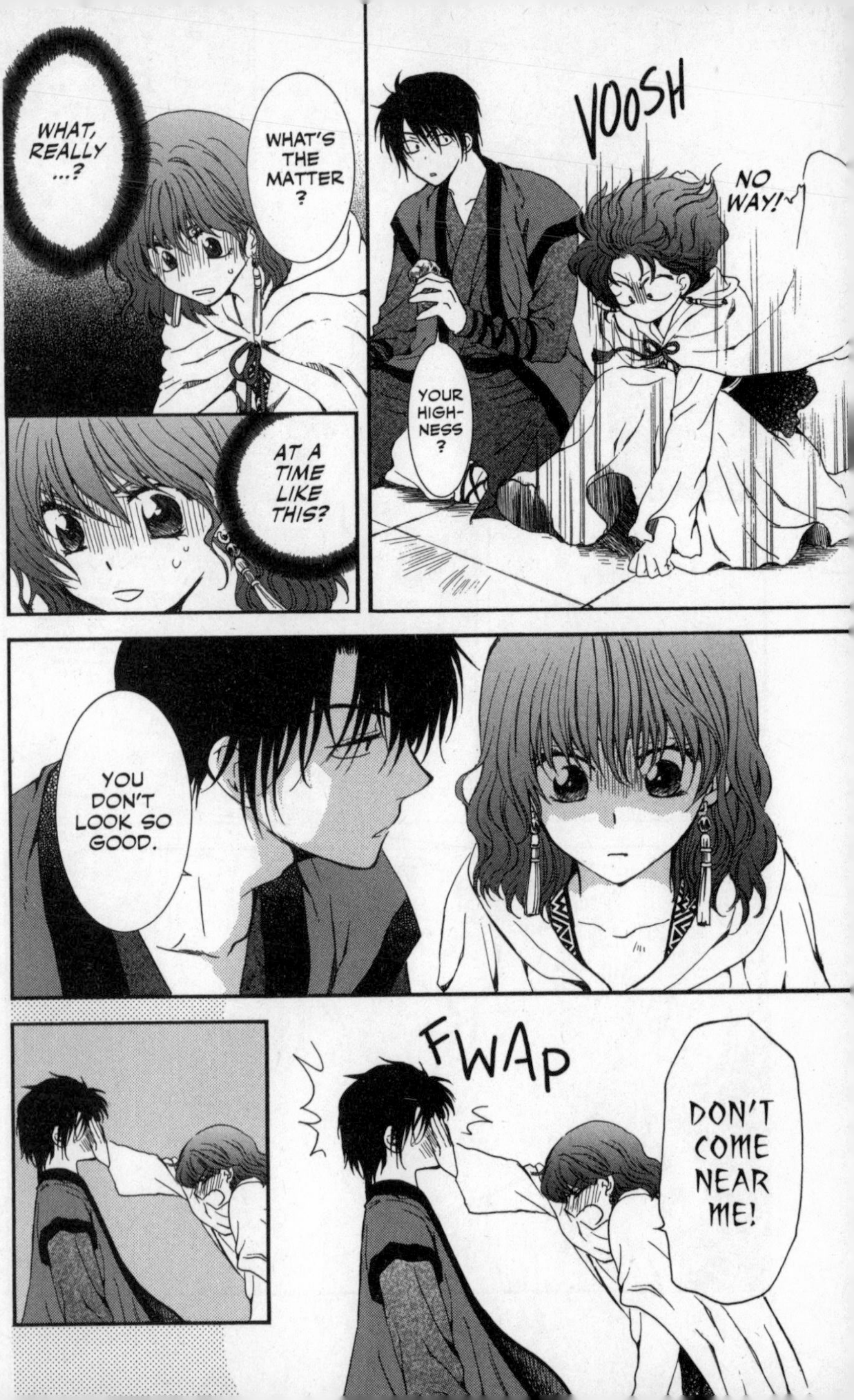
VOOSH
NO WAY!
YOUR HIGHNESS?
WHAT'S THE MATTER?
WHAT, REALLY ...?
AT A TIME LIKE THIS?
YOU DON'T LOOK SO GOOD.
FWAP
DON'T COME NEAR ME!

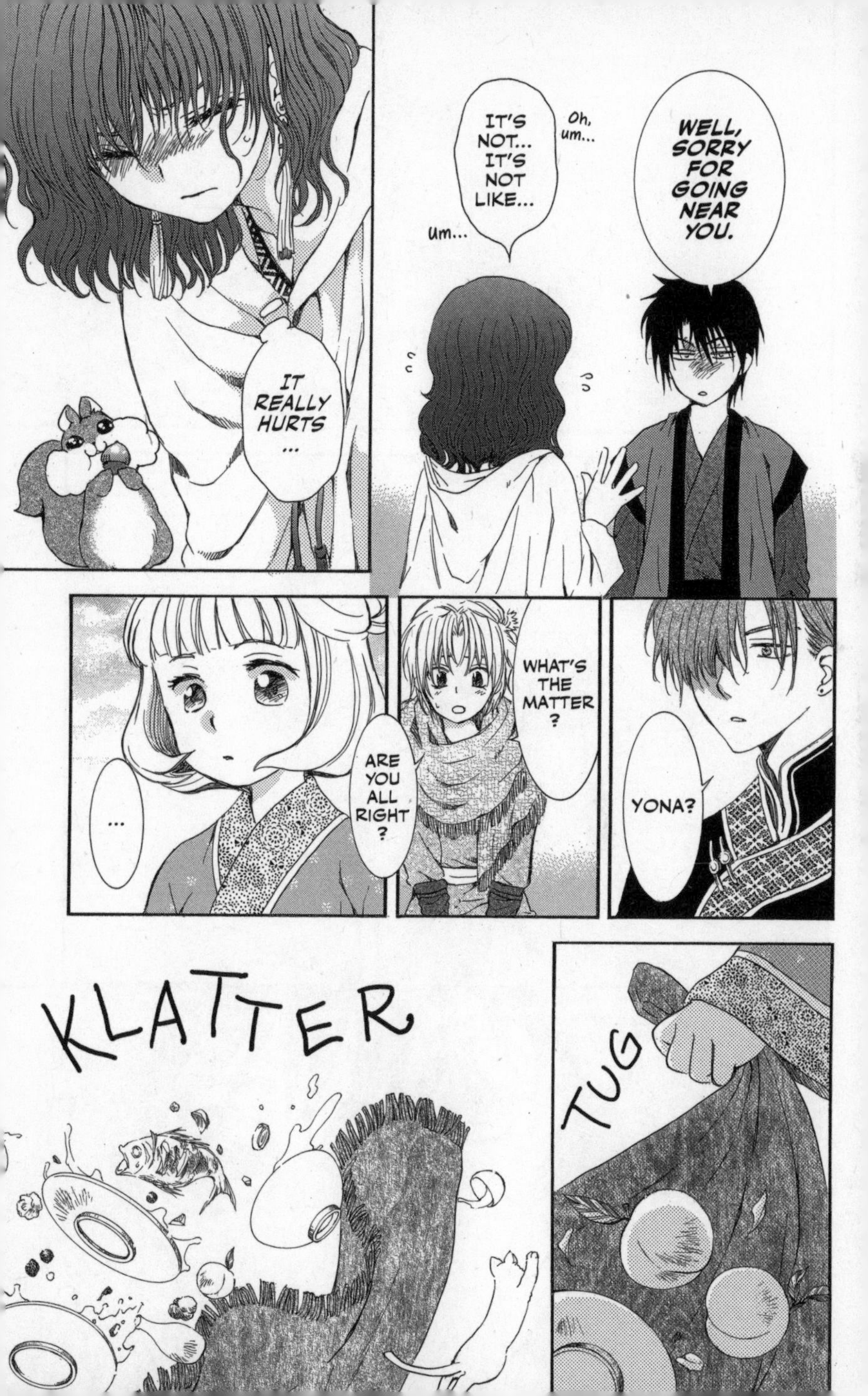
WELL, SORRY FOR GOING NEAR YOU.
Oh, um...
IT'S NOT... IT'S NOT LIKE...
um...
IT REALLY HURTS ...
YONA?
WHAT'S THE MATTER?
ARE YOU ALL RIGHT?
...
TUG
KLATTER

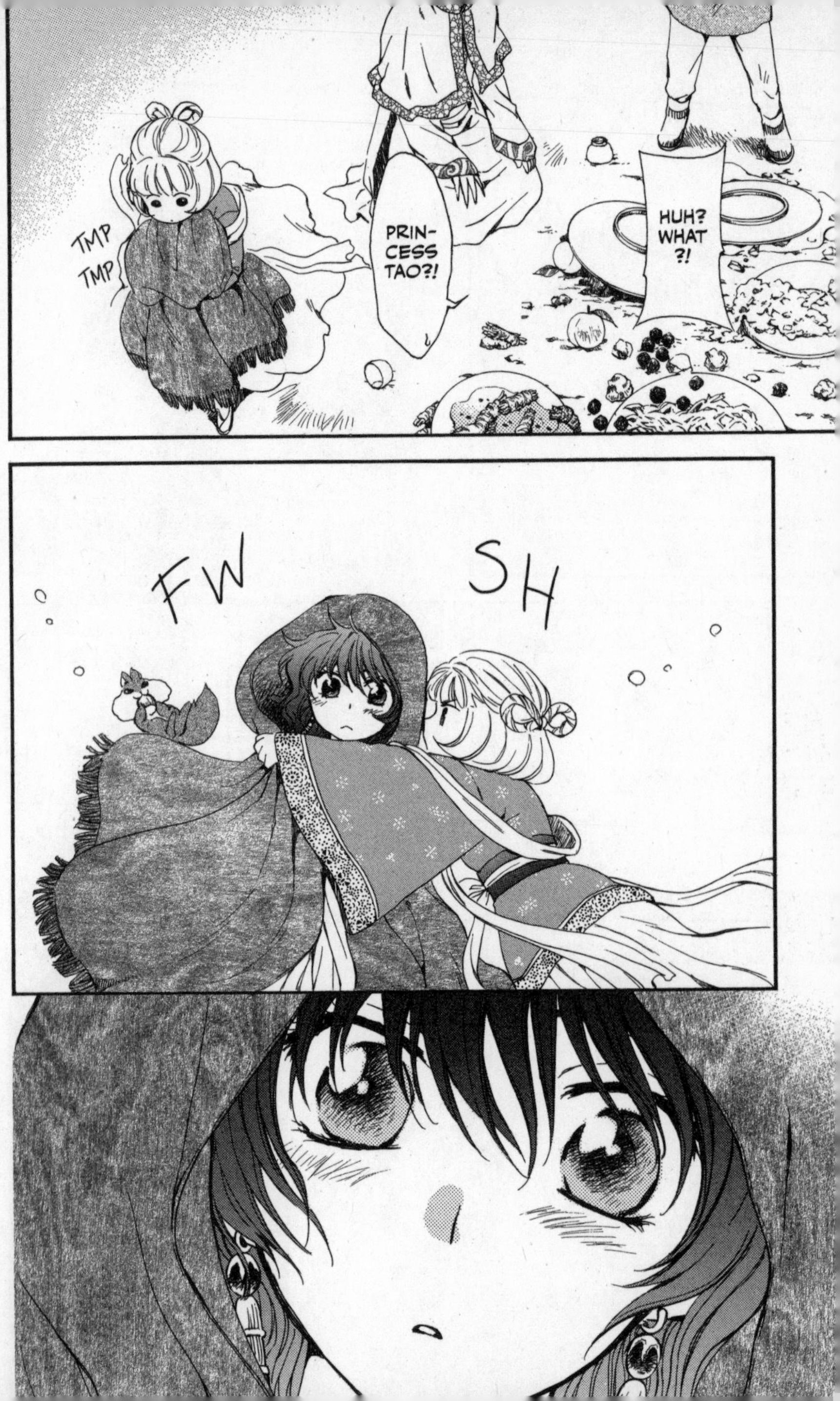
HUH? WHAT?!
PRIN-CESS TAO?!
TMP TMP
FWSH

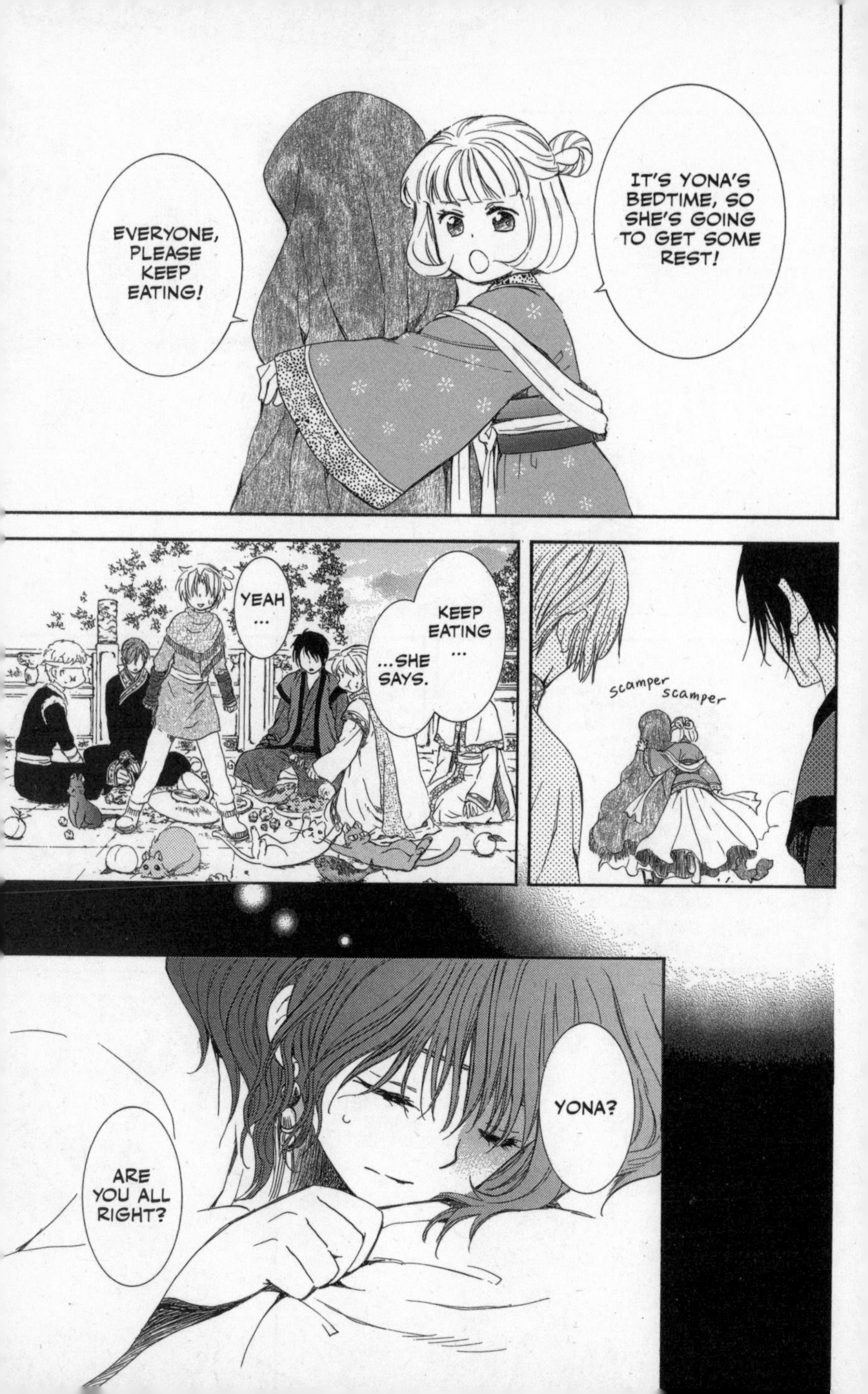
IT'S YONA'S BEDTIME, SO SHE'S GOING TO GET SOME REST!
EVERYONE, PLEASE KEEP EATING!
scamper scamper
KEEP EATING ...
...SHE SAYS.
YEAH ...
YONA?
ARE YOU ALL RIGHT?

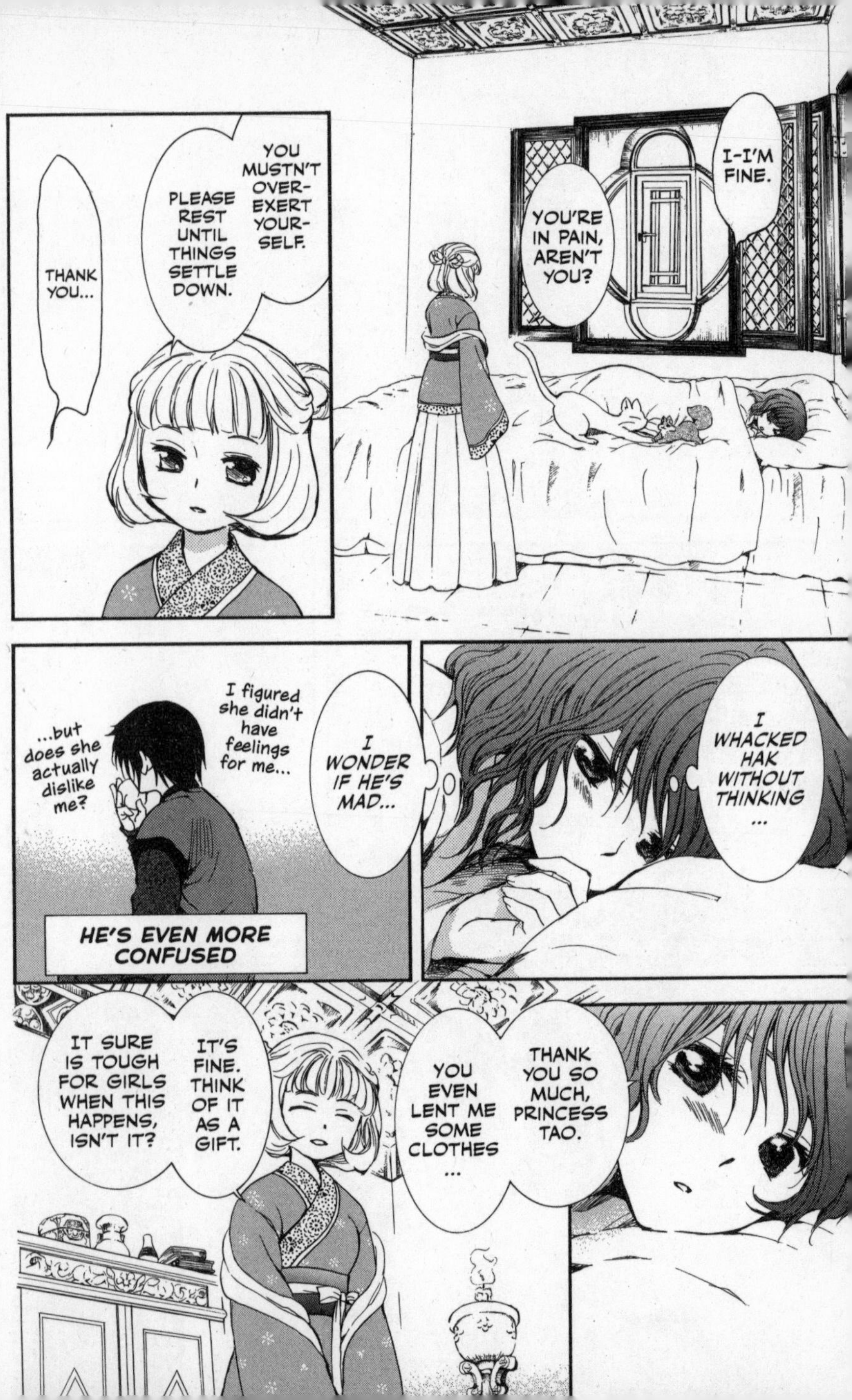
I-I'M FINE.
YOU'RE IN PAIN, AREN'T YOU?
YOU MUSTN'T OVER-EXERT YOUR-SELF.
PLEASE REST UNTIL THINGS SETTLE DOWN.
THANK YOU...
I WHACKED HAK WITHOUT THINKING...
I WONDER IF HE'S MAD...
I figured she didn't have feelings for me...
...but does she actually dislike me?
HE'S EVEN MORE CONFUSED
THANK YOU SO MUCH, PRINCESS TAO.
YOU EVEN LENT ME SOME CLOTHES...
IT'S FINE. THINK OF IT AS A GIFT.
IT SURE IS TOUGH FOR GIRLS WHEN THIS HAPPENS, ISN'T IT?

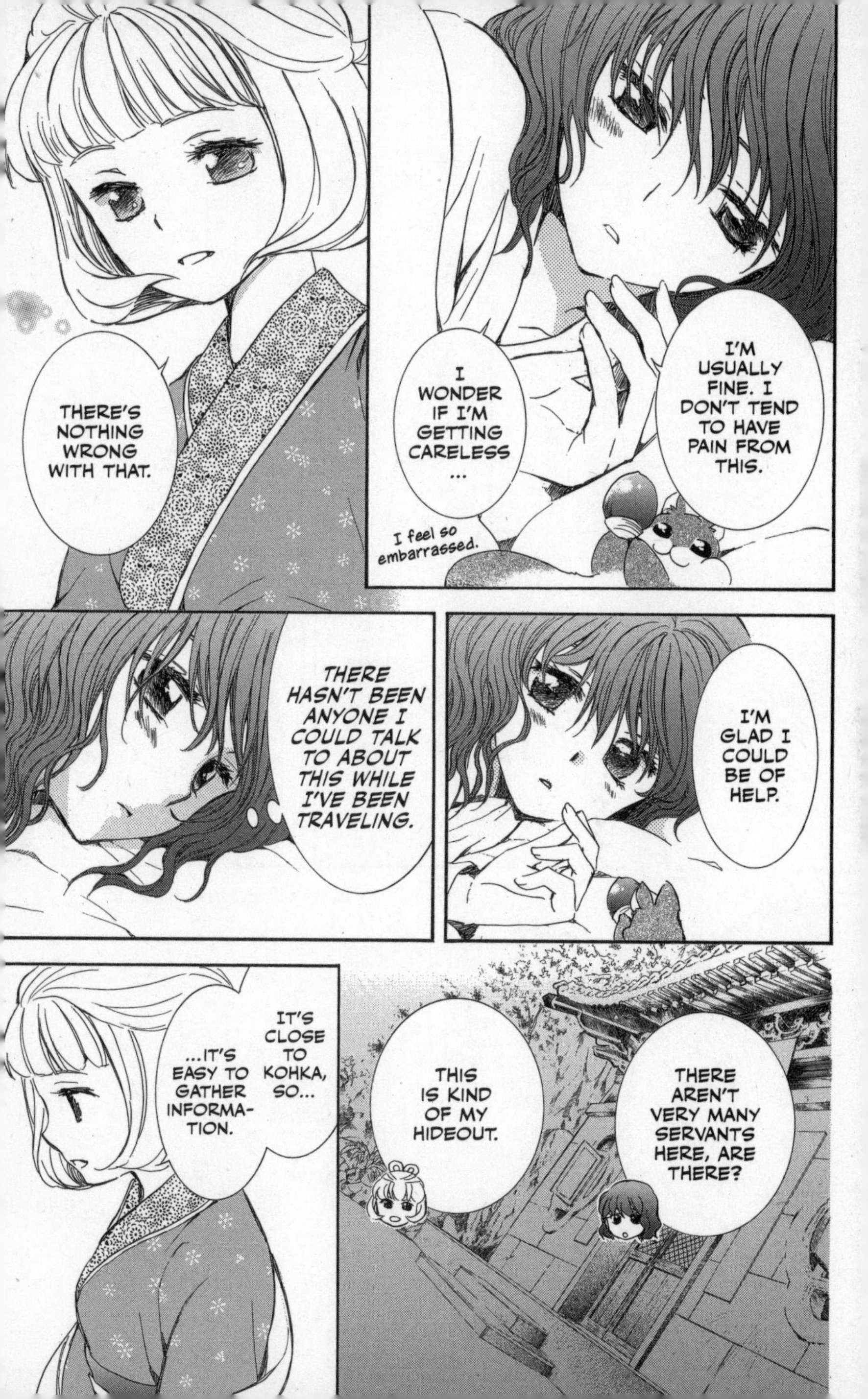
I'M USUALLY FINE. I DON'T TEND TO HAVE PAIN FROM THIS.
I WONDER IF I'M GETTING CARELESS...
I feel so embarrassed.
THERE'S NOTHING WRONG WITH THAT.
I'M GLAD I COULD BE OF HELP.
THERE HASN'T BEEN ANYONE I COULD TALK TO ABOUT THIS WHILE I'VE BEEN TRAVELING.
THERE AREN'T VERY MANY SERVANTS HERE, ARE THERE?
THIS IS KIND OF MY HIDEOUT.
IT'S CLOSE TO KOHKA, SO...
...IT'S EASY TO GATHER INFORMA-TION.

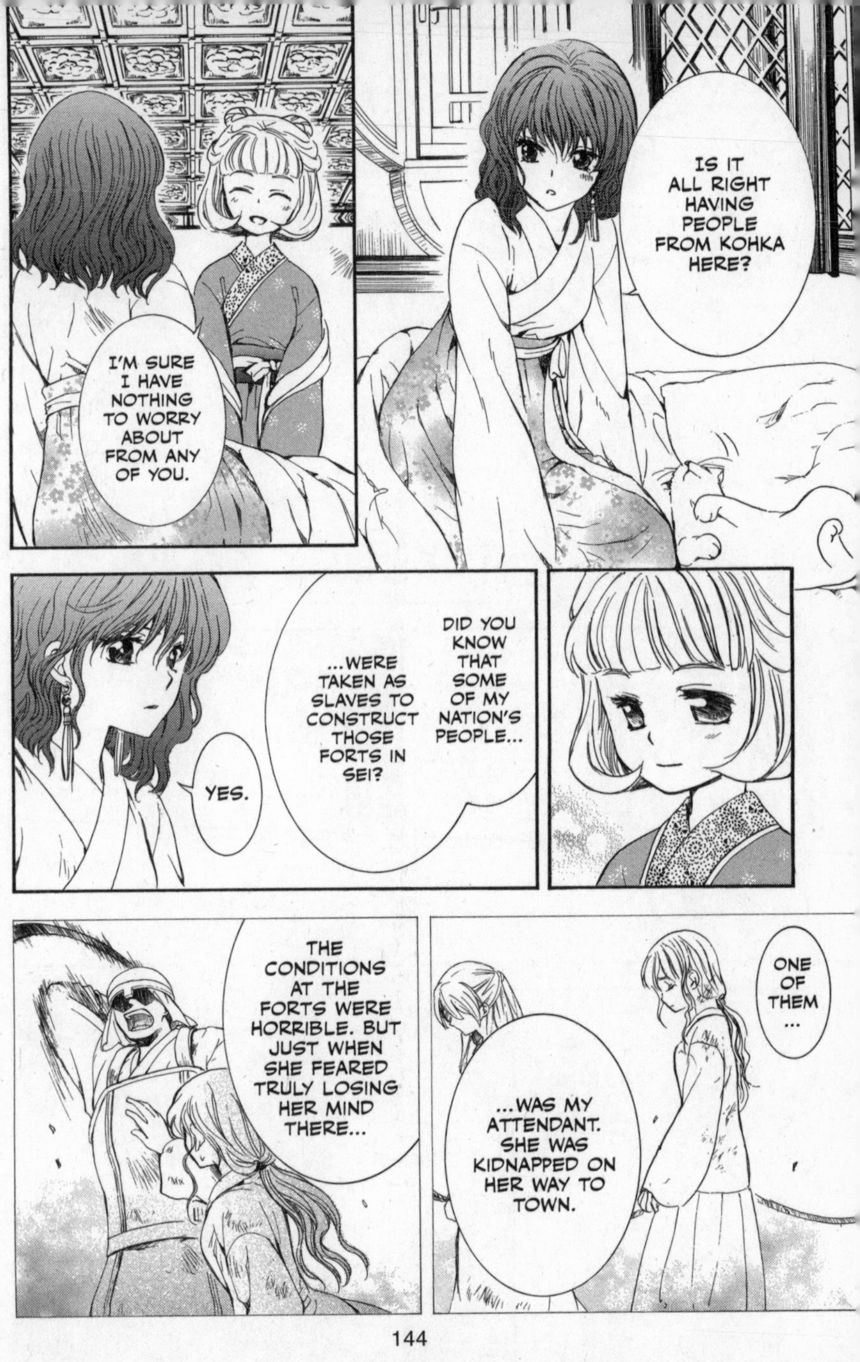
IS IT ALL RIGHT HAVING PEOPLE FROM KOHKA HERE?
I'M SURE I HAVE NOTHING TO WORRY ABOUT FROM ANY OF YOU.
DID YOU KNOW THAT SOME OF MY NATION'S PEOPLE...
...WERE TAKEN AS SLAVES TO CONSTRUCT THOSE FORTS IN SEI?
YES.
ONE OF THEM ...
...WAS MY ATTENDANT. SHE WAS KIDNAPPED ON HER WAY TO TOWN.
THE CONDITIONS AT THE FORTS WERE HORRIBLE. BUT JUST WHEN SHE FEARED TRULY LOSING HER MIND THERE...

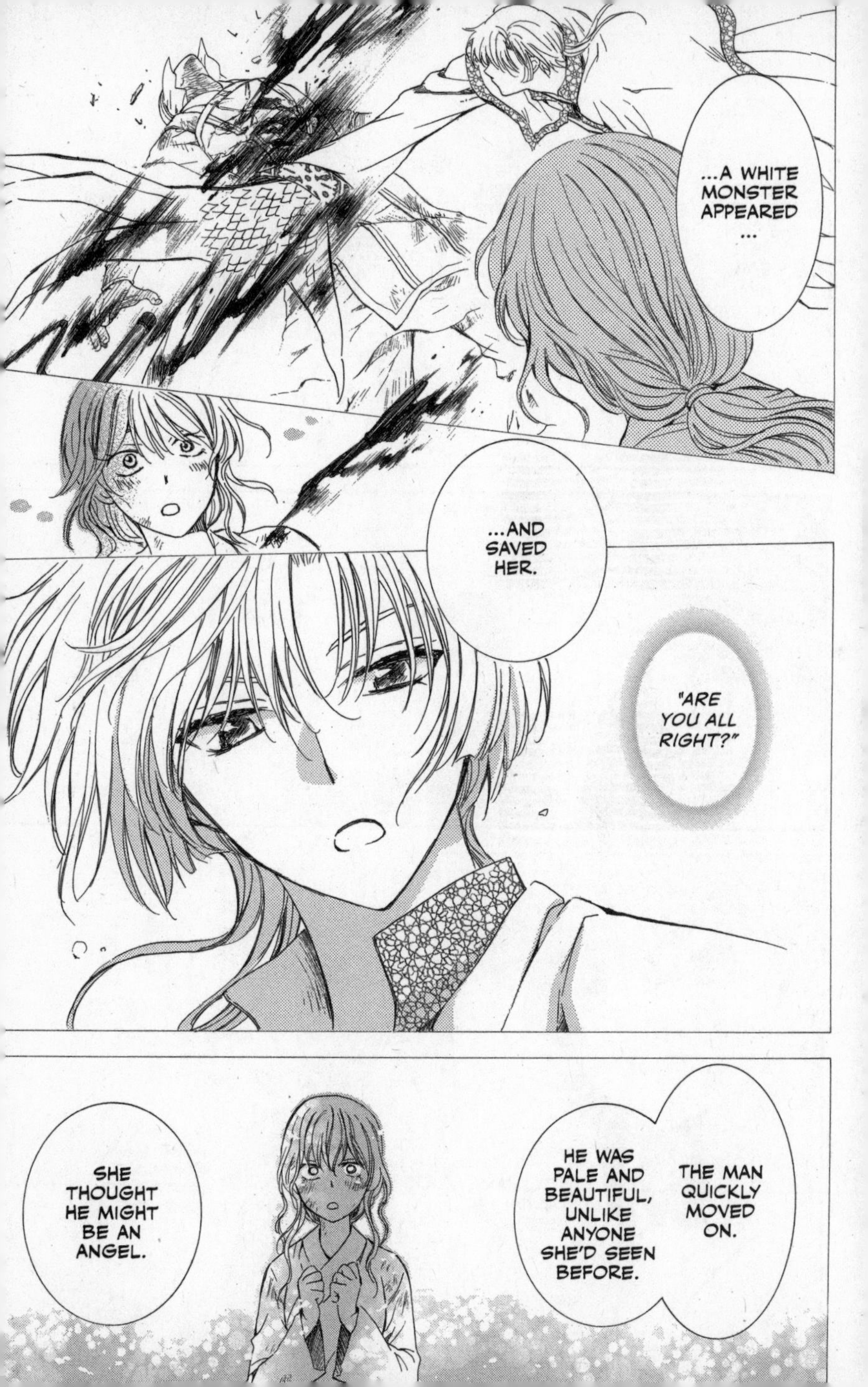
...A WHITE MONSTER APPEARED ...
...AND SAVED HER.
"ARE YOU ALL RIGHT?"
THE MAN QUICKLY MOVED ON.
HE WAS PALE AND BEAUTIFUL, UNLIKE ANYONE SHE'D SEEN BEFORE.
SHE THOUGHT HE MIGHT BE AN ANGEL.

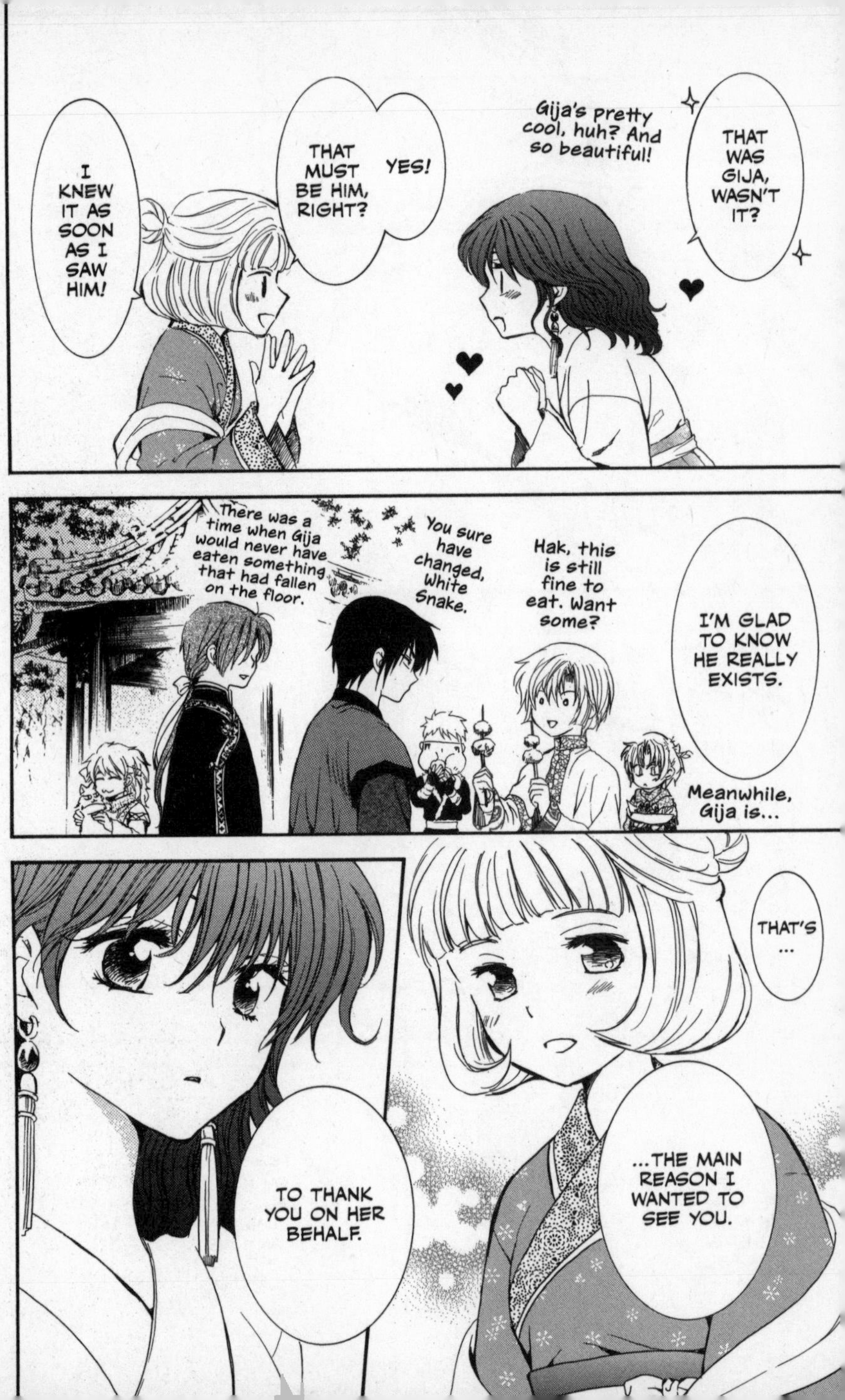
THAT WAS GIJA, WASN'T IT?
Gija's pretty cool, huh? And so beautiful!
YES!
THAT MUST BE HIM, RIGHT?
I KNEW IT AS SOON AS I SAW HIM!
I'M GLAD TO KNOW HE REALLY EXISTS.
Meanwhile, Gija is...
Hak, this is still fine to eat. Want some?
You sure have changed, White Snake.
There was a time when Gija would never have eaten something that had fallen on the floor.
THAT'S ...
...THE MAIN REASON I WANTED TO SEE YOU.
TO THANK YOU ON HER BEHALF.

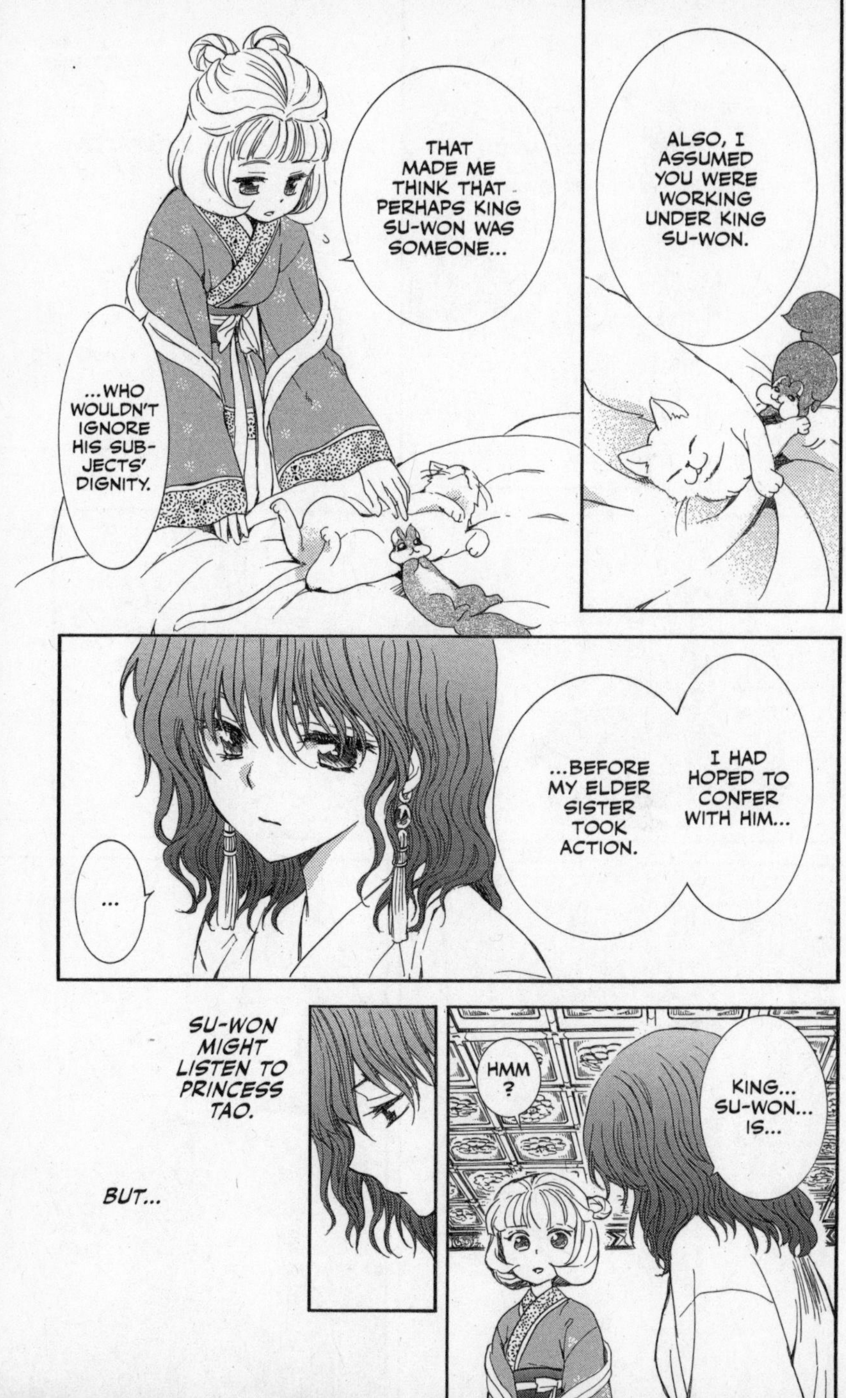
ALSO, I ASSUMED YOU WERE WORKING UNDER KING SU-WON.
THAT MADE ME THINK THAT PERHAPS KING SU-WON WAS SOMEONE...
...WHO WOULDN'T IGNORE HIS SUB-JECTS' DIGNITY.
I HAD HOPED TO CONFER WITH HIM...
...BEFORE MY ELDER SISTER TOOK ACTION.
...
KING... SU-WON... IS...
HMM?
SU-WON MIGHT LISTEN TO PRINCESS TAO.
BUT...

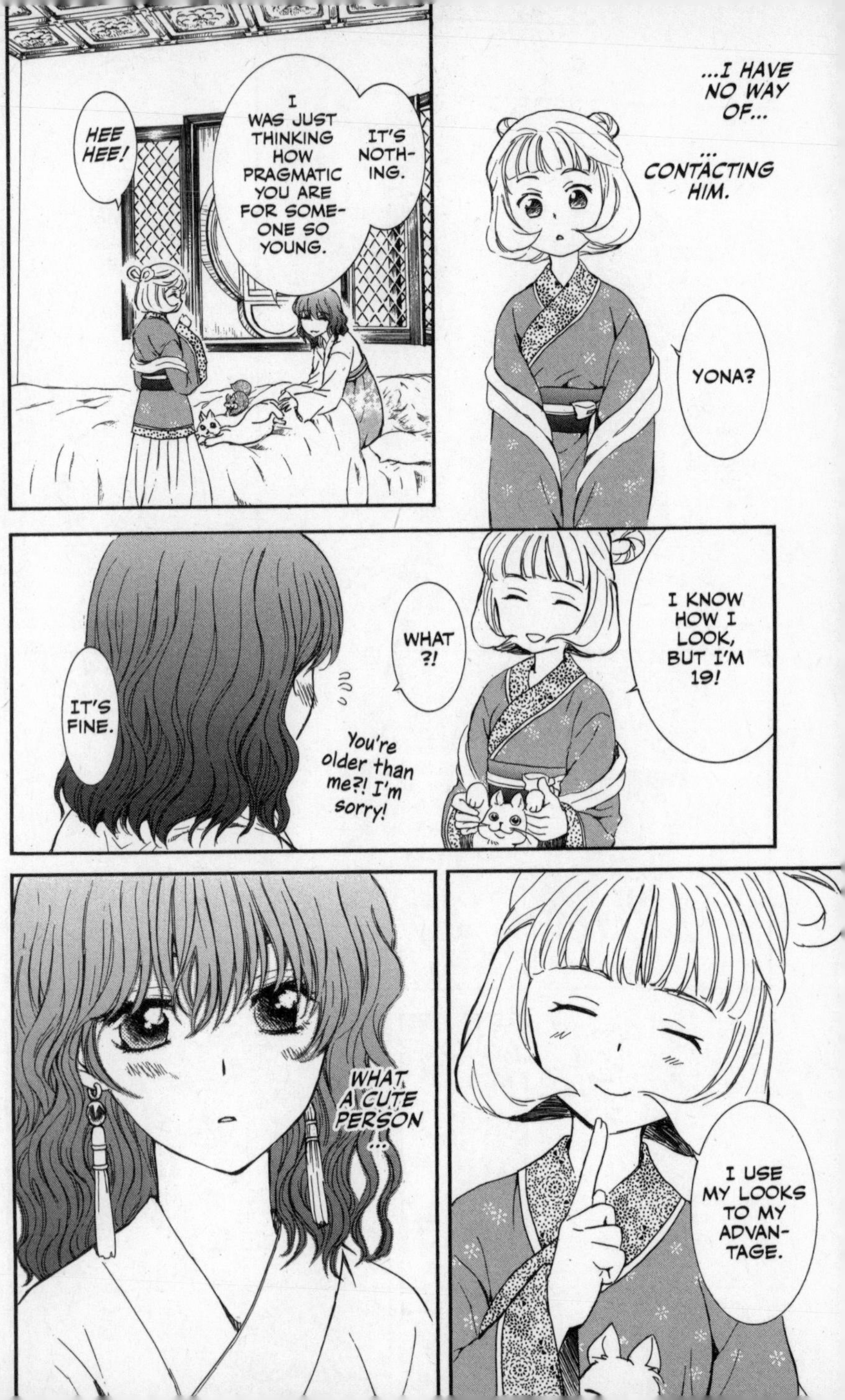
...I HAVE NO WAY OF...
... CONTACTING HIM.
YONA?
IT'S NOTH-ING.
I WAS JUST THINKING HOW PRAGMATIC YOU ARE FOR SOME-ONE SO YOUNG.
HEE HEE!
I KNOW HOW I LOOK, BUT I'M 19!
WHAT ?!
You're older than me?! I'm sorry!
IT'S FINE.
I USE MY LOOKS TO MY ADVAN-TAGE.
WHAT A CUTE PERSON ...

The Zeno arc OAD was made to be a two-parter. When the Zeno arc was published, I had no idea I'd someday get to see the original Four Dragon Warriors, the Crimson Dragon King and Kaya moving and speaking in an anime. I'm so very thankful. During that time, I was worried about whether people would enjoy the story of Zeno's past without Yona, Hak and the other three Dragons, but my readers responded better to it than I expected and enjoyed the OAD. So I'm glad I went ahead with it! ^^

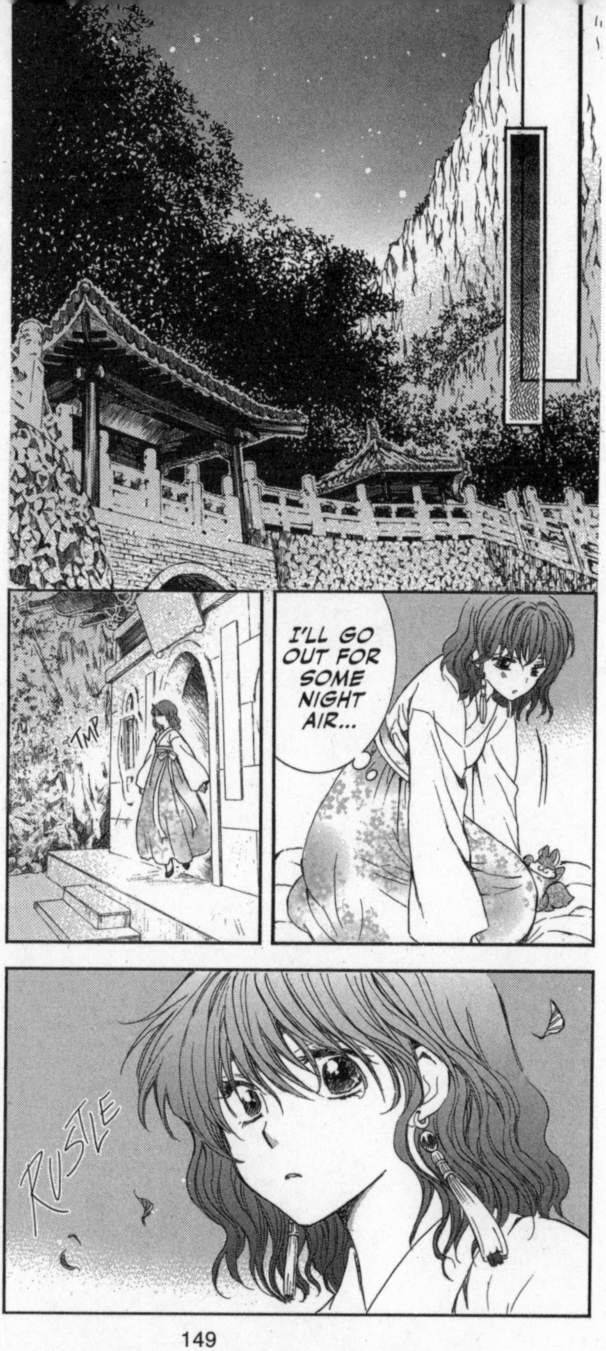
I'LL GO OUT FOR SOME NIGHT AIR...
TMP
RUSTLE

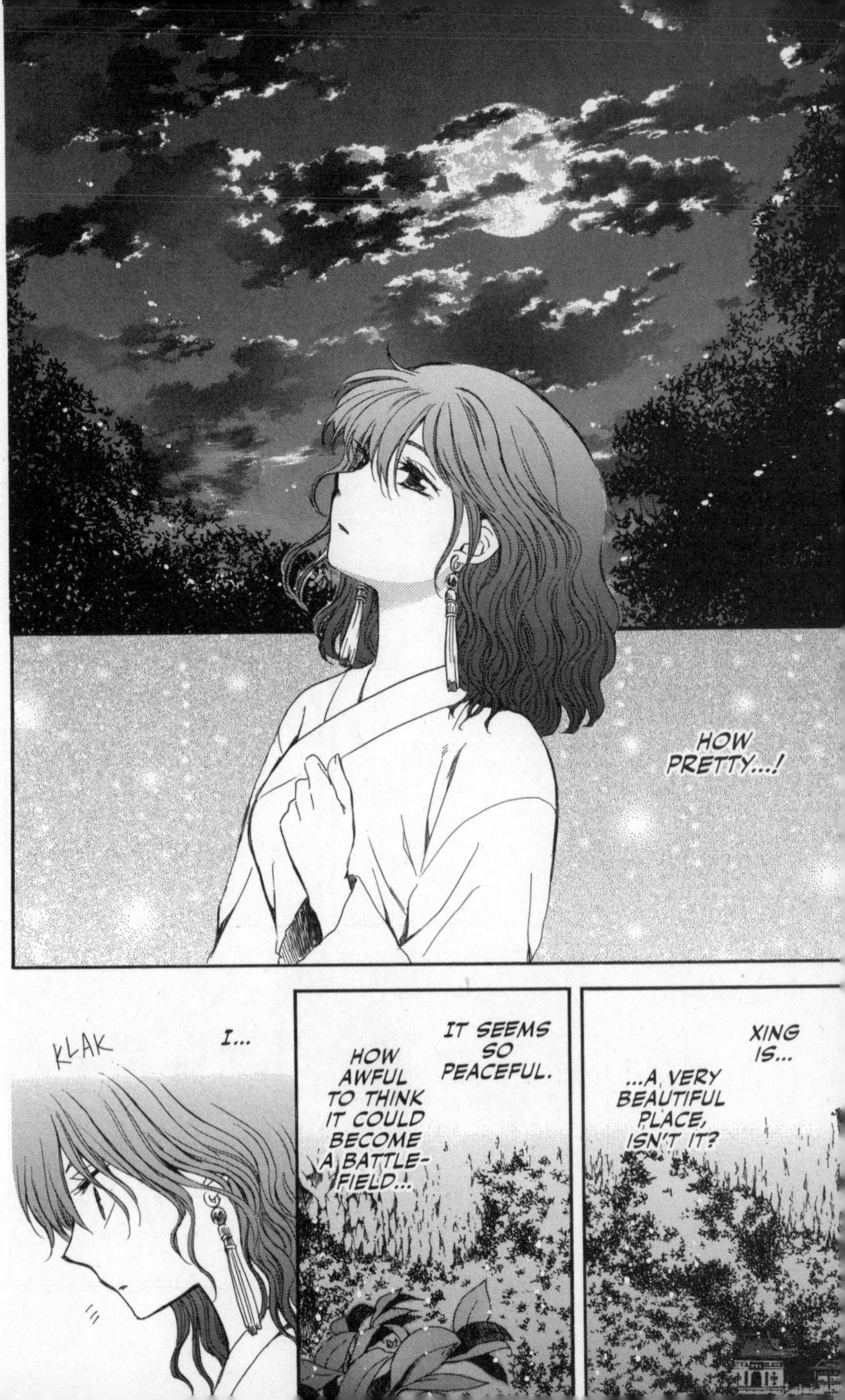
HOW PRETTY...!
XING IS...
...A VERY BEAUTIFUL PLACE, ISN'T IT?
IT SEEMS SO PEACEFUL.
HOW AWFUL TO THINK IT COULD BECOME A BATTLE-FIELD...
I...
KLAK

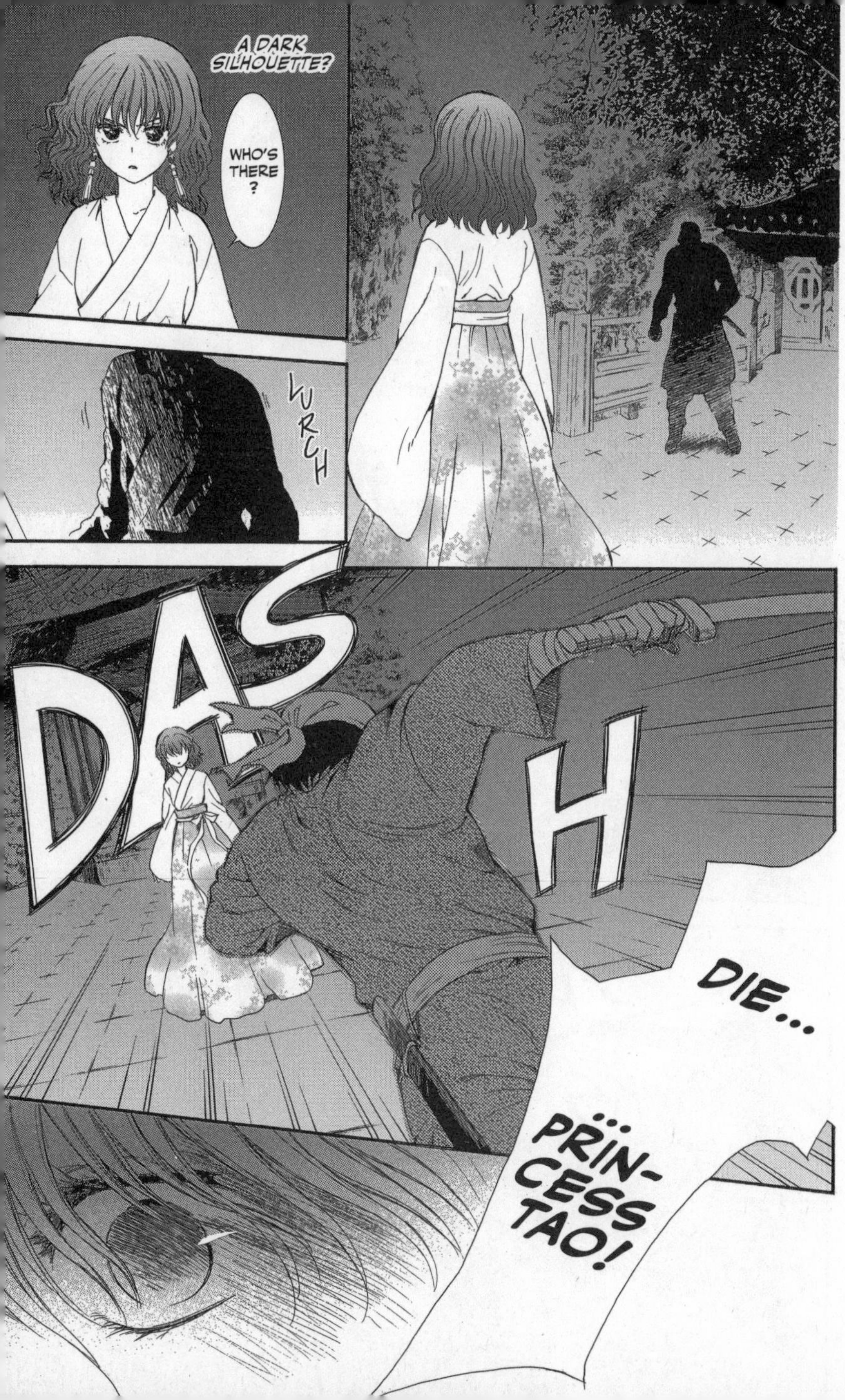
A DARK SILHOUETTE?
WHO'S THERE?
LURCH
DASH
DIE...
...PRIN-CESS TAO!

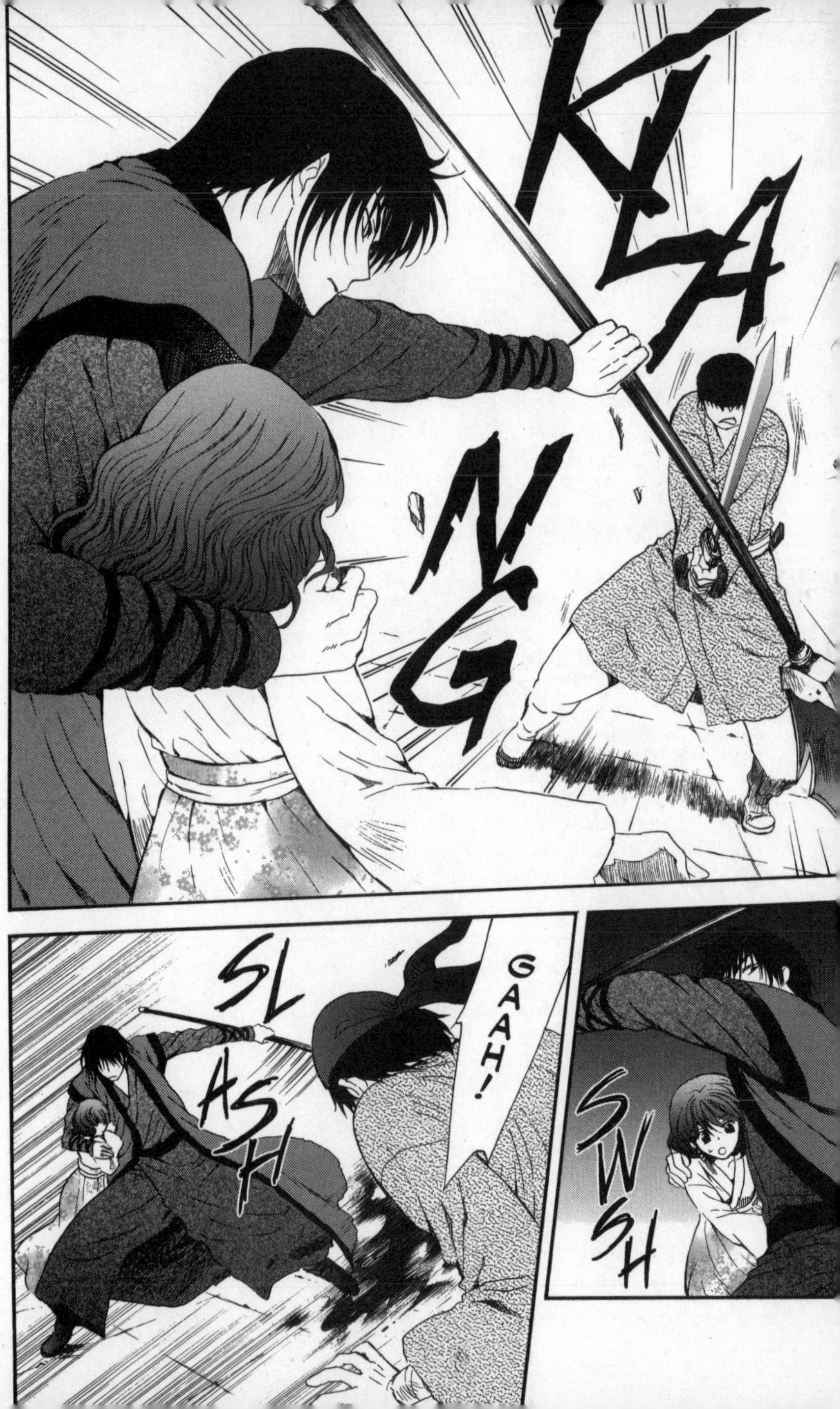
KLANG
SWSH
GAAH!
SLASH

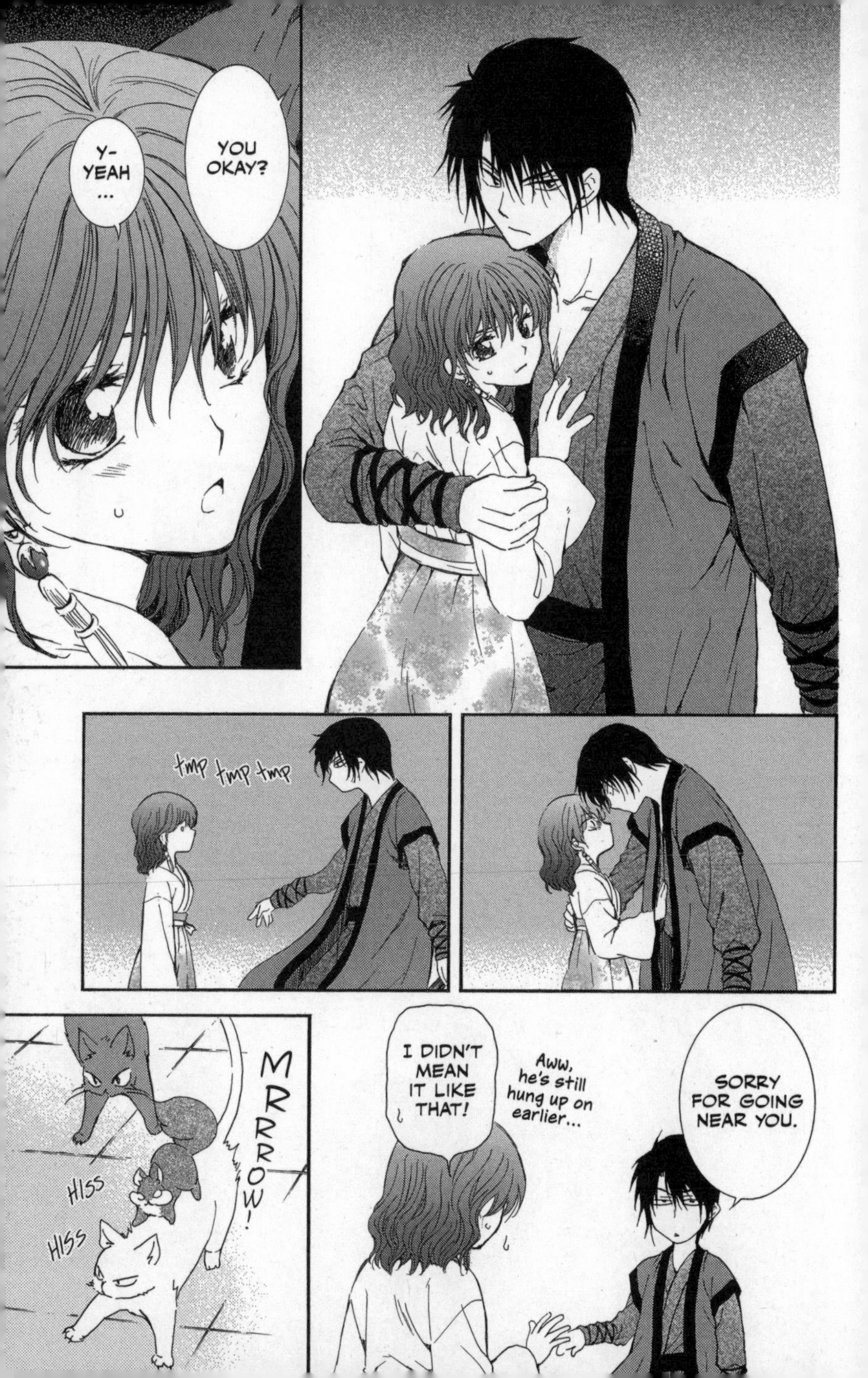
YOU OKAY?
Y-YEAH ...
tmp tmp tmp
SORRY FOR GOING NEAR YOU.
Aww, he's still hung up on earlier...
I DIDN'T MEAN IT LIKE THAT!
MRRROW!
HISS
HISS

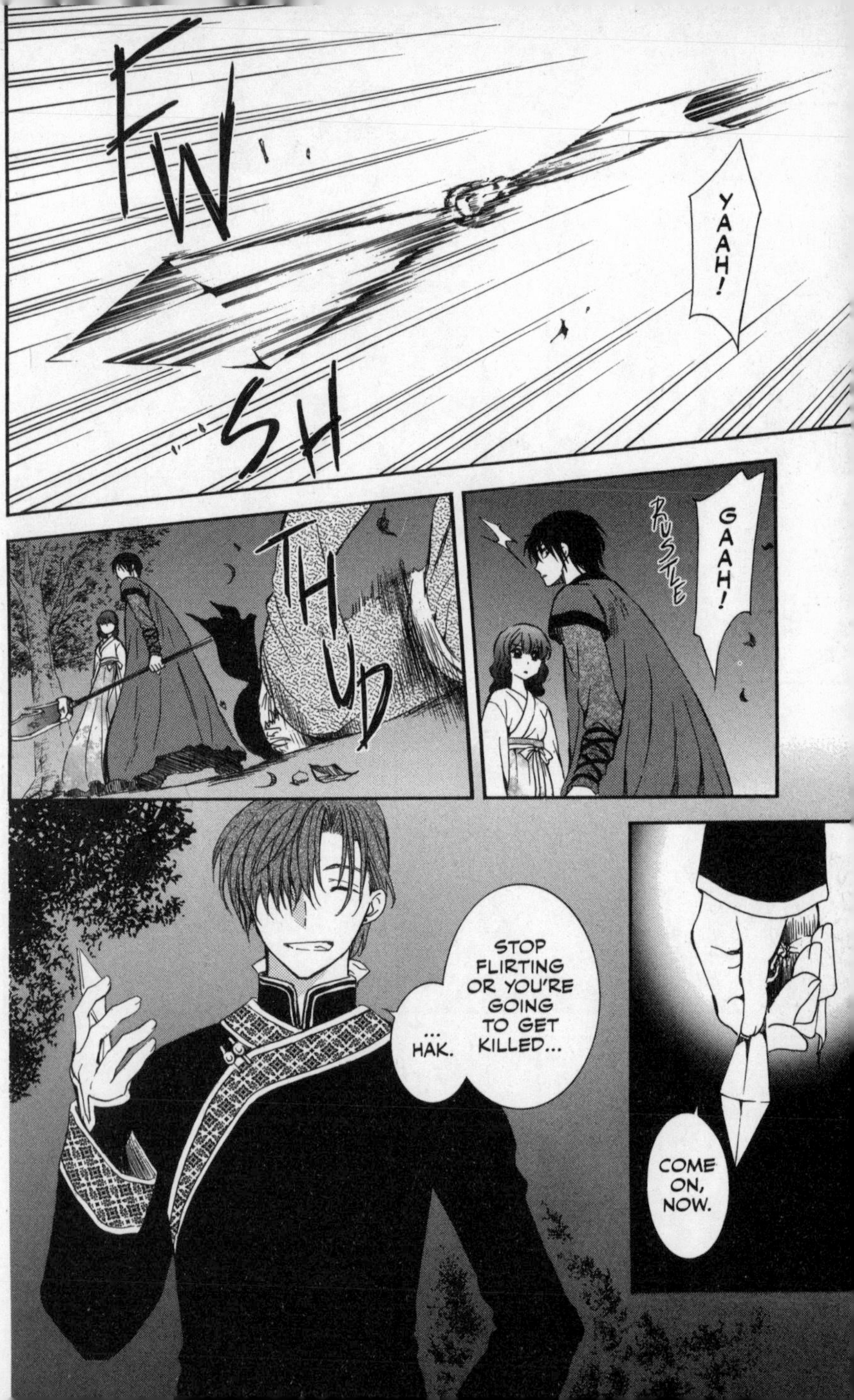
YAAH!
FW
SH
GAAH!
RUSTLE
THUD
COME ON, NOW.
STOP FLIRTING OR YOU'RE GOING TO GET KILLED...
... HAK.

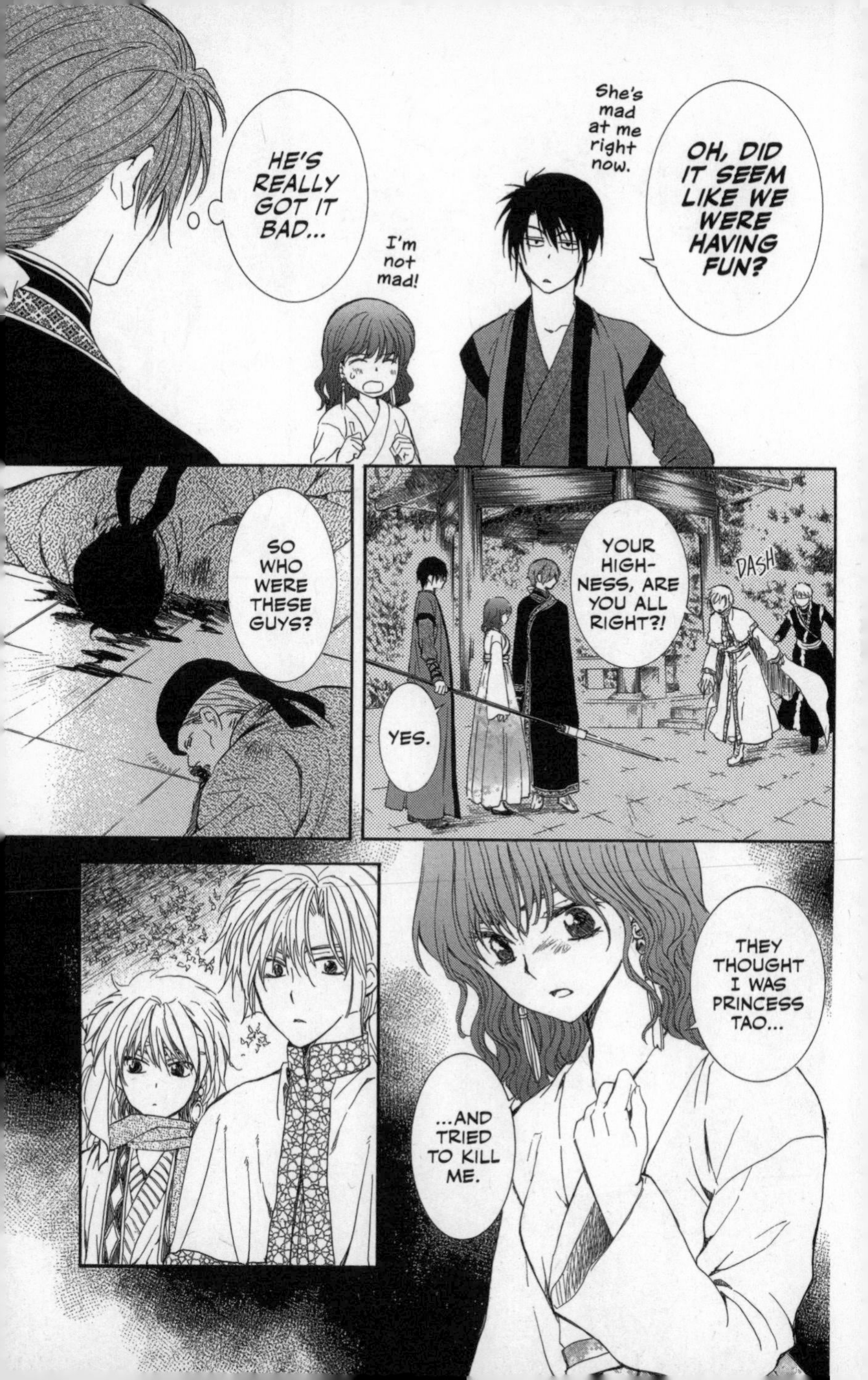
OH, DID IT SEEM LIKE WE WERE HAVING FUN?
She's mad at me right now.
I'm not mad!
HE'S REALLY GOT IT BAD...
DASH
YOUR HIGH-NESS, ARE YOU ALL RIGHT?!
YES.
SO WHO WERE THESE GUYS?
THEY THOUGHT I WAS PRINCESS TAO...
...AND TRIED TO KILL ME.

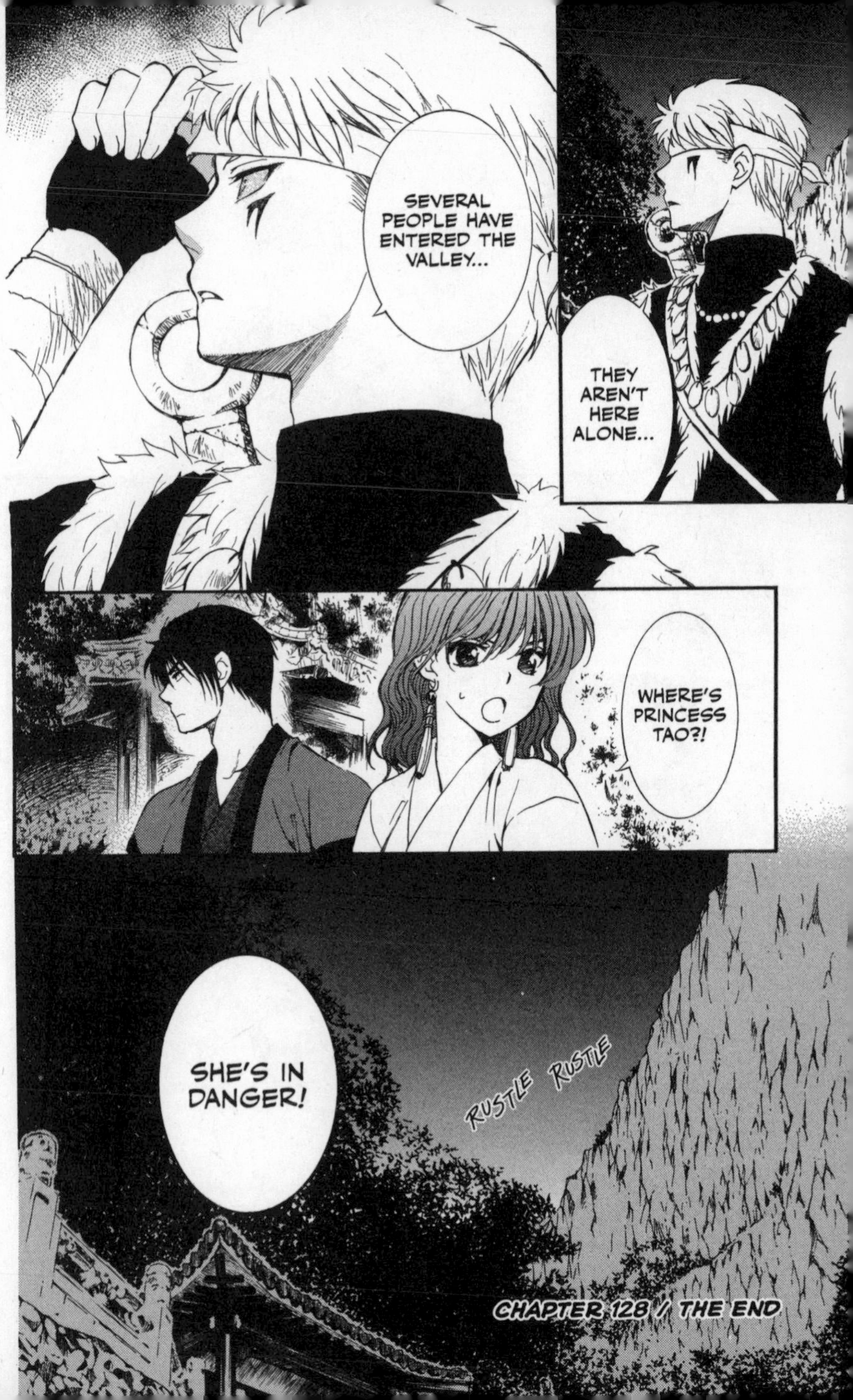
THEY AREN'T HERE ALONE...
SEVERAL PEOPLE HAVE ENTERED THE VALLEY...
WHERE'S PRINCESS TAO?!
RUSTLE RUSTLE
SHE'S IN DANGER!
CHAPTER 128 / THE END

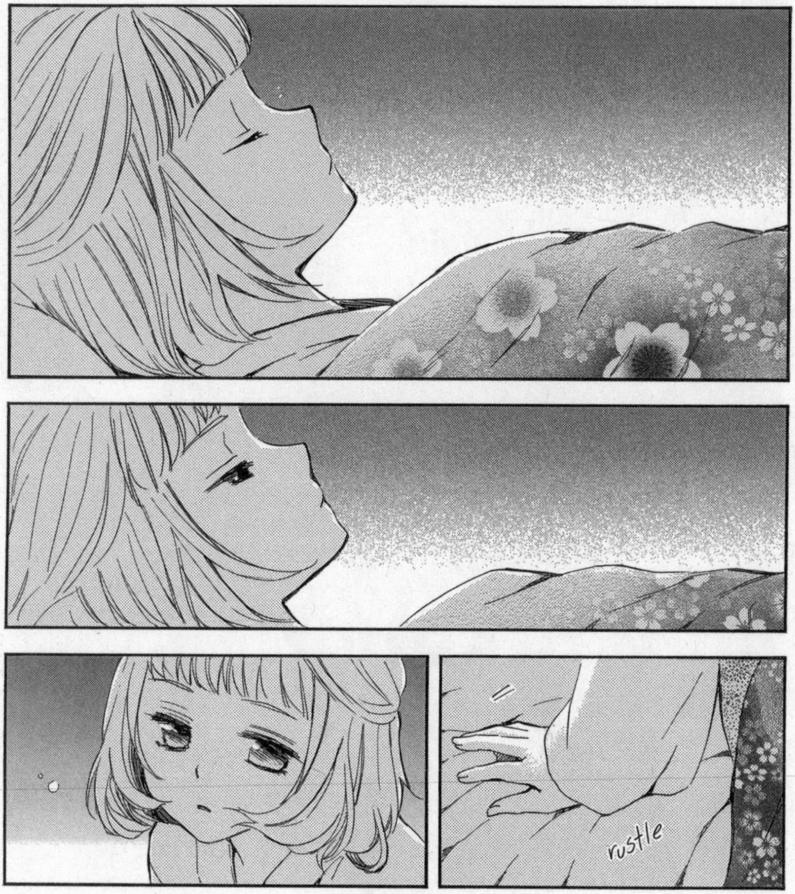
rustle

A special thanks!
My assistants → Mikorun, C.F., Ryo Sakura, Ryo, Awafuji, Oka, Eika
and my little sister...
My editor Tokushige, my previous editors and the *Hana to Yume* editorial office...
Everyone who's involved in creating and selling *Yona*-related merchandise...
My beloved family and friends who've always supported me.
And you, for reading this!
I'd also like to thank the director and staff who worked on the *Yona* anime!
I'm going to work as hard as I can while I still have energy!

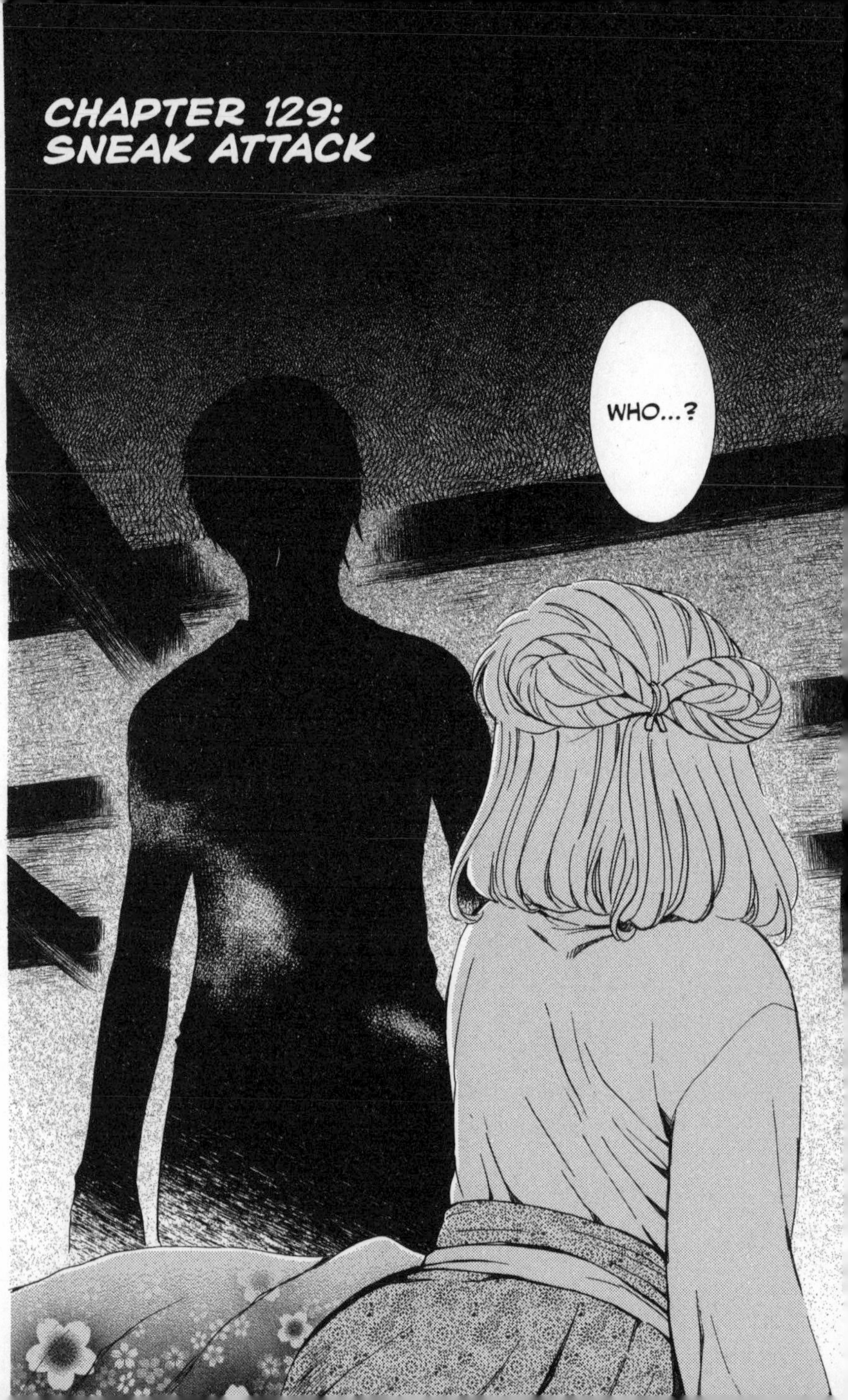
CHAPTER 129:
SNEAK ATTACK
WHO...?

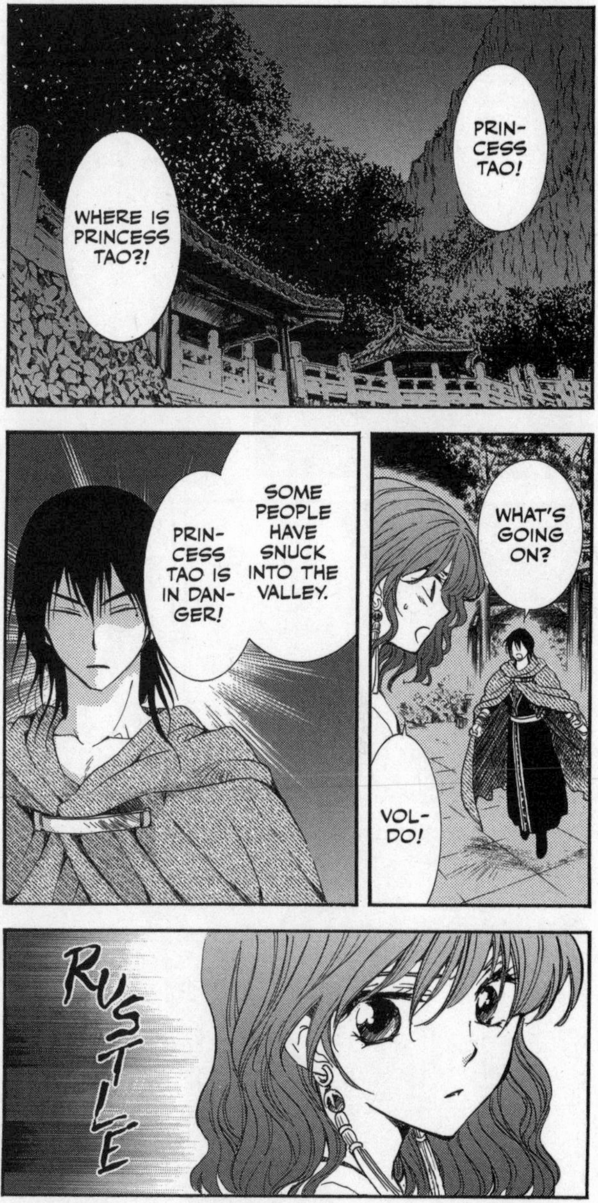
PRINCESS TAO!
WHERE IS PRINCESS TAO?!
WHAT'S GOING ON?
VOL-DO!
SOME PEOPLE HAVE SNUCK INTO THE VALLEY.
PRINCESS TAO IS IN DANGER!
RUSTLE

This year, I've been hooked on *Kodoku no Gurume*.* I don't really like eating meat unless it's ground up, but when Matsushige eats it, it looks so delicious. I also love Kusumi Sensei for his fun dialogue. I've bought seasons one through five on DVD and have watched them several times. ♥ Also, I especially love the TV talk show *Matsuko no Shiranai Sekai*, particularly the food episodes. (*Hee hee.*) I work industriously on my manuscript while watching both shows on an empty stomach. I draw some extra cover art and color drawings for *Hana to Yume* magazine. Please check them out!

Well, see you in volume 23!

*A TV SHOW ABOUT A TRAVELING SALESMAN WHO SAMPLES LOCAL CUISINE. YUTAKA MATSUSHIGE PLAYS THE MAIN CHARACTER. MASAYUKI KUSUMI IS THE AUTHOR OF THE MANGA.

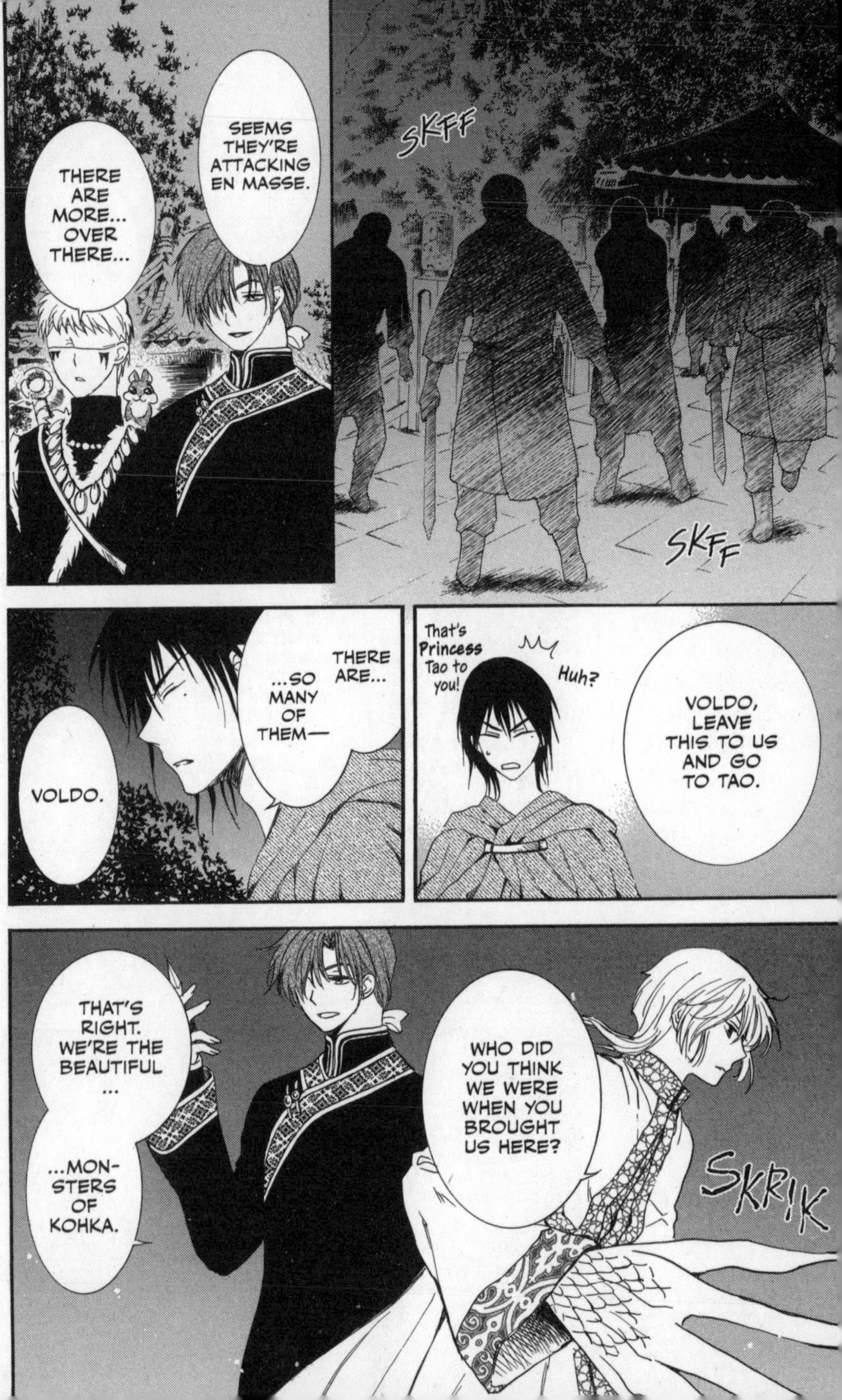
SKFF
SKFF
SEEMS THEY'RE ATTACKING EN MASSE.
THERE ARE MORE... OVER THERE...
VOLDO, LEAVE THIS TO US AND GO TO TAO.
Huh?
That's Princess Tao to you!
THERE ARE...
...SO MANY OF THEM—
VOLDO.
WHO DID YOU THINK WE WERE WHEN YOU BROUGHT US HERE?
SKRIK
THAT'S RIGHT. WE'RE THE BEAUTIFUL ...
...MONSTERS OF KOHKA.

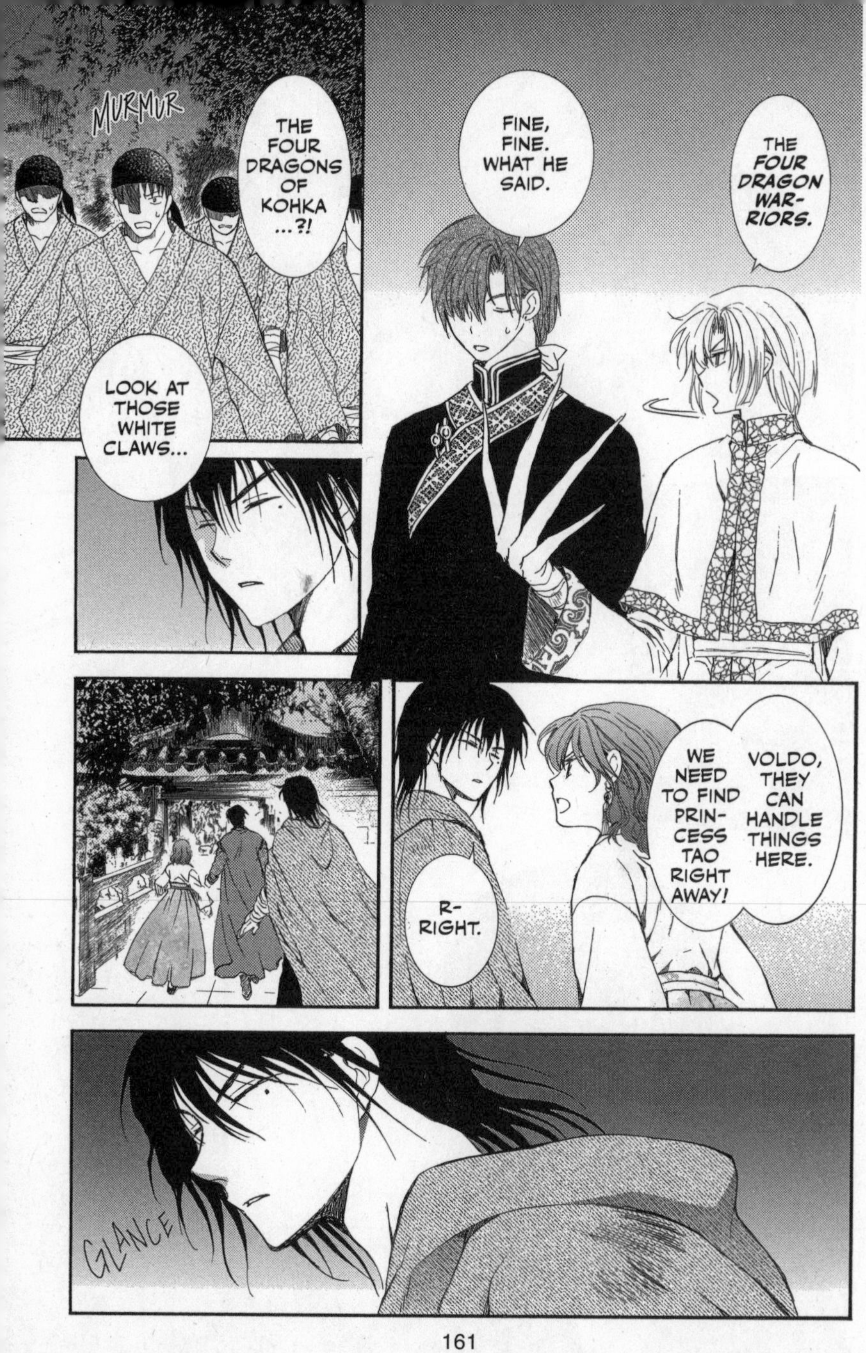
THE FOUR DRAGON WAR-RIORS.
FINE, FINE. WHAT HE SAID.
MURMUR
THE FOUR DRAGONS OF KOHKA ...?!
LOOK AT THOSE WHITE CLAWS...
VOLDO, THEY CAN HANDLE THINGS HERE.
WE NEED TO FIND PRIN-CESS TAO RIGHT AWAY!
R-RIGHT.
GLANCE

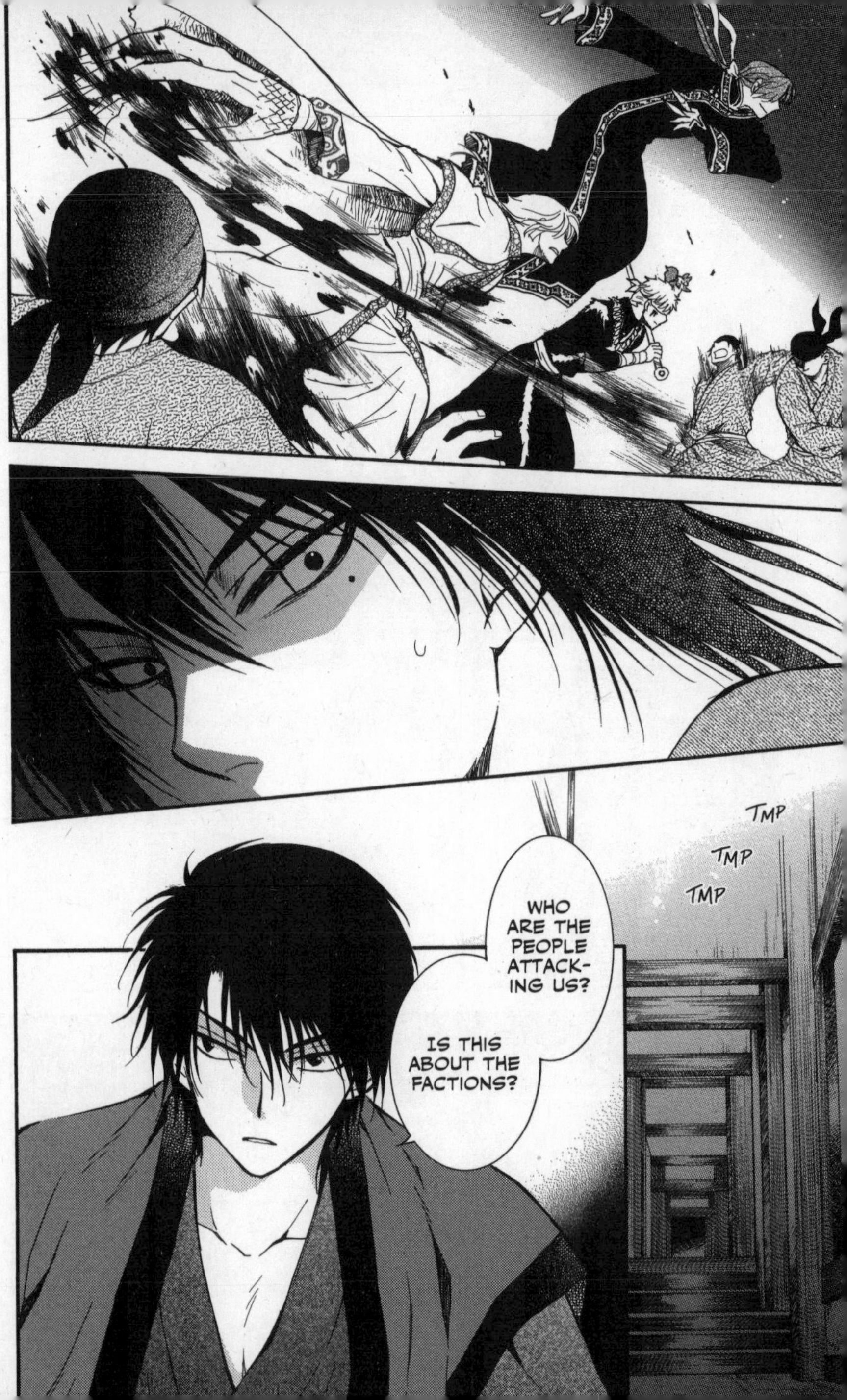
TMP
TMP
TMP
WHO ARE THE PEOPLE ATTACK-ING US?
IS THIS ABOUT THE FACTIONS?

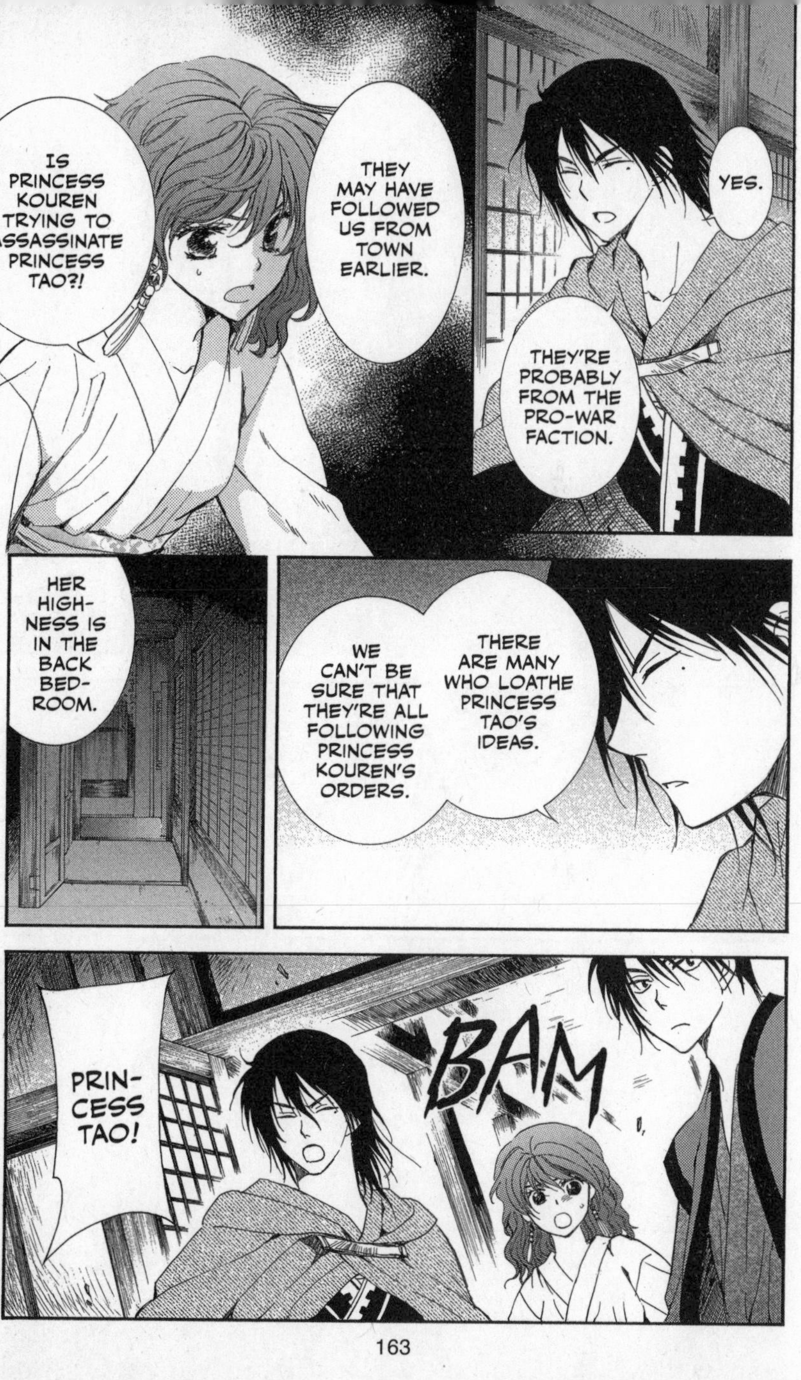
YES.
THEY'RE PROBABLY FROM THE PRO-WAR FACTION.
THEY MAY HAVE FOLLOWED US FROM TOWN EARLIER.
IS PRINCESS KOUREN TRYING TO ASSASSINATE PRINCESS TAO?!
THERE ARE MANY WHO LOATHE PRINCESS TAO'S IDEAS.
WE CAN'T BE SURE THAT THEY'RE ALL FOLLOWING PRINCESS KOUREN'S ORDERS.
HER HIGH-NESS IS IN THE BACK BED-ROOM.
BAM
PRIN-CESS TAO!

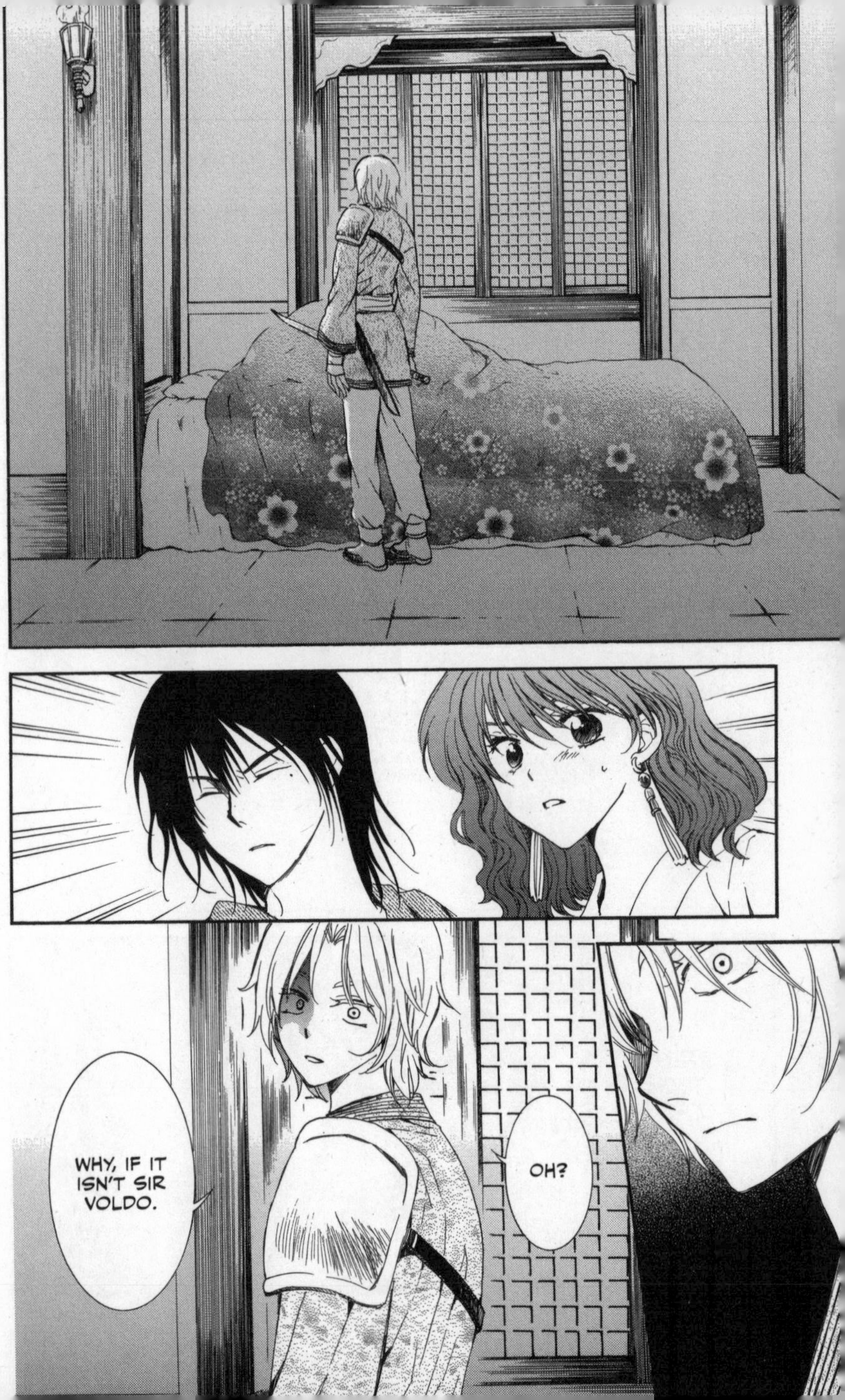
OH?
WHY, IF IT ISN'T SIR VOLDO.

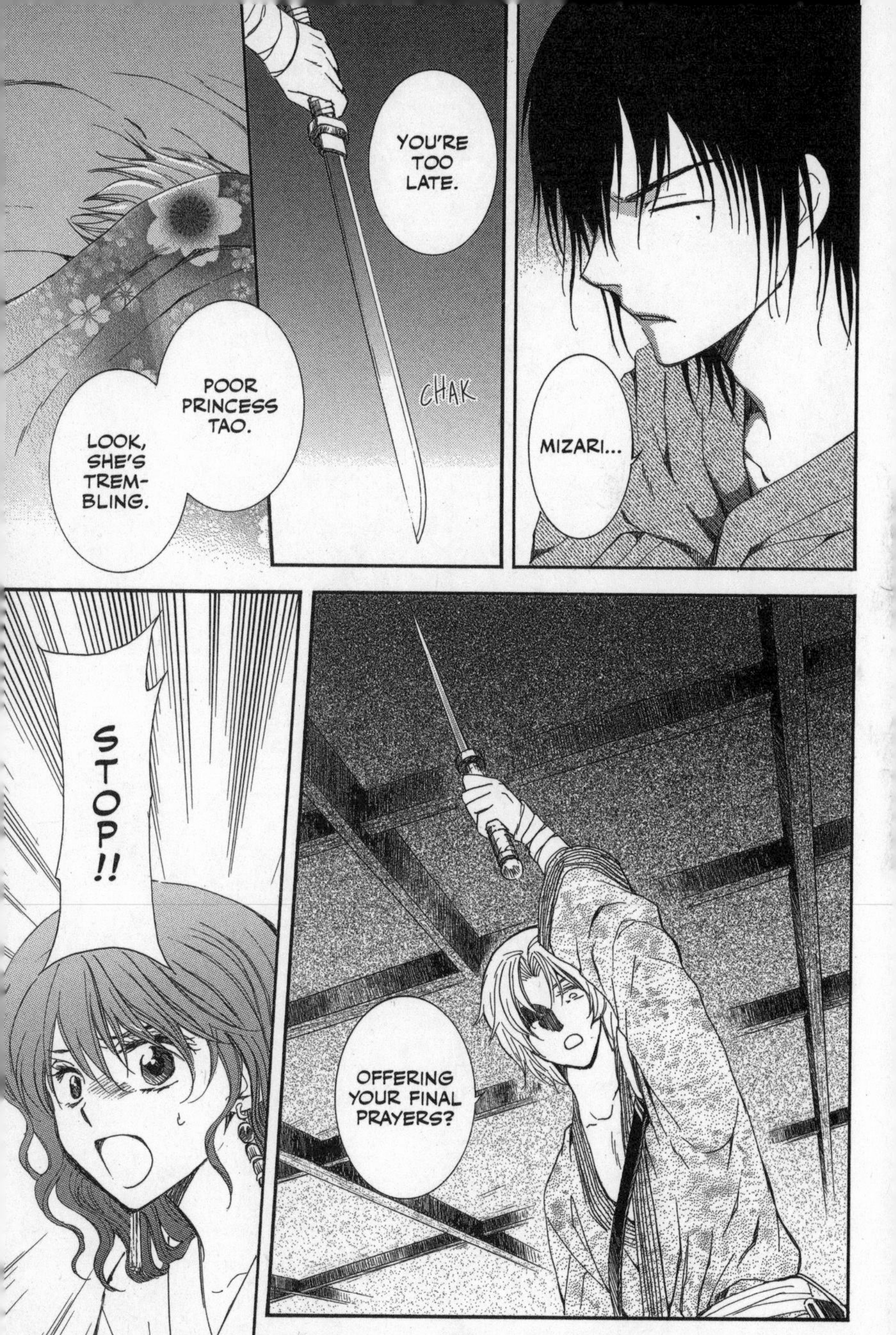
MIZARI...
YOU'RE TOO LATE.
CHAK
POOR PRINCESS TAO.
LOOK, SHE'S TREM-BLING.
OFFERING YOUR FINAL PRAYERS?
STOP!!

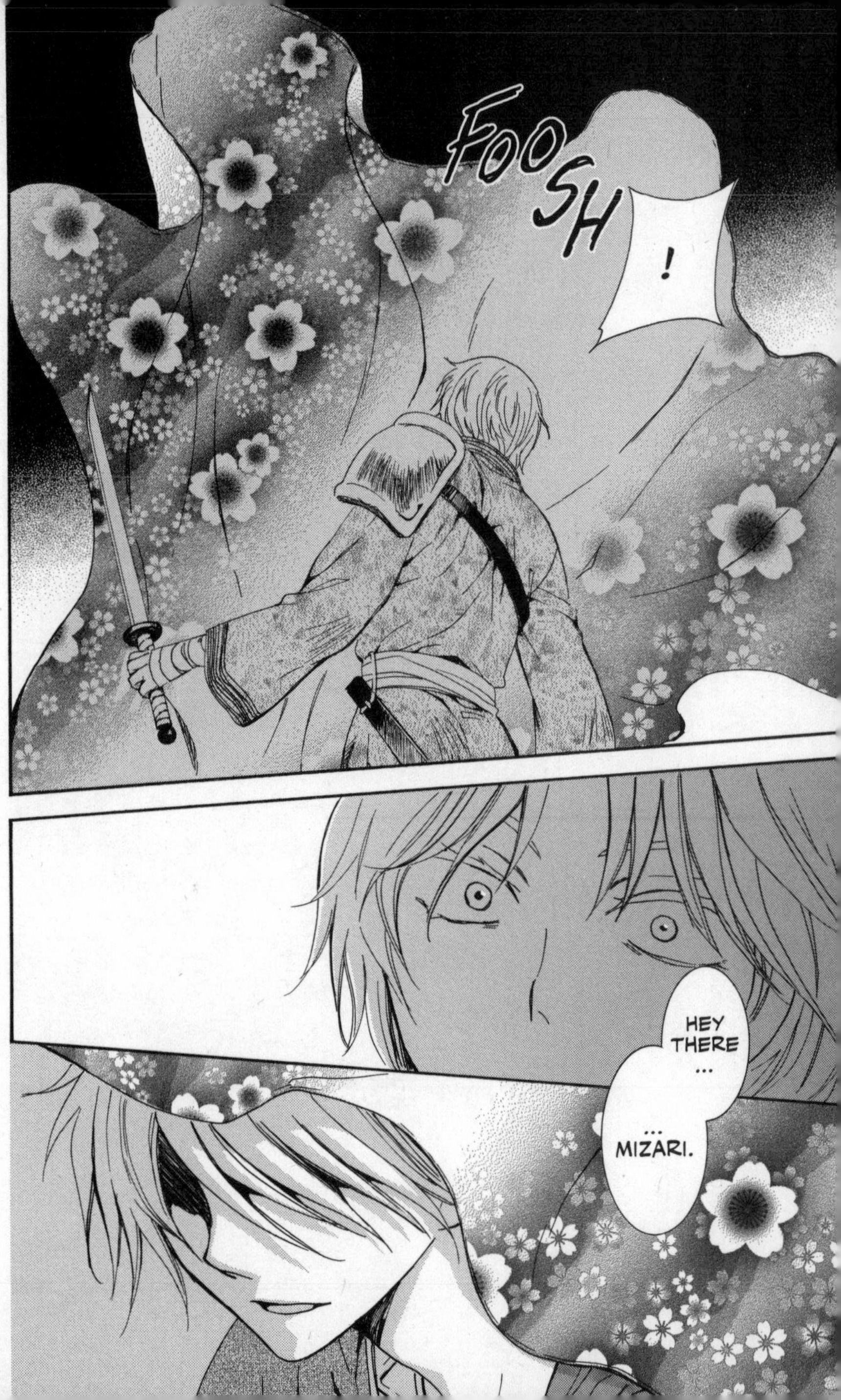
FOOSH
!
HEY THERE ...
... MIZARI.

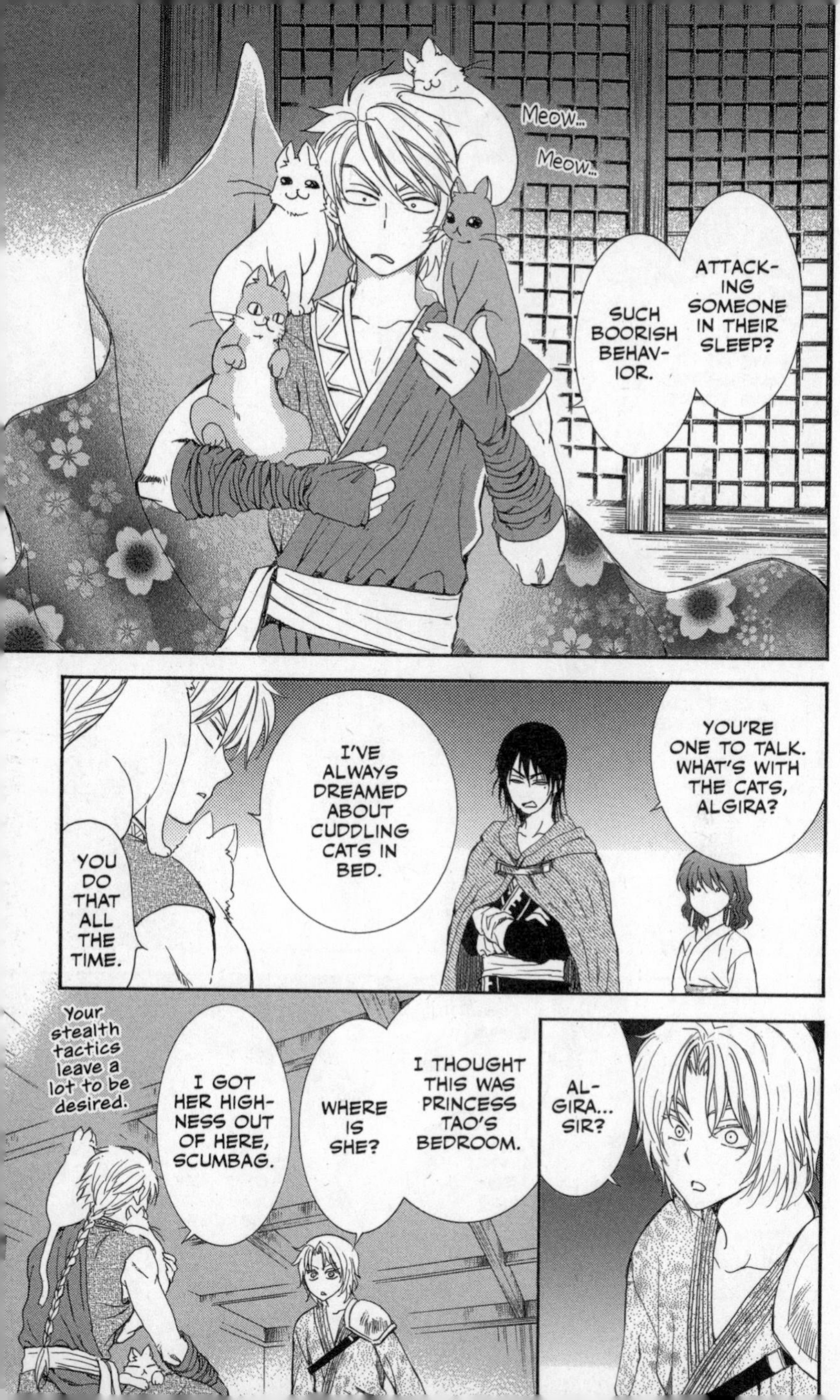
Meow...
Meow...
ATTACK-ING SOMEONE IN THEIR SLEEP?
SUCH BOORISH BEHAV-IOR.
YOU'RE ONE TO TALK. WHAT'S WITH THE CATS, ALGIRA?
I'VE ALWAYS DREAMED ABOUT CUDDLING CATS IN BED.
YOU DO THAT ALL THE TIME.
AL-GIRA... SIR?
I THOUGHT THIS WAS PRINCESS TAO'S BEDROOM.
WHERE IS SHE?
I GOT HER HIGH-NESS OUT OF HERE, SCUMBAG.
Your stealth tactics leave a lot to be desired.

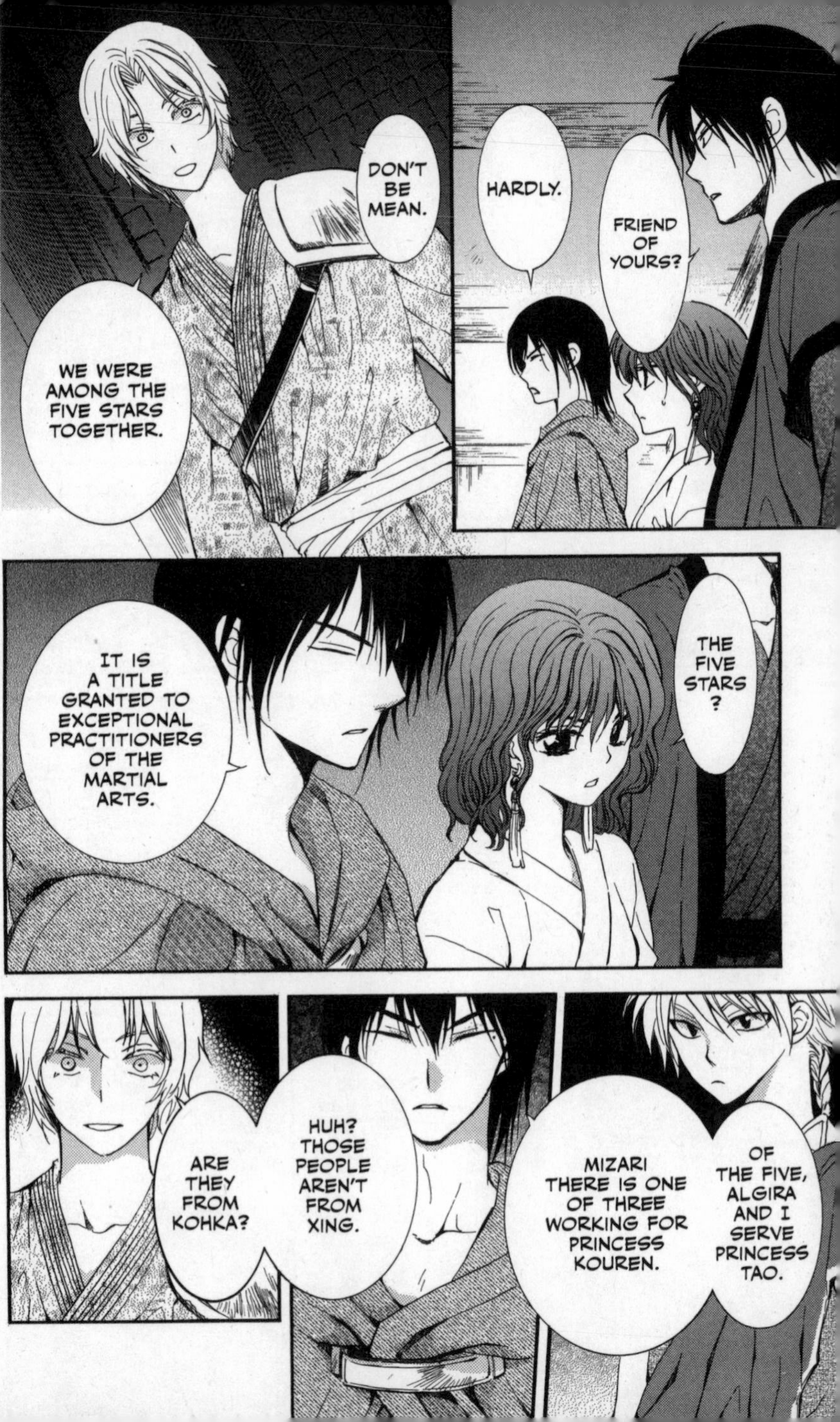
FRIEND OF YOURS?
HARDLY.
DON'T BE MEAN.
WE WERE AMONG THE FIVE STARS TOGETHER.
THE FIVE STARS?
IT IS A TITLE GRANTED TO EXCEPTIONAL PRACTITIONERS OF THE MARTIAL ARTS.
OF THE FIVE, ALGIRA AND I SERVE PRINCESS TAO.
MIZARI THERE IS ONE OF THREE WORKING FOR PRINCESS KOUREN.
HUH? THOSE PEOPLE AREN'T FROM XING.
ARE THEY FROM KOHKA?

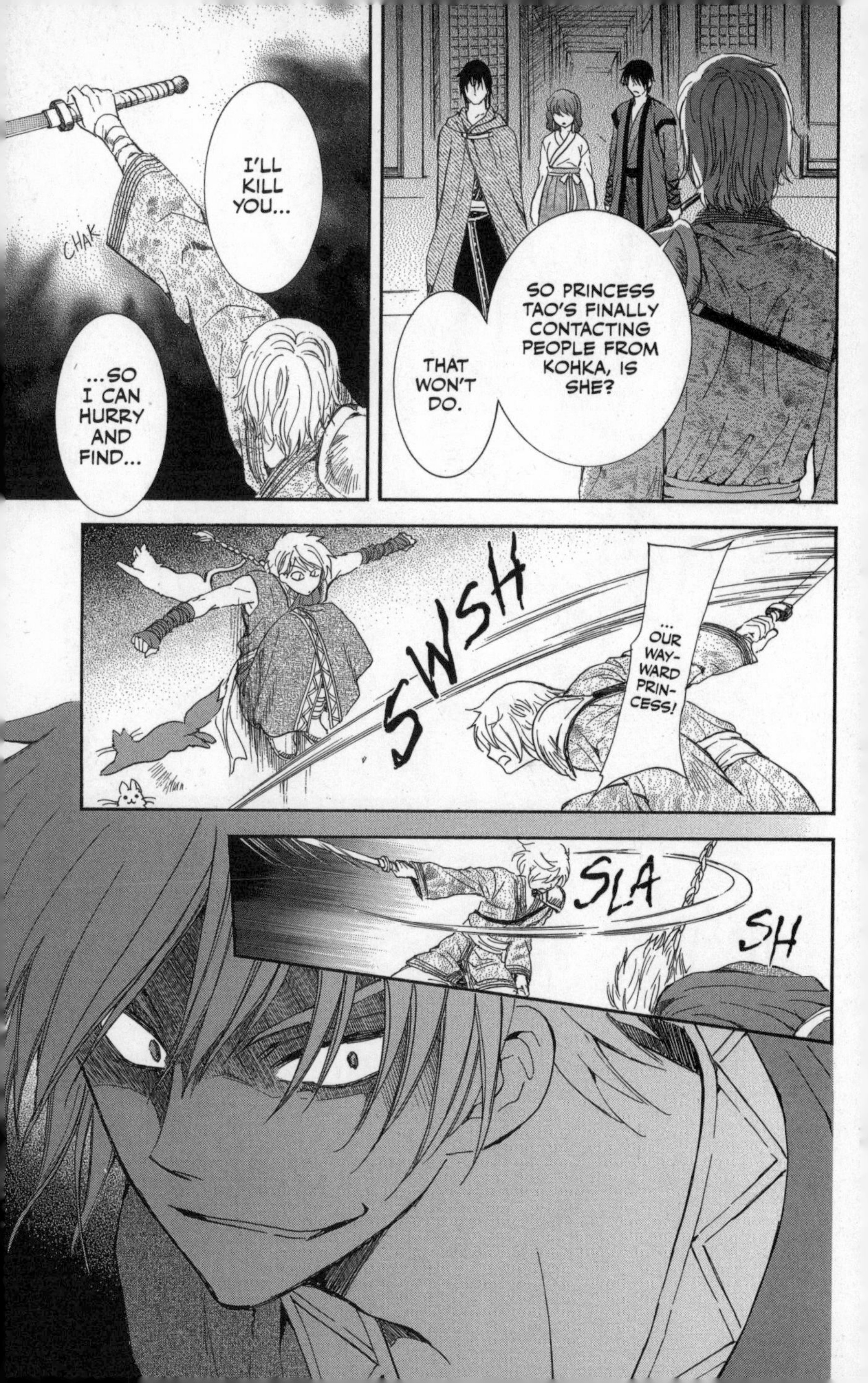
SO PRINCESS TAO'S FINALLY CONTACTING PEOPLE FROM KOHKA, IS SHE?
THAT WON'T DO.
I'LL KILL YOU...
CHAK
...SO I CAN HURRY AND FIND...
...OUR WAYWARD PRINCESS!
SWSH
SLASH

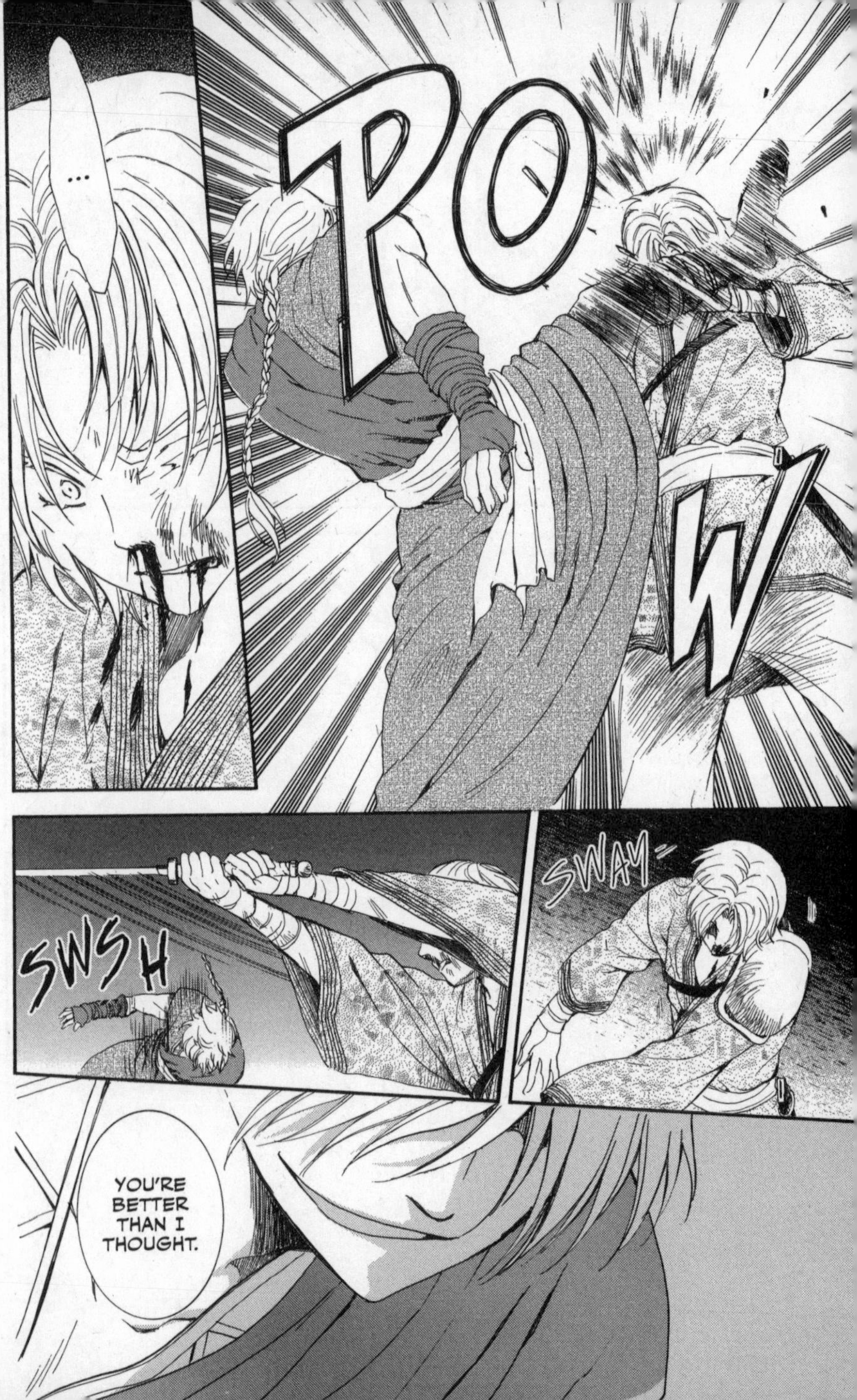
POW
...
SWAM
SWSH
YOU'RE BETTER THAN I THOUGHT.

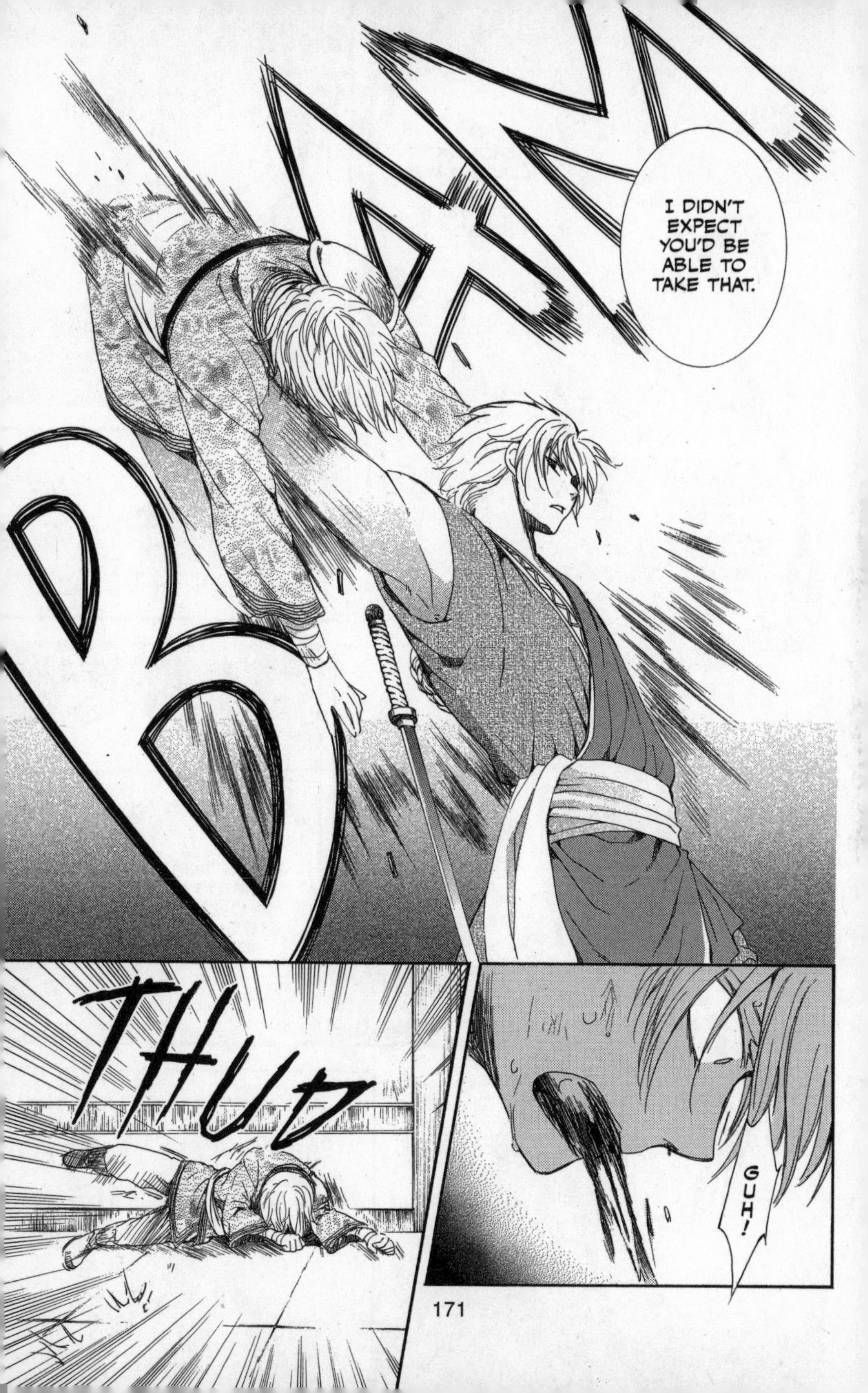
I DIDN'T EXPECT YOU'D BE ABLE TO TAKE THAT.
BAM
GUH!
THUD

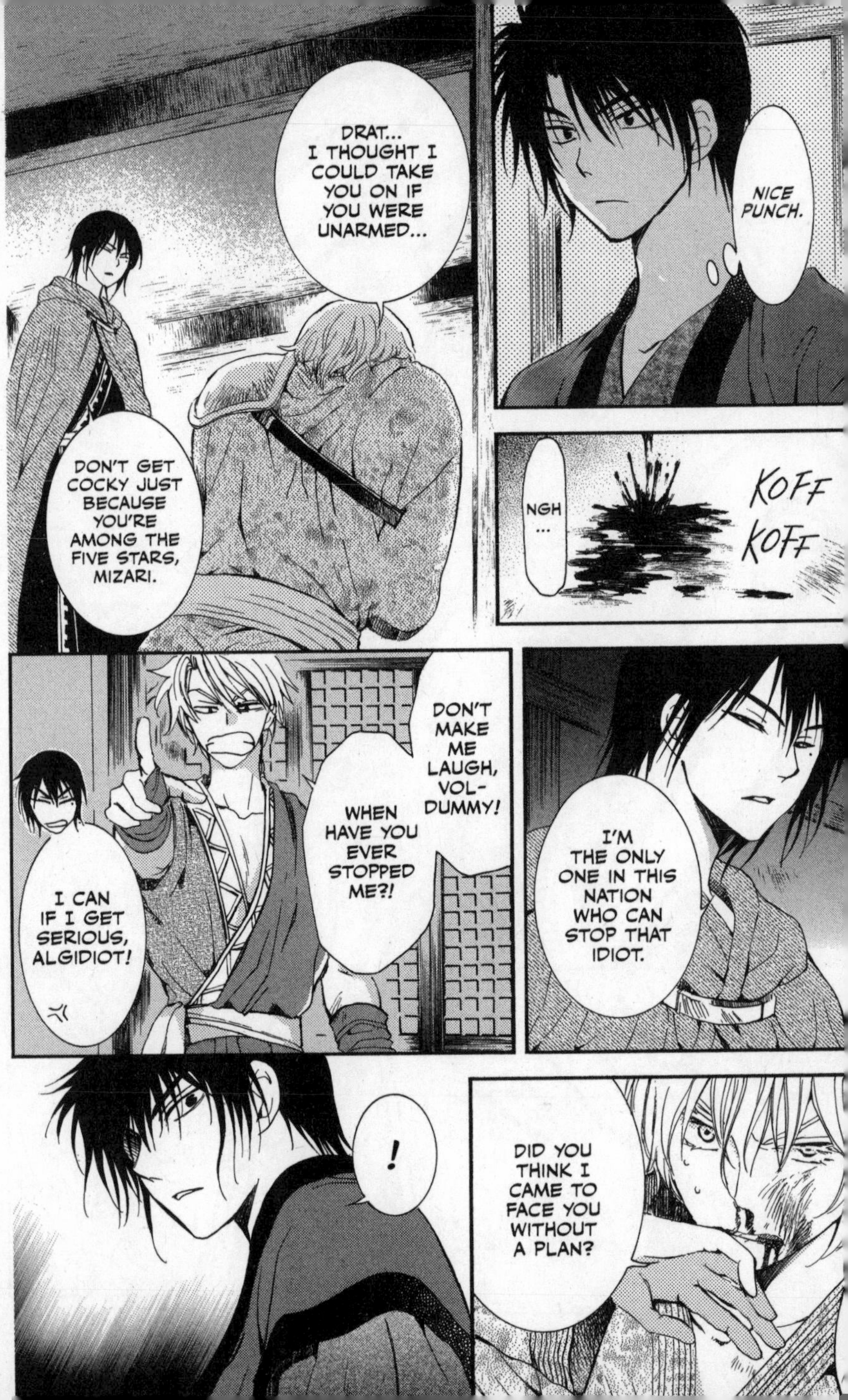
NICE PUNCH.
NGH...
KOFF KOFF
DRAT... I THOUGHT I COULD TAKE YOU ON IF YOU WERE UNARMED...
DON'T GET COCKY JUST BECAUSE YOU'RE AMONG THE FIVE STARS, MIZARI.
I'M THE ONLY ONE IN THIS NATION WHO CAN STOP THAT IDIOT.
DON'T MAKE ME LAUGH, VOL-DUMMY!
WHEN HAVE YOU EVER STOPPED ME?!
I CAN IF I GET SERIOUS, ALGIDIOT!
DID YOU THINK I CAME TO FACE YOU WITHOUT A PLAN?
!

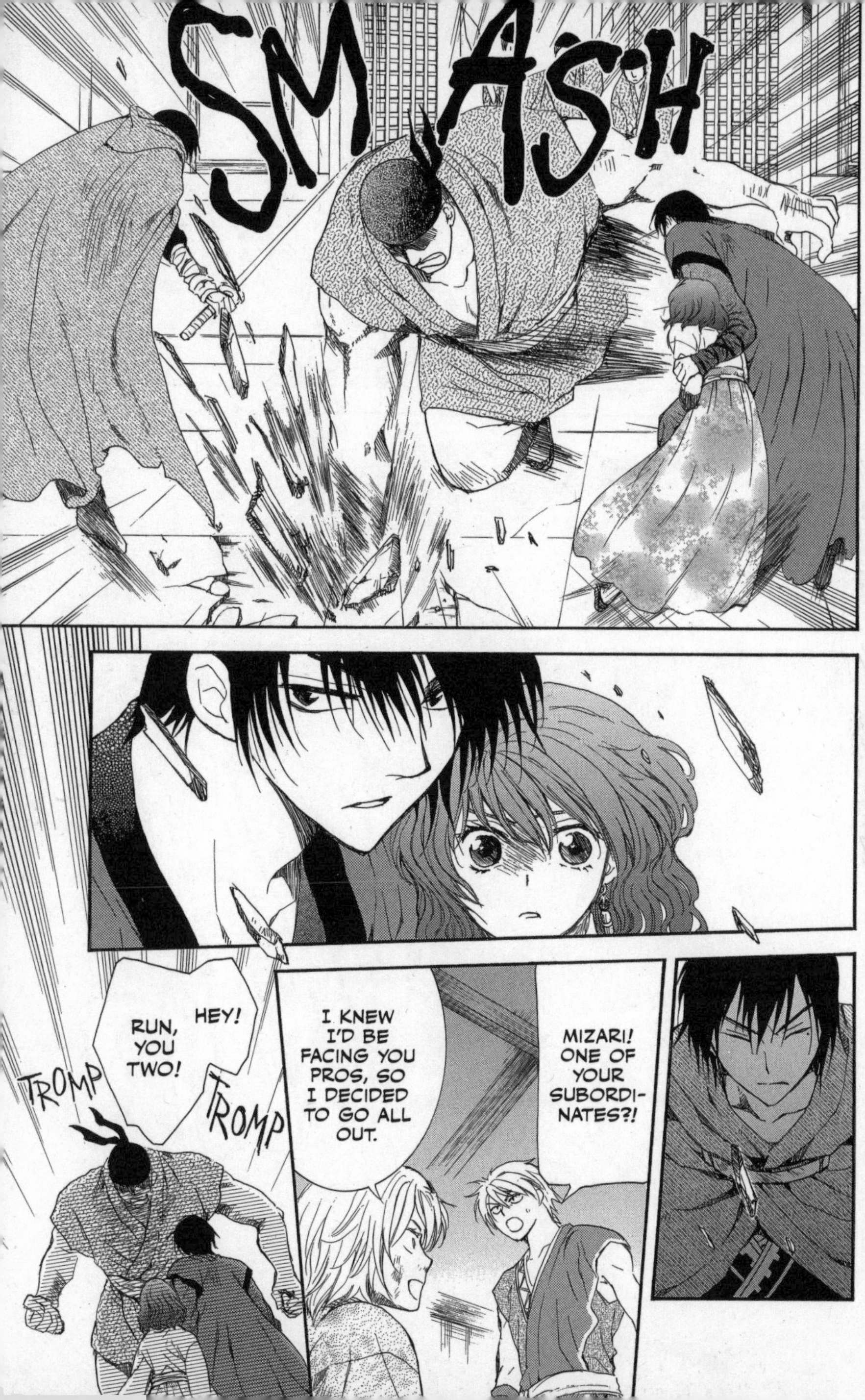
SMASH
MIZARI! ONE OF YOUR SUBORDI-NATES?!
I KNEW I'D BE FACING YOU PROS, SO I DECIDED TO GO ALL OUT.
HEY!
RUN, YOU TWO!
TROMP
TROMP

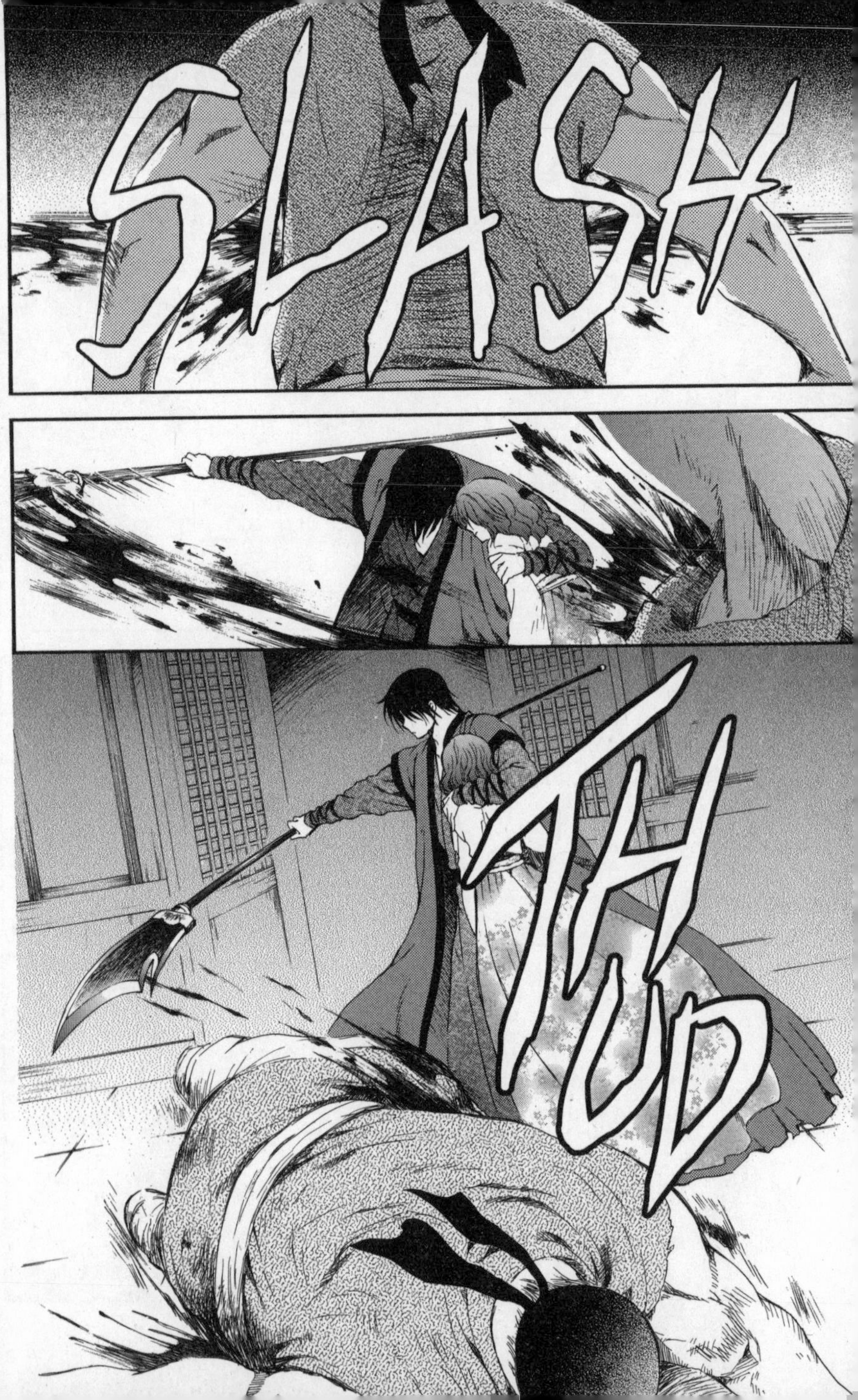
SLASH
THUD

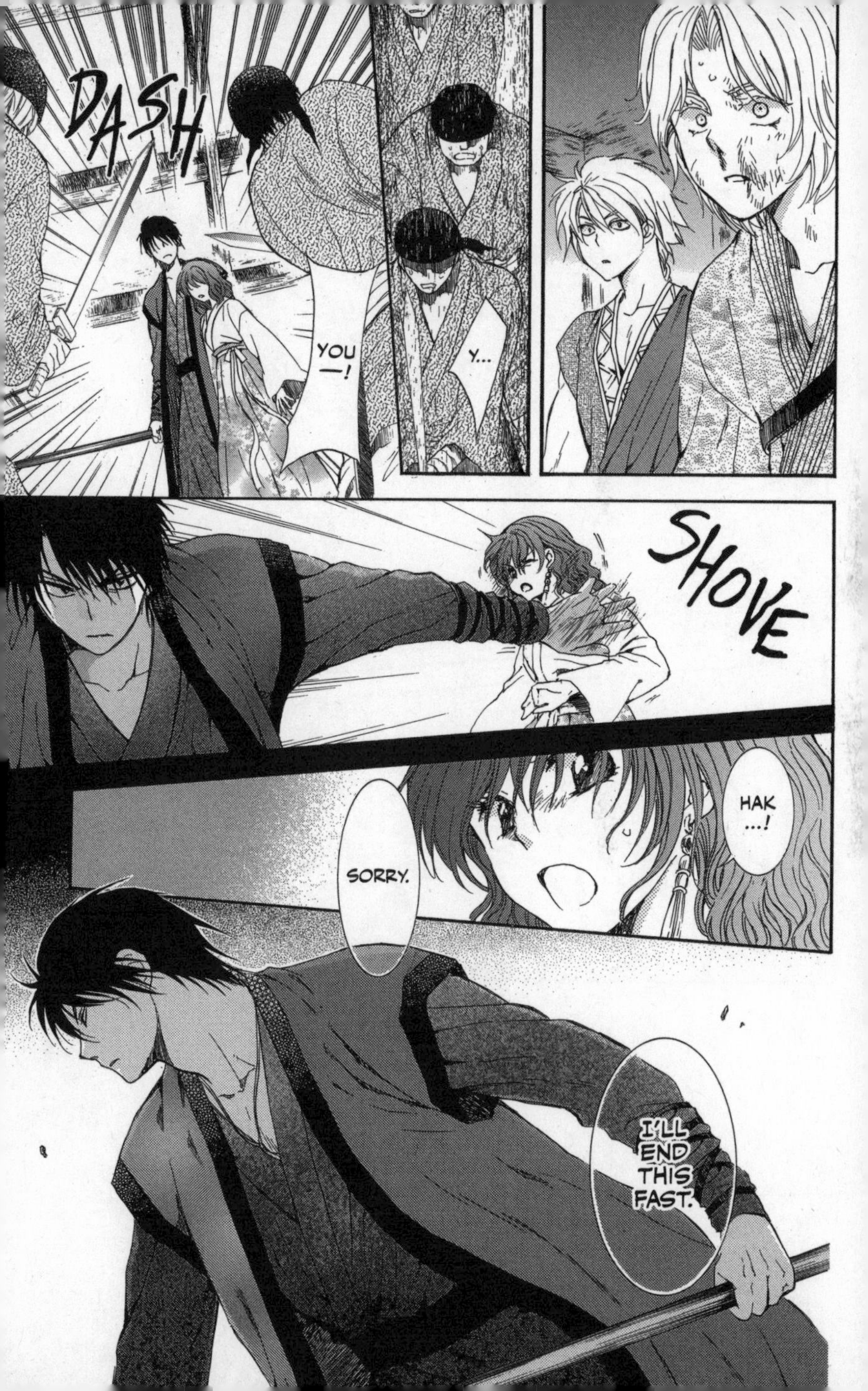
Y...
YOU —!
DASH
SHOVE
HAK ...!
SORRY.
I'LL END THIS FAST.

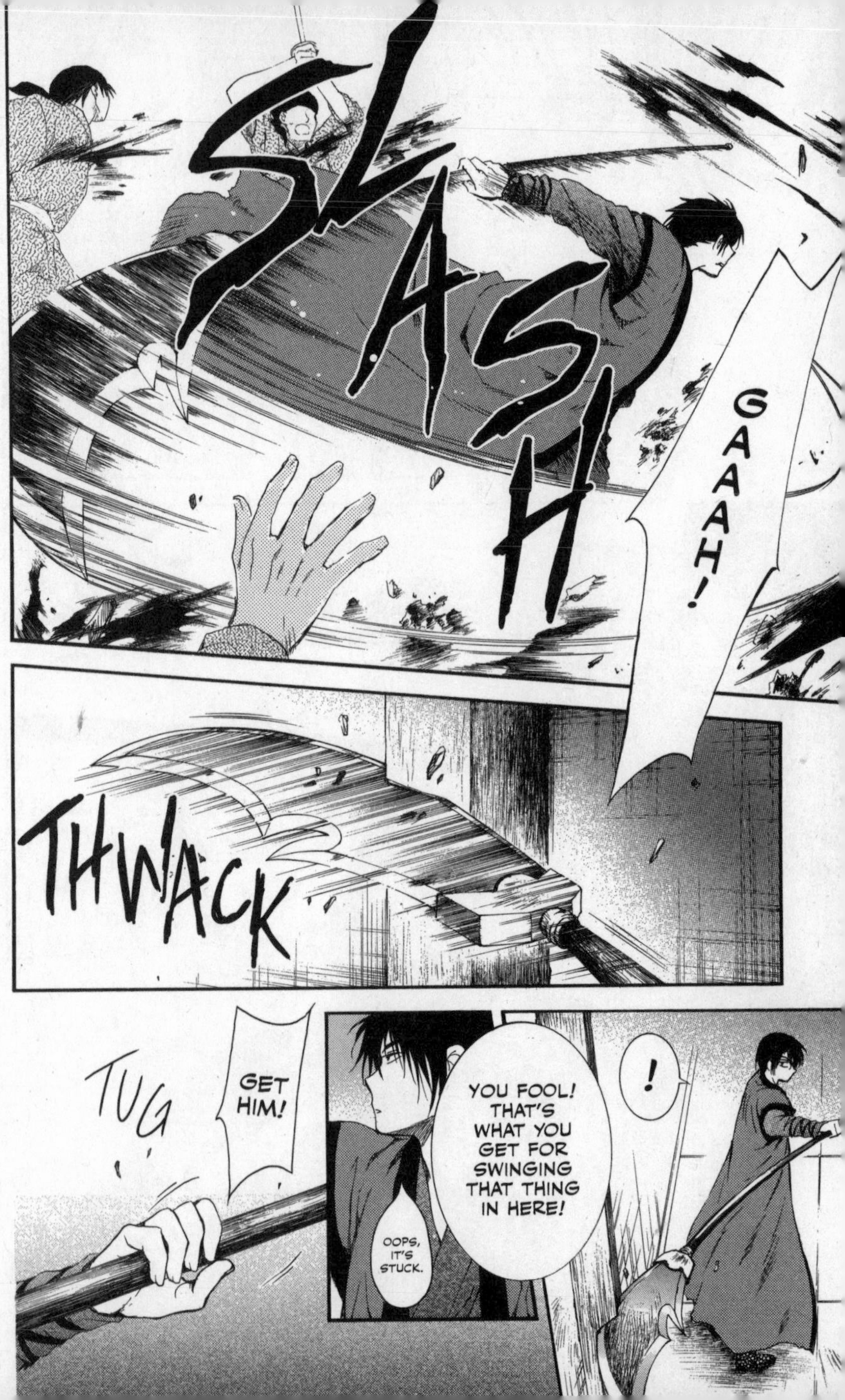
SLASH
GAAAH!
THWACK
!
YOU FOOL! THAT'S WHAT YOU GET FOR SWINGING THAT THING IN HERE!
OOPS, IT'S STUCK.
GET HIM!
TUG

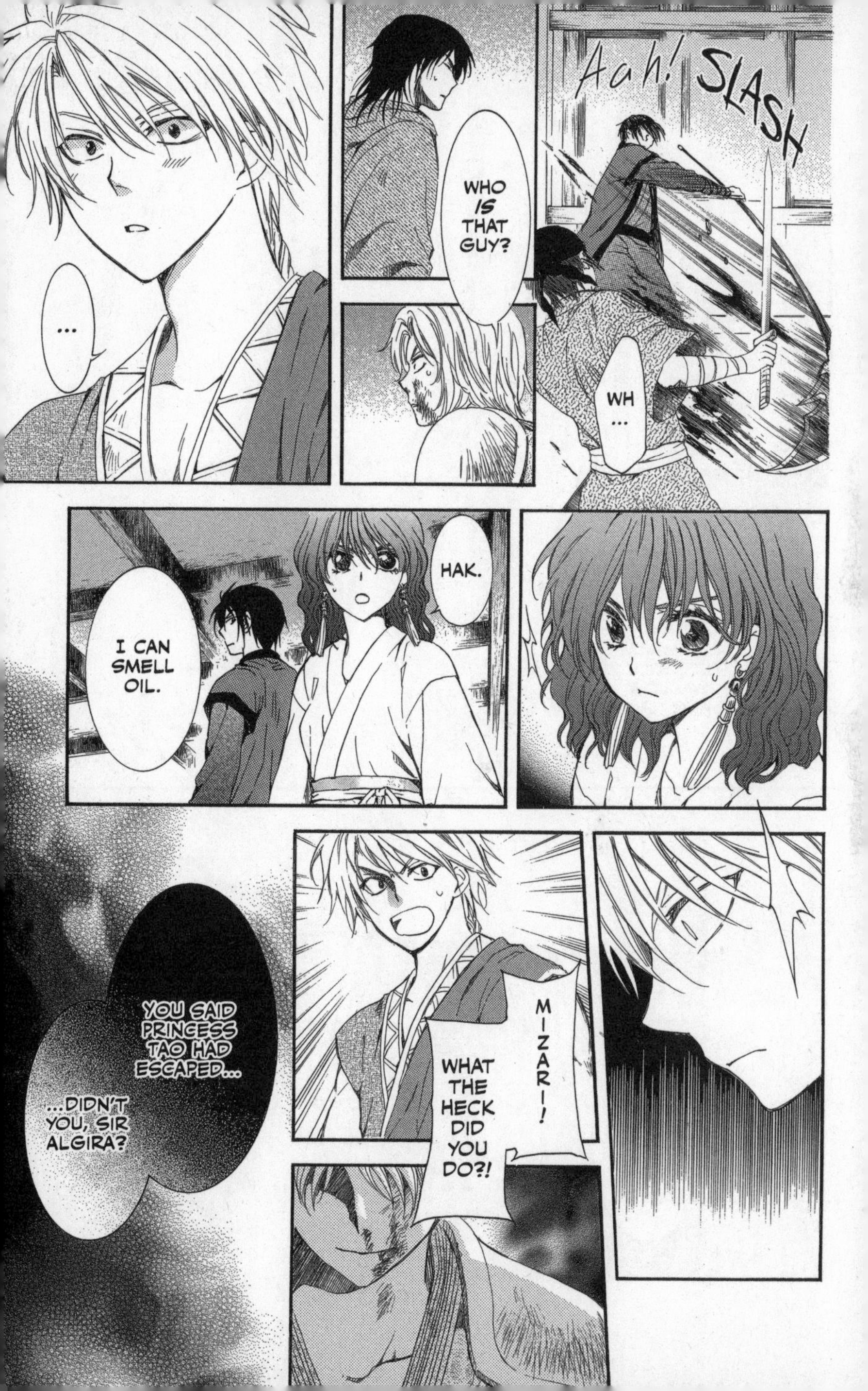
Aah! SLASH
WH...
WHO IS THAT GUY?
...
HAK.
I CAN SMELL OIL.
MIZAR!
WHAT THE HECK DID YOU DO?!
YOU SAID PRINCESS TAO HAD ESCAPED...
...DIDN'T YOU, SIR ALGIRA?

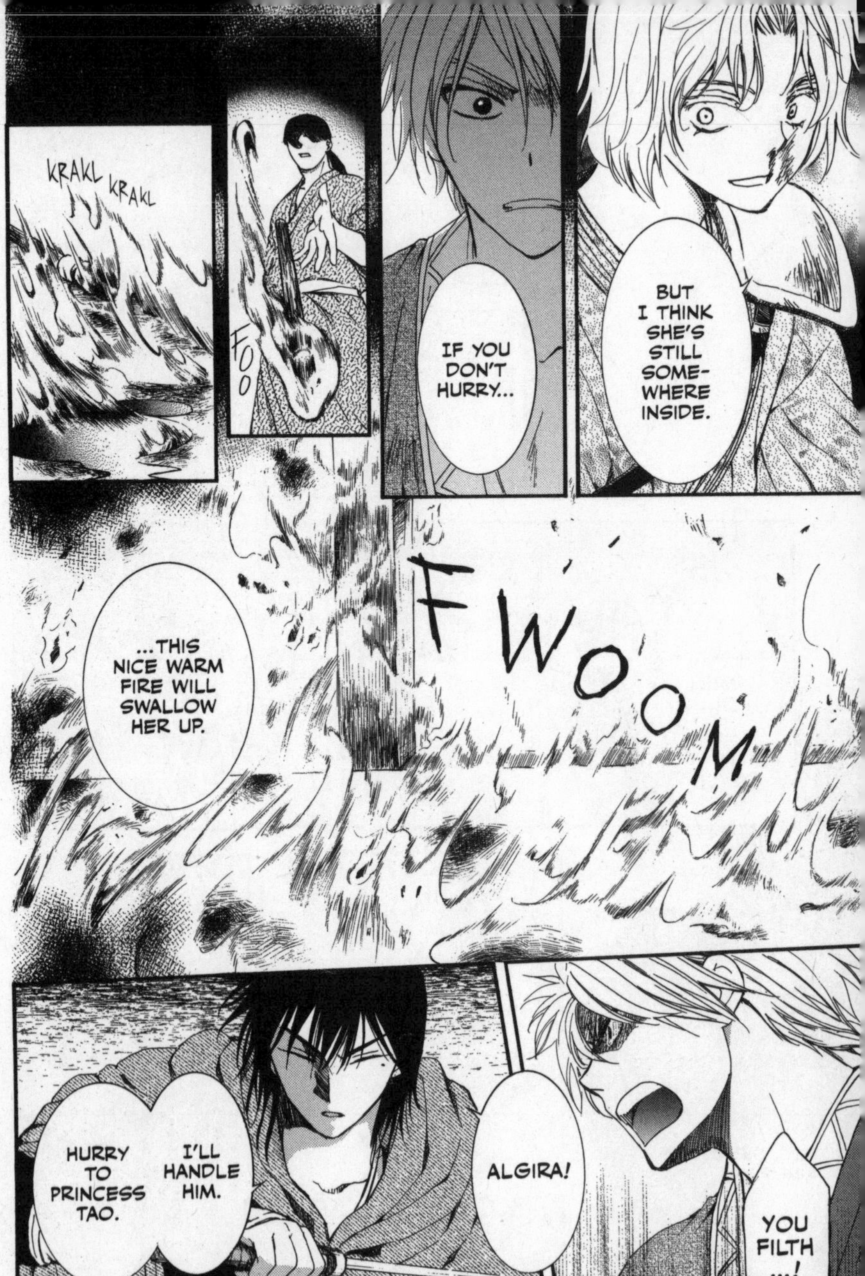
BUT I THINK SHE'S STILL SOME-WHERE INSIDE.
IF YOU DON'T HURRY...
FOO
KRAKL KRAKL
FWOOM
...THIS NICE WARM FIRE WILL SWALLOW HER UP.
YOU FILTH...!
ALGIRA!
I'LL HANDLE HIM.
HURRY TO PRINCESS TAO.

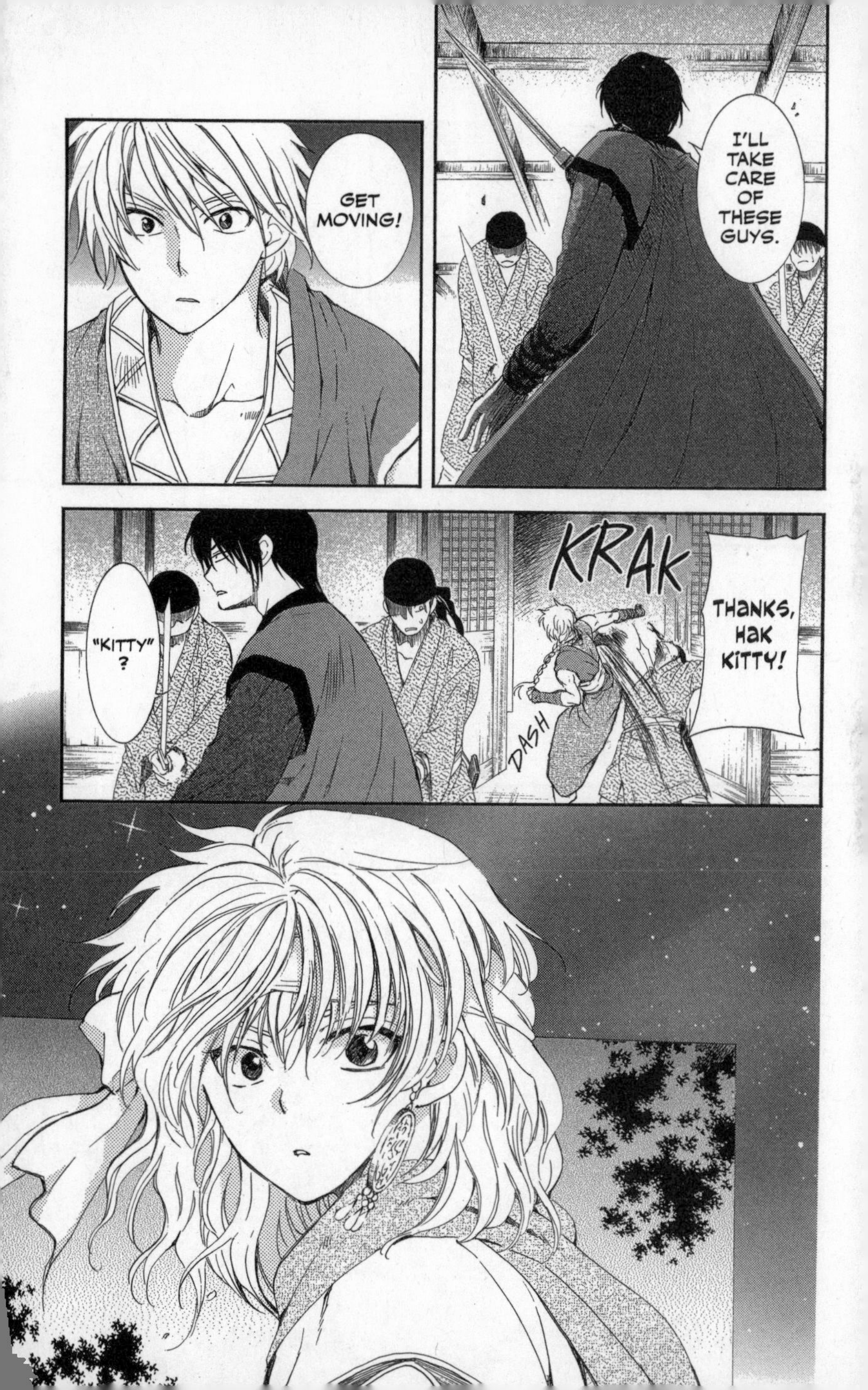
I'LL TAKE CARE OF THESE GUYS.
GET MOVING!
KRAK
THANKS, HAK KITTY!
DASH
"KITTY"?

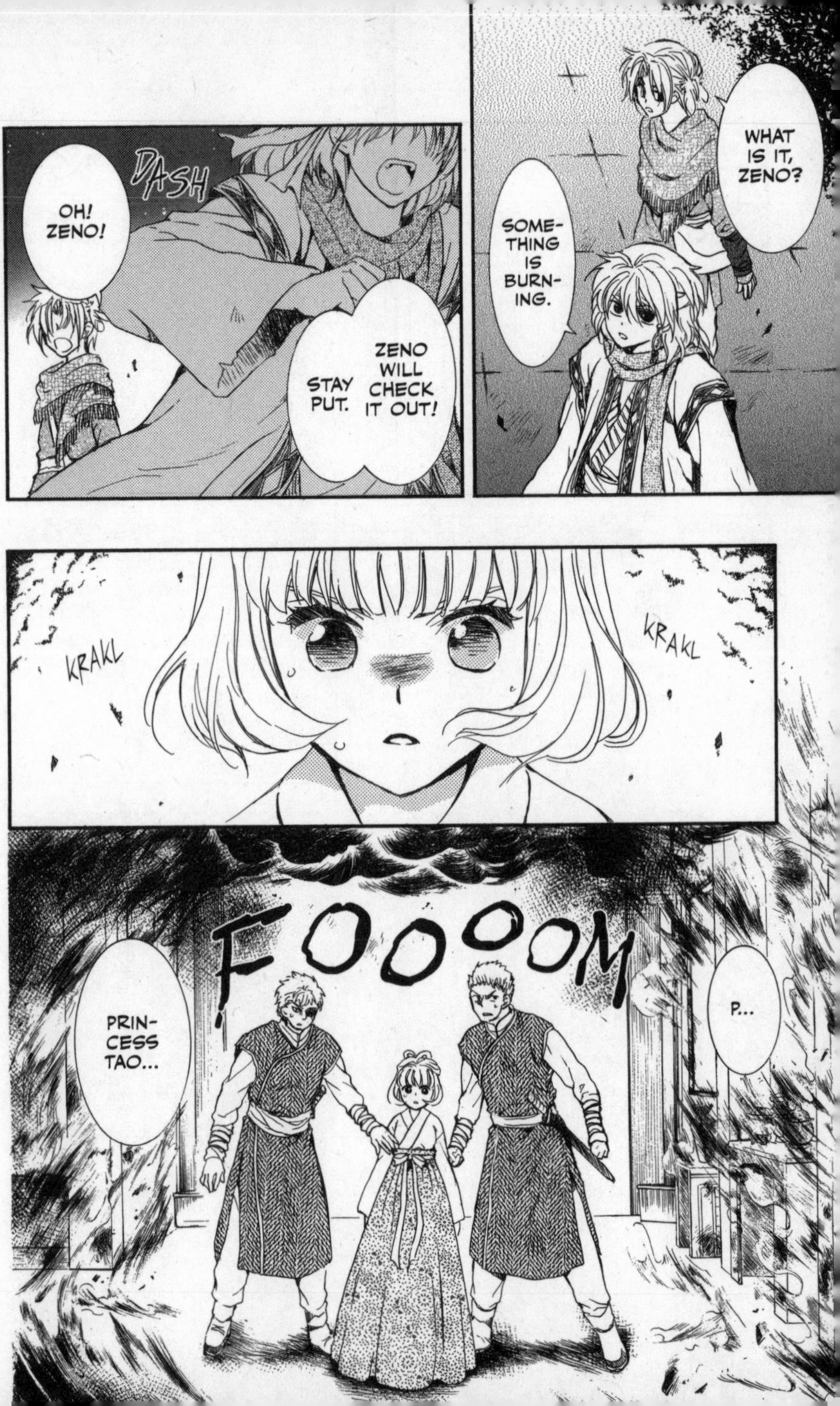
WHAT IS IT, ZENO?
SOME-THING IS BURN-ING.
ZENO WILL CHECK IT OUT!
STAY PUT.
DASH
OH! ZENO!
KRAKL
KRAKL
FOOOOM
P...
PRIN-CESS TAO...

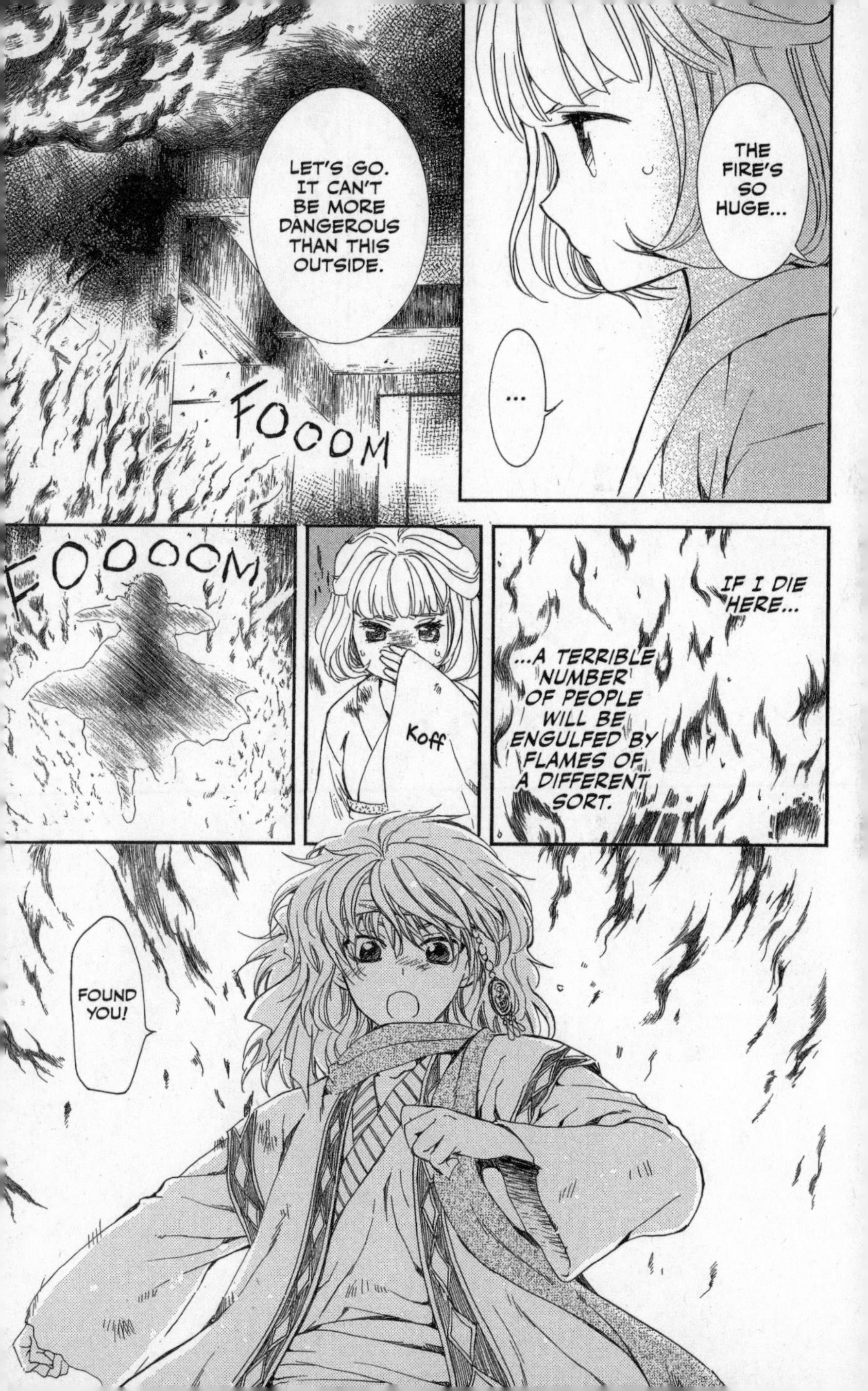
THE FIRE'S SO HUGE...
...
LET'S GO. IT CAN'T BE MORE DANGEROUS THAN THIS OUTSIDE.
FOOOM
IF I DIE HERE...
...A TERRIBLE NUMBER OF PEOPLE WILL BE ENGULFED BY FLAMES OF A DIFFERENT SORT.
Koff
FOOOOM
FOUND YOU!

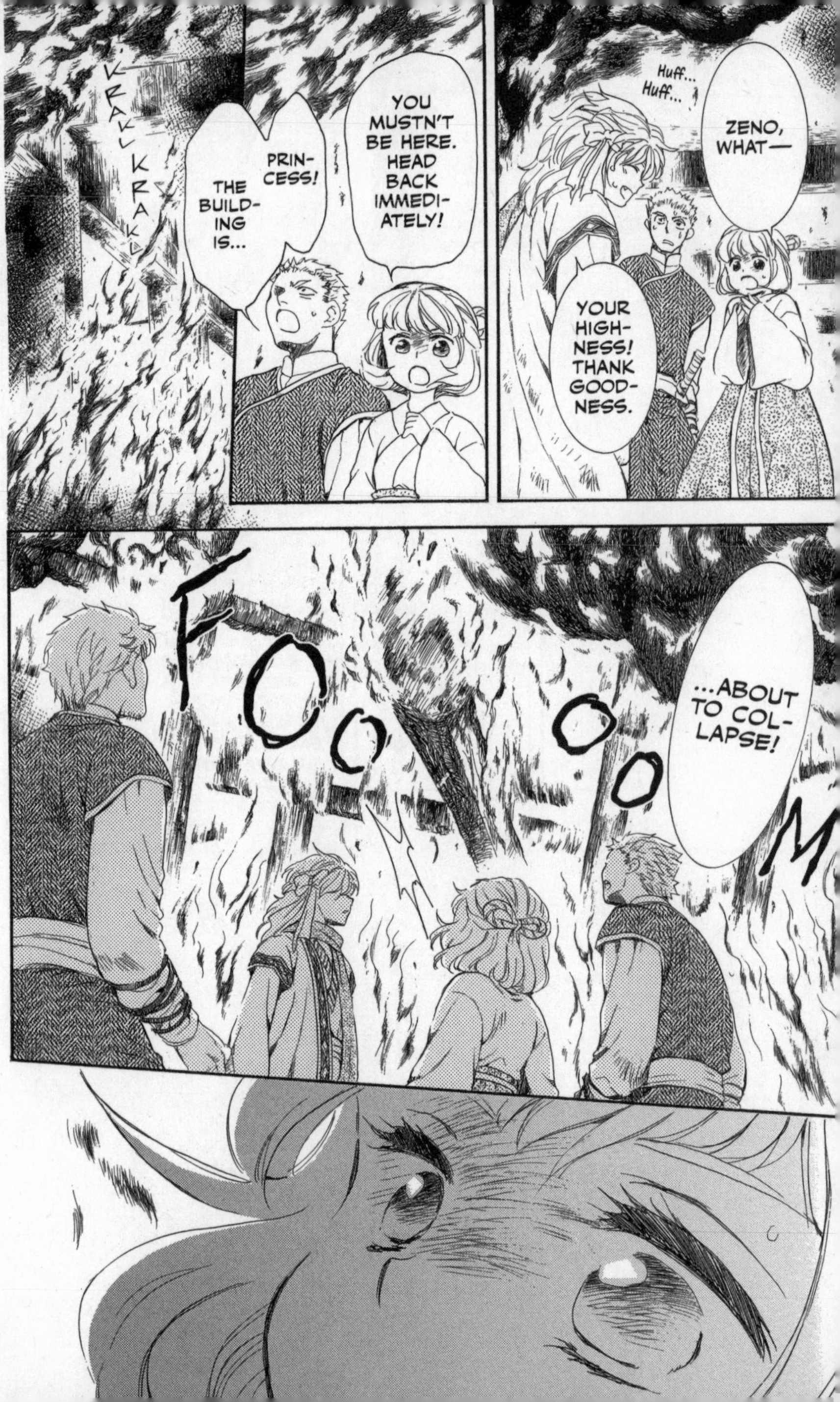
ZENO, WHAT—
Huff... Huff...
YOUR HIGHNESS! THANK GOODNESS.
YOU MUSTN'T BE HERE. HEAD BACK IMMEDIATELY!
PRINCESS!
THE BUILDING IS...
KRAK KRAK KRAK
...ABOUT TO COLLAPSE!
FOOOOOM

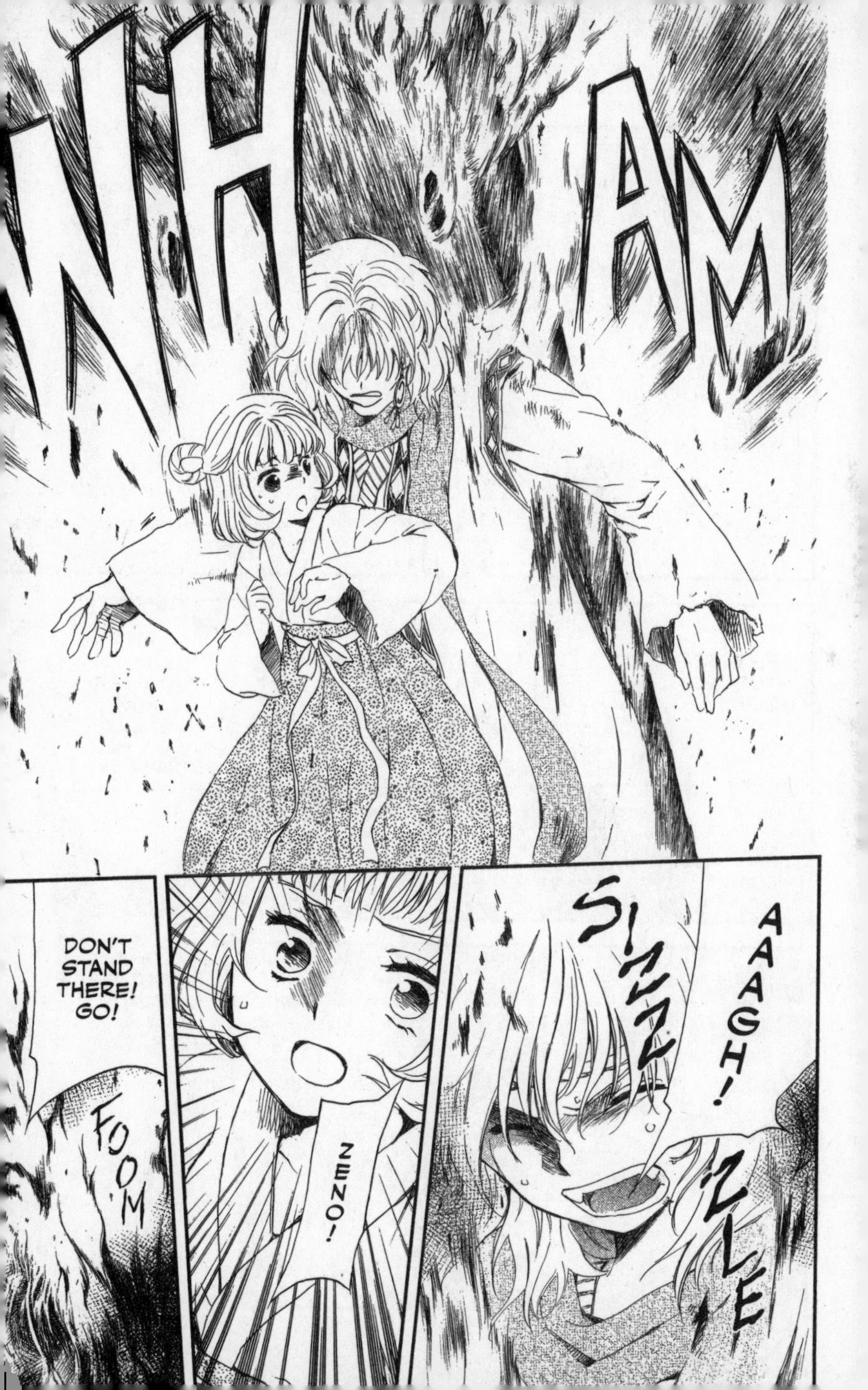
WHAM
AAAGH!
SIZZZ
ZZLE
ZENO!
DON'T STAND THERE! GO!
FOOM

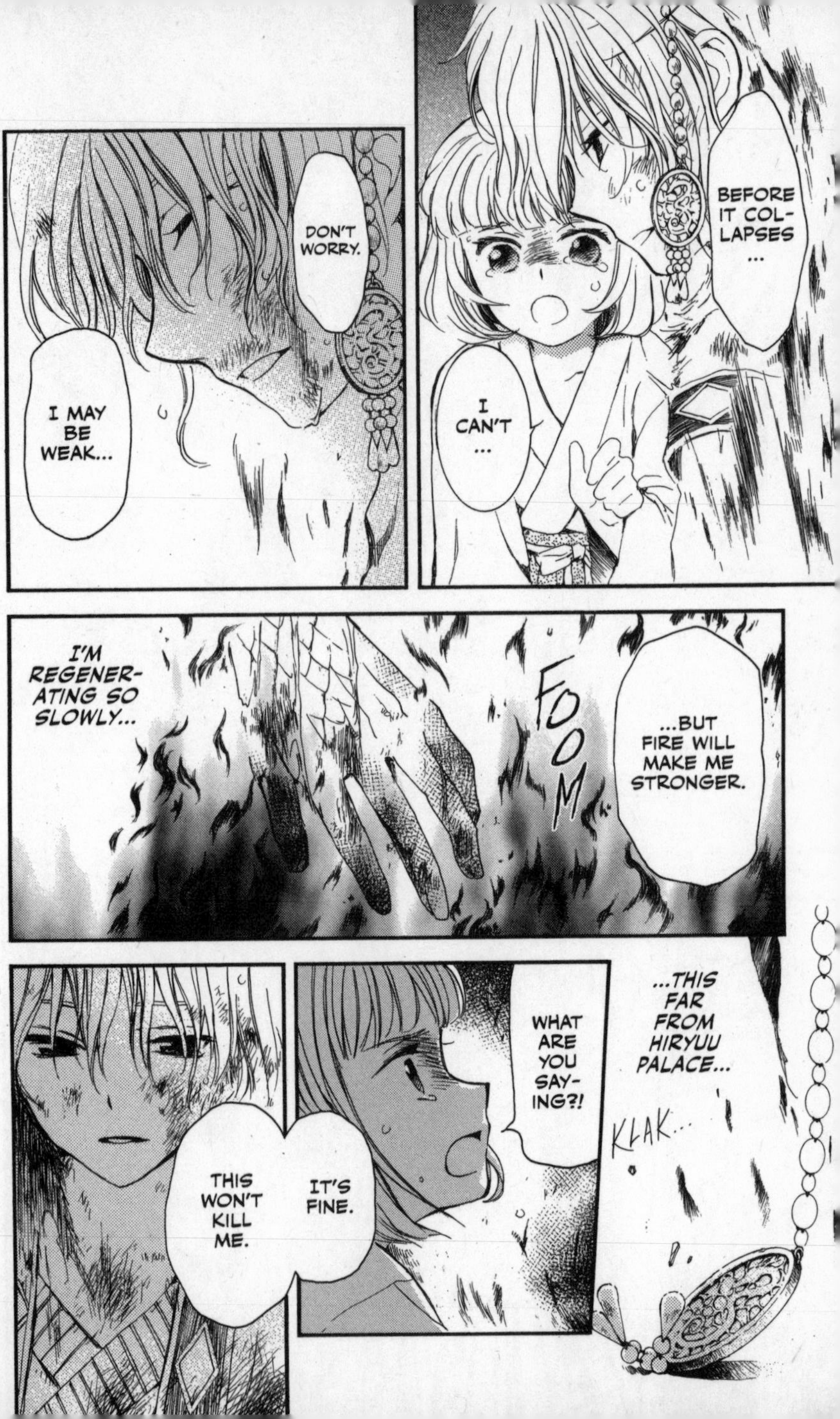
BEFORE IT COL-LAPSES...
I CAN'T...
DON'T WORRY.
I MAY BE WEAK...
I'M REGENER-ATING SO SLOWLY...
...BUT FIRE WILL MAKE ME STRONGER.
FOOM
...THIS FAR FROM HIRYUU PALACE...
KLAK...
WHAT ARE YOU SAY-ING?!
IT'S FINE.
THIS WON'T KILL ME.

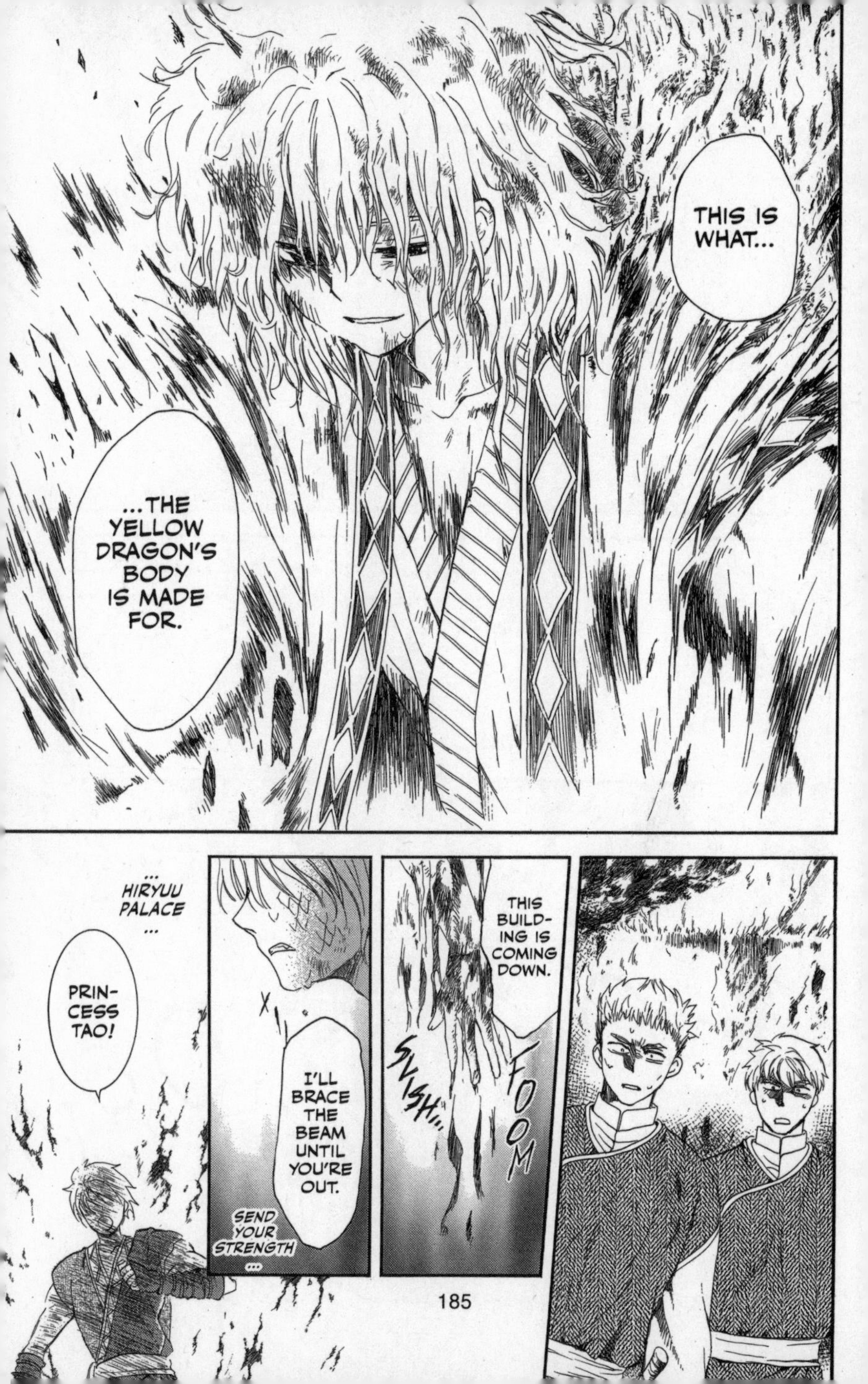
THIS IS WHAT...
...THE YELLOW DRAGON'S BODY IS MADE FOR.
THIS BUILDING IS COMING DOWN.
FOOM
SVISH...
I'LL BRACE THE BEAM UNTIL YOU'RE OUT.
SEND YOUR STRENGTH ...
...HIRYUU PALACE ...
PRIN-CESS TAO!

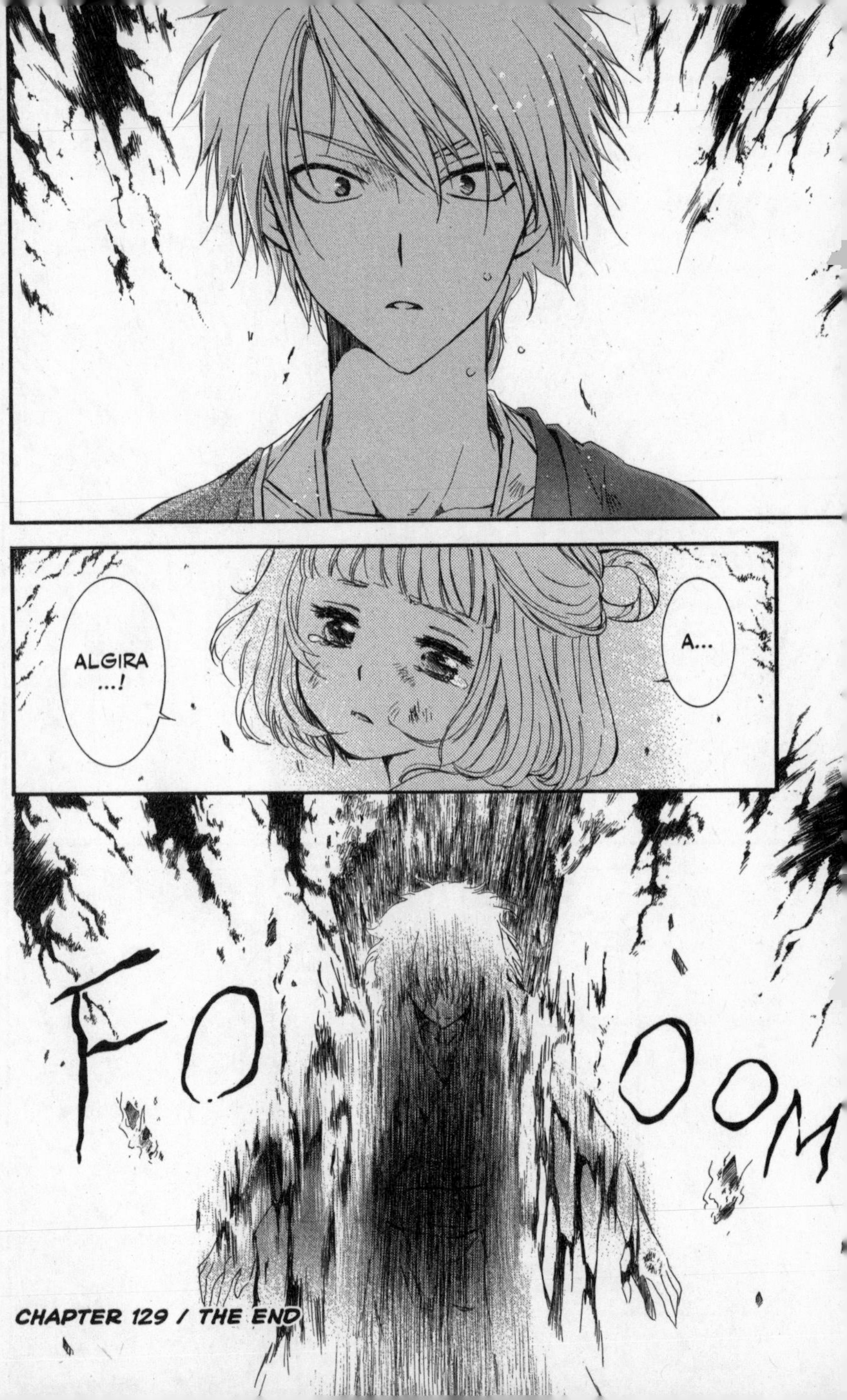
A...
ALGIRA ...!
FO OOM
CHAPTER 129 / THE END

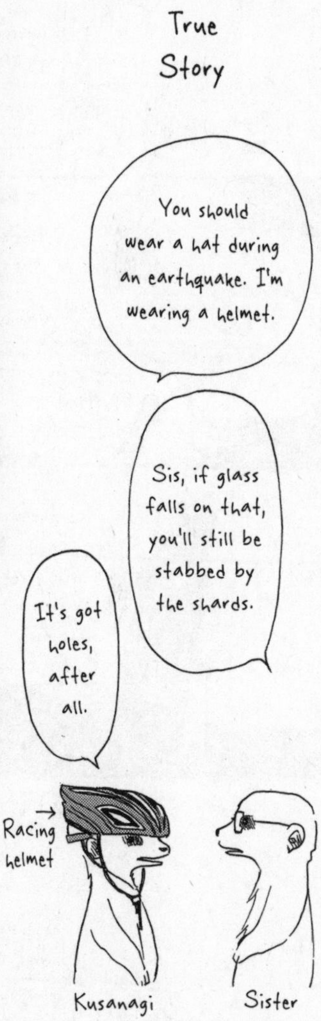
True Story
You should wear a hat during an earthquake. I'm wearing a helmet.
Sis, if glass falls on that, you'll still be stabbed by the shards.
It's got holes, after all.
Racing helmet
Kusanagi
Sister

Right After the Kumamoto Earthquake

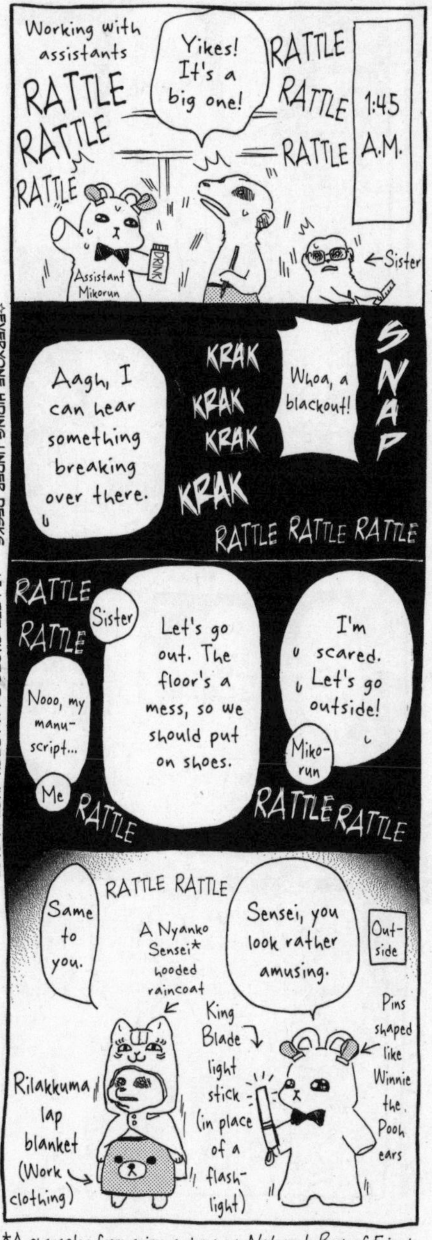
1:45 A.M.
RATTLE RATTLE RATTLE
Yikes! It's a big one!
Working with assistants
RATTLE RATTLE RATTLE
Sister
DRINK
Assistant Mikorun
SNAP
Whoa, a blackout!
KRAK KRAK KRAK KRAK
Aagh, I can hear something breaking over there.
RATTLE RATTLE RATTLE
I'm scared. Let's go outside!
Mikorun
Let's go out. The floor's a mess, so we should put on shoes.
Sister
RATTLE RATTLE
Nooo, my manu-script...
Me
RATTLE
RATTLE RATTLE
Out-side
Sensei, you look rather amusing.
RATTLE RATTLE
Same to you.
A Nyanko Sensei* hooded raincoat
Pins shaped like Winnie the Pooh ears
King Blade light stick (in place of a flash-light)
Rilakkuma lap blanket (Work clothing)

☆EVERYONE HIDING UNDER DESKS ☆I LEFT SHOES BY MY DESK JUST IN CASE

*A character from anime and manga *Natsume's Book of Friends*

Cats Don't Come When You Call Them

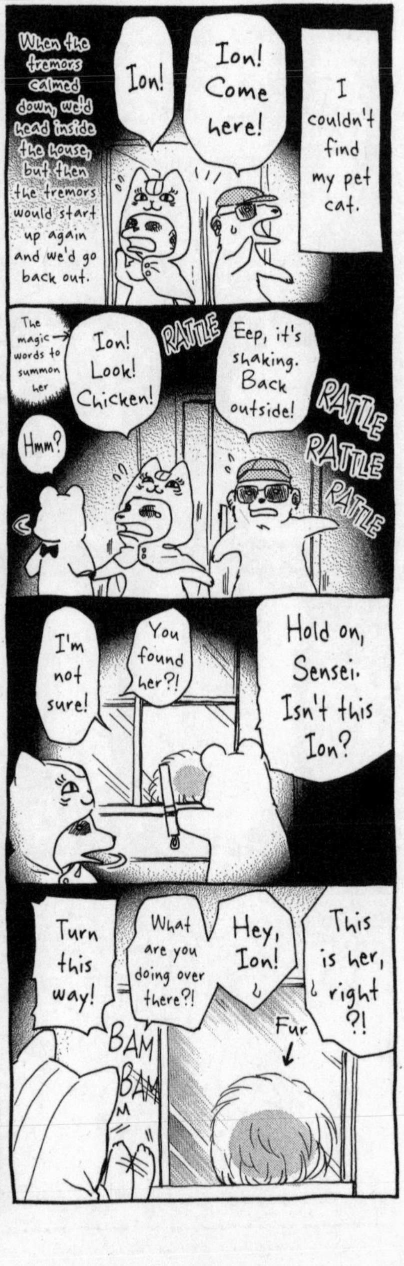
I couldn't find my pet cat.
Ion! Come here!
Ion!
When the tremors calmed down, we'd head inside the house, but then the tremors would start up again and we'd go back out.
Eep, it's shaking. Back outside!
RATTLE RATTLE RATTLE
RATTLE
Ion! Look! Chicken!
The magic words to summon her
Hmm?
Hold on, Sensei. Isn't this Ion?
You found her?!
I'm not sure!
This is her, right?!
Hey, Ion!
What are you doing over there?!
Turn this way!
Fur
BAM BAM

I love Totoro

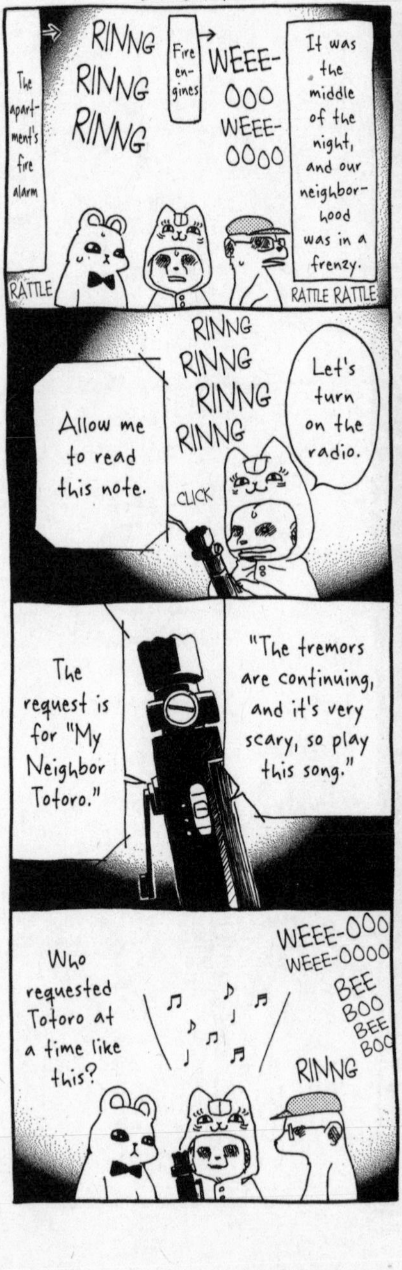
It was the middle of the night, and our neighborhood was in a frenzy.
WEEE-OOO WEEE-OOOO
Fire engines
RINNG RINNG RINNG
The apartment's fire alarm
RATTLE RATTLE
RATTLE
Let's turn on the radio.
RINNG RINNG RINNG RINNG
Allow me to read this note.
CLICK
"The tremors are continuing, and it's very scary, so play this song."
The request is for "My Neighbor Totoro."
WEEE-OOO WEEE-OOOO
BEE BOO BEE BOO
RINNG
Who requested Totoro at a time like this?

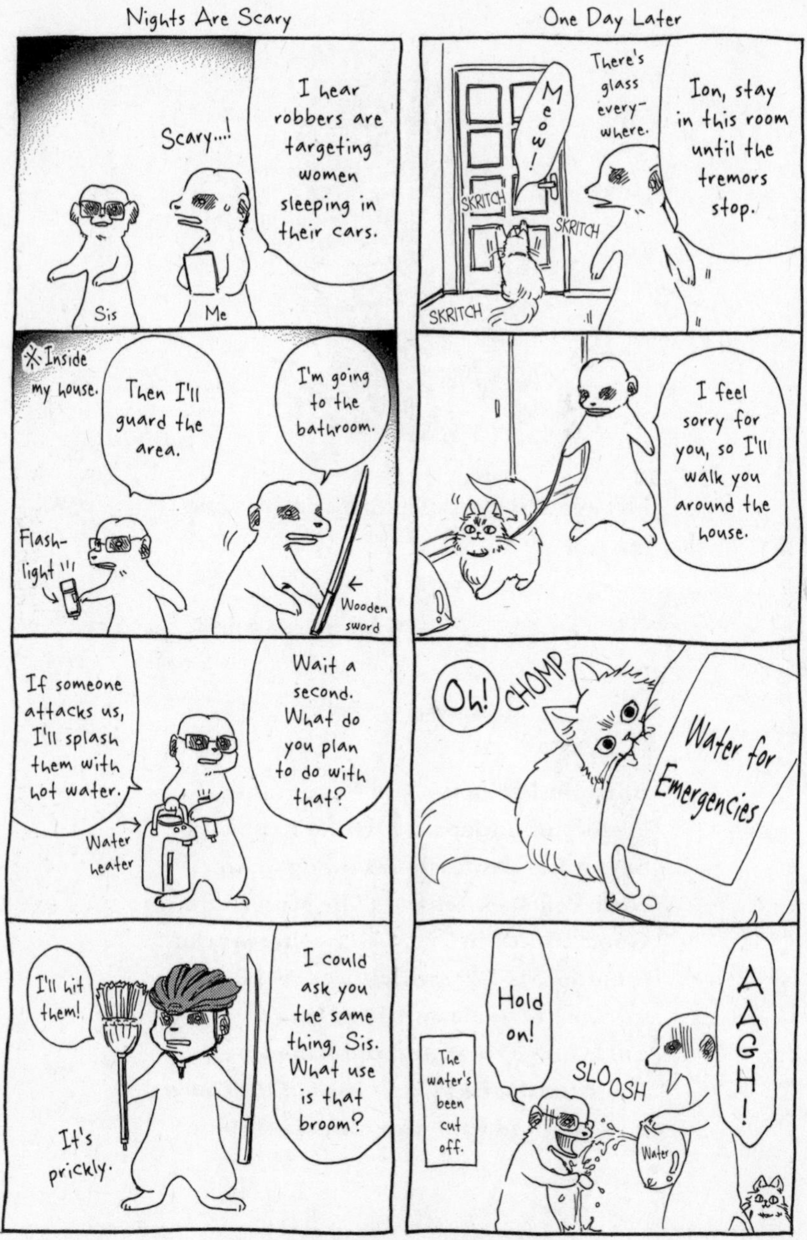
One Day Later
Ion, stay in this room until the tremors stop.
There's glass everywhere.
Meow!
SKRITCH
SKRITCH
SKRITCH
I feel sorry for you, so I'll walk you around the house.
Water for Emergencies
CHOMP
Oh!
AAGH!
Water
SLOOSH
Hold on!
The water's been cut off.
Nights Are Scary
I hear robbers are targeting women sleeping in their cars.
Scary...!
Me
Sis
I'm going to the bathroom.
Then I'll guard the area.
※Inside my house.
Wooden sword
Flashlight
Wait a second. What do you plan to do with that?
If someone attacks us, I'll splash them with hot water.
Water heater
I could ask you the same thing, Sis. What use is that broom?
I'll hit them!
It's prickly.

TRUE STORY / THE END

It'd be great if you continued to read this series this year!

—Mizuho Kusanagi

Born on February 3 in Kumamoto Prefecture in Japan, Mizuho Kusanagi began her professional manga career with *Yoiko no Kokoroe* (The Rules of a Good Child) in 2003. Her other works include *NG Life*, which was serialized in *Hana to Yume* and *The Hana to Yume* magazines and published by Hakusensha in Japan. *Yona of the Dawn* was adapted into an anime in 2014.

YONA OF THE DAWN
VOL.22
Shojo Beat Edition

STORY AND ART BY
MIZUHO KUSANAGI

English Adaptation/Ysabet Reinhardt MacFarlane
Translation/JN Productions
Touch-Up Art & Lettering/Lys Blakeslee
Design/Philana Chen
Editor/Amy Yu

Akatsuki no Yona by Mizuho Kusanagi
© Mizuho Kusanagi 2016
All rights reserved.
First published in Japan in 2016 by HAKUSENSHA, Inc., Tokyo.
English language translation rights arranged with
HAKUSENSHA, Inc., Tokyo.

Printed in the U.S.A.

Published by VIZ Media, LLC
P.O. Box 77010
San Francisco, CA 94107

10 9 8 7 6 5 4 3 2 1
First printing, February 2020

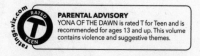

viz.com   shojobeat.com

This is the last page.

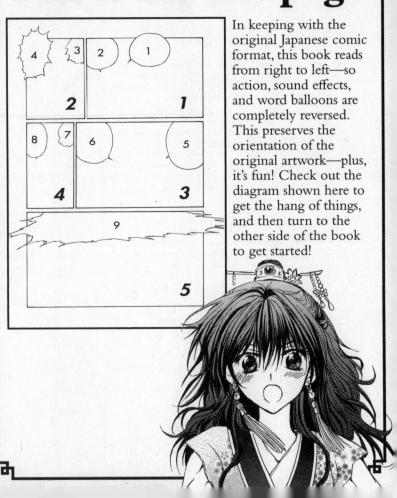

In keeping with the original Japanese comic format, this book reads from right to left—so action, sound effects, and word balloons are completely reversed. This preserves the orientation of the original artwork—plus, it's fun! Check out the diagram shown here to get the hang of things, and then turn to the other side of the book to get started!